JOHN DONNE

The Epithalamions
Anniversaries
AND
Epicedes

JOHN DONNE

The Epithalamions
Anniversaries

AND

Epicedes

EDITED WITH
INTRODUCTION AND COMMENTARY
BY

W. MILGATE

OXFORD
AT THE CLARENDON PRESS
1978

Oxford University Press, Walton Street, Oxford OX2 6DP

OXFORD LONDON GLASGOW
NEW YORK TORONTO MELBOURNE WELLINGTON
KUALA LUMPUR SINGAPORE JAKARTA HONG KONG TOKYO
DELHI BOMBAY CALCUTTA MADRAS KARACHI
IBADAN NAIROBI DAR ES SALAAM CAPE TOWN

© *Oxford University Press 1978*

British Library Cataloguing in Publication Data

Donne, John
  The epithalamions, anniversaries
  and epicedes.
  I. Title   II. Milgate, Wesley
  821'.3   PR2245   77–30423
  ISBN 0–19–812729–4

*Printed in Great Britain
at the University Press, Oxford
by Vivian Ridler
Printer to the University*

PREFACE

THIS edition of the Epithalamions, *Anniversaries*, and Epicedes of
Donne completes the series of which the earlier volumes were
Helen Gardner's editions of the Divine Poems (1952) and Love-
Poems (1965) and my own of the Satires, Epigrams, and Verse
Letters (1967). Its purposes are to examine the text in the light
of manuscripts not available to Sir Herbert Grierson for his edition
of the *Poems* in 1912, to isolate any variant readings in the poems
which might have stood in Donne's own copies, to provide as
full a commentary as possible, and generally to gather together
the results of the scholarly and critical work on the poems since
Grierson's edition appeared. I also thought it useful to print
together the epitaphs and inscriptions composed by Donne;
these compositions occupy a position mid-way between prose
and verse, and have relationships at some points with the poems.
The 'Elegies upon the Author' published in the early editions are
reprinted here, for their interest to students of Donne's early
reputation as a poet, and as verses with which Donne's own
commemorative poems may be compared.

   The text which has resulted from my scrutiny of the manuscripts
does not differ greatly from that of Grierson, except in the 'Elegy
on Prince Henry' and the *Anniversaries*, in which the choice of
different copy-texts has led to differences in the treatment of
accidents; but in all the poems it has been possible to make some
improvements on the text, and to come somewhat closer to what
might have stood in Donne's own copies of his poems. After
Professor Frank Manley's edition of the *Anniversaries* (1963)
another may seem otiose; but these poems can obviously not be
omitted from an edition of Donne's poetry which aims at com-
pleteness, and I have tried, wherever possible, to prevent my
work on the *Anniversaries* from being merely repetitive. Manley's
text is so soundly constructed, however, that mine is necessarily
almost identical with it, the chief difference being in the treatment
of the accidents. In the commentary on each poem will be found

a list of the manuscripts in which it occurs. Textual matters are usually dealt with next, with some account of the basic text and of my departures from it and from Grierson's. The Commentary is as full as reasonable limitations of space would allow, and in it I have tried to make accessible to the serious but not specialist reader verses which in their basic assumptions and methods are less in tune with modern tastes and sympathies than others among Donne's poems, but which are central to an understanding of his convictions and of his intellectual and spiritual development.

The preparation of this edition was much assisted by the award to me in 1971 of short-term grants by the trustees or governing bodies of the Henry E. Huntington Library, the Newberry Library, and the Folger Shakespeare Library; and I should like to express my warm gratitude for these opportunities to explore these (and other) collections in the United States of America, and for the courtesy and helpfulness of the directors and officers of the libraries. The resources of libraries in England were also placed at my disposal with great willingness and cordiality; and to the staff of the Bodleian Library, where much of my work was done, I owe a special debt of gratitude. I have been given permission to print material held by the libraries mentioned, and I am grateful also for a similar privilege granted by the trustees or librarians of the following: the Henry W. Berg and Albert A. Berg Collection in the New York Public Library, for permission to print variants from the Westmoreland manuscript; the George Arents Tobacco Collection in the same library for permission to print variants from the John Cave manuscript; the Houghton Library, Harvard University, for permission to quote variants from the Carnaby, Dobell, O'Flaherty, and Stephens manuscripts; and the Librarian of Trinity College, Dublin, for allowing me similarly to use the important manuscript of Donne's poems in his care. The Librarian and Benchers of Lincoln's Inn kindly allowed me to print the inscription written by Donne in the copy of a Bible which he presented to the Society's library. I acknowledge also the kindness of the Director of the Pierpont Morgan Library in allowing me to examine the Holgate manuscript, and of Mr. Clive E. Driver, who placed at my disposal the manuscript collections of seventeenth-century poetry in his care at the Rosenbach Foundation, Philadelphia. The staff of the Hertzog August Library at Wolfenbüttel assisted me in my attempts to identify Michael Corvinus.

Sir Geoffrey Keynes has continued his great services to Donne scholarship, especially by publishing the fourth edition of his *Bibliography of John Donne*. I owe him, however, particular gratitude for being permitted to collate the Leconfield and Luttrell manuscripts and to examine the commonplace-book of Edward Hyde in his library. He has also generously allowed me to print Donne's inscription in Corvinus's autograph album.

Debts of other kinds I also gratefully acknowledge. Professor Manley's edition of the *Anniversaries* has obviously been of great assistance to me. I have also made use of Professor Z. R. Sullens's study, 'Neologisms in Donne's English Poems' (1964). Mr. W. M. Lebans kindly allowed me to consult the edition of the Epicedes, now in the Bodleian Library, which he submitted as a thesis (1964); it is a pleasure to acknowledge the help he has given me, chiefly in the published articles based on his more extensive study. Mr. Alan MacColl generously made available to me the results of his collations of copies of the edition of Donne's *Poems* published in 1633, on the charitable principle that so tedious a task, once fully performed, should not have to be undertaken by another; and in addition he shared with me his lists of manuscripts in which Donne's poems severally appear. For some points in the Commentary I am indebted to Professor William A. Ringler Jr. (who brought to my notice the contents of Aberdeen University MS. 29), Professor John Wallace, Dr. C. T. Mark, and Dr. Heather D. Ousby. My colleague Professor R. St. C. Johnson helped me with the translations of the Epitaphs and Inscriptions. It is of great assistance to an editor to be aware of work being currently done by other scholars, and for such assistance I am indebted to the late Rosalie Colie and to Barbara K. Lewalski, who kindly gave me an outline of the progress of their Donne studies. Professor Lewalski's book on the *Anniversaries* has appeared opportunely, and I am grateful for having been able to make use of it.

I acknowledge the graciousness of Her Majesty the Queen

in allowing me to reproduce the miniature portrait of Donne in the royal collection; and the kindness of the Trustees of the New York Metropolitan Museum of Art in giving me permission to use the portrait of Prince Henry and Lord Harington.

My greatest debt is to Dame Helen Gardner. As the general editor of the series she has given me continual advice and assistance, but she has gone far beyond the bounds of duty. She has read the whole of my typescript and has made many valuable suggestions for the improvement of this edition. We began, indeed, to produce this book jointly, and worked on the text of the *Anniversaries* together. While circumstances made it preferable for the junior editor to proceed on his own, the sense of close collaboration has never been lacking from his labours.

For any errors and inadequacies that remain, however, I am solely responsible.

W. M.

The Australian National University
Canberra

CONTENTS

PLATES

REFERENCES AND
ABBREVIATIONS

QUOTATIONS from Donne's poems, other than those included in this volume, are taken from the following texts: the *Divine Poems* (1952) and the *Elegies and the Songs and Sonnets* (1965), edited by Helen Gardner, and the *Satires, Epigrams and Verse Letters*, edited by W. Milgate (1967). H. J. C. Grierson's edition of *The Poems of John Donne*, 2 vols. (Oxford, 1912) and Frank Manley's edition of the *Anniversaries* (Baltimore, 1963) are frequently cited. These volumes are referred to as

> Gardner, *Divine Poems*
> Gardner, *Elegies etc.*
> Milgate, *Satires etc.*
> Grierson
> Manley

Quotations from the *Sermons, Essays, Ignatius his Conclave*, and *Devotions* are from the following modern editions: *The Sermons of John Donne*, edited by G. R. Potter and Evelyn M. Simpson, 10 vols. (University of California Press, 1953–62); *Essays in Divinity*, edited by Evelyn M. Simpson (Oxford, 1952); *Ignatius his Conclave*, edited by T. S. Healy (Oxford, 1969); *Devotions upon Emergent Occasions*, edited by John Sparrow (Cambridge, 1923). For the *Paradoxes and Problems* I have used the edition by Sir Geoffrey Keynes (1923), and I sometimes cite *The Courtier's Library*, edited by Evelyn M. Simpson, with a translation by P. Simpson (London, 1930). These are referred to as

> *Sermons*
> Simpson, *Essays*
> Healy, *Ignatius his Conclave*
> Sparrow, *Devotions*
> Keynes, *Paradoxes and Problems*
> *The Courtier's Library*

Quotations rom Donne's other prose works are taken from the original editions, to which reference is made as follows:

Pseudo-Martyr	*Pseudo-Martyr.* 1610
Biathanatos	*ΒΙΑΘΑΝΑΤΟΣ* (1647)

Letters	*Letters to Severall Persons of Honour.* 1651
Tobie Mathew Collection	*A Collection of Letters, made by Sr Tobie Mathews K^t.* 1660

Other references:

Bald	*John Donne: a Life*, by R. C. Bald. Oxford, 1970
Bald, *Donne and the Drurys*	*Donne and the Drurys*, by R. C. Bald. Cambridge, 1959
Chambers	*The Poems of John Donne*, edited by E. K. Chambers (The Muses' Library). 2 vols. 1896
Gosse	*The Life and Letters of John Donne*, by Edmund Gosse. 2 vols. 1899
Grolier	*The Poems of John Donne*, edited by J. R. Lowell and C. E. Norton (The Grolier Club, New York). 2 vols. 1895
Grosart	*The Complete Poems of John Donne, D.D., Dean of St. Paul's*, edited by A. B. Grosart (Fuller Worthies Library). 2 vols. 1872
Keynes	*A Bibliography of Dr. John Donne, Dean of St. Paul's*, by Geoffrey Keynes Kt., fourth edition. Oxford, 1973
Lewalski	*Donne's 'Anniversaries' and the Poetry of Praise*, by Barbara K. Lewalski. Princeton, 1973
Burton, *Anatomy*	Robert Burton, *The Anatomy of Melancholy*, edited by H. Jackson (Everyman's Library). 3 vols. 1932
Jonson, *Works*	*Ben Jonson*, edited by C. H. Herford and Percy and Evelyn Simpson. 11 vols. Oxford, 1925–52
Migne, *P.G., P.L.*	J. Migne, *Patrologia Graeca* and *Patrologia Latina*. (The references are given to volume and column.)
Scaliger, *Exercitationes . . .*	J. C. Scaliger, *Exotericum Exercitationum Libri XV de Subtilitate ad Hieronymum Cardanum*. Frankfurt, 1607
Shakespeare	I have followed Professor Peter Alexander's edition of 1951 in using the line references of Clark and Wright's Cambridge edition
Tilley	*A Dictionary of the Proverbs in England in the Sixteenth and Seventeenth Centuries*, by M. P. Tilley. 1950

Walton, *Lives*	Unless specific reference is made to another edition, quotations are taken from the reprint of the edition of 1675 in the World's Classics Series

*　　*　　*

A.V.; *V.*	The Authorized Version, and the Vulgate text, respectively, of the Bible. Scriptural texts in English are quoted from the *A.V.*
D.N.B.	*The Dictionary of National Biography*
E.L.H.	*A Journal of English Literary History*
J.E.G.P.	*Journal of English and Germanic Philology*
M.L.N.	*Modern Language Notes*
M.L.R.	*Modern Language Review*
N. and Q.	*Notes and Queries*
O.E.D.	*Oxford English Dictionary*
P.R.O.	Public Record Office
R.E.S.	*Review of English Studies*
S.E.L.	*Studies in English Literature*
S.P.	State Papers
S.P.	*Studies in Philology*
T.L.S.	*The Times Literary Supplement*

GENERAL INTRODUCTION

JOSEPH WARTON remarked that Donne had 'noble talents for moral and ethical poesy',[1] and thus indicated the centre from which not only Donne's poetry but most of his other writings also took their principal origin. If we had none of his work but the *Satires*, it might be possible to regard the moral alertness and the critical spirit in these poems as due merely to the skilful adoption of a traditional satiric 'voice'; but one does not need to go far outside them to find proof that the *Satires*, like all Donne's writings from the earliest letters in verse and prose to his last sermon, *Deaths Duell*, show that preoccupation with moral and ethical questions which gives a focus to our view of his life and work and reveals a powerful principle of unity working beneath his apparently very various compositions and occupations. One cannot read for long in his work without coming across words like 'true', 'just', and 'perfect', which usually carry both a moral and a religious burden of meaning, since for Donne, as he wrote in a verse letter to Rowland Woodward, 'There is no Vertue, but Religion'. His moral and ethical concerns thus open out into a continual and passionate study of man's nature and of God's, and of man's physical and spiritual frailty upon which Christ had yet imposed the obligation to be perfect. Donne's thoughts and imagination return time and again to the first chapters of the book of Genesis; for in the Fall the moral life of man began. The ability, and the duty, to discriminate between good and evil thus laid upon the individual conscience, the 'discretion' to 'see, and Judge, and follow worthinesse', are frequent themes in Donne's writing. One of his favourite images is that (with all its Biblical overtones) of 'trying' or 'testing' the quality of a man's life, as of a metal by fire; and one of the chief qualities of his poetry is the ceaseless submission of 'accepted' values, conventions, and attitudes to a quizzical, ironic, or scathing scrutiny. Thus, for example, the third Satire

[1] *An Essay on the Genius and Writings of Pope*, i (1756), xi.

challenges the conventional view of 'bravery' and 'courage', and many of the verse letters and epicedes evaluate the worth and honour of those who are called 'worthy' and 'honourable'. Where virtue or religion could be found, however, Donne's full powers were exerted to salute and celebrate it.

'Our nature is Meteorique,' he wrote to Sir Henry Goodyer,[1] 'we respect (because we partake so) both earth and heaven; for as our bodies glorified shall be capable of spirituall joy, so our souls demerged into those bodies, are allowed to partake earthly pleasure. Our soul is not sent hither, only to go back again: we have some errand to do here: nor is it sent into prison, because it comes innocent: and he which sent it, is just.' Donne's concern with morality led inevitably to a study of the soul's errand and to an almost unceasing contemplation of the relation between the earthly and heavenly dimensions of man's nature. In most of the poems in this volume the 'commerce' of earth and heaven is a central part of the theme. *The First Anniversary*, for instance, rehearses (if only to lament its weakening or fracture) practically all the ways by which this commerce was manifested or by which it could be conceived. The spiritual power which works in the physical is variously a 'soul', an 'intrinsique Balme', a 'Magnetique force'; it shows itself as the 'influence' of the heavenly bodies upon man and upon earthly 'Elements', or as the 'sympathy' between celestial materials and terrestrial plants and metals (like that between the 'compassionate' turquoise and its wearer); even colour is the divine light shining through the material object. In man the 'spirits' which conveyed the controlling and unifying force of the soul to the physical members were like, or the same as, the instruments (such as Prince Henry) who diffused the spiritual influence of the monarch through the practicalities of statecraft. There were 'correspondences' between the earthly part of man and the physical universe; his spiritual part, however, repeated the order of the heavenly world—for instance, the triple and yet unified powers of the rational soul (memory, understanding, will) were a representation in man of the Trinity itself. The terms frequently used nowadays in expounding these ideas—'world-

[1] *Letters*, p. 46.

picture', 'paradigms', 'correspondences', and the like—may obscure the fact that for Donne the powers that interpenetrated the total scheme of things were *forces*; although the universe had been created whole, and although the portion of it which man could know and into which it was proper for him to inquire was limited, what he knew did not suggest that the nature of things was static. The commerce or 'trafique' between earth and heaven both within man and without was understood, and felt, as being actual and vigorous; and amid this interplay of forces the human soul must pursue its errand.

It was not, of course, without encouragement and guidance on the way. The human mind, the conscience, the creation ('creatures'), and the Scriptures were among the several 'books'[1] in which God had written out the purposes and patterns of the universe which He had planned. One of the reassuring qualities of this universe was the existence of a transforming power, so that the earthly was continually striving to become the spiritual. This part of the dynamism in things Donne frequently states through the alchemical notions that all substances seek to become gold, and that the 'virtue', 'spirit', 'quintessence', or 'tincture' of anything might be purged of dross and isolated as an 'elixir', which might itself be the means by which other things are purified and transformed. It may be that the influence of the stars is 'Imprisond in an Herbe, or Charme, or Tree', but it is—or, as the theme of *The First Anniversary* causes Donne to represent the matter (ll. 393–400), it used to be—possible for the full potentiality of this influence to be enacted in the curing of men. The human soul might in a sense be imprisoned in the body, but yet, as Donne told Goodyer, it was not 'sent into prison'; for God provides means by which it might transcend its prison and achieve its proper 'virtue', in a measure in the body, completely when it was released at the moment of death. It is not only man's soul, however, that is glorified in heaven but the body also; the biblical accounts of the resurrection and glorification of the body suggested that this process was of essentially the same kind as the alchemical transforming of physical substances. When Donne goes further

---

[1] Cf. Sparrow, *Devotions*, p. 52.

and, for example, considers the possibility that not only Mistress Bulstrode's body, but also the coffin in which it lies, will be transformed, he is (however unfortunately) bringing together inferences allowed by accepted beliefs without moving into the realms of the wholly fantastic; he is practising his doctrine that reason should not only prepare us for the acts of faith to which we commit ourselves but should work also upon the truths to which faith assents, drawing inferences which enlighten our understanding of the nature of things. These ideas concerning transformation are obviously suitable to the epicede, to both eulogy of the dead and consolation of the bereaved.

In the dynamic commerce of earth with heaven, as the converse of transformation or 'resurrection' (that which raises the earthly to the spiritual), there exists also the process by which the spiritual 'demerges' into, or is incarnated in, the physical. To behold the spiritual directly is not often given to man—perhaps in 'ecstasy' it may be so, but only briefly, since the 'death of ecstacy', if prolonged, produces death itself (as, in 'A Funeral Elegy', ll. 80–2, Donne postulates of Elizabeth Drury). Man needs a medium through which to contemplate or to 'thinke' spiritual things which he cannot 'know'. This need is satisfied primarily by the example and teaching of Christ in His incarnate life, but also by the examples of virtuous Christians; the two kinds of example, however, are virtually one, since the goodness in the souls of the virtuous is literally the Christ within them. If we think that the 'divinity' which Donne attributes to the Countess of Bedford and the other great ladies addressed in his verse letters, and to the subjects of his epicedes and *Anniversaries*, is a merely complimentary hyperbolic quality, we miss the theological truth being expressed of which the conventional compliment (also, of course, present in the poems) is a dilution. It is because all goodness is 'of' God and Christ 'liveth within' the Christian that 'I am a God; thus far a God, that by my adhering to Christ, I am made partaker of the Divine Nature'; 'every Christian truely reconciled to God . . . is a beame, and an abridgement of *Christ* himselfe'.[1] Readers have often complained that the terms in which Donne

---

[1] *Sermons*, x. 186; vi. 290.

speaks of Elizabeth Drury (and, even more, those in which he speaks of the subjects of his epicedes and obsequies) are wildly extravagant hyperboles; it is worth remembering, however, that what the Bible says of the Christian is at least as startling; for we can 'grow to bee *Filii Dei*, *The Sonnes of God*; And by that title, *Cohaeredes Christi*, *Joint-heires with Christ* [Rom. viii. 17]; And so to bee *Christi ipsi*, *Christs our selves*; as *God* calls all his *faithfull*, his *Anointed* [Ps. cv. 15], his *Christs*.'[1] Hence, as Donne says in his inscription in the autograph-book of Michael Corvinus, 'what is spoken of Christ may be said of each and every Christian'. It follows also that a virtuous person is a 'mirror' or 'glass' by means of which the divine may be mediated to our vision. The 'exemplar' subjects of the poems in this volume, like those of the verse letters, are therefore represented as objects of the poet's (and our) 'study', 'meditation', 'consideration', or 'contemplation', as means of understanding spiritual truths and the nature of virtue,[2] an idea elaborated upon in the Harington 'Obsequies'. Donne might have said to all his subjects, as he wrote to the Countess of Huntingdon, that his purpose was 'God in you to praise'. The death of a virtuous person is thus a general bereavement, since it removes from our contemplation a means of seeing and understanding divinity and goodness:

> Though God be truly'our glass, through which we see
> All, since the beeing of all things is hee,
> Yet are the trunkes which doe to us derive
> Things, in proportion fit, by perspective,
> Deeds of good men; for by their living here,
> Vertues, indeed remote, seeme to be nere.[3]

The sense of loss at the death of such 'exemplar' men and women is increased if the dead person is young as well as virtuous, and especially if he is also a Prince. It is true that Donne applies to any of his subjects figures and modes of expression which contemporary elegists reserved for the praise of royal persons (such as Queen Elizabeth and Prince Henry); for, at the level at which Donne contemplates the issues of death and celebrates the virtuous life, he takes it for granted that all Christians have been made by

---

[1] Ibid. viii. 70.   [2] See Lewalski, Chapter 2.
[3] 'Obsequies to the Lord Harington', ll. 35–40.

Christ 'kings and priests unto God and his Father' (Rev. i. 6,
v. 10); Elizabeth Drury, for example, 'was' both a state and a
church (*The Second Anniversary*, ll. 359–75). Yet in the hierarchy
of society the Prince, of course, had special spiritual responsibilities.
That King Charles should command Donne to publish a sermon
was

to make your selfe as a *Glasse*, (when the *Sun* it selfe is the *Gospell
of Christ Jesus*) to reflect, and cast them upon your *Subjects*. It was
a *Metaphor* in which, your *Majesties Blessed Father* seemd to delight;
for in the name of a *Mirroir*, a *Looking Glasse*, he sometimes presented
Himselfe, in his publique declarations and speeches to his *People*;
and a continued *Metaphor* is an *Allegory*, and holds in more. So *your
Majestie* doth more of the offices of such a *Glasse*; You doe that office
which *Moses* his *Glasses* did, at the *Brazen Sea* in the *Temple*, (for you
show others their spots, and in a Pious and unspotted life of your
owne, you show your *Subjects* their deficiencies) And you doe the
other office of such *Glasses*, by this communicating to all, the beames
which your *Majestie* receivd in your selfe.

We 'need such *Glasses* and such *Images*, as God shews us himself
in the King'.[1] The idea is elaborated in the Somerset 'Epithala-
mion', and gives added dimensions to the 'Elegy on Prince Henry',
where the praise of the Prince's exemplary virtue is more or less
taken for granted, and the main emphasis is upon the special kingly
powers that make him so important to 'Our soule's . . . long journey
of considering God'.

Both in the 'Epithalamion'[2] and in the address to King Charles
just quoted Donne shows himself ready to accept the symbols
in which James I's Court imaged itself, and there is no doubt
about his feeling for the rituals in which the ideal patterns of
royalty and of ordered society were expressed. Unhappily, fallen
man is unable to sustain the ideal in practice; he is prone to make
what God intends for physic into poison; in the latter days of the
world, he is restricted in his moral understanding by the decay
and dissolution of the ideal patterns in the world itself (as *The
First Anniversary* demonstrates) and by his own ignorance and

---

[1] *Sermons*, vii. 72, 357.
[2] See Margaret M. McGowan, ' "As through a Looking Glass" . . .', in *John Donne
Essays in Celebration*, ed. A. J. Smith (1972), pp. 175–218.

by the fallibility of the bodily instruments of knowledge (as *The Second Anniversary* shows). Even kings might not be what they should be: 'A glasse is not the lesse brittle, because a *Kings* face is represented in it; nor a King the lesse brittle, because *God* is represented in him'.[1] 'God proceeds by example, by pattern',[2] but through sin the patterns are broken, the examples harder to discern, and man himself has become less percipient. The integrity of Donne's vision ensures that he attends to the deplorable actualities of human life no less keenly than to the ideal paradigms, and the liveliness of his apprehension of things in man's nature respecting *both* earth and heaven is the chief source of the qualities in his poetry that have caused it to be characterized as 'metaphysical'. Hence arises also his insistence that man's conduct should be 'tried' and tested for its moral validity. Any discrepancy between the actual behaviour of men and the ideal patterns which are supposed to regulate it is, of course, the main source of satire; and that even the epicedes and *Anniversaries* are not without satiric qualities has often been remarked.[3]

Such a summary of the chief ideas and attitudes to be found in the poems here printed may indicate the degree of their seriousness and the nature of their central concerns; it will not make the inferior patches of verse seem any better, but it might help readers to locate more precisely the reasons for relative failure or success of the poetry at any point. At least it will not be surprising to find that the earliest written of these poems, the 'Epithalamion made at Lincoln's Inn', is strongly satirical in tone, and also has in its refrain the idea of 'perfection'. All the other poems in this volume might be called 'public' poems, written to satisfy the demands of particular occasions and more or less by command, by inescapable request, or by social and political pressure. This epithalamion, however, like practically all Donne's other poetry, was written for his own delight or satisfaction, or for the pleasure of his friends. Its primary motive seems to have been the fun of trying his hand at an epithalamion; if it were

---

[1] Sparrow, *Devotions*, p. 42.   [2] *Sermons*, iv. 98.
[3] See, e.g., Grosart, i. 98; N. Frye, *Anatomy of Criticism* (Princeton, 1957), p. 298. Desmond McCarthy thought that Donne's 'Threnodies are half satires', *Criticism* (London, 1932), p. 43.

connected with an actual marriage—and this is very doubtful—
it could hardly have been one with which Donne was closely or
seriously involved. The more likely occasion of the poem was the
publication of Spenser's 'Epithalamion'. Here the reader might
contemplate the ideal pattern of marriage, founded on true love,
related intimately to the rhythms of nature and of the heavens,
supported by both mythic apprehension and spiritual under-
standing, unfolded in poetry of joyful serenity and ritual state-
liness. To these qualities the poet in Donne could hardly fail to
respond; his poem from time to time seems to assent to, and to
express with some charm, the traditional motifs of the epithalamion,
and it is not surprising that there is a sprinkling of verbal echoes
of Spenser's poem. The stanza-form seems to owe its existence
generally to Spenser's example, and it may be that the longer
and more complex stanzas used in some of the love lyrics are due
to an interest created or renewed by Spenser's practice. It was,
however, the satirist in Donne that was especially stimulated
by Spenser's poem; for Donne could not fail to note the discrepancy
between the perfect paradigm of marriage and what weddings
were really like in the City. The mythic figure he invokes is the
highly equivocal goddess Flora; sun and moon pursue no ordered
sequence but impinge on our consciousness in the poem as ar-
bitrarily and fitfully as upon the notice of the city-dweller; the
frank celebration of physical union as an essential part of the
age-old ritual of marriage emerges as a rather violent and grotesque
bawdiness. Despite the verve and the technical skill, which Donne
apparently thought were sufficient to warrant his preserving the
poem, it is not a success as a whole. It is neither consistent satire
nor committed celebration, and its wit and its imaginative force are
uneasily divided between these purposes. As a result the references
to 'perfection' and to 'vertue' and 'truth' become rather empty
gestures. How could it be otherwise when the 'praise and fame'
due to the bride are based only on her wealth and beauty and an
(apparently) equally adventitious virginity?

It was a different matter when, seventeen and a half years
later, Donne wrote his next epithalamion. No longer is there any
uncertainty of purpose. Donne's admiration for 'the worthiest

Princess of the world',[1] Elizabeth, and her bridegroom, the universal approval of and joy in the marriage, and the realization, as fully as this world allowed, of the ideal in the actual, all combined to produce a joyous, relaxed, and almost flawless celebration of the nuptials. It is characteristic of Donne that even in such happy circumstances he has no thought to spare for the trivial jocularities customary at weddings (the breaking of the cake on the bride's head, the snatching of her garters, the scramble for the bridegroom's points, and so on[2]) but respects the deeper joy of rituals engrained in the experience of mankind, sacred to the continuance and nurture of the human race and (where royal or noble persons were involved) to the ordering of societies and nations in the way God had ordained, and expressive of the origin of Christian marriage and the indissoluble union of two persons in soul and body—a union so exalted and so 'mystical' that it could be conceived as of the same order as the marriage of 'the Body and Soule in the Creation'[3] and the union between Christ and His church. The 'solemnization' of a marriage is not, however, merely solemn, or incompatible with jollity. The play of wit in Donne's poem and the ordered movement of the intricate and skilfully wrought stanzas reflect both the gaiety and the dignified and splendid ritual of the ceremonies. The poem moves with ease and originality among the familiar images and symbolisms current in celebratory works for Court occasions, but with a coherent and harmonious ordering of these images hardly within the grasp of Donne's contemporaries who essayed poems in this genre. It was a happy instinct that led him to associate St. Valentine's Day with the Chaucerian gathering of birds in the sparkling opening of the poem; and from this flows effortlessly the sequence of images and emblems—the sparrow and the dove, the phoenix, the 'glorious flames', the gems, the stars and the spheres, and the complicated play with sun and moon, day and 'eve' and night. While the imagery is appropriately enlarged to cosmic dimensions and there are reminders of important spiritual issues, other details continue the homely, even domestic, tone from the opening stanza (with its

---

[1] *Letters*, p. 76.
[2] See *English Epithalamies*, ed. R. H. Case (London, 1896), p. xxxiv.
[3] *Sermons*, vii. 257.

mention of husband, wife, and feather-bed), and we are aware of the crowing cock, of clocks and paying debts, of tapers, sheets, and bed-curtains. Unobtrusively the poem, like the perfect marriage, reconciles, and rejoices in the reconciliation of, the parts of man's 'meteorique' nature in the union of man and wife, respecting both earth and heaven, and their claims upon the participants in the marriage.

Much of the brilliance and *élan* of this epithalamion carried Donne through his next, and last, poem in this kind—that on the marriage of Somerset. He wrote it with an odd mixture of willingness and reluctance, for about the occasion clung doubts, disapproval, and even scandal, of at least some of which he must have appreciated the force. Partly, it may be, to protect his integrity, and certainly because he would not let a lively appreciation of the idealisms concerning royalty and marriage cloud his eyes to the actualities, Donne included in his poem some uncompromising references to the circumstances of the marriage of which everyone was aware, but which possibly the King and other participants might have wished to be forgotten.[1] The spiritual meanings of rituals are not, however, invalidated by unworthiness in those who perform them, and Donne could proceed to celebrate the nuptials, approved by Church and King, for all that they might ideally represent. Flattery the poem indeed contains; but if Somerset and his bride, and even the King and certain of his bishops and courtiers, did not entirely embody the ideal, at least it is the ideal and not the failure to embody it that Donne celebrates. Hence he could write of the essence of marriage, and fill his lines with vivacity and humour, with courtly wit and compliment, and with a playful deftness and ingenuity in learned reference. The poem is beautifully attuned to the tastes and fancies of the Court, without finally sacrificing any of the solemnity of marriage or of the spiritual dimensions it calls into question. The skill with which Donne's private circumstances and convictions are reconciled to the demands of the public occasion is shown also in the induction. This is a good example of his lordly ways with traditional genres. It looks like a 'pastoral' dialogue; but it turns out that to

[1] See the notes to ll. 121, 123, 127, 166–7.

be in the country is to be in exile from the Court, the 'animation' from which is the only force that gives the country any meaning. Moreover, the form of the induction accords with the place given to the pastoral mode among the components of the mythos through which James's Court expressed itself, especially in masques presented at the Court. Donne's own hopes of preferment are delicately involved into the pattern, and also, with characteristic honesty, his sense of the irksomeness of having to make the gesture of writing the poem ('And yet I scap'd not here'). His two mature epithalamions are among the finest in English, and part of the reason is that, original as they are, they are based on a thoroughly professional and learned acquaintance with the tradition of the genre in classical and modern times, though Donne has, as usual, so absorbed earlier practice into poetry of his own cast that specific debts are almost impossible to find.[1]

This is true also of the Epicedes. In this genre, as in that of the epithalamion, Donne had essayed a poem as a young man, 'A Funeral Elegy: To L. C.' ('Sorrow, who to this house scarce knew the way'). That the poem is early is suggested both by the textual evidence[2] and by the style, which seems both immature and experimental. It is significant that among lines almost all characterized by unsteady, even ungainly, rhythms and frigid conceits the best is related to the main theme of Donne's mature poems in this genre: 'Ere rigg'd a soule for heavens discoverie'. When in 1609 the death of Lady Markham, and doubtless the wish of the Countess of Bedford, called forth his next epicede, the only sign of tentativeness in the writing of the poem is the formal sequence of the three traditional parts of the elegy (of almost equal length in Donne's poem): Lament (ll. 1–16), Consolation (ll. 17–38), and Panegyric (ll. 39–62).[3] In his other funeral elegies these three elements are freely fused or intermingled. Donne's subject-matter, the role of Lady Markham in the poem, and the cast of its imagery, however, show no hint of tentativeness; the mode he invented for his epicedes is established at once. He came

---

[1] See J. A. S. McPeek, *Catullus in Strange and Distant Britain* (Harvard, 1939), Chapter 7, and Margaret M. McGowan, op. cit.   [2] Gardner, *Elegies etc.*, pp. xxxi–xxxiii.
[3] See W. M. Lebans, 'The Influence of the Classics in Donne's *Epicedes and Obsequies*', *R.E.S.* xxiii (1972).

to it partly through his knowledge of the typology of the Bible, not only as it regarded the prefiguring of Christ in Old Testament personages, but also as it showed men and women (especially in the New Testament) as exemplars of Christian living. Thus, in a verse letter to Lady Bedford presumably concerning the death of Lady Markham ('You that are she and you'), Donne concludes by identifying the dead lady with an appropriate type of virtue: 'Yet but of *Judith* no such booke as shee.' He had already, of course, in the earlier verse letters to great ladies and in poems addressed to Woodward, Wotton, and Goodyer, worked out a mode of eulogy, courtly and yet studious of general moral and spiritual issues; and, especially, he had devised ways of celebrating the divinity that shows itself in the 'mirror' of a virtuous man or woman. Donne's epicedes therefore required that the persons whom they celebrated should be, in fact, virtuous. Mistress Bulstrode might have been an exception; but she was at least a friend of the virtuous Countess of Bedford, and might have been justly credited with a death-bed repentance. Donne's reluctance to write about the unworthy is shown by his courteous evasiveness when pressed by Sir Henry Goodyer to compose an elegy on the death (in 1619) of the rake Richard Martin;[1] the elegy was never written, and, indeed, Donne's next poem, written only a short time later, was 'A Hymn to Christ, at the Author's last going into Germany'. Acquaintance and even liking were not enough to justify the writing of an elegy. On the other hand, where virtue existed to be praised, neither acquaintance nor liking was required; Elizabeth Drury, whom he had never seen, could thus be the subject of Donne's most lengthy elegiac compositions.[2] His work in the mode of the funeral elegy which he devised was consistent and well-sustained during the years (1609–14) in which he chiefly practised it. The 'Hymn to the Saints, and to Marquess Hamilton' (1625) is a rather forced and unconvincing attempt to revive a kind of poetry which Donne had outgrown; but the mode was so firmly established from the first (in the 'Elegy on the Lady Mark-ham') that we are able to exercise the skill that Donne himself

---

[1] *Letters*, pp. 175, 224.

[2] The situation was not unparalleled; Francis Beaumont's popular elegy on Lady Mark-ham contains the statement, 'I never saw thy face'.

has taught us in judging to what extent poems or parts of poems are working successfully in the mode which he created.

The writer of epicedes is much restricted by the occasions of which he writes. Apart from touching upon particularly significant happenings in the life of the dead person, there is little the elegist can do but rehearse the traditional topics of grief, praise, and comfort. The problem arises, therefore, of giving the impression in the poem that this recent sorrow is deeply felt, while having to rely upon a limited stock of appropriate ideas and sentiments that can all too easily become flat and mechanical in effect. Most of these traditional notions recur in Donne's epicedes, and he shows great skill in giving striking modulations to the regular topics. It must be confessed, however, that Lady Markham and Mistress Bulstrode do not seem to differ in death as they certainly did in life; it was easier to differentiate among the male subjects of Donne's elegies since Prince Henry, the Prince's friend Lord Harington, and the Marquess Hamilton had opportunities to display their virtues in public affairs as the two ladies had not. In every case, however, the fact that a real person and an actual sorrow lie behind the poems gives an essential addition to their weight and their relevance to the deepest concerns of men. By treating the dead person as an 'exemplar' or 'mirror' Donne is able to include in the epicedes lines which are rather reflective or 'moral' than specifically funerary; for in praising God 'in' a virtuous person he was able to discharge the duty of a Christian poet, to set forth or 'publish' spiritual and moral doctrines, and to make clear the dimensions of the virtue allowed to men and women by God's grace. The deeper tones in the epicedes result from the continual reminders that death is the consequence of original sin and involves the whole plan of man's redemption. The best lines, indeed, tend to be those charged with weighty moral or theological 'statements'; but they are deftly woven into the texture of lament or praise or consolation by constant reference to the dead person whose life reflected these truths. So, in his 'praise' of Lady Markham, Donne discusses the 'elder' and 'younger' deaths:

> They perish both, when they attempt the just;
> For, graves our trophies are, and both deaths dust.

So, unobnoxious now, she'hath buried both;
For, none to death sinnes, that to sinne is loth . . .
Of what small spots pure white complaines! Alas,
How little poyson breaks a christall glasse!
She sinn'd, but just enough to let us see
That Gods Word must be true, All, sinners be.

It was by 'seeing' God's word exemplified in the character and behaviour of the dead person that Donne hoped to convey the depth of the grief felt by those now bereft of such an example—'my griefe, great as thy worth', as he says at the end of the Harington 'Obsequies'.

Another way of bringing the life and poignancy of sorrow to conventional and overworked basic material was by the use of imagery, like that in the passage just quoted concerning the supposed action of poison upon fine glass, so fresh and striking as to suggest the force of a sorrow that stimulated these insights. It is in part through such imagery that Donne establishes his role in the poem, as one who in his study of an exemplary person has uncovered and accepted anew the truths of God's word and the proper grounds for sorrow; these he imparts to his fellow mourners with the stamp of his own assimilation upon them. At times Donne uses larger and elaborated images or conceits as a structural device to link together various truths which the occasion of this bereavement enables him to 'publish'. Some are traditional or Biblical, and accord with the frequent use of commonplaces and proverbial sentiments appropriate to the universality of death and of mourning (the 'waters' of death; the 'triumph' of the soul; death as a 'bird of prey'). Others are more like emblems, for instance the geometrical images which open the 'Elegy on Prince Henry' and occupy ll. 105–20 of the Harington 'Obsequies', or the imagery of clocks which is worked out in ll. 131–54 of the latter poem. Sometimes the imagery reaches extravagant dimensions; one can accept the terms on which Donne is able, for example, to claim that Mistress Bulstrode's soul 'was Paradise', her heart the Burning Bush, but to conceive of Lady Markham's body as glorified into 'th'Elixar of this All' is to strain credulity, poetic good taste, and perhaps theology as well. Though always interesting, often resonant and impressive, the Epicedes are in fact patchy performances, including areas of flat and somewhat clumsy versifying. Despite their flaws the poems are, however, important as exhibiting (like the *Anniversaries*) both the central concerns of Donne throughout his life, and particularly his efforts to clarify and to find adequate expression for convictions which he was later to 'publish' as a priest of the Church.

Of the mature epicedes Donne had written only those on Lady Markham and Mistress Bulstrode when, in the earlier part of December 1610, Elizabeth Drury, the only surviving daughter of Sir Robert Drury of Hawstead, Suffolk, died in London a few weeks before her fifteenth birthday.[1] Although Donne may have met Drury earlier, it does not seem that their acquaintance could have been so intimate that Donne would write an elegy on the dead girl unprompted. It is likely that the prompting came from Donne's sister Anne, whose husband, William Lyly, had settled at Hawstead under Drury's patronage from 1598 until his death in August 1603; Anne Lyly would presumably have known Elizabeth Drury from the child's second year to her eighth, and may indeed have seen her fairly constantly until Elizabeth's death. 'A Funeral Elegy' was probably written in December 1610. The fact that it was published with *The First Anniversary* as the second poem in the volume (*1611*) has sometimes been thought to indicate that the elegy may have been written after the longer poem. This does not seem to follow; it is more likely that the elegy contained ideas which were more fully developed in *The First Anniversary* than that Donne would, or could, reuse in a sketchier form ideas which he had already elaborated in the *Anniversary*. Moreover, the opening lines of the elegy suggest that the poem was designed, or imagined, as an epitaph suitable to be pinned on the hearse over Elizabeth Drury's grave (she was buried in Hawstead church on 17 December 1610); and it is written in the same style, with images drawn frequently from the same areas (especially in the first half of the poem) as those Donne had employed in the elegies written in 1609 on Lady Markham and Mistress Bulstrode. It was presumably in response to Donne's

[1] For a full account of Donne's relations with the Drurys, see Bald, pp. 237 ff.

writing of the elegy that he was invited to compose the Latin
inscription for Elizabeth Drury's monument.[1] Both Sir Robert
and Lady Drury apparently found the poet's qualities and company
attractive, and their friendship led to his being invited to
accompany the Drurys on an extended journey in Europe, for
which a licence was granted on 2 July 1611, though it was not
until early in November that the party actually set out. During
the period of waiting Donne evidently composed *The First Anni-
versary*, which had been begun when Elizabeth Drury had been
dead for 'some months' (l. 39); the poet's 'first yeares rent' (l. 447)
was being paid in advance, and the first part of the poem ('The
entrie into the worke', ll. 1–90), among its other functions, seems
designed to apologize for the fact that though Elizabeth had been
dead for some time she had not been adequately celebrated. The
Drurys apparently urged Donne to publish the poem, and with
some reluctance he sent it to the press with 'A Funeral Elegy'
appended, and with some prefaratory verses 'To the Praise of
the Dead, and the Anatomy'.

The quality of the printing (by contrast with that in *1612*)
suggests that Donne was able to see the book through the press
himself before leaving England. The volume was not entered in
the Stationers' Register, but Sir Arthur Throckmorton's diary
shows that he received a copy from London on 21 November.
There can be little doubt that the verses 'To the Praise of the
Dead, and the Anatomy' were composed by Joseph Hall. Ben
Jonson told William Drummond of Hawthornden that Hall was
'the Herbenger to Dones Anniversarie', and, though the reference
is to 'The Harbinger to the Progress' prefixed to *The Second Anni-
versary*, the lines 'To the Praise of the Dead . . .' are so similar in
style and purpose to 'The Harbinger to the Progress' that it seems
highly unlikely that the poems are by different authors. Hall,
at the instigation of Lady Drury, had been appointed rector of
All Saints, Hawstead, in 1601 and remained there until 1607; he
had thus seen Elizabeth Drury grow from her sixth to her twelfth
year at Hawstead and probably shared some of the parents' grief
when she died. Hall's letter of resignation from Hawstead contained

---

[1] See p. 76 below.

a promise to continue his relations with the Drurys; and to take part in Donne's commemoration of their daughter would have been a way of showing that his warm feeling for them remained. The subject of *The First Anniversary* would have appealed to Hall for another reason: he had, according to Thomas Fuller, been 'noted in the University, for his ingenuous maintaining, (be it *Truth*, or *Paradox*) that *Mundus senescit, The World groweth old*'. The publisher of both *1611* and *1612*, furthermore, was Samuel Macham, who was, like Hall, a native of Ashby de la Zouche, and who had already published several books for Hall. It seems clear, therefore, that Hall played a considerable part in the publication of Donne's poems on Elizabeth Drury.[1]

Donne may have begun *The Second Anniversary* on or near the first actual anniversary of her death, since he begins by saying that 'a yeare is runne' since she died (ll. 3–6). The poem certainly belongs to the earlier part of his stay with the Drurys in Amiens, where the party had settled into a house by the end of November 1611. The last lines of the poem (511–18) make it clear that the poet is in France; and, apart from the compliment to his patron and the compelling nature of his theme, Donne's motive for supplying this his 'second yeeres true Rent' (l. 520) was probably to beguile the tedium of life in Amiens. The poem was sent to England as soon as it was finished, and was published early in 1612 by Macham with a reprint of the contents of *1611*. It is very likely that Joseph Hall, having contributed his 'Harbinger' to the new poem, and because of his associations with Macham and the Drurys, made the arrangements for the printing. Sir Arthur Throckmorton received his copy of *1612* on 10 May 1612, but already Donne had replied to criticisms of the *Anniversaries* from Paris on 14 April. To George Garrard he wrote on that day:

Of my Anniversaries, the fault that I acknowledge in my self, is to have descended to print any thing in verse, which though it have excuse even in our times, by men who professe, and practise much gravitie; yet I confesse I wonder how I declined to it, and do not pardon my self: But for the other part of the imputation of

[1] Bald, pp. 242–4.

having said too much, my defence is, that my purpose was to say
as well as I could: for since I never saw the Gentlewoman, I cannot
be understood to have bound my self to have spoken just truths,
but I would not be thought to have gone about to praise her, or
any other in rime; except I took such a person, as might be capable
of all that I could say. If any of those Ladies think that Mistris
Drewry was not so, let that Lady make her self fit for all those praises
in the book, and they shall be hers.[1]

Perhaps a day or two earlier, Donne wrote in similar terms to
Goodyer:

> I hear from *England* of many censures of my book, of M^ris· *Drury*;
> if any of those censures do but pardon me my descent in Printing
> any thing in verse, (which if they do, they are more charitable then
> my self; for I do not pardon my self, but confesse that I did it against
> my conscience, that is, against my own opinion, that I should not
> have done so) I doubt not but they will soon give over that other
> part of that indictment, which is that I have said so much; for no
> body can imagine, that I who never saw her, could have any other
> purpose in that, then that when I had received so very good tes-
> timony of her worthinesse, and was gone down to print verses, it
> became me to say, not what I was sure was just truth, but the best
> that I could conceive; for that had been a new weaknesse in me, to
> have praised any body in printed verses, that had not been capable
> of the best praise that I could give.[2]

Part of Donne's defence had already been foreshadowed in the
closing lines of 'A Funeral Elegy'. The idea that underlies it is
that on which Donne's mode of 'praise' is founded, that the
virtue exemplified in any person, since it is 'of' Christ, is worthy
of the 'best praise' that could be given; and other persons who
(Donne recognizes) might reasonably think the praise excessive
might remedy the situation best by accepting 'the gift of her
example'. If from personal observation (denied him in the case
of Elizabeth Drury) he could determine, as 'just truth', that
another lady possessed greater or more matured virtues, he was

---

[1] *Letters*, pp. 238–9; a variant text of the letter appears on p. 255.
[2] Ibid., pp. 74–5. Donne's fear that the 'censures' might include the loss of the Countess
of Bedford's patronage is shown in the unfinished verse letter to her 'begun in France'
('Though I be *dead*, and buried . . .').

not prevented from saying 'the best that he could say' of her
also—a point which Donne makes in his last complimentary poem
addressed to a lady, the verse letter to the Countess of Salisbury;
in which poem we see the last evidence of Donne's discomfiture by
criticism of the *Anniversaries*, and of the difficulty which he, like all
poets, found in reconciling a vision of the 'best' with the courtesies
and practicalities of social relationships. The criticisms of the
poems did not, however, destroy his concern for them, and when,
by the beginning of September 1612, he returned to London, he
had an errata slip placed in the unsold copies of *1612*. With the
two later editions of the *Anniversaries* in his lifetime (*1621*, *1625*)
he seems, however, to have had nothing to do. The poems ap-
parently found a wide audience, since there were four editions of
'A Funeral Elegy', and *The First Anniversary*, and three of *The
Second Anniversary*, before the first collected edition of the *Poems*
in 1633. Indeed, for readers of poetry outside the fairly restricted
band of amateurs among whom most of Donne's other poetry
circulated in manuscript he was from 1612 until 1633 the poet
of the *Anniversaries*.

Coleridge thought that 'these Anniversaries were the strangest
caprice of genius on record';[1] C. S. Lewis considered that 'scattered,
but exquisite, patches of poetry . . . appear from time to time
amidst the insanity of *The First and Second Anniversaries*'.[2] To
Donne's seventeenth-century readers, however, the poems did
not seem the products of caprice or insanity; the only adverse
contemporary criticism of which we have a record, that by Ben
Jonson, accuses them of profanity and blasphemy, but Jonson was
probably unique, and perverse, in describing their profoundly
religious basis and modes of utterance in terms so extreme. Since
the first thorough-going (and seminal) study of the poems in
modern times, by Louis L. Martz,[3] many scholars have discussed
them, all, whatever their differences in approach and inter-
pretation,[4] granting that the *Anniversaries* are of considerable

[1] *Coleridge's Miscellaneous Criticism*, ed. T. M. Raysor (1936), p. 143.
[2] 'Donne and Love Poetry in the Seventeenth Century', *Seventeenth Century Studies
presented to Sir Herbert Grierson* (1938), p. 79.
[3] *The Poetry of Meditation* (1954), pp. 219–48 (reprinted from *E.L.H.* xiv. 1947).
[4] For an account of most of these studies, see Lewalski, *passim*.

stature and beauty; and few modern readers would deny that these, Donne's most sustained compositions in verse, have claims to be considered the finest long poems written in English between *The Faerie Queene* and *Paradise Lost*. It is possible, however, that they are rather simpler, and at the same time more richly and flexibly imagined, than many modern discussions make them out to be.

In *The First Anniversary* Martz felt a lack of control and of real fusion in Donne's relation of a sense of the decay of the world to the figure of Elizabeth Drury, and other critics have shared this uneasiness. The relation which Donne makes is, I think, defensible on both logical and poetical grounds, but here and there the writing is characterized by a sense of strain and a relative lack of clarity. One wonders, indeed, if he had not conceived, or even partly written, a satiric 'anatomy', for the completion and publication of which Mistress Drury's death provided the occasion. However that may be, Donne's carefully worded title explains that it is the girl's 'untimely death' that enables him to 'represent' the 'frailty and the decay of this whole world'. The grounds on which her death can be related to the world's decay are clear and orthodox enough; the death of a specific person and the frailty and decay of the world in general are both traceable to one ultimate source, the sin of man in Eden; this truth is most poignantly brought home when an innocent person dies, for it seems that the world, corrupt and sick before, is now struck to the heart if virtue is vulnerable—the 'whole' world is mortal; even so, man is still able to restore in himself and clarify to others some part of the image of God clouded and defaced by the sin of Adam, and of this image a virtuous Christian like Elizabeth Drury can be a 'mirror', and a means of our achieving virtue by following her example. She is thus able to represent all the realities of man's spiritual and moral predicament: the consequences of his sin (of which her death showed her to be the victim), the bliss lost in Eden, and the means of recovering at least the 'twilight' of the full radiance of the image of God in man.[1]

'She' has been variously said by modern interpreters of the

[1] Cf. *The Second Anniversary*, ll. 455–8.

Anniversaries to represent the Virgin Mary, the Church (Anglican or Roman, or both), Queen Elizabeth, Astraea, the Logos, Wisdom, or St. Lucy. One's first response to these suggestions is that, if Elizabeth Drury specifically 'means' all these, then either she means nothing at all, or Donne's poems are in a hopeless state of confusion. But these are not the impressions one receives while reading the poems themselves. As a symbol of the highest spiritual potentialities of mankind, of the image of God or the Christ 'in' man, the presentation of Mistress Drury requires of a Christian poet 'all', and the 'best', that he 'could say' or 'conceive'. It was natural that Donne should make use of idealisms and techniques of praise which others had applied to the celebration of women who were envisaged as possessing and revealing the highest spiritual qualities (the Blessed Virgin, saints, Queen Elizabeth, Petrarch's Laura, Dante's Beatrice), or to the celebration of such high qualities in the figure of an allegorical or symbolic woman (Wisdom, the Church as the Bride of Christ, and perhaps mythical personifications like Astraea). To exploit poetically the details of such praises was not, however, to import into the *Anniversaries* the specific persons or ideas which were the objects of praise in other contexts. While the material presented in *The First Anniversary* is laid out systematically to suggest an 'anatomy', it is an error, I believe, to expect or to find any systematic rigidity in the spiritual significances of Donne's symbolic 'she', or in the flexible and indeed rather opportunistic imaginative uses to which he puts his symbol in various parts of the poem. He is treating fundamental issues which are antecedent, both in the history of the created world and in God's plan for it, to those in more specialized and perhaps more complex traditions in which critics have found identifications for Donne's 'she'. The rich and paradoxical significances which he draws from the figure of Mistress Drury are neither surprising nor confusing if we locate his practice in another tradition of symbolism with which he was deeply familiar. For instance, a sacrament of the Church is a ritual act which is symbolic at once of the need of grace, of the giving of grace, of the cause of it, and of its consequences. It seems to me to be in this mode that Elizabeth Drury (especially in *The First*

Anniversary) can be intelligibly used to symbolize what 'the world' has lost, the result (in death, which she suffered like all mankind) of the loss, and the cause of the world's losing it.

It is in this last idea that the element of hyperbole in Donne's 'praise' is to be found. He can say 'all' and 'the best' of Elizabeth Drury as she represents what man lost in Eden and may recover, by grace, in Christian living; and it is hardly possible to exaggerate the pathos of the untimely death of an innocent girl. That her death is the cause of the world's death, however, the last blow to its already corrupt being, does at first seem an extravagant idea, which involves the risk that we should regard Mistress Drury as literally *sui generis*, not representative of virtuous mortals in general, and hence perhaps not human at all (the hyperbole can be seen developing in 'A Funeral Elegy', ll. 27–34). The idea is almost forced upon Donne as an imaginative consequence of the main conceit of *The First Anniversary*. This is the notion that the 'world' corresponds to a human being; its body is racked by fatal illness; it dies, and becomes a corpse which may be anatomized or dissected. The operation had better be performed quickly, before the cadaver decays (ll. 439–42), Donne's sardonic way of reminding his 'hearers' that in the last days of the world they had better urgently pursue the soul's errand while there is yet time. Of this world the symbolic 'she' is represented as being the 'soul', an idea of which Donne made use for other purposes in 'A Fever' and in a prose letter to Mistress Bridget White;[1] this 'soul' is that which gives the body of the world cohesion, value, and (Donne must add) life; hence the departure of Mistress Drury's soul 'causes' the death of the world itself. One may see in the hyperbole a way of expressing the desolation of bereavement, when we feel that our world has 'gone to pieces'; there is a wider feeling of loss in that 'Any mans *death* diminishes *me*';[2] and the removal of any 'glass' of God's goodness increases the power of sin, and hence of death. Yet it is obvious that Donne's conceit contains within it significances which must inevitably come into headlong conflict: for how can the soul ('she') die as well as causing the body to die by leaving it? The paradoxes arise from Donne's

---

[1] *Letters*, p. 1.   [2] Sparrow, *Devotions*, p. 98.

determination here, as so often in his poetry, to hold together in our contemplation the original, and yet by grace still sufficiently available, bliss of man's unfallen state and the actualities of his degenerate condition. Donne concedes something to logic when he considers the objection that if the world is dead there is nobody left to write or read poems. His answer, however, that 'there's a kind of world remaining still', is quickly transformed from an ingenious semblance of logic to the deepest level of symbolism in the poem: the full 'day' of man's spiritual condition in Eden being lost, there is in 'the twi-light of her memory' a means by which fallen man might, through her example, achieve sufficient virtue for his redemption—the 'new world' turns out to be a moral and spiritual state. By these means Donne is able to find expression for matters which do not lie in the province of logic, and can be contemplated at all only in paradox and symbol. The more one studies *The First Anniversary* the more one recognizes the skill with which Donne uses the figure of Elizabeth Drury as a focus for, and as a means of expressing, every aspect of man's moral and spiritual predicament. In the result 'she' cannot be described as inhuman or *sui generis* at all, and Donne's hyperbole seems not to be, ultimately, a falsification. If even the virtuous die, virtue itself may be said to suffer death; the death of virtue is the life of sin; and sin is that which brought death to man and sowed the seeds of decay and death in the frame of the world itself.

The ideas and materials of *The First Anniversary* were all commonplaces to Donne's contemporaries. His account of the evidences of the decay and approaching end of the world differs from the many given by other writers only in being pointedly and coherently organized, and in being expressed in poetry of great imaginative freshness and force. An 'anatomy', or systematic analysis, requires the presentation in orderly form of the whole 'body' of material under scrutiny. The scale of Donne's conception demands a profusion of details, ranging over all time and space, to suggest the totality of man's knowledge of the nature of things and of his place in the moral and spiritual order; there is good poetic justification for what to Mario Praz seemed the 'ponderous redundancy' of the poem.[1] It is as if with ruthless thoroughness, contemptuous and yet anxious, the poet is answering a question asked in *The Second Anniversary*: 'Poore soule, in this thy flesh what do'st thou know?' (l. 254). What it knows is sufficiently alarming, and yet the poem is full of the agonized desire to know and an acute sense of the frustration of man's best efforts to understand; the poet must confess in the end the 'incomprehensiblenesse' of Elizabeth Drury and of all that he has seen represented in her. The fragmented and warring systems proposed by scientists and philosophers offer no hope of total comprehension. Yet the poem's final impression on the reader is not that the world is fractured into meaningless particulars. The organizing power of poetry is still possible to man; the principle of reordering is still present in the 'memory' of a moral and spiritual harmony against which the vivid picture of fragmentation is constantly set (what is said to be gone is as present in the poem as what remains); the universe is still an 'organ' set in tune by the virtuous. Donne's often brilliant imagery is itself a factor of co-ordinating vision, reinforcing, and sometimes almost indistinguishable from, the accepted 'correspondences' that show the ordered pattern of the creation. The deep pathos of the realization that 'The heart being perish'd, no part can be free' is set against a confidence in our power to be 'none of' the world and to attain to the joys of heaven as they are available to us, in proportion, both here and in the hereafter.

There is another tone in the complex emotional orchestration of the poem—the satiric. The word 'anatomy' implies a realistic analysis which places the anatomist in a position of superiority to his material; it leads naturally to disparagement; and when this disparagement is directed at earthly frailties from the vantage-point of spiritual wisdom the resulting satire accommodates both acidic wit and grim disdainful humour, rather of the kind displayed by St. Laurence on the grid-iron and Donne's ancestor Sir Thomas More on the chopping-block:

> We are borne ruinous: poore mothers crie,
> That children come not right, nor orderly,

---

[1] 'Donne's Relation to the Poetry of his Time', *A Garland for John Donne*, ed. T. Spencer 1931), p. 73.

> Except they headlong come, and fall upon
> An ominous precipitation.
> How witty's ruine! how importunate
> Upon mankinde!   (ll. 95–100)

This tone plays over much of *The First Anniversary* (and is by no means absent from the companion poem). It rises naturally in the texture of the verse, which, in much of the poem, is packed, terse, witty, civilized, tending to epigram and responding skilfully to the rhetorical possibilities of the couplet. Pope seems to have learned much from Donne's practice.

The handling of materials so multifarious, of ideas so fundamental and so charged with paradox, and of feelings so complex, requires very considerable skill in organization and structure. Even in short poems (for example, 'The Canonization') Donne tends to use several methods of organization simultaneously; and in the *Anniversaries* the structural methods are more numerous than can be set out simply in a scheme of headings or a skeleton outline of topics treated in the poems. Donne himself initiated the making of such outlines[1] by his side-notes, hardly necessary, but appropriate to the conception of *The First Anniversary* as a systematic 'anatomy' and continued, for uniformity, in the second poem. Summaries of their contents have been based on interpretations of the *Anniversaries* as examples of formal meditation, of epideictic poetry, or of the funeral elegy; *The First Anniversary* has been compared in form to the classical oration;[2] Donne himself calls the first poem a 'Song' and both poems 'Hymns'. None of these conceptions of the genre of the poems takes account of the substructures which develop as Donne organizes details concerning a topic that arises in the course of his reflections (for example, *The First Anniversary*, ll. 418–24, and *The Second Anniversary*, ll. 359–74), a technique to be found in some of the epicedes, especially in the Harington 'Obsequies'. Moreover, if one compares the schemes proposed for the *Anniversaries*, although there is agreement that some large areas of the poems are 'sections' concerned with

---

[1] For examples, see Grierson, ii. 188; Martz, loc. cit.; O. B. Hardison, *The Enduring Monument* (1962), pp. 176–83; W. M. Lebans, 'Donne's Anniversaries and the Tradition of the Funeral Elegy', *E.L.H.* xxxix (1972).

[2] See H. Love, 'The Argument of Donne's *First Anniversary*', *Mod. Philology*, lxiv (1966).

one main topic, there is a good deal of fuzziness around the edges, and opinions differ as to the exact points at which one 'section' ends and another begins.[1] I am not sure that the experience of reading the poems involves an awareness of any rigid underlying 'plan', except where Donne draws attention to it by the refrain ('Shee, shee is dead . . .'). He creates a genre for each poem as the theme and purpose require, and, although he was clearly familiar with the traditions of meditation, praise, elegy, oratory, the hymn, and so on, he seems to exploit them with the same poetic opportunism as, to meet the emergencies of the moment, he develops substructures in smaller areas of the poems. No limiting conception of genre or structure breaks the flow of this discursive and meditative verse. The only 'genre' which can accommodate all the qualities to be found in the poems and which can include hymn, praise, condemnation, meditation, oration, satire, and vision, is, indeed, the sermon of the kind which Donne himself composed.

Ben Jonson remarked to William Drummond 'that Dones Anniversarie was profane and full of Blasphemies / that he told Mr Donne, if it had been written of *th*e Virgin Marie it had been something to which he answered that he described the idea of a Woman and not as she was.'[2] If Drummond reported Jonson, and Jonson Donne, correctly, Donne's remark seems to be the typically incomplete statement of a defensive poet suddenly confronted by an uncomprehending critic. It is true that Elizabeth Drury is something like a Platonic 'idea'—'best, and first originall of all faire copies' (*The First Anniversary*, ll. 227-8); but, more precisely, as part of her function in the poem she symbolizes the 'Idea' by which God created man when He made him in His own image. The marred image of God in a man or woman may be restored only by grace through Christ: 'If thou wilt be a new Creature . . . then Christ is thy *Idæa*, thy Pattern, thine Original.'[3] Thus it seems likely that Donne's defence of the *Anniversaries* states a primary fact about them—that in celebrating Elizabeth Drury he was praising the Christ within her.[4] The real Elizabeth Drury

[1] See Lewalski, pp. 247 ff., 280 ff. [2] Jonson, *Works*, i. 133.
[3] *Sermons*, iv. 99. [4] See Lewalski, pp. 111-15.

is hardly individualized in *The First Anniversary*; there is nothing specifically womanly about what she represents in the poem; indeed, to remember her womanliness is to increase the embarrassment at certain points caused by the fact that Donne's symbol has to be called 'she' (ll. 99–110, 176–80). Yet she is not an inhuman abstraction; as in the verse letters to ladies and in the epicedes Donne's centre of concentration is on the individual man or woman as a 'mirror' of Christian virtue; the *Anniversaries* therefore require that we remember the existence of Elizabeth Drury as an actual person. Donne's flexible handling of his symbolic 'she', however, enables him to represent in her much more than the 'Idea' just defined; she is rather his imaginative instrument for describing the Idea of Man—the whole human condition as it respects both earth and heaven.

This is Donne's basic subject in both the poems. In *The Second Anniversary*, however, the figure of Elizabeth Drury changes; a good deal of reference is made to the virtues of her outlook and conduct while she was alive (for instance, in ll. 449–67), and she is much more an idealized woman than in the earlier poem. Nevertheless, the change is not really radical; the ideal virtue which Donne praises 'in' her is still that which in the person of one living on earth 'mirrors' the nature of Christ. She is still an example mediated to us for our imitation, a pattern like that provided by any 'saint'—not as the Roman Church understands that word (ll. 511–16) but in its Protestant and primary New Testament reference to any committed Christian. The Christ 'in' such a person can be the 'Idea', 'Pattern', and 'Original' in the lives of others. Dryden, indeed, thought that the 'Design' of Donne's 'Panegyrick . . . was to raise an Emulation of the living, to Copy out the Example of the dead';[1] although this statement of the 'design' is too limited, it may be said that the death of such an exemplar is not, in a sense, 'untimely' if the living do imitate the example. Partly to this end, *The Second Anniversary* devotes a good deal of attention to Elizabeth Drury's religious life on earth. Hence its title states that her 'religious' death is the occasion for a 'contemplation' of the restrictions and discomforts experienced by

---

[1] Preface to *Eleanora* (1692).

the human soul in this life and of 'her exaltation' in the next. The ambiguity of 'her' in the title and the double reference of the word 'she' in the body of the poem are ways of suggesting that what is said of the 'progress' of Elizabeth Drury's soul applies to the progress of his own, and to that of the soul of any virtuous Christian; this generality of reference is conveyed also in the strategic uses of the pronouns ('she', 'I', 'we', and 'thou') and in the telescoping of tenses (for example, in the opening lines), to suggest that God's eternal design of salvation is applicable to any who will accept the 'progress' exemplified in the poem. *The Second Anniversary* is not correctly described, as was sometimes formerly asserted, as an account of 'the ascent of the soul'; most of the poem is concerned with the soul's errand on earth, with the limits which man's restricted bodily organs of sense and faint powers of understanding place upon the soul's earthly progress, and with the contemplation of the joys which the soul will share in heaven as they may be envisaged by one still living on earth. In the 'refrain' (so far as Donne sustains it) 'she' is not 'dead' (as in *The First Anniversary*) but 'gone' where only the 'contemplation' of the poet can follow her. Instead of the agonized attempt to 'know' in the earlier poem, this 'contemplation' is expressed as the more joyful power of being able to 'think' of spiritual dimensions beyond the reach of knowledge (a distinction which Donne elaborates in a different way in the 'Elegy on Prince Henry'). In this mood, tones enter the poem which were not heard in *The First Anniversary*, and which often impart great beauty to the verse:

> Thinke then, my soule, that death is but a Groome,
> Which brings a Taper to the outward roome,
> Whence thou spiest first a little glimmering light,
> And after brings it nearer to thy sight:
> For such approches doth Heaven make in death.   (ll. 85–9)

Donne clearly considered the *Anniversaries* as companion poems. He takes care to re-establish in the later poem the basic conceptions expressed in the earlier: the world is still a 'Carkas', Elizabeth Drury its 'forme'; the 'weedlesse Paradises' produced by imitation of her virtues in the first poem are recalled in the statement in the second that 'Paradise adhear'd' to her person; 'the twi-light of her memory' is caught up by 'after this sunnes set'; the exhortation that because the world is 'rotten at the hart' we should be 'none of it' is restated in the poet's direction to his soul to 'Forget this rotten world' which is 'not worth a thought'. In fact, however, a good deal of thought is given to the world in *The Second Anniversary*; the actualities of human life are never obscured by the longing for perfection. The deepest motive of the poem seems to be expressed in the prayer 'so to see thee, in all thy *Glasses*, in all thy representations of thy selfe to us here, as that hereafter we may see thee *face to face*, and as thou art in thy self, in thy kingdome of glory'; 'And as thou hast maryed in us *two natures*, mortall and immortall, mary in us also, the knowledge, and the practise of all duties belonging to both conditions, that so this world may be our *Gallery* to the next'.[1] Of the achievement of these aims Elizabeth Drury is both an example and a symbol. *The Second Anniversary* (like its companion poem) is crammed with instances of men doing 'all duties'—prince, groom, sergeant, anchorite, divine, libeller, physician, author, and so on—confusedly, for good or ill; they are balanced by the picture of the ordered and glorious company of heaven. The earthly nature of man is associated with fragmentation and disease, his spiritual potentialities with harmony and health and with the virtual identity of wholeness and wholesomeness, whether in man's body, the world's, or the body-politic; and of the latter combination of qualities Elizabeth Drury is also the imaginative representation. Donne also calls upon the tradition of scepticism (a tradition almost unbroken from classical times to the Renaissance) to expose the fallibility of the senses and of the knowledge possible in this life; a good deal of the poem examines satirically the results of education and the ignorance of the learned; it asserts with great power and imaginative resource the triviality of what can be 'known' by observation and reason, and the joy and value of 'thinking' what is ordered, certain, and lasting. The distinction is resolved by our 'progress' here, and our attaining perfectly hereafter, to 'th'Art of knowing Heaven'; the soul is

[1] *Sermons*, viii. 94–5.

not finally sent into prison, for at the end of its progress, after death, the virtuous soul will find that 'knowing' and 'thinking' become the same when (like Elizabeth Drury) it is given the supreme joy of the sight of God.

The Second Anniversary presents a very full account of the progress of a soul, from its first infusion into the foul body, its absorption of the two inferior souls, its education, its experience among the vicissitudes and limitations of life on earth, to the process of death and the soul's release from the body. The movement of the poem does not, however, follow this progress as the principle of its ordering. After the introductory lines (1–84, corresponding to the first ninety of *The First Anniversary*) in which the themes and symbolic mode of the poem are adumbrated, the poet's 'contemplation' flows through six phases disposed in an ascending order of blessings available to the soul after death. Each of the six topics is treated on the same general plan: consideration of the soul's 'incommodities' in this life; a contrasting picture of the soul's 'exaltation' in heaven; the representation of Elizabeth Drury as having shown the virtues of a regenerate soul on earth which foreshadow their perfection in heaven; and an exhortation to the poet's soul, and to all those who seek to 'know' heaven, to follow her there by learning from her example. The poem ends with a passage full of wit and confidence; Elizabeth Drury bears God's stamp or image as does the poem itself; it is His will that she should 'for life, and death, a patterne bee' to those who live after her, and God, who gave her the power to live virtuously and to 'progress' to the sight of Him, gives the poet the power to write of her, and to summon the attention of his hearers to learn, as his 'contemplation' has taught him, the truths that her 'religious death' proclaims.

In the *Anniversaries* Donne studies the issues of 'life, and death' of which the figure of Elizabeth Drury affords in various ways a 'patterne'. The poems range through all space and through every 'world'; all time is present at any moment; all the inhabitants of earth and heaven are brought to our minds; many conceptions in which mankind has sought to express a sense of an ideal spiritual state are recalled. It has been said of T. S. Eliot's *The Waste Land*

that it is 'the equivalent in content to an epic',[1] and this is certainly
true of the *Anniversaries*, though it was left to Milton to write the
full epic statement of the themes which Donne considers. The
inclusiveness of Donne's poems is not, however, merely a matter
of the scope of their materials and themes; they present feelings
doubtless shared by many of Donne's contemporaries confronted
by profound disturbances (in religion, science, and politics)
of the long-established order, and aware of differing attitudes
in a world charged with a sense of disintegration. In another way,
too, the *Anniversaries* are a kind of *summa*; they contain many
similarities in idea and phrasing to passages in Donne's earlier
poetry and rehandle many of his former themes and images;[2] and
in addition they prefigure numerous passages in the *Sermons*. It is as
if during the years when the urgency of finding a vocation pressed
upon him, especially if it were to be a vocation as a priest of the
Church, Donne set down all that could be 'known' and 'thought',
and in various ways poetically expressed, about man's 'meteorique'
nature, of which he almost desperately felt the limitations and
the hard-won possibilities; the grim humour and the relentless
realism of the picture of man's earthly state no less than the
earnest celebration of the joys of heaven suggest that he used
this period of relative leisure and security to 'try' to the depths
his spiritual resources. The *Anniversaries* are moving evidence
of this self-examination, which ensured that when Donne at
length went up into the pulpit to proclaim the word of God the
trumpet gave forth no uncertain sound.

[1] I. A. Richards, *Principles of Literary Criticism* (1926), p. 291.
[2] See P. Crutwell, *The Shakespearean Moment* (1954), Chapter 3.

TEXTUAL INTRODUCTION

WITH the exception of the three poems published by Donne and referred to as the *Anniversaries* in his letters and of the 'Elegy on Prince Henry', the poems in this volume were first printed after the poet's death. In establishing their texts it is therefore necessary to consider manuscript copies which antedate the first edition of 1633, especially since the editor of 1633 used for the printer's copy manuscripts belonging to two of the main groups, which *a priori* had no more authority than exemplars of these two manuscript traditions which are extant. The editor of 1633 corrected the text of one of his main manuscripts by comparing it with that of the other, and appears to have referred to another source in order to make good deficiencies shared by his two main manuscripts; and he seems to have occasionally altered readings on his own initiative in order to 'improve' the meaning and the rhythm. Though 1633 is the only one of the early editions which has any authority, the value of its readings varies with the source for the moment being employed; and its text must be continually checked against the evidence of the surviving manuscripts. This theory of the texts was put forward by Sir Herbert Grierson in 1912 and developed by Helen Gardner in her editions of the *Divine Poems* (1952) and *The Elegies and the Songs and Sonnets* (1965). Manuscripts to which I refer are more fully discussed in these last two volumes, and in Milgate, *Satires etc.* Confirmation of the general soundness of Grierson's basic theory, and of the refinements that have later been made upon it, has been given in the text of the verse letter 'To the Lady Carey, and Mrs. Essex Rich' in a copy in Donne's handwriting discovered in 1970.[1] In this edition I therefore follow the same principles as those adopted in earlier volumes in the series, dealing at length only with the comparatively few problems in the text of the poems here presented.

[1] See the facsimile, with commentary by Helen Gardner, published by the Bodleian Library and the Scolar Press in 1972, and the discussion by N. Barker, *The Book Collector*, xxii (1973), 487–93. The holograph is Bodleian MS. *Eng. Poet. d. 197*.

I. EPITHALAMIONS AND EPICEDES

(i)

One of the manuscripts used by the editor of *1633* belonged to a group designated Group I, of which five members are extant: *C 57*, *D*, *H 49*, *Lec* and *SP*.[1] They derive from a common ancestor (*X*), which contained a collection of poems probably made by Donne himself in 1614. The relationships of the surviving manuscripts of the Group can be summarized by the following stemma:

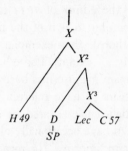

All these manuscripts omit lines in 'Obsequies to the Lord Harington' (end of l. 159 to the middle of l. 161). Since none of them contains the 'Epithalamion made at Lincoln's Inn', 'Elegy on the Death of Mistress Bulstrode' ('Language thou art too narrow'), the 'Elegy on Prince Henry', or 'An Hymn to the Saints, and to Marquess Hamilton', it may be presumed that these four poems were not in the original collection (*X*). Another manuscript, *H 40*, though it cannot be considered as part of Group I because it does not descend from *X*, has close connections with the Group. It shares with *RP 31* a miscellaneous collection of poems (including seven certainly by Donne); but it adds thirty-nine of Donne's poems not found in *RP 31*, including the elegies on Lady Markham and Mrs. Bulstrode ('Death I recant'), which are found in the Group I collection. The text, and other features, of the poems by Donne in *H 40* suggest that all but one ('The Flea') descend from

---

[1] For a key to sigla, shelf-marks, and present locations of manuscripts, see the list on pp. lxv–lvii. The Group I manuscripts are described in Gardner, *Divine Poems*, pp. lvii–lxvi, and *Elegies etc.*, pp. lxiv–lxv; see also Margaret Crum, 'Notes on the Physical Characteristics of Some Manuscripts of the Poems of Donne and of Henry King', *The Library* (June 1961).

portions of the same collection of loose sheets and quires (presumably Donne's own copies) used by the compiler of X.[1]

The editor of *1633* sought his text of verses missing from his Group I manuscript in a manuscript belonging to another main group, Group II, of which four members are extant: *A 18*, *N*, *TCC* and *TCD*.[2] *A 18* is a copy of *TCC* and *N* is a copy of *TCD*. Since *TCD* contains more poems than *TCC*, has a better text, and is sometimes better arranged, it cannot descend from *TCC* but must descend, like *TCC*, from a collection of Donne's works designated *Y*. *TCC* differs from *TCD* in omitting the Epithalamion for Princess Elizabeth's marriage, the 'Elegy on Prince Henry', and 'Obsequies to the Lord Harington'; it is possible that these poems were in *Y* and were ignored by the copyist of *TCC*. It has been plausibly suggested that *Y* was, or was derived from, a collection of his writings entrusted by Donne to his friend Sir Robert Ker (later Earl of Ancrum) just before leaving England in 1619 as chaplain to the embassy of Viscount Doncaster.[3] This suggestion is supported by the inclusion in the Group II manuscripts of the unfinished poem 'Resurrection'; for poets do not usually circulate unfinished poems, though they may keep them among their papers. It is also interesting that the 'Hymn to the Saints, and to Marquess Hamilton', written at Ker's request in 1625, is added in *TCC* (after a blank page) and in *TCD* (in a hand different from that in which most of the poems were transcribed); the omission of the poem from *N* shows that *N* was copied from *TCD* before the 'Hymn' was added. Another manuscript, *L 74*, apparently represents a smaller collection from which *Y* grew by accretion; it has a good text agreeing with that in the Group II manuscripts but free from their characteristic errors.[4] Of

[1] For a fuller discussion of *H 40*, see Gardner, *Elegies etc.*, pp. lxv–lxvii.

[2] The Group II manuscripts are described in Gardner, *Divine Poems*, pp. lxvi–lxvii, and *Elegies etc.*, p. lxvii. I follow Grierson in using the siglum *TC* for readings shared by *TCC* and *TCD*.

[3] See Alan MacColl, *Essays in Criticism*, xvii (1967) at p. 259, and 'The Circulation of Donne's Poems in Manuscript' in *John Donne: Essays in Celebration*, ed. A. J. Smith (London, 1972), pp. 32–5. Donne's apprehensions at the prospect of extensive travels (Bald, pp. 341–5) led him to send to Ker his own copy of *Biathanatos* and 'the Poems, of which you took a promise' (*Letters*, p. 21). William Drummond, writing to Ker in 1621, says that he will continue corresponding 'so long as Daniell lastes (who, dying as I heare, bequeathed to you his scrolls) or Done, who in his travells lefte you his' (*Correspondence of Sir Robert Ker, first Earl of Ancram*, ed. D. Laing (Edinburgh, 1875), i. 24).

[4] *L 74* is described by Grierson, ii. civ–cv, and in Gardner, *Elegies etc.*, pp. lxviii–lxx.

the poems in the present volume, *L 74* contains only the 'Elegy on the Lady Markham' and the two epicedes on Mistress Bulstrode. The relationship of another manuscript, *DC*, to Group II is less clear, since leaves have been lost from it, and with them a good deal of textual evidence. The 'Epithalamion made at Lincoln's Inn' breaks off at the foot of a page at l. 72, and its completion, and the other two epithalamions, were presumably copied on leaves now missing. The text resumes with ll. 45–62 of the 'Elegy on the Lady Markham', which are followed by 'Elegie Mis Bolstred' ('Death I recant') and the first eighty-seven lines of 'Elegy on Prince Henry'. Two more leaves are missing, and the text begins again at l. 109 of 'Obsequies to the Lord Harington'. The manuscript apparently never included the Hamilton 'Hymn' or the other elegy on Mistress Bulstrode ('Language thou art too narrow'). The text of *DC* is occasionally very poor (as in the Harington 'Obsequies'). It is basically that of Group II, but in some readings it agrees with *1633* against Group II.[1] In establishing the text of the poems in this volume *DC* is of little use.

The other manuscripts containing collections of Donne's poems were said by Grierson to constitute Group III, with the exception of *W*, which stands apart from the rest. This manuscript is a fair copy in the hand of Donne's friend Rowland Woodward of three groups of the poet's writings. The first section of *W* contains no poem (with one explicable exception) known to have been composed after 1598, and it includes the 'Epithalamion made at Lincoln's Inn' (but the manuscript contains none of the epicedes or the other epithalamions). The text is good, and must derive closely from Donne's own copy of the poem.

Among the other manuscripts which represent a tradition of the text different from that in Groups I and II there are four large collections of his poetry which can be more properly designated 'Group III': *Dob, Lut, O'F*, and *S 96*.[2] The poems which they have in common (except the *Satires*) have a text which derives from a

---

[1] See the discussion of *DC* in Gardner, *Elegies etc.*, pp. lxx–lxxi, lxxxviii, where the conclusion reached is that 'Its connexions must be with the manuscript that provided the copy for *1633* at a stage before the "editor" had made his final corrections and improvements.'

[2] For descriptions of these manuscripts, see Gardner, *Divine Poems*, pp. lxix–lxxiv, and *Elegies etc.*, pp. lxxi–lxxv.

common original. All contain the three epithalamions, but of the epicedes *Dob* lacks the 'Elegy upon the Death of Mistress Bulstrode' ('Language thou art too narrow') and both *Dob* and *S 96* lack the 'Elegy on Prince Henry' and the Hamilton 'Hymn'. These two manuscripts represent the collection at an earlier stage than *Lut* (copied 1631–2) and *O'F* (dated 12 October 1632), which contain poems added from a Group II manuscript. The writer of *Lut* was conscious of difficulties in the text; he occasionally records an alternative reading in the margin, he sometimes makes corrections, and it is probable that he has silently incorporated into the text readings from his Group II manuscript and elsewhere, and 'corrections' of his own. *O'F*, which (like *Lut*) contains all the epithalamions and epicedes, derives from *Lut*. The compiler of *O'F* added some more poems and the *Paradoxes and Problems*, and achieved the fullest and best arranged of the surviving manuscripts of Donne's work. Two correctors have been at work in the manuscript, one possibly the original scribe, altering many, though by no means all, readings different from those in *1633* to the wording of the edition. It seems very probable that *O'F* was being prepared for an edition of Donne's poems, and that the compiler was forestalled by the appearance of *1633*. Even the scribe of *Lut* seems to have had publication in mind, and noted that the 'Elegy on Prince Henry' was 'since in print but out of print'. The compiler of *O'F* had no reason to be totally discouraged by the publication of *1633*, since he had many more poems than had appeared in the edition. It looks as if either he entered into an arrangement with the publisher of *1633*, John Marriott, or Marriott acquired *O'F*; for the second edition of the *Poems* in 1635 obviously had *O'F* as one of its main sources.[1] Despite the differences among them due to error and sophistication, however, in the poems they share *Dob*, *Lut*, *O'F*, and *S 96* clearly belong to a third tradition of the manuscripts.

Four other collections are related to one another in a way which shows that they are surviving members of a fourth group: *Cy*, *HK 2*, *O2*, and *P*.[2] Their general relationship is not, however, demonstrable from the poems in the present volume, since *HK 2*

[1] See Appendix A.
[2] See Gardner, *Elegies etc.*, pp. lxxv–lxxviii. *HK 2* is the second part of the Haslewood–Kingsborough manuscript, the earlier-written and textually more interesting

contains only the epithalamion for the marriage of Princess Elizabeth
(in a good text). The text of this poem in *O2* and *P* seems to derive
from the same source as that in *HK 2*; *O2* and *P* also contain the
Lincoln's Inn 'Epithalamion' in a text rather less good. *Cy*, *O2*, and
P have the 'Elegy on the Lady Markham' and the two elegies on
Mistress Bulstrode, clearly taken from the same near source.
Cy opens with the 'Elegy on Prince Henry' (not in *O2* and *P*),
and its copyist may have included this from a separate text of the
poem before beginning to transcribe his main collection; the
manuscript peters out at l. 38 of 'A Valediction: of my Name
in the Window', so that the scribe's main source might have
contained other poems. None of the four manuscripts includes
the Harington 'Obsequies'.

    The other manuscript collections of Donne's poems seem to have
no uniform relations to one another or to the groups just discussed.
Most show signs of contamination of one tradition by another,
and all have a good many erroneous or sophisticated readings.
Several have been put together from a variety of sources. *A 25*,
for example, was written by many copyists,[1] the poems by Donne
having been apparently acquired in batches (occasionally, perhaps,
singly). Probably the earliest scribe to work in the manuscript
wrote in three poems, one of which was the Harington 'Obsequies'
(the letter accompanying which appears forty leaves later in a
different hand). Another scribe copied the 'Elegy on Mrs. Bulstrode'
('Death I recant'), and yet another many of Donne's poems,
including the 'Elegy on the Lady Markham' and the Epithalamion
for Princess Elizabeth's wedding. The Epithalamion and 'Death I
recant' have a mixed text, the primary source of which is impossible
to determine; the copy of the 'Elegy on the Lady Markham' is
most like that in *Cy*, *O2*, and *P*. Lines 110, 203–4, and 185–8 are
omitted from the Harington 'Obsequies', and though *JC* also
omits ll. 185–8 this is probably due to independent eye-slip on
the part of the respective copyists, for the text in *A 25* seems
basically like that in *S*. *A 25* illustrates very well the hazards that

collection. Both *HK 2* and *HK 1* contain collections of Donne's poems within a miscellany
of verse by other writers.

    [1] See Grierson, ii. clii–cliii, and Gardner, *Elegies etc.*, pp. lxxviii–lxxix. *C* consists of
passages selected from the texts in *A 25*.

threatened the text of Donne's poems in the compilation of manu-
script collections of his work. *JC* opens with a poem by its first
owner, John Cave, on Donne's *Satires* dated 3 June 1620; a copy
of the manuscript, *D 17*, is dated 1625. Yet even by this time
Cave had managed to assemble a collection that came from various
sources, with a text which gives evidence of the influence of
different traditions and which in one way or another has fallen
into errors found nowhere else. His manuscript contains rather
poor copies of the Epithalamion for Princess Elizabeth's marriage,
the 'Elegy on the Lady Markham', and the Harington 'Obsequies'.
S is dated at the end 19 July 1620, and includes the two epicedes
on Mistress Bulstrode and 'Obsequies to the Lord Harington'.
The variants in the text of these poems are not so numerous as to
allow a certain judgement about the sources of the texts in *S*; but
it follows in them the same pattern as in other poems it contains,
its textual relations varying from poem to poem. The texts of the
elegies on Mistress Bulstrode vary between those of *O'F* and *Cy*;
in the Harington 'Obsequies' the basic text seems to be like that
in *Dob*, but it has been contaminated with Group I readings.
B, a much larger collection of Donne's poems (with the *Paradoxes
and Problems*), obviously aiming at completeness, includes the
three epithalamions and four epicedes (omitting the 'Elegy on
Prince Henry' and the Hamilton 'Hymn'). The text is very careless,
but seems basically that of Group III, in the epicedes resembling
that of *O'F* and in the epithalamions that of *Dob*; like *Dob*, *B*
omits ll. 226–35 of the Somerset 'Epithalamion'. *Hd* (which
includes a poem on the death of Sir John Burroughs, 1627) offers
fairly good texts of the epithalamions on Princess Elizabeth's
marriage and on Somerset's (ll. 1–170 only), and of the 'Elegy on
the Lady Markham'; in the elegy its text is like that in *Cy*, *O2*, *P*, in
the epithalamions like that in *Dob*. Two other manuscripts are
late. *HK 1* was not copied much before 1640, but a section mainly
of Donne's poems, each initialled 'L. C.', probably comes from a
collection which antedates the earlier editions; it contains an
extremely poor copy of the Harington 'Obsequies' and better
texts of the 'Elegy upon the Death of Mistress Bulstrode' ('Lan-
guage thou art too narrow') and the Somerset 'Epithalamion'

(ll. 1–170). *O1* has a poor text of the 'Elegy on the Lady Markham', the two elegies on Mistress Bulstrode, and the Harington 'Obsequies' (without the last ten lines, which were copied on the lost last leaf of the manuscript). One or more of the epithalamions and epicedes appear from time to time in miscellanies, and I have listed these at the beginning of the commentary on each poem; they are textually uninteresting, but give some indication of the extent to which each of the poems circulated.

Much more interesting are some copies made nearer to the dates of composition of various poems. William Drummond of Hawthornden obtained copies of some poems 'belonging' to Donne, and transcribed them in *HN*;[1] the manuscript has good copies of the two elegies on Mistress Bulstrode. A somewhat expanded collection depending in part on the same source as *HN* is found in *Wed*,[2] which, however, drops one elegy on Mistress Bulstrode ('Language thou art too narrow') and adds a respectable text of the 'Elegy on the Lady Markham'. Surviving copies of single poems bring us close to the manner in which Donne's verses on important occasions circulated in Court circles. One is a good text, unfortunately damaged, among the Conway papers (*A 23*), of the Somerset 'Epithalamion'; it is in the hand of Donne's friend Sir Henry Goodyer, who corresponded with Conway.[3] The other, also on a single leaf, is among the State papers of Sir Joseph Williamson in the Public Record Office: a text of the Hamilton 'Hymn' (S.P. *9/51*).[4] Though slightly damaged, the copy is almost entirely accurate. It was in very similar form that John Chamberlain saw the poem fairly soon after its composition; and Sir Robert Ker, for whom it was written, clearly lost little time in circulating Donne's tribute to Hamilton among the amateurs of poetry at Court.

Since (apart from the 'Epithalamion made at Lincoln's Inn') the epithalamions and epicedes were composed for patrons, it

---

[1] See Milgate, *Satires etc.*, pp. li–lii.

[2] *Wed* was first described by A. MacColl, 'A New Manuscript of Donne's poems', *R.E.S.*, N.S. xix (1968).

[3] *Letters*, p. 34. The handwriting was identified as Goodyer's by Mr. A. MacColl, in his thesis, 'The Circulation of Donne's Poems in Manuscript' (1967), in the Bodleian Library.

[4] First noted by B. W. Whitlock, 'A Note on Two Donne Manuscripts', *Renaissance News*, xviii (1965).

would have been discourteous for Donne to have reissued them in a revised form, even if he desired to improve them. The manuscript copies, as might be expected, offer no evidence of revision. As the text of the holograph of Donne's verse letter to Lady Carey and her sister suggests, however, there might have occurred minor variations in separate copies which Donne made of any poem. It is highly improbable that the Rich sisters allowed a copy of the verse letter to be taken, or that any lover of poetry would have known of its existence; it seems clear that the copy lay undisturbed among the family papers until recent times. The manuscript texts of the letter must descend from a copy which Donne kept in his letter-book or among his papers. The two small variations in wording are of the kind which it is almost impossible to avoid when transcribing a text, especially, perhaps, if a poet is making another copy of his own work. It seems very probable that Donne also kept copies of the poems he wrote for great public occasions, and perhaps also of those he composed for the Countess of Bedford on the deaths of her friends and relatives. Variations in these copies may have found their way into manuscript collections, and I have included in the textual apparatus all variations which cannot be shown to be erroneous. It is possible to give a fair account of the variants by citing representative manuscripts; and I quote, for Group I, *C 57* and *H 49*; for Group II, *TCC*, *TCD*, and a related text, *L 74*; for Group III, *Dob* and *O'F*; and in the Lincoln's Inn 'Epithalamion', *W* because of its good authority. The other manuscripts provide a general check on the readings quoted, sometimes by showing how error has occurred, and any point of interest in them is noted in the Commentary.

(ii)

The editor (if indeed there was only one) of *1633* used his Group I manuscript for the epithalamions and epicedes which it contained. For his texts of the Lincoln's Inn 'Epithalamion', the 'Elegy upon the Death of Mistress Bulstrode' ('Language thou art too narrow'), the 'Elegy on Prince Henry', and the Hamilton 'Hymn', he went to a Group II manuscript. His Group I manuscript was clearly like *C 57* and *Lec*, and it sometimes led

the editor into error; indeed, readings of *1633* supported only by
C 57 and *Lec* must be rejected. The editor also emended his
Group I copy from his Group II manuscript, and sometimes
probably from another text, and, whatever his primary source,
altered readings on his own initiative (sometimes mistakenly)
to improve the sense. He was interested in the rhythm as well,
and took care over elision marks.[1] Indeed, the volume is remarkable
for the evidence it provides of constant supervision even during
printing, as is shown by the attention given to wording, punc-
tuation, and elisions as the sheets passed through the press.

In the second edition of 1635, new poems were added, the
contents were rearranged (under the headings which *O'F* took
from *Lut*), and a considerable number of changes were made
from the text of *1633*. Among the titles added to poems (in-
cluding some titles not found in any extant manuscript) was the
inappropriate one, 'Elegie XI. Death', assigned to the epicede
on Mistress Bulstrode beginning 'Language thou art too narrow'
(which in *1633* had been entitled simply 'Elegie'). The connection
of the edition with *O'F* is, however, very close; alterations to
the text, although mostly to readings which *O'F* shares with
other Group III (or in certain poems, Group II) manuscripts,
are sometimes to a reading which is found only in *Lut* and *O'F*,
or in *O'F* alone.[2] It will be remembered that many readings in
O'F itself had been corrected to those in *1633*. The edition of
1635, therefore, cannot be regarded, in the main, as being sub-
stantive, being a reprint of the first edition conflated with readings
from *O'F*. It is sometimes useful, however, in punctuating the
poems; and for three of the 'Elegies upon the Author' it provides
the appropriate copy-text. The subsequent editions of Donne's
Poems in the seventeenth century are of no interest to the editor
of the poems in the present volume; their variants may be found,
if required, in Grierson's edition.

(iii)

The 'Elegy on Prince Henry' is in a special position. It is the
only poem printed in Donne's lifetime from autograph which is

---

[1] See the 'Note on Versification', p. 108.   [2] See Appendix A.

also transmitted independently in manuscripts. The text in the manuscript tradition is very probably descended from a copy of the poem which Donne kept among his papers. The copy which he sent, or, as Joshua Sylvester would have us believe, which found its way surreptitiously, to be included in the third edition (1613) of *Lachrymae Lachrymarum*,[1] was presumably (like nearly all contemporary 'printer's copy') destroyed. Sylvester's volume, connected with a topic of great general interest, doubtless very soon went (as the scribe of *Lut* notes) out of print, and it was worth the while of collectors of Donne's poetry to transcribe this Elegy along with the rest of the poems available to them. I note in the apparatus to the poem any variants in the manuscript tradition which might conceivably have stood in a copy which Donne transcribed for himself. Since, however, the text in *1613* is that which he wished, or allowed, to be printed, I take it as the copy-text. Comparison with the first printed texts of the *Anniversaries* suggests that through Sylvester's vibrant typography one can frequently discern the spelling and punctuation used by Donne himself.

II. THE *ANNIVERSARIES*

The *Anniversaries* are the only poems printed in Donne's lifetime with whose printing we can be certain that he was concerned.[2] There are, as is to be expected with poems that their author sent to press, no manuscript copies whose witness has to be weighed against the witness of the printed text.[3] These poems, therefore, require rather different editorial treatment from that required for posthumously printed poems where the text was derived from manuscript copies of the poet's works.

What became in the second edition *The First Anniversary* was first published in a small octavo volume entitled *An Anatomy of the World*, printed (probably by Humfrey Lownes the elder) for

---

[1] See the commentary on the poem, p. 190.

[2] The Latin verses on *Volpone* were printed with the play in 1607, the verses on Coryat in the *Crudities* (1611) and in *The Odcombian Banquet* (1611), and the 'Elegy on Prince Henry' in Sylvester's volume. Three of the *Songs and Sonnets* were printed in song-books. In none of these cases can we assume that Donne had any concern with the printing.

[3] There is a copy of 'A Funeral Elegy' in a Bodleian manuscript, *Eng. Poet. e 37*, but the text is taken from the edition of 1621; ll. 1–8 and 75–6 of the poem are copied into Brit. Lib. MS. *Harley 3991* also from a printed text.

Samuel Macham in 1611.[1] It appeared, under this title, in italic type, preceded by a poem 'To the Praise of the Dead, and the Anatomy' (almost certainly by Joseph Hall), in roman type, and followed by Donne's 'A Funeral Elegy', also in roman type. The obvious care taken in the printing and proof-reading (four corrections being made while the book was being printed off[2]) makes it very probable that Donne himself passed the proofs before leaving for the Continent with the Drurys about the beginning of November 1611.[3]

The Second Anniversary ('Of the Progress of the Soul') was composed while Donne was in France with the Drurys and printed by the beginning of April 1612.[4] It was published in a small octavo, and followed a reprint of the contents of the volume of 1611 provided with a new title-page which added the heading 'The First Anniversary' above the original title. *The Second Anniversary* was given a separate title-page and Donne's poem was preceded by 'The Harbinger to the Progress' by Joseph Hall.[5] The publisher was again Samuel Macham, but the press-work was done by another printer, Melchisadec Bradwood. The typographical distinction of the edition of 1611 was reversed in 1612: the two *Anniversaries* were printed in roman type, the supplementary poems in italic.[6] Marginal notes were supplied to both *Anni-*

---

[1] Only two copies are known to have survived, each in different ways defective; one is in the Henry E. Huntington Library, the other in the collection of Sir Geoffrey Keynes. By combining pages from the two copies and repairing a deficiency in both with a wood-block used elsewhere by Macham, Sir Geoffrey was able to make a perfect facsimile, published for the Roxburghe Club (1951); see the Postscript to this facsimile, and Keynes, *Bibliography*, pp. 171–80.   [2] See ll. 117, 133, 237, and 385.

[3] Sir Arthur Throckmorton received his copy of the book from London on 21 November (A. L. Rowse, *Raleigh and the Throckmortons* (1962), p. 288). Donne was very careful of accuracy in the printing of works he published later (see E. M. Simpson, 'A Note on Donne's Punctuation', *R.E.S.* iv. 1928), and was presumably not less punctilious here. For the dates and circumstances of composition of the poems, see the General Introduction, pp. xxix–xxxiii.

[4] Donne refers to criticisms of his *Anniversaries* in a letter to George Garrard from Paris, dated 14 April 1612 (*Letters*, pp. 237–9). His use of the word 'Anniversaries' makes it clear that it is the volume of 1612 and not *An Anatomy of the World* of 1611 that he is defending.

[5] Jonson told Drummond that Joseph Hall was 'the Herbenger to Dones Anniversarie' (*Works*, i. 149). It seems safe to assume with Grierson that he also wrote the poem 'To the Praise of the Dead, and the Anatomy', prefacing *An Anatomy of the World*. For Hall's relations with Donne, see the General Introduction, pp. xxx–xxxi.

[6] Grierson wrongly stated that 'The Praise of the Dead' as well as *An Anatomy of the World* were in italic in *1611* and went on to suppose that both were regarded as merely introductory to 'A Funeral Elegy' in roman, but that when the idea of Anniversary poems emerged these were regarded as the main works and printed in roman and the other poems in italic. The most probable explanation of the change in *1612* is shortage of italic type.

versaries, probably, though not certainly, on Donne's instructions. We may assume that the general title of *Anniversaries* given to the two main poems was Donne's.

The printing of the volume of 1612 was careless, and neither the printer nor Joseph Hall, who probably saw it through the press, made any attempt to correct its errors.[1] One surviving copy, however, contains an errata slip.[2] That this was compiled by Donne himself is suggested by the inclusion of seven errors in the text of *The First Anniversary* in addition to corrections of one in 'The Harbinger to the Progress' and of twenty in *The Second Anniversary* itself. The printer had set up his text of *The First Anniversary* and the poems that accompanied it directly from the edition of 1611, and would not presumably have had a manuscript of these poems to refer to; indeed, his lack of interest in the correctness of the text suggests that he would in any case have made no such reference. Furthermore, some of the corrections in the errata list (e.g. of 'then' to 'there', twice in the earlier poem, once in *The Second Anniversary*) cannot easily be attributed to anyone but the man who had written the manuscript, since a printer who had misread the words in the first place would hardly have been confident enough to correct errors in an errata slip, if indeed it could ever have occurred to him that he had made them. Only the author would have been likely to change 'Towres' in l. 262 of *The First Anniversary* (in both editions) to 'Townes', or 'Hydroptique' and 'to'rect' in *The Second Anniversary* (ll. 48, 417) to 'Hydropique' and 't'erect'. The errata slip fails to correct other errors; but the only plausible explanation for its existence is that on returning from the Continent early in September 1612 Donne himself noted some of the mistakes and insisted on the insertion of the slip in the unsold copies. This would account for the rarity of the errata slip and for the failure

---

[1] The only variation I have noticed is in the last line of p. 2 (A5^v), where, instead of 'there is', the copy in the Folger Shakespeare Library reads 'therei s'; this may be due either to a movement of the type or to the casual adjustment of an error in type-setting during the printing of the book.

[2] First noted by Mr. John Sparrow, *T.L.S.* (29 June 1946), p. 312. Grierson replied in the issue of 20 July 1946. Six of the seven surviving copies are in United States libraries; that containing the errata slip is in the collection of Sir Geoffrey Keynes. Keynes adds a seventh copy (in the library of R. S. Pirie) to the six listed by Manley. The slip is reproduced in Keynes, f. p. 172.

of the printers of the later seventeenth-century editions to make use of it.[1]

For *The First Anniversary*, 'A Funeral Elegy', and 'To the Praise of the Dead, and the Anatomy', therefore, the 1611 edition is the only possible copy-text; and for *The Second Anniversary* and Hall's 'Harbinger to the Progress', the edition of 1612.[2] The readings of the errata slip must, however, be accepted into the text. Otherwise, an editor has little to do but offer his author his services as press-reader and proof-corrector; except that changes in spelling and punctuation must be made sparingly, since the printed texts probably reflect Donne's own practice in the manuscripts supplied to the printer (for example, in the care—not complete—with which rhyming syllables are wherever possible spelt alike), and, where Donne's practice is apparently inconsistent, the editor will choose the alternative least distracting to a modern reader.

In this edition broken, turned, or wrong fount letters are silently corrected, contractions are silently expanded, and ligatures and digraphs are not reproduced. The use of *u/v*, *i/j*, *vv*, and long *ſ* is normalized to modern practice. Otherwise all variations from the copy-text, including the correction of actual misprints and of all errors corrected in the errata slip, are recorded in the apparatus. Some obvious errors that escaped the notice of the compiler of the errata slip have been corrected, and the use of contracted forms and marks of elision is made consistent in the relatively few places where this was necessary.[3] The punctuation has required rather more correction. In most cases the alteration has the support of later editions, and is, I hope, obvious and self-justifying.

The Anniversaries with the accompanying poems were reprinted twice in Donne's lifetime, in 1621[4] and 1625. There is no evidence

---

[1] Manley, pp. 53–5.

[2] These are represented in the apparatus and Commentary by the sigla *1611* and *1612*.

[3] In the 580 lines of *The First Anniversary* and 'A Funeral Elegy' it has been necessary to make a contraction only on six occasions and to supply an elision mark between words on eight. In the 528 lines of *The Second Anniversary* fifteen contracted forms and fifteen elision marks have been supplied. The difference supports the view that Donne oversaw the printing of the edition of 1611, and that in writing out his poems for the press he was careful to indicate contracted forms and elisions.

[4] The Bodleian copy of the edition of 1621 has some interesting but unauthoritative annotations.

that Donne himself took any interest in the text of these editions. Their variant readings have, therefore, no authority. The same is true of the variants in the text of the posthumous *Poems* of 1633. The editor of the edition of 1633 followed the practice of previous printers in using as his copy-text the most recent edition of the *Anniversaries*, that of 1625. Attempts were made to correct its errors, so that in addition to preserving misprints from previous editions the text of *1633* includes a number of editorial sophistications, where a more or less intelligent guess has been made at what would give a required sense. But although editions subsequent to *1611* and *1612* are of no value in establishing the text, their readings have been recorded in the apparatus. The text of *1633* has historic importance as the first collected edition of Donne's poems and the source of all later editions, and it was the basis of Grierson's text, the *textus receptus*. Inclusion of its readings makes it necessary to include the readings of the intermediate editions of 1621 and 1625, since many of the readings of *1633* derive from them or are attempts to correct them. In this section of this edition I depart from the practice of recording in the apparatus only readings that merit consideration. A complete collation of the editions allows those interested to see the editor of *1633* at work on an extant source. His care and good sense are apparent in making obvious corrections of the errors in *1625*, his corrections often restoring the original reading and, on occasion, agreeing with the errata slip. On other occasions we see him making guesses of varying merit. Readings from editions subsequent to *1633* are not recorded,[1] with the exception that the readings of Grierson's text are noted wherever it differs substantially from the text in this edition.

III. CONCLUSIONS

The copy-text for each of the poems is the first printed text. Apart from the 'Elegy on Prince Henry' and the *Anniversaries* (and three of the 'Elegies upon the Author'), this is the text of *1633*. While *1633* is superior to any single manuscript, however,

[1] Readings from editions from 1635 to 1669 may be found, if required, in Manley, pp. 109–12.

it must be corrected from the manuscripts, where it misprints or has obviously misread the 'copy'. In addition, readings in which *1633* follows *C 57* and *Lec* against the other manuscripts of Group I must be regarded as errors derived from the Group I manuscript used in compiling *1633*, and must be corrected. Further, any readings in *1633* that do not have manuscript support must be regarded as editorial emendations and (unless the reasons that would appear to have swayed the first editor are still valid) must be rejected. The careful printing of *1633*, which follows the best contemporary practice, makes it a good model; readings adopted into the text are regularized to the editor's practice elsewhere in the edition; and where he has failed to be consistent I have tried to achieve uniformity.

In printing all the poems, from whatever printed source, I follow the spelling and usually the punctuation of the copy-text, but abandon long *s* and ligatures; printers' contractions have been expanded; the use of *i/j*, *u/v*, and *vv* is normalized to modern practice. In titles the typography is regularized. The lavish use of italic and upper-case letters in Sylvester's text (*1613*) of the 'Elegy on Prince Henry' has been abandoned in favour of the general practice of *1633*. It is clear from the holograph of Donne's verse letter to Lady Carey and her sister that he punctuated fairly heavily, and wished his poems to be read slowly, with pauses for the full effect of the phrasing to be appreciated. I have tried to benefit from this example, though in the main I have emended the punctuation sparingly; for the changes I have made there is nearly always warrant in one or more of the more careful manuscripts or in editions later than *1633*. For some suggestions I am indebted to Grierson, who had a sensitive understanding of seventeenth-century punctuation.

In the textual apparatus I name the copy-text for each poem and the printed or manuscript texts from which variant readings are given. Where a manuscript has been corrected by someone after the scribe had finished his copying I give the original reading, adding '(*b.c.*)', that is, 'before correction'; with reference to *O'F* the meaning is 'before its correction to the reading of *1633*'. The manuscripts from which readings are given have been chosen to represent the groups in which the poem is found, or the main traditions of the text. I have adopted Grierson's convenient siglum *TC* to show that the reading of *TCD* is also that of *TCC*; when they differ I quote each separately. In quoting variants I give the spelling of the first manuscript named (normalizing the use of *u* and *v*), unless the reading has been adopted into the text; differences of spelling among the manuscripts are ignored, unless there is some point in recording them. The apparatus notes all variations from the copy-text. It also seeks to record, in the form of group readings, any variation in the text which could possibly be authentic. To this end it has been pruned of readings that can be proved wrong, and as far as possible of scribal errors and sophistications. Where there is any doubt, however, I have preferred not to be dogmatic, but to present the evidence to the reader's judgement. Readings of the early collected editions later than the first are not given, having been based on those in *1635*, the nature of whose text is shown in Appendix A. I quote readings from Grierson's edition of 1912 (*Gr*), however, where it differs from mine.

Variations made in the copy-texts as the sheets were being printed are also recorded in the apparatus. Such variations are fairly numerous in *1633* and often affect small details easy to miss without some aid to the wearying human eye. I am, therefore, most grateful to Mr. Alan MacColl for allowing me to use the results of his comparison of thirteen copies of *1633* for press variants on the collating machine at the British Library.[1] Some of the changes made in the edition seem to me to have been ill advised, and I occasionally prefer the reading of the uncorrected state.

In the Commentary I list all the texts in which, so far as I know, a particular poem is to be found.[2] Variants of the title are discussed,

---

[1] The copies are those in the British Library (2), Bodleian Library (2), All Souls, Balliol, Brasenose, Christ Church, Corpus Christi, Queen's, St. John's, Wadham, and Worcester Colleges, Oxford.

[2] I have inspected most of them, but for a few I rely on photographs or on reports from those who have been able to examine the manuscripts, notably Professor J. T. Shawcross, who has a valuable list in his edition of *The Complete Poetry of John Donne* (New York, 1967), and Mr. A. MacColl, who kindly lent me a list which he had made for his own purposes.

in order to avoid cluttering the textual apparatus. Textual matters are dealt with near the beginning of the commentary on each poem so that readers not interested in the subject may avoid the discussions of them. The notes on the poems are as full as considerations of space decently allow. Those on the 'Elegies upon the Author', however, are restricted to points which might interest students, not of the writers of the elegies, but of Donne himself.

LIST OF SIGLA

Classified List of Manuscripts of the Epithalamions
and Epicedes

(i) MSS. containing collections of Donne's poems

GROUP I

C 57 Cambridge University Library, Add. MS. 5778.

D Dowden MS. Bodleian Library, MS. Eng. Poet. e 99 (formerly
     in the library of Mr. Wilfred Merton).

H 49 British Library, Harleian MS. 4955.

Lec Leconfield MS. In the library of Sir Geoffrey Keynes.

SP St. Paul's Cathedral Library, MS. 49 B 43.

H 40 British Library, Harleian MS. 4064.

GROUP II

A 18 British Library, Add. MS. 18647.

N Norton MS. Harvard College Library, MS. Eng. 966/3 (formerly
     MS. Nor. 4503).

TCC Trinity College, Cambridge, MS. R 3 12.

TCD Trinity College, Dublin, MS. 877 (formerly G 2 21).

L 74 British Library, Lansdowne MS. 740.

DC National Library of Wales, Dolau Cothi MS.

GROUP III

Dob Dobell MS. Harvard College Library, MS. Eng. 966/4 (formerly
     MS. Nor. 4506).

Lut Luttrell MS. In the library of Sir Geoffrey Keynes.

O'F¹ O'Flaherty MS. Harvard College Library, MS. Eng. 966/5
     (formerly MS. Nor. 4504).

S 96 British Library, Stowe MS. 961.

---

¹ *O'F (b.c.)*: O'Flaherty, before correction. This indicates that the reading cited has been
corrected to the reading of *1633*.

IV

W   Westmoreland MS. Berg Collection, New York Public Library.

V

HK 2   Haslewood–Kingsborough MS., second part, Huntington Library,
           MS. HM 198.

(a)

Cy   Carnaby MS. Harvard College Library, MS. Eng. 966/1 (formerly
           MS. Nor. 4502).

O 2   Osborn Collection, Yale University, MS. b 148.

P   Phillipps MS. Bodleian Library, MS. Eng. Poet. f 9.

(b)

A 25   British Library, Add. MS. 25707.

B   Bridgewater MS. Huntington Library, MS. EL 6893.

C   Cambridge University Library, Add. MS. 29.

D 17   Victoria and Albert Museum, Dyce Collection, MS. D 25 F 17.

JC   John Cave MS. George Arents Tobacco Collection, New
           York Public Library. (Formerly in the library of Richard
           Jennings.)

O 1   Osborn Collection, Yale University, MS. b 114 (formerly King
           MS.; Raphael King, Catalogue 51, Item 73).

S   Stephens MS. Harvard College Library, MS. Eng. 966/6 (formerly
           MS. Nor. 4500).

(ii) MSS. containing copies of single poems

A 23   British Library, Add. MS. 23229.

S.P. 9/51 Public Record Office, State Papers Misc. 9/51/17.

(iii) MSS. containing Donne's poems with those of other authors[1]

EH   Edward Hyde MS. In the library of Sir Geoffrey Keynes.

Grey   S. African Public Library, Cape Town, MS. Grey 2 a 11.

Hd   Harvard College Library, MS. Eng. 966/7.

HK 1   Haslewood–Kingsborough MS., first part, Huntington Library,
           MS. HM 198.

---

[1] This is a select list, containing only those miscellanies that have a substantial number
of poems by Donne and a few that are of special interest.

HN	Hawthornden MS. National Library of Scotland, MS. 2067.
Hol	Holgate MS. Pierpont Morgan Library, New York, MS. MA 1057.
La	Edinburgh University Library, Laing MS. iii. 493.
RP 31	Bodleian Library, Rawlinson Poetical MS. 31.
RP 117 (2)	Bodleian Library, Rawlinson Poetical MS. 117, second part.
S 962	British Library, Stowe MS. 962.
TCD (2)	Trinity College, Dublin, MS. 877, second part.
Wed	Wedderburn MS. National Library of Scotland, MS. 6504.
Wel	Welbeck MS. In the library of the Duke of Portland, deposited in the library of the University of Nottingham; MS. PwV 37.

Seventeenth-century editions of the poems are cited under their dates: *An Anatomy of the World* (1611) as *1611*, the completed *Anniversaries* as *1612*, *1621*, and *1625*; Sylvester's *Lachrymae Lachrymarum* (1613) as *1613*; and the editions of Donne's *Poems* from 1633 to 1699 as *1633*, *1635*, etc.

The Poems of John Donne, ed. H. J. C. Grierson, 2 vols. (Oxford, 1912) is cited as *Gr*.

The symbol *Σ* is used in the apparatus when the majority of the manuscripts cited agree in a reading; those which do not are specified.

PLATE I

John Donne in 1616; from the miniature by Isaac Oliver at Windsor Castle; by gracious permission of Her Majesty the Queen

EPITHALAMIONS
ANNIVERSARIES
AND
EPICEDES

EPITHALAMIONS

Epithalamion made at Lincolnes Inne

THE Sun-beames in the East are spred,
    Leave, leave, faire Bride, your solitary bed,
  No more shall you returne to it alone,
It nourseth sadnesse, and your bodies print,
Like to a grave, the yielding downe doth dint;   5
    You and your other you meet there anon;
  Put forth, put forth that warme balme-breathing thigh,
Which when next time you in these sheets wil smother,
      There it must meet another,
  Which never was, but must be, oft, more nigh;   10
Come glad from thence, goe gladder then you came,
To day put on perfection, and a womans name.

    Daughters of London, you which bee
Our Golden Mines, and furnish'd Treasurie,
  You which are Angels, yet still bring with you   15
Thousands of Angels on your mariage daies,
Help with your presence, and devise to praise
    These rites, which also unto you grow due;
  Conceitedly dresse her, and be assign'd,
By you, fit place for every flower and jewell,   20
      Make her for love fit fewell,
  As gay as Flora, and as rich as Inde;
So may shee faire, rich, glad,'and in nothing lame,
To day put on perfection, and a womans name.

EPITHALAMIONS. *Text from 1633. Readings are given from representative MSS. named in the apparatus for each epithalamion.*

  Epithalamion made etc. *MSS.*: *TC* (*TCD with TCC*); *Dob, O'F; W. Title from 1633, TC*: Epithalamium on a Citizen *Dob, O'F*: Epithalamium *W.*   4 bodies] body *1633 uncorrected*   8 these] those *Dob, O'F*   smother,] smother *1633*   10 must ... oft] oft must be *Dob, O'F*   12 *day*] night *Dob, O'F (b.c.)*   21 fewell,] fewell *1633*   23 faire ... in *TC, W (no elision mark)*: faire and rich, in *1633, Dob, O'F*   24 *To day*] omit *Dob, O'F (b.c.)*

And you frolique Patricians,   25
Sonnes of these Senators wealths deep oceans,
Ye painted courtiers, barrels of others wits,
Yee country men, who but your beasts love none,
Yee of those fellowships whereof hee's one,
Of study'and play made strange Hermaphrodits,   30
Here shine; This Bridegroom to the Temple bring.
Loe, in yon path, which store of straw'd flowers graceth,
The sober virgin paceth;
Except my sight faile, 'tis no other thing;
Weep not nor blush, here is no griefe nor shame,   35
To day put on perfection, and a womans name.

Thy two-leav'd gates, faire Temple,'unfold,
And these two in thy sacred bosome hold,
Till, mystically joyn'd, but one they bee;
Then may thy leane and hunger-starved wombe   40
Long time expect their bodies and their tombe,
Long after their owne parents fatten thee;
All elder claimes, and all cold barrennesse,
All yeelding to new loves bee far for ever,
Which might these two dissever,   45
All waies, all th'other may each one possesse;
For, the best Bride, best worthy'of praise and fame,
To day puts on perfection, and a womans name.

Oh winter dayes bring much delight,
Not for themselves, but for they soon bring night;   50
Other sweets wait thee then these diverse meats,
Other disports then dancing jollities,
Other love tricks then glancing with the eyes,
But that the Sun still in our halfe Spheare sweates;

25 Patricians,] Patricians *1633*   26 Sonnes of these *W*: Some of these *1633*:
Sonnes of those *Dob, O'F*: Some of those *TC*   28 who] which *Dob, O'F*   30
study'and] study and *1633*   31 bring.] bring *1633*   32 Loe] So *Dob, O'F*
(b.c.)   path,] path *1633*   straw'd] *omit Dob, O'F*   37 gates, ... unfold] gates
faire Temple unfold *1633*   39 but] both in *Dob, O'F (b.c.)*   43 cold] old
Dob, O'F (b.c.)   46 All waies *W*: Alwaies *1633*, *Σ*   all ... each] th'each other
may th'each *Dob, O'F (b.c.)*   47 worthy'of] worthy of *1633*   49 Oh *O'F, W*:
our *Dob*: *omit 1633, TC*   51 these] those *Dob, O'F*   53 eyes,] eyes; *1633*
54 that] yf *Dob, O'F (b.c.)*

Hee flies in winter, but now he stands still, 55
Yet shadowes turne; Noone point he hath attain'd,
His steeds will bee restrain'd,
But gallop lively downe the Westerne hill;
Thou shalt, when he hath runne the worlds half frame,
To night put on perfection, and a womans name. 60

The amorous evening starre is rose,
Why should not then our amorous starre inclose
Her selfe in her wish'd bed? Release your strings
Musicians, and dancers take some truce
With these your pleasing labours, for great use 65
As much wearinesse as perfection brings;
You, and not only you, but all toyl'd beasts
Rest duly; at night all their toyles are dispens'd;
But in their beds commenc'd
Are other labours, and more dainty feasts; 70
She goes a maid, who, least she turne the same,
To night puts on perfection, and a womans name.

Thy virgins girdle now untie,
And in thy nuptiall bed (loves altar) lye
A pleasing sacrifice; now dispossesse 75
Thee of these chaines and robes which were put on
T'adorne the day, not thee; for thou, alone,
Like vertue'and truth, art best in nakednesse;
This bed is onely to virginitie
A grave, but, to a better state, a cradle; 80
Till now thou wast but able
To be what now thou art; then that by thee
No more be said, *I may bee,* but, *I am,*
To night put on perfection, and a womans name.

55 now he *Dob, O'F, W*: he now *1633, TC, Gr*   57 will] nill *W, Gr; see note*
59 runne *Dob, O'F, W*: come *1633, TC*   60 To night] *omit Dob, O'F (b.c.)*   put *Σ*:
but *1633*   62 should not then *Σ*: . . . thou *TCC*: then should not *1633, Gr*
63 your] the *Dob, O'F*   65 these] those *Dob, O'F*   68–9 dispens'd . . .
commenc'd] dispensed . . . commenced *1633*   73 virgins] Virgin *Dob, O'F*
74 (loves altar)] [loves alter] *1633*   76 these *1633, W*: those *TC, Dob, O'F*   were]
wee *1633 corrected*

Ev'n like a faithfull man content,   85
That this life for a better should be spent,
So, shee a mothers rich stile doth preferre,
And at the Bridegroomes wish'd approach doth lye,
Like an appointed lambe, when tenderly
The priest comes on his knees t'embowell her;   90
Now sleep or watch with more joy; and O light
Of heaven, to morrow rise thou hot, and early;
This Sun will love so dearely
Her rest, that long, long we shall want her sight;
Wonders are wrought, for shee which had no maime,   95
To night puts on perfection, and a womans name.

An Epithalamion, or Mariage Song on the Lady Elizabeth, and Count Palatine being married on St. Valentines Day

I

HAILE Bishop Valentine, whose day this is,
        All the Aire is thy Diocis,
        And all the chirping Choristers
And other birds are thy Parishioners,
        Thou marryest every yeare   5
The lirique Larke, and the grave whispering Dove,
The Sparrow that neglects his life for love,
        The household Bird, with the red stomacher,
        Thou mak'st the Blackbird speed as soone,
As doth the Goldfinch, or the Halcyon;   10
The husband Cocke lookes out, and straight is sped,
And meets his wife, which brings her feather-bed.

---

85 Ev'n] Even *1633*   86 spent,] spent; *1633*   95 maime, *1633, W*: maime
1633 uncorrected: name *TC, Dob, O'F (b.c.)*

  An Epithalamion etc. *MSS.: C 57, H 49; TCD; Dob, O'F. Title from 1633, C 57: . . .*
and Fredericke count . . ., beeing St. . . . *H 49*: Epithalamium *TCD*: Vpon the marriage
of the Prince Palatine and the Lady Elizabeth on . . . *Dob*: Vpon Frederick Count Palatine
and the Lady Elizabeth maryed on . . . *O'F*   6 lirique] Lirique *1633*   9 Blackbird]
black bird *1633*   11 Cocke] cocke *1633*   straight] soone *Dob, O'F*

This day more cheerfully then ever shine,
This day, which might enflame thy self, Old Valentine.

II

Till now, Thou warmd'st with multiplying loves   15
  Two larkes, two sparrowes, or two Doves;
  All that is nothing unto this,
For thou this day couplest two Phoenixes,
  Thou mak'st a Taper see
What the sunne never saw, and what the Arke   20
(Which was of foules, and beasts, the cage, and park,)
Did not containe, one bed containes, through Thee,
  Two Phoenixes, whose joyned breasts
Are unto one another mutuall nests,
Where motion kindles such fires, as shall give   25
Yong Phoenixes, and yet the old shall live;
Whose love and courage never shall decline,
But make the whole year through, thy day, O Valentine.

III

Up then faire Phoenix Bride, frustrate the Sunne,
  Thy selfe from thine affection   30
  Tak'st warmth enough, and from thine eye
All lesser birds will take their jollitie.
  Up, up, faire Bride, and call,
Thy starres, from out their severall boxes, take
Thy Rubies, Pearles, and Diamonds forth, and make   35
Thy selfe a constellation, of them All,
  And by this blazing, signifie,
That a Great Princess falls, but doth not die;
Bee thou a new starre, that to us portends
Ends of much wonder; And be Thou those ends.   40
Since thou dost this day in new glory shine,
May all men date Records, from this thy Valentine.

13 shine,] shine. *1633* 16 Doves;] Doves, *1633* 25 Where] Whose *Dob, O'F*
(*b.c.*) 26 live;] live. *1633* 31 Tak'st] Takest *1633* 32 jollitie] Jollitie *1633*
37 this *H 49, TCD, Dob, O'F* (*b.c.*): their *1633, C 57, Gr* 40 ends.] ends, *1633*

IV

Come forth, come forth, and as one glorious flame
        Meeting another, growes the same,
        So meet thy Fredericke, and so   45
To an unseparable union growe.
          Since separation
Falls not on such things as are infinite,
Nor things which are but one, can disunite,
You'are twice inseparable, great, and one;   50
        Goe then to where the Bishop staies,
To make you one, his way, which divers waies
Must be effected; and when all is past,
And that you'are one, by hearts and hands made fast,
You two have one way left, your selves to'entwine,   55
Besides this Bishops knot, or Bishop Valentine.

V

But oh, what ailes the Sunne, that here he staies,
        Longer to day, then other daies?
        Staies he new light from these to get?
And finding here such store, is loth to set?   60
         And why doe you two walke,
So slowly pac'd in this procession?
Is all your care but to be look'd upon,
And be to others spectacle, and talke?
        The feast, with gluttonous delaies,   65
Is eaten, and too long their meat they praise,
The masquers come too late, and'I thinke, will stay,
Like Fairies, till the Cock crow them away.
        Alas, did not Antiquity assigne
A night, as well as day, to thee, O Valentine?   70

44 another] Another *1633*   46 growe *H 49, TCD, Dob, O'F*: goe *1633 (with comma),*
C 57 49 disunite,] disunite. *1633*   56 or *MSS.*: O *1633*   59 these] thee *TCD, Dob*
67 too late *1633, C57, H 49*: late *TCD, Dob, O'F*

VI

They did, and night is come; and yet wee see
      Formalities retarding thee.
      What meane these Ladies, which (as though
They were to take a clock in peeces,) goe
      So nicely'about the Bride;   75
A Bride, before a good night could be said,
Should vanish from her cloathes, into her bed,
As Soules from bodies steale, and are not spy'd.
      But now she'is laid; What though shee bee?
Yet there are more delayes, For, where is he?   80
He comes, and passes through Spheare after Spheare,
First her sheetes, then her Armes, then any where.
Let not then this day, but this night be thine,
Thy day was but the eve to this, O Valentine.

VII

Here lyes a shee Sunne, and a hee Moone here,   85
      She gives the best light to his Spheare,
      Or each is both, and all, and so
They unto one another nothing owe,
      And yet they doe, but are
So just and rich in that coyne which they pay,   90
That neither would, nor needs forbeare, nor stay;
Neither desires to be spar'd, nor to spare,
      They quickly pay their debt, and then
Take no acquittances, but pay again;
They pay, they give, they lend, and so let fall   95
No such occasion to be liberall.
      More truth, more courage in these two do shine,
Then all thy turtles have, and sparrows, Valentine.

75 nicely'about] nicely about *1633*   79 she'is] she is *1633*   81–2 Spheare, . . .
where.] Spheare. . . . where, *1633*   83 then this day *C 57, H 49, TCD*: this day, then
1633, Dob, Gr: this day *O'F*   84 the] thy *C 57, H 49, TCD*   91 nor stay] or stay
Dob, O'F   stay;] stay, *1633*   94 acquittances *TCD, Dob, O'F*: acquittance *1633,
C 57, H 49*

VIII

And by this act of these two Phenixes
    Nature againe restored is,   100
    For since these two, are two no more,
Ther's but one Phenix still, as was before.
        Rest now at last, and wee
As Satyres watch the Sunnes uprise, will stay
Waiting, when your eyes open'd, let out day,   105
Onely desir'd, because your face wee see;
        Others neare you shall whispering speake,
And wagers lay, at which side day will breake,
And win by'observing, then, whose hand it is
That opens first a curtaine, hers or his;   110
    This will be try'd to morrow after nine,
Till which houre, wee thy day enlarge, O Valentine.

Epithalamion at the Marriage of the Earl of Somerset

Ecclogue

1613. December 26.

Allophanes *finding* Idios *in the country in Christmas time, reprehends his absence from court, at the mariage of the Earle of Sommerset,* Idios *gives an account of his purpose therein, and of his absence thence.*

Allophanes.

UNSEASONABLE man, statue of ice,
    What could to countries solitude entice

101 two,] two *1633*   105 open'd] opened *1633*   day,] day. *1633*   111 try'd] tryed *1633*

   Epithalamion etc. *MSS.:* C 57, H 49; *TC (TCD with TCC)*; *Dob, O'F. Covering title supplied, adapted from TC*   *Ecclogue . . . thence. 1633,* C 57: . . . thys Christmas reprehends . . . from the Court . . . Actions there. *H 49*: Eclogue Induceing an Epithalamion at the Marriage of the E: of S: Allophanes . . . that Christmas, reprehends . . . at that marriage; Idios . . . actions there. *TC*: Eclogue. Allophanes . . . this Christmas, reprehends . . . and his Actions there. *Dob:* . . . in the Christmas, reprehends . . . Actions (*corr. by scribe from* Absence) there. *O'F*   ECCLOGUE] ECCLOGVE *1633 corrected*   mariage of] mariage Of *1633*   2 countries] Countrey *TC*

Thee, in this yeares cold and decrepit time?
Natures instinct drawes to the warmer clime
Even small birds, who by that courage dare,   5
In numerous fleets, saile through their Sea, the aire.
What delicacie can in fields appeare,
Whil'st Flora'herselfe doth a freeze jerkin weare?
Whil'st windes do all the trees and hedges strip
Of leafes, to furnish roddes enough to whip   10
Thy madnesse from thee; and all springs by frost
Have taken cold, and their sweet murmure lost;
If thou thy faults or fortunes would'st lament
With just solemnity, do it in Lent;
At Court the spring already'advanced is,   15
The Sunne stayes longer up; and yet not his
The glory is, farre other, other fires:
First, zeale to Prince and State; then loves desires
Burne in one brest, and like heavens two great lights,
The first doth governe dayes, the other nights.   20
And then that early light, which did appeare
Before the Sunne and Moone created were,
The Princes favour is defus'd o'r all,
From which all Fortunes, Names, and Natures fall;   24
Then from those wombes of starres, the Brides bright eyes,
At every glance, a constellation flyes,
And sowes the Court with starres, and doth prevent
In light and power, the all-ey'd firmament;
First her eyes kindle other Ladies eyes,
Then from their beames, their jewels lusters rise,   30
And from their jewels, torches do take fire,
And all is warmth, and light, and good desire;
Most other Courts, alas, are like to hell,
Where in darke plotts, fire without light doth dwell:
Or but like Stoves, for lust and envy get   35
Continuall, but artificiall heat;

12 murmure Σ: murmures *1633*, *C 57*   15 already'advanced] already advanced *1633*
17 fires :] fires. *1633*   22 were,] were; *1633*   29 kindle Σ: kindles *1633, C 57*
30–1 beames, . . . jewels, torches] beames . . . jewels torches *1633*   34 plotts Σ:
places *1633, C 57*

Here zeale and love growne one, all clouds disgest,
And make our Court an everlasting East.
And can'st thou be from thence?
Idios.   No, I am there.
As heaven, to men dispos'd, is every where,   40
So are those Courts, whose Princes animate,
Not onely all their house, but all their State.
Let no man thinke, because he'is full, he'hath all,
Kings (as their patterne, God) are liberall
Not onely'in fulnesse, but capacitie,   45
Enlarging narrow men, to feele and see,
And comprehend the blessings they bestow.
So, reclus'd hermits often times do know
More of heavens glory, then a wordling can.
As man is of the world, the heart of man,   50
Is an epitome of Gods great booke
Of creatures, and man need no farther looke;
So is the Country'of Courts, where sweet peace doth,
As their one common soule, give life to both;
I am not then from Court.
Allophanes.   Dreamer, thou art.   55
Think'st thou, fantastique, that thou hast a part
In the East-Indian fleet, because thou hast
A little spice, or amber in thy taste?
Because thou art not frozen, art thou warme?
Seest thou all good because thou seest no harme?   60
The earth doth in her inward bowels hold
Stuffe well dispos'd, and which would faine be gold,
But never shall, except it chance to lye,
So upward, that heaven gild it with his eye;
As, for divine things, faith comes from above,   65
So, for best civill use, all tinctures move
From higher powers; From God religion springs,

39 there.] there *1633*   42 State.] State, *1633*   43 he'is . . . he'hath] he is . . .
he hath *1633*   45 onely'in] onely in *1633*   53 Country'of] Country of *1633*
54 one] owne *C 57, TC, Dob, O'F (b.c.)*   both;] both, *1633*   55 art.] art, *1633*
56 thou, fantastique,] thou fantastique *1633*   57 East-Indian *H 49, Dob*: East Indian
C 57, TC: East India *O'F*: Indian *1633*   58 amber] Amber *1633*   61 inward
MSS.: inner *1633*

Wisdome, and honour from the use of Kings.
Then unbeguile thy selfe, and know with mee,
That Angels, though on earth employd they bee,   70
Are still in heav'n, so is hee still at home
That doth, abroad, to honest actions come.
Chide thy selfe then, O foole, which yesterday
Might'st have read more then all thy books bewray;
Hast thou a history, which doth present   75
A Court, where all affections do assent
Unto the Kings, and that, that Kings are just?
And where it is no levity to trust?
Where there is no ambition, but to'obey,
Where men need whisper nothing, and yet may;   80
Where the Kings favours are so plac'd, that all
Finde that the King therein is liberall
To them, in him, because his favours bend
To vertue, to the which they all pretend?
Thou hast no such; yet here was this, and more,   85
An earnest lover, wise then, and before.
Our little Cupid hath sued Livery,
And is no more in his minority,
Hee is admitted now into that brest
Where the Kings Counsells and his secrets rest.   90
What hast thou lost, O ignorant man?
Idios.   I knew
All this, and onely therefore I withdrew.
To know and feele all this, and not to have
Words to expresse it, makes a man a grave
Of his owne thoughts; I would not therefore stay   95
At a great feast, having no Grace to say.
And yet I scap'd not here; for being come
Full of the common joy, I utter'd some;
Reade then this nuptiall song, which was not made

75 present] represent *TC*   77 that, that *1633, C 57, H 49, TCD*: that the *TCC,
Dob, O'F*   78 trust?] trust. *1633*   84 pretend?] pretend. *1633*   86 before.]
before, *1633 uncorrected*   90 Counsells] Counsayle *TC*   91 knew] knew,
1633 uncorrected   92 onely therefore] therefore only *TC*   withdrew.] withdrew
1633   96 Grace] grace *1633 uncorrected*   say.] say, *1633*   98 joy, . . . some;]
joy; . . . some, *1633*

Either the Court or mens hearts to invade,   100
But since I'am dead, and buried, I could frame
No Epitaph, which might advance my fame
So much as this poore song, which testifies
I did unto that day some sacrifice.

Epithalamion

I

The time of the Mariage.

THOU art repriv'd, old yeare, thou shalt not die,   105
    Though thou upon thy death bed lye,
      And should'st within five dayes expire,
   Yet thou art rescu'd by a mightier fire,
      Then thy old Soule, the Sunne,
When he doth in his largest circle runne.   110
The passage of the West or East would thaw,
And open wide their easie liquid jawe
To all our ships, could a Promethean art
Either unto the Northerne Pole impart
The fire of these inflaming eyes, or of this loving heart.   115

II

Equality of persons.

But undiscerning Muse, which heart, which eyes,
    In this new couple, dost thou prize,
      When his eye as inflaming is
As hers, and her heart loves as well as his?
      Be try'd by beauty,'and than   120
The bridegroome is a maid, and not a man.
If by that manly courage they be try'd,

101–2 buried, . . . fame] buried . . . fame, _1633 uncorrected_   _After_ 104 _Epithalamion_
Σ: _omit 1633, TC_   105 repriv'd,] repriv'd _1633_   107 expire,] expire
_1633_   120 try'd . . . beauty,'and] tryed . . . beauty and _1633_   121–2 man. . . .
try'd] man, . . . tryed _1633_

Which scornes unjust opinion; then the bride
Becomes a man. Should chance or envies Art
  Divide these two, whom nature scarce did part?   125
Since both have both th'enflaming eyes, and both the loving
 heart.

III

Raysing of the Bridegroome.

Though it be some divorce to thinke of you
  Singly, so much one are you two,
   Yet let me here contemplate thee,
First, cheerfull Bridegroome, and first let mee see,   130
   How thou prevent'st the Sunne,
  And his red foming horses dost outrunne,
How, having laid downe in thy Soveraignes brest
All businesses, from thence to reinvest
Them, when these triumphs cease, thou forward art   135
To shew to her, who doth the like impart,
The fire of thy inflaming eyes, and of thy loving heart.

IV

Raising of the Bride.

But now, to Thee, faire Bride, it is some wrong,
  To thinke thou wert in Bed so long,
   Since soone thou lyest downe first, tis fit   140
Thou in first rising should'st allow for it.
   Pouder thy Radiant haire,
  Which if without such ashes thou would'st weare,
Thou, which, to all which come to looke upon,
Art meant for Phoebus, would'st be Phaëton.   145
For our ease, give thine eyes, th'unusuall part
Of joy, a Teare; so quencht, thou maist impart,
To us that come, thy'inflaming eyes, to him, thy loving heart.

126 have both Σ: have *1633*, *C 57* eyes *H 49*, *TC*, *Dob*, *O'F* (*b.c.*): eye *1633*, *C 57*
128 Singly Σ: Single *1633*, *C 57* 129 Yet let *O'F*: Let *1633*, Σ; *see note* 140 soone]
Soone *1633* 141 it.] it, *1633* 144 all which] all that *Dob*, *O'F* 145 Art
TCC, *Dob*: Are *1633*, *C 57*, *H 49*, *TCD*: Wert *O'F* for . . . Phaëton.] for, . . . Phaëton,
1633 148 thy'inflaming] thy inflaming *1633*

V

Her Apparrelling.

Thus thou descend'st to our infirmitie,
    Who can the Sun in water see.   150
      Soe dost thou, when in silke and gold,
Thou cloudst thy selfe; since wee which doe behold,
      Are dust, and wormes, 'tis just
Our objects be the fruits of wormes and dust;
    Let every Jewell be a glorious starre,   155
Yet starres are not so pure, as their spheares are.
And though thou stoope, to'appeare to us, in part,
    Still in that Picture thou intirely art,
Which thy inflaming eyes have made within his loving heart.

VI

Going to the Chappell.

Now from your Easts you issue forth, and wee,   160
    As men which through a Cipres see
      The rising sun, doe thinke it two,
Soe, as you goe to Church, doe thinke of you,
      But that vaile being gone,
By the Church rites you are from thenceforth one.   165
The Church Triumphant made this match before,
    And now the Militant doth strive no more;
Then, reverend Priest, who Gods Recorder art,
    Doe, from his Dictates, to these two impart
All blessings, which are seene, or thought, by Angels eye or
    heart.   170

167 more;] more, *1633*   170 or thought] Or . . . *1633*

VII

The Benediction.

Blest payre of Swans, Oh may you interbring
    Daily new joyes, and never sing,
    Live, till all grounds of wishes faile,
Till honor, yea till wisedome grow so stale,
        That, new great heights to trie,   175
It must serve your ambition, to die;
Raise heires, and may here, to the worlds end, live
Heires from this King, to take thankes, you, to give,
Nature and grace doe all, and nothing Art;
    May never age, or error overthwart   180
With any West, these radiant eyes, with any North, this heart.

VIII

Feasts and Revells.

But you are over-blest. Plenty this day
    Injures; it causes time to stay;
    The tables groane, as though this feast
Would, as the flood, destroy all fowle and beast.   185
        And were the doctrine new
That the earth mov'd, this day would make it true;
For every part to dance and revell goes;
They tread the ayre, and fal not where they rose.
Though six houres since, the Sunne to bed did part,   190
The masks and banquets will not yet impart
A sunset to these weary eyes, a Center to this heart.

178 from *1633*, *TC*, *Dob*: for *C 57*, *H 49*, *O'F* (*b.c.*)   you] yours *Dob*, *O'F* (*b.c.*)
179 Art;] Art, *1633*   183 causes *MSS.*: causeth *1633*, *Gr*   188 goes;] goes.
1633   192 a Center] A Center *1633*

IX

The Brides going to bed.

What mean'st thou Bride, this companie to keep?
  To sit up, till thou faine wouldst sleep?
   Thou maist not, when thou'art laid, doe so. 195
Thy selfe must to him a new banquet grow,
   And you must entertaine
And doe all this daies dances o'r againe.
Know that if Sun and Moone together doe
Rise in one point, they doe not set so too. 200
Therefore thou maist, faire Bride, to bed depart,
Thou art not gone, being gone; where e'r thou art,
Thou leav'st in him thy watchfull eyes, in him thy loving heart.

X

The Bridegroomes comming.

As he that sees a starre fall, runs apace,
  And findes a gellie in the place, 205
   So doth the Bridegroome hast as much,
Being told this starre is falne, and findes her such.
   And as friends may looke strange,
  By a new fashion, or apparrells change,
Their soules, though long acquainted they had beene, 210
These clothes, their bodies, never yet had seene;
Therefore at first shee modestly might start,
But must forthwith surrender every part,
As freely,'as each to each before, gave either eye or heart.

195 thou'art] thou art *1633* 200 too.] to. *1633* 202 being gone;] ...
gone, *1633* 207 such.] such, *1633* 211 seene;] seene. *1633* 214
freely,'as] freely, as˝*1633*

XI

The good-night.

Now, as in Tullias tombe, one lampe burnt cleare,   215
   Unchang'd for fifteene hundred yeare,
   May these love-lamps we here enshrine,
In warmth, light, lasting, equall the divine.
   Fire ever doth aspire,
And makes all like it selfe, turnes all to fire,   220
But ends in ashes, which these cannot doe,
For none of them is fuell, but fire too;
This is joyes bonfire, then, where loves strong Arts
Make of so noble individuall parts
One fire of foure inflaming eyes, and of two loving hearts.   225

Idios.

As I have brought this song, that I may doe
A perfect sacrifice, I'll burne it too.

Allophanes.

No, Sir. This paper I have justly got,
For, in burnt incense, the perfume is not
His only that presents it, but of all;   230
What ever celebrates this Festivall
Is common, since the joy thereof is so.
Nor may your selfe be Priest: But let me goe,
Backe to the Court, and I will lay'it upon
Such Altars, as prize your devotion.   235

218–22 divine. . . . too;] divine; . . . too. *1633*   222 them *Σ*.: these *1633, TC,*
Gr 223 where] when *TC, Dob* 226–35 *omit Dob* 228 No, Sir.]
No Sᵗ. *1633* 230 all;] all, *1633*

THE FIRST ANNIVERSARIE

AN ANATOMY OF THE WORLD

Wherein, by Occasion of the Untimely Death of
Mistris Elizabeth Drury the Frailty and
the Decay of this whole World is
Represented.

To the Praise of the Dead, and the Anatomy

WEl dy'de the world, that we might live to see
    This world of wit, in his Anatomee:
No evill wants his good: so wilder heyres
Bedew their fathers Toombs with forced teares,
Whose state requites their los: whils thus we gain   5
Well may we walk in blacks, but not complaine.
Yet, how can I consent the world is dead
While this Muse lives? which in his spirits stead
Seemes to informe a world: and bids it bee,
In spight of losse, or fraile mortalitee?   10
And thou the subject of this wel-borne thought,
Thrise noble maid, couldst not have found nor sought
A fitter time to yeeld to thy sad Fate,
Then whiles this spirit lives; that can relate
Thy worth so well to our last nephews eyne,   15
That they shall wonder both at his, and thine:
Admired match! where strives in mutuall grace
The cunning Pencill, and the comely face:
A taske, which thy faire goodnes made too much
For the bold pride of vulgar pens to tuch;   20

THE FIRST ANNIVERSARIE. *1611. Collations from 1612, the errata slip in one copy of 1612, 1621,
1625, 1633. Titles from 1611, except head-title,* The First Anniversarie, *added in 1612* To
the Praise of the Dead *etc. Printed in roman in 1611, italic in 1612*   12 *maid,*] maid;
1611

Enough is us to praise them that praise thee,
And say that but enough those praises bee,
Which had'st thou liv'd, had hid their fearefull head
From th'angry checkings of thy modest red:
Death bars reward and shame: when envy's gone,   25
And gaine, 'tis safe to give the dead their owne.
As then the wise Egyptians wont to lay
More on their Tombs, then houses: these of clay,
But those of brasse, or marble were; so wee
Give more unto thy Ghost, then unto thee.   30
Yet what we give to thee, thou gav'st to us,
And maist but thanke thy selfe, for being thus:
Yet what thou gav'st, and wert, O happy maid,
Thy grace profest all due, where 'tis repayd.
So these high songs that to thee suited bine,   35
Serve but to sound thy makers praise, in thine,
Which thy deare soule as sweetly sings to him
Amid the Quire of Saints and Seraphim,
As any Angels tongue can sing of thee;
The subjects differ, tho the skill agree: 40
For as by infant-yeares men judge of age,
Thy early love, thy vertues, did presage
What an hie part thou bear'st in those best songs
Whereto no burden, nor no end belongs.
Sing on, thou Virgin soule, whose lossefull gaine   45
Thy love-sicke Parents have bewayl'd in vaine;
Never may thy name be in our songs forgot
Till we shall sing thy ditty, and thy note.

26 *gaine,*] gaine; *1611*   34 *where*] were *1612–1625*   36 *in*] and *1633*
43 *What an hie . . . best songs*] What hie . . . best songs *1621, 1625:* What hie . . . best of
songs *1633*

An Anatomy of the World

WHEN that rich soule which to her Heaven is gone, *The entrie*
   Whom all they celebrate, who know they'have one, *worke.* *into the*
(For who is sure he hath a soule, unlesse
It see, and Judge, and follow worthinesse,
And by Deedes praise it? He who doth not this,   5
May lodge an In-mate soule, but 'tis not his.)
When that Queene ended here her progresse time,
And, as t'her standing house, to heaven did clymbe,
Where, loth to make the Saints attend her long,
Shee's now a part both of the Quire, and Song,   10
This world, in that great earth-quake languished;
For in a common Bath of teares it bled,
Which drew the strongest vitall spirits out:
But succour'd then with a perplexed doubt,
Whether the world did loose or gaine in this,   15
(Because since now no other way there is
But goodnes, to see her, whom all would see,
All must endevour to be good as shee,)
This great consumption to a fever turn'd,
And so the world had fits; it joy'd, it mournd.   20
And, as men thinke, that Agues physicke are,
And th'Ague being spent, give over care,
So thou, sicke world, mistak'st thy selfe to bee
Well, when alas, thou'rt in a Letargee.
Her death did wound, and tame thee than, and than   25
Thou mightst have better spar'd the Sunne, or Man;
That wound was deepe, but 'tis more misery,
That thou hast lost thy sense and memory.
'Twas heavy then to heare thy voyce of mone,
But this is worse, that thou art speechlesse growne.   30

An Anatomy of the World. Italic in 1611, roman in 1612   *Marginal notes added*
in 1612: 1625, 1633 omit the first   2 Whom] Who *1633*   all they] all doe *1621–*
1633, Gr   they'have] they have *1611*   6 'tis tis *1611*   29 'Twas] T'was *1611*

Thou hast forgot thy name, thou hadst; thou wast
Nothing but she, and her thou hast o'repast.
For as a child kept from the Font, untill
A Prince, expected long, come to fulfill
The Ceremonies, thou unnam'd hadst laid,   35
Had not her comming, thee her Palace made:
Her name defin'd thee, gave thee forme and frame,
And thou forgetst to celebrate thy name.
Some months she hath beene dead (but being dead,
Measures of times are all determined)   40
But long shee'ath beene away, long, long, yet none
Offers to tell us who it is that's gone.
But as in states doubtfull of future heyres,
When sickenes without remedy, empayres
The present Prince, they're loth it should be said,   45
The Prince doth languish, or the Prince is dead:
So mankind feeling now a generall thaw,
A strong example gone equall to law,
The Cyment which did faithfully compact
And glue all vertues, now resolv'd, and slack'd,   50
Thought it some blasphemy to say sh'was dead;
Or that our weakenes was discovered
In that confession; therefore spoke no more
Then tongues, the soule being gone, the losse deplore.
But though it be too late to succour thee,   55
Sicke world, yea dead, yea putrified, since shee
Thy'ntrinsique Balme, and thy preservative,
Can never be renew'd, thou never live,
I (since no man can make thee live) will trie,
What we may gaine by thy Anatomy.   60
Her death hath taught us dearely, that thou art
Corrupt and mortall in thy purest part.
Let no man say, the world it selfe being dead,
'Tis labour lost to have discovered
The worlds infirmities, since there is none   65
Alive to study this dissectione;

39 months] moneths *1611*

For there's a kind of world remaining still,   *What life*
Though shee which did inanimate and fill   *the world*
The world, be gone, yet in this last long night,   *hath still*
Her Ghost doth walke; that is, a glimmering light,   70
A faint weake love of vertue and of good
Reflects from her, on them which understood
Her worth; And though she have shut in all day,
The twi-light of her memory doth stay;
Which, from the carcasse of the old world, free,   75
Creates a new world; and new creatures be
Produc'd: The matter and the stuffe of this,
Her vertue, and the forme our practise is.
And though to be thus Elemented, arme
These Creatures, from home-borne intrinsique harme,   80
(For all assum'd unto this Dignitee,
So many weedlesse Paradises bee,
Which of themselves produce no venemous sinne,
Except some forraine Serpent bring it in)
Yet, because outward stormes the strongest breake,   85
And strength it selfe by confidence growes weake,
This new world may be safer, being told
The dangers and diseases of the old: *The sicknesses*
For with due temper men do then forgoe,   *of the world.*
Or covet things, when they their true worth know.   90
There is no health; Physitians say that we   *Impossibility*
At best, enjoy, but a neutralitee.   *of health.*
And can there be worse sickenesse, then to know
That we are never well, nor can be so?
We are borne ruinous: poore mothers crie,   95
That children come not right, nor orderly,
Except they headlong come, and fall upon
An ominous precipitation.
How witty's ruine! how importunate
Upon mankinde! It labour'd to frustrate   100
Even Gods purpose; and made woman, sent

67 *Margin*: *What . . . still*] *omit 1625, 1633*   79 though] *thought 1621–1633*
80 home-borne] hom-borne *1611*   88 *Margin*: sicknesses] sicknesse *1621–1633*
world] *Word 1625*   99–100 ruine! . . . mankinde!] ruine? . . . mankinde? *1611*

For mans reliefe, cause of his languishment.
They were to good ends, and they are so still,
But accessory, and principall in ill.
For that first mariage was our funerall: 105
One woman at one blow, then kill'd us all,
And singly, one by one, they kill us now.
We doe delightfully our selves allow
To that consumption; and profusely blinde,
We kill our selves, to propagate our kinde.   110
And yet we doe not that; we are not men:
There is not now that mankinde, which was then
When as the Sunne, and man, did seeme to strive,
(Joynt tenants of the world) who should survive.   *Shortnesse
When Stag, and Raven, and the long-liv'd tree,   of life.*
Compar'd with man, dy'de in minoritee.   116
When, if a slow-pac'd starre had stolne away
From the observers marking, he might stay
Two or three hundred yeares to see't againe,
And then make up his observation plaine;   120
When, as the age was long, the sise was great:
Mans grouth confess'd, and recompenc'd the meat:
So spacious and large, that every soule
Did a faire Kingdome, and large Realme controule:
And when the very stature thus erect,   125
Did that soule a good way towards Heaven direct.
Where is this mankind now? who lives to age,
Fit to be made *Methusalem* his page?
Alas, we scarse live long enough to trie
Whether a new made clocke runne right, or lie.   130
Old Grandsires talke of yesterday with sorrow,
And for our children we reserve to morrow.
So short is life, that every peasant strives,
In a torne house, or field, to have three lives.   134
And as in lasting, so in length is man,   *Smalnesse
Contracted to an inch, who was a span.   of stature.*

117 slow-pac'd] slow pac'd *1611 uncorrected*   121 the sise] the the sise *1612*
129 trie] trie; *1611*   130 new *1611, 1612 errata:* true *1612–1633, Gr*
133 every] enery *1611 uncorrected*   135 man,] man *1611*

For had a man at first, in Forrests stray'd,
Or shipwrack'd in the Sea, one would have laid
A wager that an Elephant, or Whale
That met him, would not hastily assaile   140
A thing so equall to him: now alas,
The Fayries, and the Pigmies well may passe
As credible; mankind decayes so soone,
We're scarse our Fathers shadowes cast at noone.
Onely death addes t'our length: nor are we growne   145
In stature to be men, till we are none.
But this were light, did our lesse volume hold
All the old Text; or had we chang'd to gold
Their silver; or dispos'd into lesse glas,
Spirits of vertue, which then scattred was.   150
But 'tis not so: w'are not retir'd, but dampt;
And as our bodies, so our mindes are cramp't:
'Tis shrinking, not close-weaving, that hath thus,
In minde and body both bedwarfed us.
We seeme ambitious, Gods whole worke t'undoe;   155
Of nothing he made us, and we strive too,
To bring our selves to nothing backe; and we
Do what we can, to do't so soone as hee.
With new diseases on our selves we warre,
And with new phisicke, a worse Engin farre.   160
Thus man, this worlds Vice-Emperor, in whom
All faculties, all graces are at home;
And if in other Creatures they appeare,
They're but mans ministers, and Legats there,
To worke on their rebellions, and reduce   165
Them to Civility, and to mans use:
This man, whom God did wooe, and loth t'attend
Till man came up, did downe to man descend,
This man, so great, that all that is, is his,
Oh what a trifle, and poore thing he is!   170
If man were any thing, he's nothing now:

144 scarse *1612 errata, 1625, 1633*: scarsc *1611*: searse *1612, 1621*   153 close-weaving]
close-weaning *1611, 1612*: close weaning *1621, 1625*: close weaving *1633*   164 there
thers *1621*: theres *1625*   166 use:] use. *1611*

Helpe, or at least some time to wast, allow
T'his other wants, yet when he did depart
With her, whom we lament, he lost his hart.
She, of whom th'Auncients seem'd to prophesie,   175
When they call'd vertues by the name of shee,
She in whom vertue was so much refin'd,
That for Allay unto so pure a minde
Shee tooke the weaker Sex, she that could drive
The poysonous tincture, and the stayne of *Eve*,   180
Out of her thoughts, and deeds; and purifie
All, by a true religious Alchimy;
Shee, shee is dead; shee's dead; when thou knowst this,
Thou knowst how poore a trifling thing man is.
And learn'st thus much by our Anatomee,   185
The heart being perish'd, no part can be free.
And that except thou feed (not banquet) on
The supernaturall food, Religion,
Thy better Grouth growes withered, and scant;
Be more then man, or thou'rt lesse then an Ant.   190
Then, as mankinde, so is the worlds whole frame
Quite out of joynt, almost created lame:
For, before God had made up all the rest,
Corruption entred, and deprav'd the best:
It seis'd the Angels, and then first of all   195
The world did in her Cradle take a fall,
And turn'd her braines, and tooke a generall maime
Wronging each joynt of th'universall frame.
The noblest part, man, felt it first; and than   199

Both beasts and plants, curst in the curse of man.   *Decay of*
So did the world from the first houre decay,   *nature in*
That evening was beginning of the day,   *other parts.*
And now the Springs and Sommers which we see,
Like sonnes of women after fifty bee.
And new Philosophy cals all in doubt,   205
The Element of fire is quite put out;

The Sunne is lost, and th'earth, and no mans wit
Can well direct him, where to looke for it.
And freely men confesse, that this world's spent,
When in the Planets, and the Firmament   210
They seeke so many new; they see that this
Is crumbled out againe t'his Atomis.
'Tis all in pieces, all cohaerence gone;
All just supply, and all Relation:
Prince, Subject, Father, Sonne, are things forgot,   215
For every man alone thinkes he hath got
To be a Phoenix, and that there can bee
None of that kinde, of which he is, but hee.
This is the worlds condition now, and now
She that should all parts to reunion bow,   220
She that had all Magnetique force alone,
To draw, and fasten sundred parts in one;
She whom wise nature had invented then
When she observ'd that every sort of men
Did in their voyage in this worlds Sea stray,   225
And needed a new compasse for their way;
Shee that was best, and first originall
Of all faire copies; and the generall
Steward to Fate; shee whose rich eyes, and brest,
Guilt the West Indies, and perfum'd the East;   230
Whose having breath'd in this world, did bestow
Spice on those Isles, and bad them still smell so,
And that rich Indie which doth gold interre,
Is but as single money, coyn'd from her:
She to whom this world must it selfe refer,   235
As Suburbs, or the Microcosme of her,
Shee, shee is dead; shee's dead: when thou knowst this,
Thou knowst how lame a cripple this world is.
And learnst thus much by our Anatomy,
That this worlds generall sickenesse doth not lie   240
In any humour, or one certaine part;

But, as thou saw'st it rotten at the hart,
Thou seest a Hectique fever hath got hold
Of the whole substance, not to be contrould,
And that thou hast but one way, not t'admit   245
The worlds infection, to be none of it.
For the worlds subtilst immateriall parts
Feele this consuming wound, and ages darts.
For the worlds beauty is decayd, or gone,   249
Beauty, that's colour, and proportion.   *Disformity*
We thinke the heavens enjoy their Sphericall   *of parts.*
Their round proportion embracing all.
But yet their various and perplexed course,
Observ'd in divers ages doth enforce
Men to finde out so many'Eccentrique parts,   255
Such divers downe-right lines, such overthwarts,
As disproportion that pure forme. It teares
The Firmament in eight and fortie sheeres,
And in those constellations there arise
New starres, and old do vanish from our eyes: 260
As though heav'n suffred earth-quakes, peace or war,
When new Townes rise, and olde demolish'd are.
They have empayld within a Zodiake
The free-borne Sunne, and keepe twelve signes awake
To watch his steps; the Goat and Crabbe controule,   265
And fright him backe, who els to eyther Pole,
(Did not these Tropiques fetter him) might runne:
For his course is not round; nor can the Sunne
Perfit a Circle, or maintaine his way
One inche direct; but where he rose to day   270
He comes no more, but with a cousening line,
Steales by that point, and so is Serpentine:
And seeming weary with his reeling thus,
He meanes to sleepe, being now falne nearer us.
So, of the starres which boast that they do runne   275

242 saw'st] sawest *1611*   244 contrould,] contrould. *1611*   255 many'Eccen-
trique] many Eccentrique *1611*   259 those] these *1612–1633, Gr*   there *1612*
errata : then *1611–1633, Gr*   262 Townes *1612 errata* : Towres *1611–1633, Gr*
273 reeling] recling *1611*   275 starres] stares *1611*

In Circle still, none ends where he begunne.
All their proportion's lame, it sinks, it swels.
For of Meridians, and Parallels,
Man hath weav'd out a net, and this net throwne
Upon the Heavens, and now they are his owne.   280
Loth to goe up the hill, or labor thus
To goe to heaven, we make heaven come to us.
We spur, we raine the stars, and in their race
They're diversly content t'obey our pace.
But keepes the earth her round proportion still?   285
Doth not a Tenarif, or higher Hill
Rise so high like a Rocke, that one might thinke
The floating Moone would shipwracke there, and sink?
Seas are so deepe, that Whales being strooke to day,
Perchance to morrow, scarse at middle way   290
Of their wish'd journeys end, the bottom, dye.
And men, to sound depths, so much line untie,
As one might justly thinke, that there would rise
At end thereof, one of th'Antipodies:
If under all, a Vault infernall be,   295
(Which sure is spacious, except that we
Invent another torment, that there must
Millions into a strait hote roome be thrust)
Then solidnes, and roundnes have no place.
Are these but warts, and pock-holes in the face   300
Of th'earth? Thinke so: But yet confesse, in this
The worlds proportion disfigur'd is,
That those two legges whereon it doth relie,   *Disorder in the*
Reward and punishment are bent awrie.   *world.*
And, Oh, it can no more be questioned,   305
That beauties best, proportion, is dead,
Since even griefe it selfe, which now alone
Is left us, is without proportion.
Shee by whose lines proportion should bee
Examin'd, measure of all Symmetree,   310

Whom had that Ancient seen, who thought soules made
Of Harmony, he would at next have said
That Harmony was shee, and thence infer,
That soules were but Resultances from her,
And did from her into our bodies go,   315
As to our eyes, the formes from objects flow:
Shee, who if those great Doctors truely said
That th'Arke to mans proportions was made,
Had beene a type for that, as that might be
A type of her in this, that contrary   320
Both Elements, and Passions liv'd at peace
In her, who caus'd all Civill warre to cease.
Shee, after whom, what forme soe're we see,
Is discord, and rude incongruitee,
Shee, shee is dead, shee's dead; when thou knowst this   325
Thou knowst how ugly'a monster this world is:
And learnst thus much by our Anatomee,
That here is nothing to enamor thee:
And that, not onely faults in inward parts,
Corruptions in our braines, or in our harts,   330
Poysoning the fountaines, whence our actions spring,
Endanger us: but that if every thing
Be not done fitly'nd in proportion,
To satisfie wise, and good lookers on,
(Since most men be such as most thinke they bee)   335
They're lothsome too, by this Deformitee.
For good, and well, must in our actions meete:
Wicked is not much worse then indiscreet.
But beauties other second Element,
Colour, and lustre now, is as neere spent.   340
And had the world his just proportion,
Were it a ring still, yet the stone is gone.
As a compassionate Turcoyse which doth tell
By looking pale, the wearer is not well,
As gold fals sicke being stung with Mercury,   345
All the worlds parts of such complexion bee.

318 proportions] proportion *1621–1633*   326 ugly'a] ugly a *1611*

When nature was most busie, the first weeke,
Swadling the new-borne earth, God seemd to like,
That she should sport herselfe sometimes, and play,
To mingle,'and vary colours every day.   350
And then, as though she could not make inow,
Himselfe his various Rainbow did allow.
Sight is the noblest sense of any one,
Yet sight hath onely color to feed on,
And color is decayd: summers robe growes   355
Duskie, and like an oft dyed garment showes.
Our blushing redde, which us'd in cheekes to spred,
Is inward sunke, and onely'our soules are redde.
Perchance the world might have recovered,
If she whom we lament had not beene dead: 360
But shee, in whom all white, and redde, and blue
(Beauties ingredients) voluntary grew,
As in an unvext Paradise; from whom
Did all things verdure, and their lustre come,
Whose composition was miraculous,   365
Being all color, all Diaphanous,
(For Ayre, and Fire but thicke grosse bodies were,
And liveliest stones but drowsie,'and pale to her,)
Shee, shee is dead; shee's dead: when thou knowst this,
Thou knowst how wan a Ghost this our world is: 370
And learnst thus much by our Anatomee,
That it should more affright, then pleasure thee.
And that, since all faire color then did sinke,
'Tis now but wicked vanity to thinke,   374
To color vitious deeds with good pretence,   *Weaknesse*
Or with bought colors to illude mens sense.   *in the want of*
Nor in ought more this worlds decay appeares,   *correspondence*
Then that her influence the heav'n forbeares,   *of heaven and*
Or that the Elements doe not feele this,   *earth.*
The father, or the mother barren is.   380
The clouds conceive not raine, or doe not powre

350 mingle,'and] mingle, and *1611*   351 inow] enough *1633*   358 onely'our]
onely our *1611*   362 voluntary] volantary *1611*   368 drowsie,'and] drowsie, and
1611   374 'Tis] Tis *1611*   378 *Margin: earth.*] earth *1612*

In the due birth-time, downe the balmy showre.
Th'Ayre doth not motherly sit on the earth,
To hatch her seasons, and give all things birth.
Spring-times were common cradles, but are toombes;   385
And false-conceptions fill the generall wombs.
Th'Ayre showes such Meteors, as none can see,
Not onely what they meane, but what they bee.
Earth such new wormes, as would have troubled much,
Th'Egyptian Mages to have made more such.   390
What Artist now dares boast that he can bring
Heaven hither, or constellate any thing,
So as the influence of those starres may bee
Imprisond in an Herbe, or Charme, or Tree,
And doe by touch, all which those starres could do?   395
The art is lost, and correspondence too.
For heaven gives little, and the earth takes lesse,
And man least knowes their trade, and purposes.
If this commerce twixt heaven and earth were not
Embarr'd, and all this trafique quite forgot,   400
Shee, for whose losse we have lamented thus,
Would worke more fully'and pow'rfully on us.
Since herbes, and roots by dying, lose not all,
But they, yea Ashes too, are medicinall,
Death could not quench her vertue so, but that   405
It would be (if not follow'd) wondred at:
And all the world would be one dying Swan,
To sing her funerall prayse, and vanish than.
But as some Serpents poison hurteth not,
Except it be from the live Serpent shot,   410
So doth her vertue need her here, to fit
That unto us; she working more then it.
But she, in whom, to such maturity,
Vertue was growne, past growth, that it must die,
She from whose influence all Impressions came,   415
But, by Receivers impotencies, lame,
Who, though she could not transubstantiate

All states to gold, yet guilded every state,
So that some Princes have some temperance;
Some Counsaylors some purpose to advance   420
The common profite; and some people have
Some stay, no more then Kings should give, to crave;
Some women have some taciturnity;
Some Nunneries, some graines of chastity.
She that did thus much, and much more could doe,   425
But that our age was Iron, and rusty too,
Shee, shee is dead; shee's dead: when thou knowst this,
Thou knowst how drie a Cinder this world is.
And learnst thus much by our Anatomy,
That 'tis in vaine to dew, or mollifie   430
It with thy Teares, or Sweat, or Bloud: no thing
Is worth our travaile, griefe, or perishing,
But those rich joyes, which did possesse her hart,
Of which shee's now partaker, and a part.   434
But as in cutting up a man that's dead,   *Conclusion.*
The body will not last out to have read
On every part, and therefore men direct
Their speech to parts, that are of most effect;
So the worlds carcasse would not last, if I
Were punctuall in this Anatomy.   440
Nor smels it well to hearers, if one tell
Them their disease, who faine would think they're wel.
Here therefore be the end: And, blessed maid,
Of whom is meant what ever hath beene said,
Or shall be spoken well by any tongue,   445
Whose name refines course lines, and makes prose song,
Accept this tribute, and his first yeares rent,
Who till his darke short tapers end be spent,
As oft as thy feast sees this widowed earth,
Will yearely celebrate thy second birth,   450
That is, thy death. For though the soule of man
Be got when man is made, 'tis borne but than
When man doth die. Our body's as the wombe,

428 knowst] knowest *1611*   442 they're] thy're *1633*

And as a mid-wife death directs it home.
And you her creatures, whom she workes upon   455
And have your last, and best concoction
From her example, and her vertue,'if you
In reverence to her, doe thinke it due,
That no one should her prayses thus reherse,
As matter fit for Chronicle, not verse,   460
Vouchsafe to call to minde, that God did make
A last, and lastingst peece, a song. He spake
To *Moses*, to deliver unto all,
That song: because he knew they would let fall,
The Law, the Prophets, and the History,   465
But keepe the song still in their memory.
Such an opinion (in due measure) made
Me this great Office boldly to invade.
Nor could incomprehensiblenesse deterre
Me, from thus trying to emprison her.   470
Which when I saw that a strict grave could do,
I saw not why verse might not doe so too.
Verse hath a middle nature: heaven keepes soules,
The grave keeps bodies, verse the fame enroules.

A Funerall Elegie

'TIS lost, to trust a Tombe with such a ghest,
    Or to confine her in a Marble chest.
Alas, what's Marble, Jeat, or Porphiry,
Priz'd with the Chrysolite of eyther eye,
Or with those Pearles, and Rubies which shee was?   5
Joyne the two Indies in one Tombe, 'tis glas;
And so is all to her materials,
Though every inche were ten escurials.
Yet shee's demolish'd: Can we keepe her then

457 vertue,'if] vertue, if *1611*   474 fame *1612 errata, 1633*: same *1611–1625*
    A Funerall Elegie. *1611 indents alternate lines*   Roman in *1611*; italic in *1612*
1 'Tis] Tis *1611*

In workes of hands, or of the wits of men?   10
Can these memorials, ragges of paper, give
Life to that name, by which name they must live?
Sickly, alas, short-liv'd, aborted bee
Those Carkas verses, whose soule is not shee.
And can shee, who no longer would be shee,   15
Being such a Tabernacle, stoope to bee
In paper wrap't; Or, when she would not lie
In such a house, dwell in an Elegie?
But 'tis no matter; we may well allow
Verse to live so long as the world will now.   20
For her death wounded it. The world containes
Princes for armes, and Counsailors for braines,
Lawyers for tongues, Divines for hearts, and more,
The Rich for stomachs, and for backes the Pore;
The Officers for hands, Merchants for feet   25
By which remote and distant Countries meet.
But those fine spirits, which doe tune and set
This Organ, are those peeces which beget
Wonder and love; And these were shee; and shee
Being spent, the world must needes decrepit bee.   30
For since death will proceed to triumph still,
He can finde nothing, after her, to kill,
Except the world it selfe, so great as shee.
Thus brave and confident may Nature bee,
Death cannot give her such another blow,   35
Because shee cannot such another show.
But must we say shee's dead? May't not be said
That as a sundred Clocke is peece-meale laid,
Not to be lost, but by the makers hand
Repolish'd, without error then to stand,   40
Or as the Affrique Niger streame enwombs
It selfe into the earth, and after comes,
(Having first made a naturall bridge, to passe
For many leagues,) farre greater then it was,

May't not be said, that her grave shall restore   45
Her, greater, purer, firmer, then before?
Heaven may say this, and joy in't; but can wee
Who live, and lacke her, here this vantage see?
What is't to us, alas, if there have beene
An Angell made a Throne, or Cherubin?   5c
We lose by't: And as aged men are glad
Being tastlesse growne, to joy in joyes they had,
So now the sicke starv'd world must feed upone
This joy, that we had her, who now is gone.
Rejoyce then nature, and this world, that you   55
Fearing the last fires hastning to subdue
Your force and vigor, ere it were neere gone,
Wisely bestow'd, and layd it all on one.
One, whose cleare body was so pure, and thin,
Because it neede disguise no thought within.   60
'Twas but a through-light scarfe, her minde t'enroule,
Or exhalation breath'd out from her soule.
One, whom all men who durst no more, admir'd;
And whom, who ere had worth enough, desir'd;
As when a Temple's built, Saints emulate   65
To which of them, it shall be consecrate.
But as when Heav'n lookes on us with new eyes,
Those new starres ev'ry Artist exercise,
What place they should assigne to them they doubt,
Argue,'and agree not, till those starres go out: 70
So the world studied whose this peece should be,
Till she can be no bodies else, nor shee:
But like a Lampe of Balsamum, desir'd
Rather t'adorne, then last, shee soone expir'd,
Cloath'd in her Virgin white integrity;   75
For mariage, though it doe not staine, doth dye.
To scape th'infirmities which waite upone
Woman, shee went away, before sh'was one.
And the worlds busie noyse to overcome,

47 in't] int's *1625*   61 'Twas] T'was *1611*   64 worth] worke *1633*
70 Argue,'and] Argue, and *1611*   74 expir'd,] expir'd; *1611*   76 it doe] it doth
1633

Tooke so much death, as serv'd for *opium*.   80
For though she could not, nor could chuse to die,
Shee'ath yeelded to too long an Extasie.
He which not knowing her sad History,
Should come to reade the booke of destiny,
How faire and chast, humble and high shee'ad beene,   85
Much promis'd, much perform'd, at not fifteene,
And measuring future things by things before,
Should turne the leafe to reade, and read no more,
Would thinke that eyther destiny mistooke,
Or that some leafes were torne out of the booke.   90
But 'tis not so: Fate did but usher her
To yeares of Reasons use, and then infer
Her destiny to her selfe; which liberty
She tooke but for thus much, thus much to die.
Her modesty not suffering her to bee   95
Fellow-Commissioner with destinee,
Shee did no more but die; if after her
Any shall live, which dare true good prefer,
Every such person is her delegate,
T'accomplish that which should have beene her fate.   100
They shall make up that booke, and shall have thankes
Of fate and her, for filling up their blanks.
For future vertuous deeds are Legacies,
Which from the gift of her example rise.
And 'tis in heav'n part of spirituall mirth,
To see how well, the good play her, on earth.

FINIS

83 sad] said *1612–1633, Gr*   90 leafes] leaues *1612–1633, Gr*   FINIS] *omit*
1633, Gr

THE SECOND ANNIVERSARIE

OF THE PROGRES OF THE SOULE

Wherein: by Occasion of the Religious Death of
Mistris Elizabeth Drury, the Incommodities
of the Soule in this Life and her
Exaltation in the Next,
are Contemplated.

The Harbinger to the Progres

Two soules move here, and mine (a third) must move
Paces of admiration, and of love;
Thy soule (Deare Virgin) whose this tribute is,
Mov'd from this mortall sphere to lively blisse;
And yet moves still, and still aspires to see   5
The worlds last day, thy glories full degree:
Like as those starres which thou ore-lookest farre,
Are in their place, and yet still moved are:
No soule (whiles with the lugage of this clay
It clogged is) can follow thee halfe way;   10
Or see thy flight; which doth our thoughts outgoe
So fast, that now the lightning moves but slow:
But now thou art as high in heaven flowne
As heav'ns from us; what soule besides thine owne
Can tell thy joyes, or say he can relate   15
Thy glorious Journals in that blessed state?
I envie thee (Rich soule) I envy thee,
Although I cannot yet thy glory see:
And thou (Great spirit) which her's follow'd hast
So fast, as none can follow thine so fast;   20
So farre as none can follow thine so farre,

THE SECOND ANNIVERSARIE. *1612. Collations from 1612 errata slip, 1621, 1625, 1633. Titles
from 1612–1633*   8 *are:] are 1612*   15 *relate 1621–1633: re-relate 1612*

(*And if this flesh did not the passage barre*
Had'st raught her) *let me wonder at thy flight*
Which long agone had'st lost the vulgar sight
And now mak'st proud the better eyes, that thay   25
Can see thee less'ned in thine aery way;
So while thou mak'st her soules Hy progresse knowne
Thou mak'st a noble progresse of thine owne,
From this worlds carcasse having mounted hie
To that pure life of Immortalitie;   30
Since thine aspiring thoughts themselves so raise
That more may not beseeme a creatures praise,
Yet still thou vow'st her more; and every yeare
Mak'st a new progresse, while thou wandrest here;
Still upwards mount; and let thy makers praise   35
Honor thy Laura, and adorne thy laies.
And since thy Muse her head in heaven shrouds
Oh let her never stoope below the clouds:
And if those glorious sainted soules may know
Or what we doe, or what we sing below,   40
Those acts, those songs shall still content them best
Which praise those awfull powers that make them blest.

23 *raught*] *caught 1621–1633, Gr*   27 *soules Hy 1612 errata: soules by 1612:*
soule by 1621–1633, Gr   28 *owne,*] *owne. 1612*   35 *upwards*] *upward*
1621–1633, Gr

Of the Progres of the Soule

NOTHING could make mee sooner to confesse   *The entrance.*
   That this world had an everlastingnesse,
Then to consider, that a yeare is runne,
Since both this lower worlds, and the Sunnes Sunne,
The Lustre, and the vigor of this All,   5
Did set; 'twere Blasphemy, to say, did fall.
But as a ship which hath strooke saile, doth runne,
By force of that force which before, it wonne,
Or as sometimes in a beheaded man,
Though at those two Red seas, which freely ran,   10
One from the Trunke, another from the Head,
His soule be saild, to her eternall bed,
His eies will twinckle, and his tongue will roll,
As though he beckned, and cal'd backe his Soul,
He graspes his hands, and he puls up his feet,   15
And seemes to reach, and to step forth to meet
His soule; when all these motions which we saw,
Are but as Ice, which crackles at a thaw:
Or as a Lute, which in moist weather, rings
Her knell alone, by cracking of her strings: 20
So strugles this dead world, now shee is gone;
For there is motion in corruption.
As some Daies are, at the Creation nam'd,
Before the sunne, the which fram'd Daies, was fram'd,
So after this sunnes set, some show appeares,   25
And orderly vicisitude of yeares.
Yet a new Deluge, and of Lethe flood,
Hath drown'd us all, All have forgot all good,
Forgetting her, the maine Reserve of all;
Yet in this Deluge, grosse and generall,   30
Thou seest mee strive for life; my life shalbe,

---

1 confesse] confesse. *1612*   *Margin*: The entrance.] *omit 1625, 1633*   6 'twere]
t'were *1612*   10 Though *1612 errata, 1633*: Through *1612–1625*   12 be] he
1621–1633   13 twinckle] twincke *1625*   16 meet] meet. *1612*   17 soule;]
soule, *1612*   20 strings:] strings. *1612*   29 all;] all, *1612*

To bee hereafter prais'd, for praysing thee,
Immortal Mayd, who though thou wouldst refuse
The name of Mother, be unto my Muse
A Father, since her chast Ambition is,   35
Yearely to bring forth such a child as this.
These Hymnes may worke on future wits, and so
May great Grand-children of thy praises grow.
And so, though not Revive, embalme, and spice
The world, which else would putrify with vice.   40
For thus, Man may extend thy progeny,
Untill man doe but vanish, and not die.
These Hymns thy issue, may encrease so long,
As till Gods great Venite change the song.   44
Thirst for that time, O my insatiate soule,   *A just*
And serve thy thirst, with Gods safe-sealing Bowle. *disestimation*
Bee thirsty still, and drinke still till thou goe;   *of this world.*
'Tis th'onely Health, to be Hydropique so.
Forget this rotten world; And unto thee,
Let thine owne times as an old story be;   50
Be not concern'd: study not why, nor whan;
Do not so much, as not beleeve a man;
For though to erre, be worst, to try truths forth,
Is far more busines, then this world is worth.
The World is but a Carkas; thou art fed   55
By it, but as a worme, that carcas bred;
And why shouldst thou, poore worme, consider more,
When this world will grow better then before,
Then those thy fellow-wormes doe thinke upone
That carkasses last resurrectione.   60
Forget this world, and scarse thinke of it so,
As of old cloaths, cast off a yeare agoe.
To be thus stupid is Alacrity;
Men thus lethargique have best Memory.

34-5 Muse ... Father,] Muse, ... Father *1612*   37 Hymnes] Hymes *1612*
41 For] for *1612*   42 vanish] banish *1625*   43 thy] they *1621, 1625*
45 *Margin: disestimation*] estimation *1625*   46 safe-sealing] safe-fealing *1612-*
1633   47 till *1612 errata, 1621-1633*: till, *1612*   48 'Tis *1612 errata*: T'o
1612: To *1621-1633, Gr*   Hydropique *1612 errata*: Hydroptique *1612-1633, Gr*
50 be;] be *1612*   52 man;] man. *1612*   62 off] of *1612*

Looke upward; that's towards her, whose happy state   65
We now lament not, but congratulate.
Shee, to whom all this world was but a stage,
Where all sat harkning how her youthfull age
Should be emploid, because in all, shee did,
Some Figure of the Golden times, was hid.   70
Who could not lacke, what ere this world could give,
Because shee was the forme, that made it live;
Nor could complaine, that this world was unfit,
To be staid in, then when shee was in it;
Shee that first tried indifferent desires   75
By vertue,'and vertue by religious fires,
Shee to whose person Paradise adhear'd,
As Courts to Princes; shee whose eies enspheard
Star-light inough, t'have made the South controll,
(Had shee beene there) the Star-full Northern Pole,   80
Shee, shee is gone; shee's gone; when thou knowst this,
What fragmentary rubbidge this world is
Thou knowst, and that it is not worth a thought;
He honors it too much that thinks it nought.   84
Thinke then, my soule, that death is but a Groome,   *Contemplation*
Which brings a Taper to the outward roome,   *of our state*
Whence thou spiest first a little glimmering light,   *in our death-bed.*
And after brings it nearer to thy sight:
For such approches doth Heaven make in death.
Thinke thy selfe laboring now with broken breath,   90
And thinke those broken and soft Notes to bee
Division, and thy happiest Harmonee.
Thinke thee laid on thy death bed, loose and slacke;
And thinke that but unbinding of a packe,
To take one precious thing, thy soule, from thence.   95
Thinke thy selfe parch'd with fevers violence,
Anger thine Ague more, by calling it
Thy Physicke; chide the slacknesse of the fit.

---

67 was *1612 errata, 1633*: twas *1612–1625*   76 vertue,'and] vertue,and *1612*
81 shee's . . . knowst] she is . . . knowest *1612*   82 is] is. *1612*   83 knowst]
knowest *1612*   85 my] My *1612*   86 roome] romme *1612*   96 parch'd]
pach'd *1625*: patch'd *1633*

Thinke that thou hearst thy knell, and thinke no more,
But that, as Bels cal'd thee to Church before,   100
So this, to the Triumphant Church, cals thee.
Thinke Satans Sergeants round about thee bee,
And thinke that but for Legacies they thrust;
Give one thy Pride, to'another give thy Lust:
Give them those sinnes which they gave thee before,   105
And trust th'immaculate blood to wash thy score.
Thinke thy frinds weeping round, and thinke that thay
• Weepe but because they goe not yet thy way.
Thinke that they close thine eyes, and thinke in this,
That they confesse much in the world, amisse,   110
Who dare not trust a dead mans eye with that,
Which they from God, and Angels cover not.
Thinke that they shroud thee up, and thinke from thence
They reinvest thee in white innocence.
Thinke that thy body rots, and (if so lowe,   115
Thy soule exalted so, thy thoughts can goe,)
Thinke thee a Prince, who of themselves create
Wormes which insensibly devoure their state.
Thinke that they bury thee, and thinke that rite
Laies thee to sleepe but a saint Lucies night.   120
Thinke these things cheerefully: and if thou bee
Drowsie or slacke, remember then that shee,
Shee whose Complexion was so even made,
That which of her Ingredients should invade
The other three, no Feare, no Art could guesse: 125
So far were all remov'd from more or lesse.
But as in Mithridate, or just perfumes,
Where all good things being met, no one presumes
To governe, or to triumph on the rest,
Onely because all were, no part was best: 130
And as, though all doe know, that quantities
Are made of lines, and lines from Points arise,
None can these lines or quantities unjoynt,

113 shroud] shourd *1621, 1625*   116 goe,] goe. *1612*   117 thee] the *1612*
119 rite *1612 errata*: right *1612–1633*, Gr   129 on] no *1612*   130 best:] best.
1612

And say this is a line, or this a point:
So though the Elements and Humors were   135
In her, one could not say, this governes there.
Whose even constitution might have wonne
Any disease to venter on the Sunne,
Rather then her: and make a spirit feare
That he to disuniting subject were.   140
To whose proportions if we would compare
Cubes, th'are unstable; Circles, Angulare;
Shee who was such a Chaine, as Fate emploies
To bring mankind, all Fortunes it enjoies,
So fast, so even wrought, as one would thinke,   145
No Accident, could threaten any linke,
Shee, shee embrac'd a sicknesse, gave it meat,
The purest Blood, and Breath, that ere it eat.
And hath taught us that though a good man hath
Title to Heaven, and plead it by his Faith,   150
And though he may pretend a conquest, since
Heaven was content to suffer violence,
Yea though he plead a long possession too,
(For they'are in Heaven on Earth, who Heavens workes do,)
Though he had right, and power, and Place before,   155
Yet Death must usher, and unlocke the doore.
Thinke further on thy selfe, my soule, and thinke   *Incommodities*
How thou at first wast made but in a sinke;   *of the Soule*
Thinke that it argued some infermitee,   *in the Body.*
That those two soules, which then thou foundst in mee,   160
Thou fedst upon, and drewst into thee, both
My second soule of sence, and first of growth.
Thinke but how poore thou wast, how'obnoxious,
Whom a small lump of flesh could poison thus.
This curded milke, this poore unlittered whelpe   165
My body, could, beyond escape, or helpe,
Infect thee with originall sinne, and thou

134 point:] point, *1612*   137 wonne *1612 errata, 1633*: worne *1612–1625*
140 to] too *1633*   141 proportions] proportious *1612*   153 a long *1621–1633*:
along *1612*   157 thinke] thinke; *1612*   *Margin*: Incommodities . . . Body.] omit
1625, 1633   161 and] And *1612*   163 how'obnoxious] how obnoxious *1612*

Couldst neither then refuse, nor leave it now.
Thinke that no stubborne sullen Anchorit,
Which fixt to'a Pillar, or a Grave doth sit   170
Bedded and Bath'd in all his Ordures, dwels
So fowly as our soules, i'their first-built Cels.
Thinke in how poore a prison thou didst lie
After, enabled but to sucke, and crie.
Thinke, when 'twas growne to most, 'twas a poore Inne,   175
A Province Pack'd up in two yards of skinne,
And that usurped, or threatned with the rage
Of sicknesses, or their true mother, Age.
But thinke that Death hath now enfranchis'd thee,   *Her liberty*
Thou hast thy'expansion now and libertee;   *by death.*
Thinke that a rusty Peece, discharg'd, is flowne   181
In peeces, and the bullet is his owne,
And freely flies: This to thy soule allow,
Thinke thy shell broke, thinke thy Soule hatch'd but now.
And thinke this slow-pac'd soule, which late did cleave   185
To'a body,'and went but by the bodies leave,
Twenty, perchance, or thirty mile a day,
Dispatches in a minute all the way,
Twixt Heaven, and Earth: shee staies not in the Ayre,
To looke what Meteors there themselves prepare;   190
Shee carries no desire to know, nor sense,
Whether th'Ayrs middle Region be intense,
For th'Element of fire, shee doth not know,
Whether shee past by such a place or no;
Shee baits not at the Moone, nor cares to trie,   195
Whether in that new world, men live, and die.
Venus retards her not, to'enquire, how shee
Can, (being one Star) Hesper, and Vesper bee;
Hee that charm'd Argus eies, sweet Mercury,
Workes not on her, who now is growne all Ey;   200

171 Bedded] Beddded *1612*   172 i'their] in their *1612*   175 'twas . . . 'twas]
t'was . . . t'was *1612*   176 skinne,] skinne. *1612*   177 the] a *1633*
180 expansion *1612 errata, 1625, 1633*: expausion *1612, 1621*   181 flowne] flowen
1612   184 shell] sheel *1612*: sheell *1621, 1625*   185 cleave] cleave, *1612*
186 body,'and] body, and *1612*   197 retards *1612 errata, 1633*: recards *1612–1625*
198 bee;] bee, *1612*   200 growne] growen *1612*

Who, if shee meete the body of the Sunne,
Goes through, not staying till his course be runne;
Who finds in Mars his Campe, no corps of Guard;
Nor is by Jove, nor by his father bard;
But ere shee can consider how shee went,   205
At once is at, and through the Firmament.
And as these stars were but so many beades
Strunge on one string, speed undistinguish'd leades
Her through those spheares, as through the beades, a string,
Whose quicke succession makes it still one thing: 210
As doth the Pith, which, least our Bodies slacke,
Strings fast the little bones of necke, and backe;
So by the soule doth death string Heaven and Earth,
For when our soule enjoyes this her third birth,
(Creation gave her one, a second, grace,)   215
Heaven is as neare, and present to her face,
As colours are, and objects, in a roome
Where darknesse was before, when Tapers come.
This must, my soule, thy long-short Progresse bee;
To'advance these thoughts, remember then, that shee,   220
Shee, whose faire body no such prison was,
But that a soule might well be pleas'd to passe
An Age in her; shee whose rich beauty lent
Mintage to others beauties, for they went
But for so much, as they were like to her;   225
Shee, in whose body (if wee dare prefer
This low world, to so high a mark, as shee,)
The Westerne treasure, Easterne spiceree,
Europe, and Afrique, and the unknowen rest
Were easily found, or what in them was best;   230
And when w'have made this large Discoveree,
Of all in her some one part there will bee
Twenty such parts, whose plenty'and riches is
Inough to make twenty such worlds as this;
Shee, whom had they knowne, who did first betroth   235

    220 shee,] shee *1612*   224 others] other *1633, Gr*   228 Easterne
1625, 1633: Esterne *1612, 1621*   232 there *1612 errata*: then *1612–1633, Gr*
233 plenty'and] plenty and *1612*

The Tutelar Angels, and assign'd one, both
To Nations, Cities, and to Companies,
To Functions, Offices, and Dignities,
And to each severall man, to him, and him,
They would have given her one for every limme;   240
Shee, of whose soule, if we may say, 'twas Gold,
Her body was th'Electrum, and did hold
Many degrees of that; we understood
Her by her sight, her pure and eloquent blood
Spoke in her cheekes, and so distinctly wrought,   245
That one might almost say, her bodie thought,
Shee, shee, thus richly,'and largely hous'd, is gone:
And chides us slow-pac'd snailes, who crawle upon
Our prisons prison, earth, nor thinke us well
Longer, then whil'st we beare our brittle shell.   250
But 'twere but little to have chang'd our roome,   *Her ignorance*
If, as we were in this our living Tombe   *in this life*
Oppress'd with ignorance, we still were so.   *and knowledge*
                                                        in the next.
Poore soule, in this thy flesh what do'st thou know?
Thou know'st thy selfe so little,'as thou know'st not,   255
How thou did'st die, nor how thou wast begot.
Thou neither knowst, how thou at first cam'st in,
Nor how thou took'st the poyson of mans sin.
Nor dost thou, (though thou knowst, that thou art so)
By what way thou art made immortall, know.   260
Thou art too narrow, wretch, to comprehend
Even thy selfe: yea though thou wouldst but bend
To know thy body. Have not all soules thought
For many ages, that our body'is wrought
Of Ayre, and Fire, and other Elements?   265
And now they thinke of new ingredients.
And one soule thinkes one, and another way
Another thinkes, and 'tis an even lay.

236 assign'd] assigned *1612*   241 'twas] t'was *1612*   243 we] (we *1612–1625*
understood] unstood *1621, 1625*   245 distinctly] distinckly *1612*   247 richly,'and]
richly, and *1612*   251 'twere] t'were *1612*   *Margin: Her ignorance . . . next.] omit*
1633   253 so.] so, *1612*   254 soule, . . . know?] soule . . . know. *1612*
255 little,'as] little, as *1612*   257 cam'st] camest *1612*   261 too] to *1612–1625*
268 'tis] ty's *1612, 1621*   lay.] lay *1612*

Knowst thou but how the stone doth enter in
The bladders Cave, and never breake the skin?   270
Knowst thou how blood, which to the hart doth flow,
Doth from one ventricle to th'other go?
And for the putrid stuffe, which thou dost spit,
Knowst thou how thy lungs have attracted it?
There are no passages so that there is   275
(For ought thou knowst) piercing of substances.
And of those many'opinions which men raise
Of Nailes and Haires, dost thou know which to praise?
What hope have we to know our selves, when wee
Know not the least things, which for our use bee?   280
We see in Authors, too stiffe to recant,
A hundred controversies of an Ant.
And yet one watches, starves, freeses, and sweats,
To know but Catechismes and Alphabets
Of unconcerning things, matters of fact;   285
How others on our stage their parts did Act;
What Caesar did, yea, and what Cicero said.
Why grasse is greene, or why our blood is red,
Are mysteries which none have reach'd unto.
In this low forme, poore soule, what wilt thou doe?   290
When wilt thou shake off this Pedantery,
Of being taught by sense, and Fantasy?
Thou look'st through spectacles; small things seeme great,
Below; But up unto the watch-towre get,
And see all things despoyld of fallacies: 295
Thou shalt not peepe through lattices of eies,
Nor heare through Laberinths of eares, nor learne
By circuit, or collections to discerne.
In Heaven thou straight know'st all, concerning it,
And what concerns it not, shalt straight forget.   300
There thou (but in no other schoole) maist bee
Perchance, as learned, and as full, as shee,
Shee who all Libraries had throughly red

270 breake] brake *1621–1633*   277 many'opinions] many opinions *1612*
281 recant,] recant. *1612*   290 soule,] soule *1612*   291 off] of *1612*
292 taught *1612 errata, 1633*: thought *1612–1625*   300 shalt *1633*: shall *1612–1625*

At home, in her owne thoughts, and practised
So much good as would make as many more: 305
Shee whose example they must all implore,
Who would or doe, or thinke well, and confesse
That aye the vertuous Actions they expresse,
Are but a new, and worse edition,
Of her some one thought, or one action: 310
Shee, who in th'Art of knowing Heaven, was growne
Here upon Earth, to such perfection,
That shee hath, ever since to Heaven shee came,
(In a far fairer print,) but read the same:
Shee, shee, not satisfied with all this waite,   315
(For so much knowledge, as would over-fraite
Another, did but Ballast her) is gone,
As well t'enjoy, as get perfectione.
And cals us after her, in that shee tooke,
(Taking herselfe) our best, and worthiest booke.   320
Returne not, my soule, from this extasee,   *Of our comp-*
And meditation of what thou shalt bee,   *any in this*
To earthly thoughts, till it to thee appeare,   *life and in*
With whom thy conversation must be there.   *the next.*
With whom wilt thou Converse? what station   325
Canst thou choose out, free from infection,
That wil nor give thee theirs, nor drinke in thine?
Shalt thou not finde a spungy slack Divine
Drinke and sucke in th'Instructions of Great men,
And for the word of God, vent them agen?   330
Are there not some Courts, (And then, no things bee
So like as Courts) which, in this let us see,
That wits and tongues of Libellars are weake,
Because they doe more ill, then these can speake?
The poyson'is gone through all, poysons affect   335
Chiefly the cheefest parts, but some effect
In Nailes, and Haires, yea excrements, will show;

304 and] And *1612*   308 aye] aie *1612, 1621*: are *1625*: all *1633, Gr*
311 growne] growen *1612*   314 print *1612 errata*: point *1612–1633*
323 earthly] early *1625*   326 choose] chose *1633*   327 nor . . . nor] not . . .
nor *1625, 1633, Gr*

So will the poyson of sinne, in the most low.
Up, up, my drowsie soule, where thy new eare
Shall in the Angels songs no discord heare;   340
Where thou shalt see the blessed Mother-maid
Joy in not being that, which men have said,
Where shee'is exalted more for being good,
Then for her interest, of mother-hood.
Up to those Patriarckes, which did longer sit   345
Expecting Christ, then they'have enjoy'd him yet.
Up to those Prophets, which now gladly see
Their Prophecies growne to be Historee.
Up to th'Apostles, who did bravely runne
All the Sunnes course, with more light then the Sunne.   350
Up to those Martyrs, who did calmely bleed
Oyle to th'Apostles lamps, dew to their seed.
Up to those Virgins, who thought that almost
They made joyntenants with the Holy Ghost,
If they to any should his Temple give.   355
Up, up, for in that squadron there doth live
Shee, who hath carried thether, new degrees
(As to their number) to their dignitees.
Shee, who beeing to herselfe a state, enjoyd
All royalties which any state emploid,   360
For shee made wars, and triumph'd; reson still
Did not o'erthrow, but rectifie her will:
And shee made peace, for no peace is like this,
That beauty'and chastity together kisse:
Shee did high justice; for shee crucified   365
Every first motion of rebellious pride:
And shee gave pardons, and was liberall,
For, onely'her selfe except, shee pardond all:
Shee coynd, in this, that her impressions gave
To all our actions all the worth they have: 370

338 will 1612 errata: wise 1612–1625: lyes 1633, Gr   339 Up,] Up 1612
342 said,] said. 1612   348 growne] growen 1612   349 runne] runne, 1612
353 thought 1612 errata, 1633: thoughts 1612–1625   359 herselfe ... state,] her-
selfe, ... state 1612   361 triumph'd;] triumph'd, 1612   362 o'erthrow] over-
throw 1612–1625   364 beauty'and] beauty and 1612   368 onely'her selfe] onely
her selfe 1612   369 impressions] impression 1633

Shee gave protections; the thoughts of her brest
Satans rude Officers could nere arrest.
As these prerogatives being met in one,
Made her a soveraigne state, religion
Made her a Church; and these two made her all.   375
Shee who was all this All, and could not fall
To worse, by company; (for shee was still
More Antidote, then all the world was ill,)
Shee, shee doth leave it, and by Death, survive
All this, in Heaven; whither who doth not strive   380
The more, because shee'is there, he doth not know
That accidentall joyes in Heaven doe grow.

Of essentiall joy in this life and in the next.

But pause, my soule, and study ere thou fall
On accidentall joyes, th'essentiall.
Still before Accessories doe abide   385
A triall, must the principall be tride.
And what essentiall joy canst thou expect
Here upon earth? what permanent effect
Of transitory causes? Dost thou love
Beauty? (And Beauty worthyest is to move)   390
Poore couse'ned cose'nor, that she, and that thou,
Which did begin to love, are neither now.
You are both fluid, chang'd since yesterday;
Next day repaires, (but ill) last daies decay.
Nor are, (although the river keep the name)   395
Yesterdaies waters, and to daies the same.
So flowes her face, and thine eies, neither now
That saint, nor Pilgrime, which your loving vow
Concernd, remaines; but whil'st you thinke you bee
Constant, you'are howrely in inconstancee.   400
Honour may have pretence unto our love,
Because that God did live so long above
Without this Honour, and then lov'd it so,
That he at last made Creatures to bestow
Honor on him; not that he needed it,   405

378 ill,)] ill, *1612*   380 whither *1612 errata*: whether *1612–1633*   383 my]
My *1612*   395 although] Although *1612*   398 vow *1612 errata, 1633*: row
1612–1625   399 remaines;] remaines, *1612*   404 to] to to *1612*

But that, to his hands, man might grow more fit.
But since all honors from inferiors flow,
(For they doe give it; Princes doe but show
Whom they would have so honord) and that this
On such opinions, and capacities   410
Is built, as rise, and fall, to more and lesse,
Alas, 'tis but a casuall happinesse.
Hath ever any man to'himselfe assign'd
This or that happinesse, to'arrest his minde,
But that another man, which takes a worse,   415
Thinke him a foole for having tane that course?
They who did labour Babels tower t'erect,
Might have considerd, that for that effect,
All this whole solid Earth could not allow
Nor furnish forth Materials enow;   420
And that this Center, to raise such a place
Was far too little, to have beene the Base;
No more affoords this world, foundatione
T'erect true joye, were all the meanes in one.
But as the Heathen made them severall gods,   425
Of all Gods Benefits, and all his Rods,
(For as the Wine, and Corne, and Onions are
Gods unto them, so Agues bee, and war)
And as by changing that whole precious Gold
To such small copper coynes, they lost the old,   430
And lost their onely God, who ever must
Be sought alone, and not in such a thrust,
So much mankind true happinesse mistakes;
No Joye enjoyes that man, that many makes.
Then, soule, to thy first pitch worke up againe;   435
Know that all lines which circles doe containe,
For once that they the center touch, do touch
Twice the circumference; and be thou such.
Double on Heaven, thy thoughts on Earth emploid;

412 'tis] tis *1612*   413 assign'd] assigned *1612*   416 Thinke] Thinks *1633*, *Gr*
417 t'erect *1612 errata*: to'rect *1612*   420 enow] enough *1633*   421 this] his
1621–1633   422 too] to *1612*   423 world *1633*: worlds *1612–1625*
424 T'erect] To erect *1612*   429 that] the *1625*   435 up *1633*: upon *1612–1625*

All will not serve; Onely who have enjoyd   440
The sight of God, in fulnesse, can thinke it;
For it is both the object, and the wit.
This is essentiall joye, where neither hee
Can suffer Diminution, nor wee;
'Tis such a full, and such a filling good;   445
Had th'Angels once look'd on him, they had stood.
To fill the place of one of them, or more,
Shee whom we celebrate, is gone before.
Shee, who had Here so much essentiall joye,
As no chance could distract, much lesse destroy;   450
Who with Gods presence was acquainted so,
(Hearing, and speaking to him) as to know
His face, in any naturall Stone, or Tree,
Better then when in Images they bee:
Who kept, by diligent devotion,   455
Gods Image, in such reparation,
Within her heart, that what decay was grown,
Was her first Parents fault, and not her own:
Who being solicited to any Act,
Still heard God pleading his safe precontract;   460
Who by a faithfull confidence, was here
Betroth'd to God, and now is married there,
Whose twilights were more cleare, then our mid day,
Who dreamt devoutlier, then most use to pray;
Who being heare fild with grace, yet strove to bee,   465
Both where more grace, and more capacitee
At once is given: shee to Heaven is gone,
Who made this world in some proportion
A heaven, and here, became unto us all,
Joye, (as our joyes admit) essentiall.   470
But could this low world joyes essentiall touch,   *Of accidentall*
Heavens accidentall joyes would passe them much.   *joyes in both*
                                                         places.
How poore and lame, must then our casuall bee?
If thy Prince will his subjects to call thee

---

445 'Tis] Tis *1612*   449 ioye,] ioye. *1612*   457 grown] growen *1612*
462 Betroth'd] Betrothed *1612*

My Lord, and this doe swell thee, thou art than,   475
By being a greater, growne to be lesse Man.
When no Physician of Redresse can speake,
A joyfull casuall violence may breake
A dangerous Apostem in thy brest;
And whilst thou joy'st in this, the dangerous rest,   480
The bag may rise up, and so strangle thee.
What aye was casuall, may ever bee.
What should the Nature change? Or make the same
Certaine, which was but casuall, when it came?
All casuall joye doth loud and plainly say,   485
Onely by comming, that it can away.
Onely in Heaven joies strength is never spent;
And accidentall things are permanent.
Joy of a soules arrivall nere decaies;
For that soule ever joyes, and ever staies.   490
Joy that their last great Consummation
Approches in the resurrection;
When earthly bodies more celestiall
Shalbe, then Angels were, for they could fall;
This kind of joy doth every day admit   495
Degrees of grouth, but none of loosing it.
In this fresh joy, 'tis no small part, that shee,
Shee, in whose goodnesse, he that names degree,
Doth injure her; ('Tis losse to be cald best,
There where the stuffe is not such as the rest)   500
Shee, who left such a body,'as even shee
Onely in Heaven could learne, how it can bee
Made better; for shee rather was two soules,
Or like to full, on both sides written Rols,
Where eies might read upon the outward skin,   505
As strong Records for God, as mindes within;
Shee, who by making full perfection grow,

476 a greater] greater *1625, 1633, Gr*   growne] growen *1612*   Man.] Man, *1612*
477 Redresse *1612 errata, 1633*: Reders *1612–1625*   480 joy'st] joyest *1612*
482 aye] eie *1612*: eye *1621, 1625*: e'r *1633, Gr*   489 nere] neere *1612–1625*: ne'r
1633   497–9 'tis . . . 'Tis] tis . . . Tis *1612*   501 body,'as] body, as *1612*
even] ever *1625*   506 within;] within, *1612*

Peeces a Circle, and still keepes it so,
Long'd for, and longing for'it, to heaven is gone,
Where shee receives, and gives addition.   510
Here in a place, where mis-devotion frames   *Conclusion.*
A thousand praiers to saints, whose very names
The ancient Church knew not, Heaven knowes not yet,
And where, what lawes of poetry admit,
Lawes of religion have at least the same,   515
Immortall Maid, I might invoque thy name.
Could any Saint provoke that appetite,
Thou here shouldst make mee a French convertite.
But thou wouldst not; nor wouldst thou be content,
To take this, for my second yeeres true Rent,   520
Did this Coine beare any'other stampe, then his,
That gave thee power to doe, me, to say this.
Since his will is, that to posteritee,
Thou shouldst for life, and death, a patterne bee,
And that the world should notice have of this,   525
The purpose, and th'Autority is his;
Thou art the Proclamation; and I ame
The Trumpet, at whose voice the people came.

FINIS

515 religion] religion, *1612*   516 invoque *1612 errata, 1633*: inroque *1612–1625*
518 French] french *1612*   521 any'other] any other *1612*   522 doe, *1612 errata,*
1633: doe *1612–1625*   524 shouldst] shouldest *1612*   FINIS] *omit 1633, Gr*

EPICEDES AND OBSEQUIES

Elegie on the Lady Marckham

MAN is the World, and death the Ocean,
    To which God gives the lower parts of man.
This Sea invirons all, and though as yet
God hath set markes, and bounds, twixt us, and it,
Yet doth it rore, and gnaw, and still pretend,   5
And breaks our bankes, when ere it takes a friend.
Then our land waters (teares of passion) vent;
Our waters, then, above our firmament,
(Teares which our Soule doth for her sin let fall)
Take all a brackish tast, and Funerall,   10
And even those teares, which should wash sin, are sin.
We, after Gods *Noe*, drowne our world againe.
Nothing but man of all invenom'd things
Doth worke upon itselfe, with inborne stings.
Teares are false Spectacles, we cannot see   15
Through passions mist, what wee are, or what shee.
In her, this sea of death hath made no breach,
But as the tide doth wash the slimie beach,
And leaves embroderd workes upon the sand,
So is her flesh refin'd by deaths cold hand.   20
As men of China,'after an ages stay,
Do take up Porcelane, where they buried Clay;
So at this grave, her limbecke, which refines
The Diamonds, Rubies, Saphires, Pearles, and Mines,
Of which this flesh was, her soule shall inspire   25
Flesh of such stuffe, as God, when his last fire

Elegie on the Lady Marckham. *1633. MSS.*: *C 57, H 49; L 74, TC; Dob, O'F. Title
from 1633, C 57, H 49*: An Elegie uppon the death of yᵉLa:... *L 74, TC*: A funerall
Elegy on (*O'F* upon) the Death of yᵉ ... *Dob, O'F*   1 the Ocean] th'Ocean *1633,
C 57, Gr*   3 This *1633, L 74, TC, Dob*: The *C 57, H 49, O'F (b.c.)*   4 hath] have
H 49, Dob   us,] us *1633*   6 bankes *Σ*: banke *1633, L 74, TCD*   8 firma-
ment,] firmament. *1633*   9 sin *Σ*: sins *1633, Gr*   10 Funerall,] Funerall. *1633*
11 those] these *C 57, H 49, Gr*   12 our *Σ*: the *1633, TCC, Dob*   16 or] nor
L 74, TC   17 her,] her *1633*   21 stay,] stay *1633*   25 which] which, *1633*

Annuls this world, to recompence it, shall,
Make and name then, th'Elixar of this All.
They say, the sea, when it gaines, loseth too;
If carnall Death (the yonger brother) doe   30
Usurpe the body,'our soule, which subject is
To th'elder death, by sinne, is freed by this;
They perish both, when they attempt the just;
For, graves our trophies are, and both deaths dust.
So, unobnoxious now, she'hath buried both;   35
For, none to death sinnes, that to sinne is loth,
Nor doe they die, which are not loth to die;
So hath she this, and that virginity.
Grace was in her extremely diligent,
That kept her from sinne, yet made her repent.   40
Of what small spots pure white complaines! Alas,
How little poyson breaks a christall glasse!
She sinn'd, but just enough to let us see
That Gods Word must be true, All, sinners be.
So much did zeale her conscience rarifie,   45
That, extreme truth lack'd little of a lye,
Making omissions, acts; laying the touch
Of sinne, on things that sometimes may be such.
As *Moses* Cherubines, whose natures doe
Surpasse all speed, by him are winged too: 50
So would her soule, already'in heaven, seeme then,
To clyme by teares, the common staires of men.
How fit she was for God, I am content
To speake, that Death his vaine hast may repent.
How fit for us, how even, and how sweet,   55
How good in all her titles, and how meet,
To have reform'd this forward heresie,
That women can no parts of friendship bee;
How Morall, how Divine shall not be told,

    34 both] both, *1633*   deaths] dead *C 57, H 49, Dob*   36 that . . . is] w^{ch} . . .
are *L 74, TC*   loth,] loth. *1633*   37 die;] die, *1633*   38 hath she] she hath
L 74, TC   42 breaks *Σ*: cracks *1633, Gr*   glasse!] glasse? *1633*   44–5 *omit*
1633   45 rarifie *L 74, TC, O'F (corrected)*: rectifye *C 57, H 49, Dob, O'F (uncorrec-
ted)*   54 Death] death *1633*   55 even,] even *1633*   58 women *MSS.*:
woman *1633*

Lest they that heare her vertues, thinke her old,   60
And lest we take Deaths part, and make him glad
Of such a prey, and to his tryumphs adde.

Elegie on M^ris Boulstred

DEATH I recant, and say, unsaid by mee
     What ere hath slip'd, that might diminish thee.
Spirituall treason, atheisme 'tis, to say,
That any can thy Summons disobey.
Th'earths face is but thy Table; there are set   5
Plants, cattell, men, dishes for Death to eate.
In a rude hunger now hee millions drawes
Into his bloody,'or plaguy, or sterv'd jawes.
Now hee will seeme to spare, and doth more wast,
Eating the best first, well preserv'd to last.   10
Now wantonly he spoiles, and eates us not,
But breakes off friends, and lets us peecemeale rot.
Nor will this earth serve him; he sinkes the deepe,
Where harmelesse fish monastique silence keepe,
Who (were Death dead) by Roes of living sand,   15
Might spunge that element, and make it land.
He rounds the aire, and breakes the hymnique notes
In birds, Heavens choristers, organique throats,
Which (if they did not dye) might seeme to bee
A tenth ranke in the heavenly hierarchie.   20
O strong and long-liv'd death, how cam'st thou in?
And how without Creation didst begin?
Thou hast, and shalt see dead, before thou dyest,
All the foure Monarchies, and Antichrist.
How could I thinke thee nothing, that see now   25

---

60 old,] old. *1633*   62 tryumphs *MSS.*: tryumph *1633, Gr*

Elegie on M^ris Boulstred. *1633. MSS.*: *C 57, H 49*; *L 74, TC*; *Dob, O'F. Title from*
1633, C 57, H 49: An Elegie upon the death of M^ris.... *L 74, TC*: On Mrs Bulstrod.
Dob: Upon the death of M^rs.... *O'F*   5 there are set] and thie meate *L 74*:
and the meate *TC*   6 dishes] dish'd *L 74, TC, O'F*   8 bloody,'or] bloody,
or *1633*   10 first] fruite *H 49, L 74, TCD*: fruicts *TCC*   13 deepe,] deepe *1633*
14 keepe,] keepe. *1633*

In all this All, nothing else is, but thou.
Our births and life, vices, and vertues, bee
Wastfull consumptions, and degrees of thee.
For, wee to live, our bellowes weare, and breath,
Nor are wee mortall, dying, dead, but death.   30
And though thou beest, O mighty bird of prey,
So much reclaim'd by God, that thou must lay
All that thou kill'st at his feet, yet doth hee
Reserve but few, and leaves the most to thee.
And of those few, now thou hast overthrowne   35
One whom thy blow makes, not ours, nor thine own.
She was more stories high: hopelesse to come
To'her Soule, thou'hast offer'd at her lower roome.
Her Soule and body was a King and Court:
But thou hast both of Captaine mist and fort.   40
As houses fall not, though the King remove,
Bodies of Saints rest for their soules above.
Death gets 'twixt soules and bodies such a place
As sinne insinuates 'twixt just men and grace,
Both worke a separation, no divorce.   45
Her Soule is gone to usher up her corse,
Which shall be'almost another soule, for there
Bodies are purer, then best Soules are here.
Because in her, her virtues did outgoe
Her yeares, would'st thou, O emulous Death, do so?   50
And kill her young to thy losse? must the cost
Of beauty,'and wit, apt to doe harme, be lost?
What though thou found'st her proofe 'gainst sins of youth?
Oh, every age a diverse sinne pursueth.
Thou should'st have stay'd, and taken better hold,   55
Shortly, ambitious; covetous, when old,
She might have prov'd: and such devotion
Might once have stray'd to superstition.
If all her vertues must have growne, yet might
Abundant virtue'have bred a proud delight.   60

27 life] lifes *Dob*: lives *O'F*, *Gr*   32 by] of *L 74*, *TC*   36 blow] blow, *1633*
38 To'her] To her *1633*   45 worke *1633*, *O'F*: workes *H 49*, *L 74*, *TC*, *Dob*: makes
C 57   50 Death] death *1633*   56 Shortly, ambitious;] Shortly ambitious, *1633*

Had she persever'd just, there would have bin
Some that would sinne, mis-thinking she did sinne;
Such as would call her friendship, love, and faine
To sociablenesse, a name profane;
Or sinne, by tempting, or, not daring that,   65
By wishing, though they never told her what.
Thus might'st thou'have slain more soules, had'st thou not
    crost
Thy selfe, and to triumph, thine army lost.
Yet though these wayes be lost, thou hast left one,
Which is, immoderate griefe that she is gone.   70
But we may scape that sinne, yet weepe as much,
Our teares are due, because we are not such.
Some teares, that knot of friends, her death must cost,
Because the chaine is broke, though no linke lost.

Elegie upon the Death of
Mistress Boulstred

LANGUAGE thou art too narrow, and too weake
    To ease us now; great sorrow cannot speake;
If we could sigh out accents, and weepe words,
Griefe weares, and lessens, that tears breath affords.
Sad hearts, the lesse they seeme, the more they are,   5
(So guiltiest men stand mutest at the barre)
Not that they know not, feele not their estate,
But extreme sense hath made them desperate.
Sorrow, to whom we owe all that we bee,
Tyrant, in'the fift and greatest Monarchy,   10
Was't, that she did possesse all hearts before,
Thou hast kil'd her, to make thy Empire more?

62 did sinne;] . . . sinne. *1633*   64 profane;] profane. *1633*   74 though *Σ*:
but *1633, C 57, H 49*

Elegie etc. *1633. MSS.: L 74, TC*; *O'F. Title from TC*: Another Elegie . . . *L 74*:
Another upon the same M*rs*. . . . *O'F*: Elegie. *1633*: Elegie. *Death. Gr*   5 seeme,]
seeme *1633*   8 desperate.] desperate; *1633*   9 bee,] bee; *1633*   10 in'the]
in the *1633*

Knew'st thou some would, that knew her not, lament,
As in a deluge perish th'innocent?
Was't not enough to have that palace wonne,   15
But thou must raze it too, that was undone?
Had'st thou staid there, and look'd out at her eyes,
All had ador'd thee that now from thee flies,
For they let out more light, then they tooke in,
They told not when, but did the day beginne.   20
She was too Saphirine, and cleare for thee;
Clay, flint, and jeat now thy fit dwellings be;
Alas, shee was too pure, but not too weake;
Who e'r saw Christall Ordinance but would break?
And if wee be thy conquest, by her fall   25
Th'hast lost thy end, for in her perish all;
Or if we live, we live but to rebell,
They know her better now, that knew her well.
If we should vapour out, and pine, and die;
Since, shee first went, that were not miserie.   30
Shee chang'd our world with hers; now she is gone,
Mirth and prosperity is oppression;
For of all morall vertues she was all,
The Ethicks speake of vertues Cardinall.
Her soule was Paradise; the Cherubin   35
Set to keepe it was grace, that kept out sinne;
Shee had no more then let in death, for wee
All reape consumption from one fruitfull tree;
God tooke her hence, lest some of us should love
Her, like that plant, him and his lawes above,   40
And when wee teares, hee mercy shed in this,
To raise our mindes to heaven where now she is;
Who if her vertues would have let her stay
Wee'had had a Saint, have now a holiday.
Her heart was that strange bush, where, sacred fire,   45
Religion, did not consume, but'inspire

20 beginne.] beginne; *1633*   21 for *MSS.*: to *1633*   28 well.] well; *1633*
29 and pine, and] or . . . and *L 74, TCC*: or . . . or *O'F*   30 miserie.] miserie; *1633*
34 Cardinall.] Cardinall; *1633*   44 have] *omit L 74, TC, O'F (b.c.)*   holiday.]
holiday; *1633*

Such piety, so chast use of Gods day,
That what we turne to feasts, she turn'd to pray,
And did prefigure here, in devout tast,
The rest of her high Sabaoth, which shall last.   50
Angels did hand her up, who next God dwell,
(For she was of that order whence most fell)
Her body left with us, lest some had said,
Shee could not die, except they saw her dead;
For from lesse vertue, and lesse beautiousnesse,   55
The Gentiles fram'd them Gods and Goddesses.
The ravenous earth that now wooes her to be
Earth too, will be *Lemnia*; and the tree
That wraps that christall in a wooden Tombe,
Shall be tooke up spruce, fill'd with diamond;   60
And we her sad glad friends all beare a part
Of griefe, for all would waste a Stoicks heart.

Elegie on Prince Henry

LOOK to me, Faith; and look to my Faith, God:
      For, both my centres feel this period.
Of waight, one centre; one, of greatness is:
And Reason is that centre; Faith is this.
For, into'our Reason flowe, and there doe end,   5
All that this naturall world doth comprehend;
Quotidian things, and equi-distant hence,
Shut-in for men in one circumference:
But, for th'enormous greatnesses, which are
So disproportion'd and so angulare,   10
As is God's essence, place, and providence,
Where, how, when, what, soules do departed hence:

48 feasts] feast *1633*: *feast Gr*; *see note*   50 last.] last; *1633*   57 wooes]woes
1633   be] be, *1633*   58 *Lemnia* Σ: a *Lemnia 1633, Gr*   61 sad glad] glad sadd
L 74, O'F

Elegie etc. *Lachrymae Lachrymarum . . . 1613 (with typography normalized). Collations
with 1633 and MSS.*: *TCD, O'F*. Title from *1633, O'F*: Elegie Prince . . . *TCD*: Elegie
on the untimely Death of the incomparable Prince, . . . *1613*   5 into'our] into our
1613   8 men] man *1633, TCD, O'F, Gr*

These things (eccentrique else) on Faith do strike;
Yet neither all, nor upon all alike:
For, Reason, put t'her best extension,   15
Almost meetes Faith, and makes both Centres one:
And nothing ever came so neer to this,
As contemplation of the Prince wee misse.
For, all that Faith could credit mankinde could,
Reason still seconded that this Prince would.   20
If then, least movings of the centre make
(More then if whole hell belcht) the world to shake,
What must this doo, centres distracted so,
That wee see not what to beleeve or knowe?
Was it not well believ'd, till now; that hee,   25
Whose reputation was an extasie
On neighbour States; which knew not why to wake
Till hee discoverd what wayes hee would take:
For whom what Princes angled (when they tryed)
Mett a torpedo, and were stupefied: 30
And others studies, how hee would be bent,
Was his great father's greatest instrument,
And activ'st spirit to convey and tye
This soule of peace through Christianitie.
Was it not well believ'd, that hee would make   35
This general peace th'eternall overtake?
And that his times might have stretcht out so far
As to touch those of which they emblems are?
For, to confirm this just belief, that now
The last dayes came, wee saw Heav'n did allow   40
That but from his aspect and exercise,
In peace-full times, rumors of warrs should rise.
But now this faith is heresie: wee must
Still stay, and vexe our great-grand-mother, dust.
Oh! Is God prodigall? Hath He spent his store   45
Of plagues on us? and only now, when more

18 the] that *1633*, *TCD*, *O'F*, *Gr*   19 could credit] might credit *1633*, *TCD*, *O'F*, *Gr*
21 movings] moving *1633*, *Gr*   34 Christianitie.] CHRISTIANITIE? *1613*   40 came,]
came; *1613*   Heav'n] Heaven *1613*   41 exercise] Excercise *1613*   42 warrs]
war *1633*, *Gr*   should] did *1633*, *TCD*, *Gr*

Would ease us much, doth he grudge miserie,
And will not lett's enjoy our curse, to dye?
As, for the earth throw'n lowest downe of all,
'T were an ambition to desire to fall: 50
So God, in our desire to dye, dooth know
Our plot for ease, in beeing wretched so.
Therfore wee live: though such a life wee have
As but so manie mandrakes on his grave.

What had his growth and generation donne?   55
When what wee are, his putrefaction
Sustains in us, earth; which griefs animate:
Nor hath our world now other soule then that.
And could grief gett so high as Heav'n, that quire
Forgetting this, their new joy, would desire   60
(With grief to see him) hee had staid belowe,
To rectifie our errors they foreknowe.

Is th'other centre, Reason, faster, then?
Where should wee look for that, now w'are not men?
For, if our Reason be'our connexion   65
With causes, now to us there can be none.
For, as, if all the substances were spent,
'T were madnes to enquire of accident:
So is't to looke for Reason, hee being gone,
The only subject Reason wrought upon.   70

If Fate have such a chaine, whose divers links
Industrious man discerneth, as he thinks,
When miracle dooth joine, and so steal in
A new link, man knowes not where to begin:
At a much deader fault must Reason bee,   75
Death having broke off such a link as hee.
But, now, for us with busie proofs to come
That w'have no Reason, would prove we had some:
So would just lamentations. Therfore wee

47 ease us] ease as *1633 uncorrected*, *O'F*: eate as *TCD*   60 joy,] Ioy *1613*
65 be'our] be our *1613*   66 With] Of *1633, TCD, O'F, Gr*   71 Fate Σ: *Faith*
1613   73 joine,] ioine; *1613*: come, *1633, TCD, O'F, Gr*   so steal in Σ: to steal-in
1613   74 link,] link *1613*   76 broke off] broke-off *1613*   77 proofs] proofe
1633, TCD, O'F, Gr

May safelier say, that wee are dead, then hee.   80
So, if our griefs wee doo not well declare,
W'have double'excuse; hee is not dead, wee are.
Yet would not I dye yet; for though I bee
Too narrow, to think him, as hee is hee
(Our soule's best bayting and mid-period   85
In her long journey of considering God)
Yet (no dishonor) I can reach him thus;
As hee embrac't the fires of love with us.
Oh! May I (since I live) but see or hear
That shee-intelligence which mov'd this sphear,   90
I pardon fate my life. Who-e'r thou bee
Which hast the noble conscience, thou art shee,
I conjure thee by all the charmes hee spoke,
By th'oathes which only you two never broke,
By all the soules you sigh'd; that if you see   95
These lines, you wish I knew your historie:
So, much as you two mutual Heav'ns were here,
I were an angel singing what you were.

Obsequies to the Lord Harrington, brother to the Countesse of Bedford

FAIRE soule, which wast, not onely,'as all soules bee,
    Then when thou wast infused, harmony,
But did'st continue so; and now dost beare
A part in Gods great organ, this whole Spheare:
If looking up to God; or downe to us,   5
Thou finde that any way is pervious,
Twixt heav'n and earth, and that mens actions doe

---

82 double'excuse] double Excuse *1613*   wee] and we *1633*, *TCD*, *O'F*, *Gr*   83 would
not I] I would not *1633*, *TCD*, *O'F*, *Gr*   92 shee,] shee. *1613*   95 soules you]
soules yee *1633*, *Gr*   sigh'd] sigh't *1613*   97 Heav'ns] *Heavens 1613*

   Obsequies etc. *1633*. *MSS*.: *C 57*, *H 49*; *TCD*; *Dob*, *O'F*. *Title from C 57*, *H 49*:
Obsequies . . . Harringtons brother. To . . . *1633*: Elegie Lo: Harrington *TCD*: . . .
on the L. Harrington brō: to yᵉ La: Lucy Countesse . . . *Dob*: . . . upon the Lord Harrington
the last that dyed *O'F*   1 onely,'as] onely, as *1633*   7 mens *TCD*, *Dob*, *O'F*:
mans *1633*, *C 57*, *H 49*, *Gr*

PLATE II

Prince Henry and Lord Harington in 1604; from the painting by Robert Peake the elder; by kind permission of the Trustees of the Metropolitan Museum of Art, New York

Come to your knowledge, and affections too,
See, and with joy, mee to that good degree
Of goodnesse growne, that I can studie thee,   10
And, by those meditations refin'd,
Can unapparell and enlarge my minde,
And so can make by this soft extasie,
This place a map of heav'n, my selfe of thee.
Thou seest mee here at midnight, now all rest;   15
Times dead-low water; when all mindes devest
To morrows businesse, when the labourers have
Such rest in bed, that their last Church-yard grave,
Subject to change, will scarce be'a type of this,
Now when the clyent, whose last hearing is   20
To morrow, sleeps, when the condemned man,
(Who when hee opes his eyes, must shut them than
Againe by death,) although sad watch hee keepe,
Doth practice dying by a little sleepe,
Thou at this midnight seest mee, and as soone   25
As that Sunne rises to mee, midnight's noone,
All the world growes transparent, and I see
Through all, both Church and State, in seeing thee;
And I discerne by favour of this light,
My selfe, the hardest object of the sight.   30
God is the glasse; as thou when thou dost see
Him who sees all, seest all concerning thee,
So, yet unglorified, I comprehend
All, in these mirrors of thy wayes, and end;
Though God be truly'our glass, through which we see   35
All, since the beeing of all things is hee,
Yet are the trunkes which doe to us derive
Things, in proportion fit, by perspective,
Deeds of good men; for by their living here,
Vertues, indeed remote, seeme to be nere.   40
But where can I affirme, or where arrest

11 those *Σ*: these *1633, C 57, Gr*   31 as] as *1633 uncorrected*   34 these] those *TCD,
Dob, O'F*   wayes] waye *TCD, Dob, O'F*   35 truly'our (*without elision-mark*) *Σ*: our true
1633, Gr   see] see. *1633 corrected*   38 fit,] fit *1633*   39 men;] men, *1633*
40 nere.] nere; *1633*

My thoughts on his deeds? which shall I call best?
For fluid vertue cannot be look'd on,
Nor can endure a contemplation.
As bodies change, and as I do not weare   45
Those spirits, humors, blood I did last yeare,
And, as if on a streame I fixe mine eye,
That drop, which I look'd on, is presently
Pusht with more waters from my sight, and gone,
So in this sea of vertues, can no one   50
Bee'insisted on; vertues, as rivers, passe,
Yet still remaines that vertuous man there was.
And as if man feed on mans flesh, and so
Part of his body to another owe,
Yet at the last two perfect bodies rise,   55
Because God knowes where every Atome lyes;
So, if one knowledge were made of all those,
Who knew his minutes well, hee might dispose
His vertues into names, and ranks; but I
Should injure Nature, Vertue,'and Destinie,   60
Should I divide and discontinue so,
Vertue, which did in one intirenesse grow.
For as, hee that would say, spirits are fram'd
Of all the purest parts that can be nam'd,
Honours not spirits halfe so much, as hee   65
Which sayes, they have no parts, but simple bee;
So is't of vertue; for a point and one
Are much entirer, then a million.
And had Fate meant to have his vertues told,
It would have let him live to have beene old;   70
So, then that vertue'in season, and then this,
We might have seene, and said, that now he is
Witty, now wise, now temperate, now just:
In good short lives, vertues are faine to thrust,

44 contemplation.] contemplation; *1633*   46 spirits] Spirits *1633*   48 which . . . on]
on wch I look'd *TCD, Dob, O'F*   look'd] looked *1633*   50–1 vertues, can . . . as]
Vertues, as *C 57*   51 on;] on, *1633*   52 was.] was; *1633*   53 feed *Σ*: feeds *1633*,
C 57   60 Vertue,'and] Vertue, and *1633*   63 fram'd] fram'd, *1633 uncorrected*
66 Which] Who *Dob, O'F*   68 entirer,] entirer *1633 corrected*   70 old;] old, *1633*
71 So, then . . . vertue'in] So then, . . . vertue in *1633*

And to be sure betimes to get a place,   75
When they would exercise, lacke time, and space.
So was it in this person, forc'd to bee
For lack of time, his owne epitomee:
So to exhibit in few yeares as much,
As all the long breath'd Chronicles can touch.   80
As when an Angell down from heav'n doth flye,
Our quick thought cannot keepe him company,
Wee cannot thinke, now hee is at the Sunne,
Now through the Moon, now he through th'aire doth run,
Yet when he's come, we know he did repaire   85
To all twixt Heav'n and Earth, Sunne, Moon, and Aire;
And as this Angell in an instant, knowes,
And yet wee know, this sodaine knowledge growes
By quick amassing severall formes of things,
Which he successively to order brings;   90
When they, whose slow-pac'd lame thoughts cannot goe
So fast as hee, thinke that he doth not so;
Just as a perfect reader doth not dwell,
On every syllable, nor stay to spell,
Yet without doubt, hee doth distinctly see,   95
And lay together every A, and B;
So, in short liv'd good men, is'not understood
Each severall vertue, but the compound, good;
For, they all vertues paths in that pace tread,
As Angells goe, and know, and as men read.   100
O why should then these men, these lumps of Balme
Sent hither, this worlds tempests to becalme,
Before by deeds, they are diffus'd and spred,
And so make us alive, themselves be dead?
O Soule, O circle, why so quickly bee   105
Thy ends, thy birth and death, clos'd up in thee?

76 exercise] exercse *1633 uncorrected*: encrease *C 57, H 49*: exercis'd *Dob*   time] Roome
TCD, Dob, O'F   78 epitomee:] epitomee. *1633 uncorrected*: epitome. *1633 corrected*
80 touch.] touch; *1633*   81 when an] whe ann *1633 uncorrected*   85 he's] he is
1633 uncorrected   86 Aire;] Aire. *1633*   95 see,] see *1633 corrected*
97 is'not] is not *1633 uncorrected*   98 compound, good;] compound good. *1633*
102 this *Σ*: the *1633, C 57*   tempests *H 49, TCD*: tempest *1633, C 57, Dob, O'F*
103 deeds,] deeds *1633 corrected*   106 death,] death *1633*

Since one foot of thy compasse still was plac'd
In heav'n, the other might securely'have pac'd
In the most large extent, through every path,   109
Which the whole world, or man, the'abridgment hath.
Thou knowst, that though the tropique circles have
(Yea and those small ones which the Poles engrave,)
All the same roundnesse, evennesse, and all
The endlesnesse of the'equinoctiall;
Yet, when we come to measure distances,   115
How here, how there, the Sunne affected is,
Where he doth faintly worke, and where prevaile,
Onely great circles, then, can be our scale:
So, though thy circle to thy selfe expresse
All, tending to thy endlesse happinesse,   120
And wee, by our good use of that, may trye,
Both how to live well young, and how to die,
Yet, since we must be old, and age endures
His Torrid Zone at Court, and calentures
Of hot ambitions, irreligions ice,   125
Zeales agues, and hydroptique avarice,
Infirmities which need the scale of truth,
As well, as lust and ignorance of youth;
Why did'st thou not for these give medicines too,
And by thy doing tell us what to doe?   130
Though as small pocket-clocks, whose every wheele
Doth each mismotion and distemper feele,
Whose *hand* gets shaking palsies, and whose *string*
(His sinewes) slackens, and whose Soule, the *spring*,
Expires, or languishes, whose pulse, the *flye*,   135
Either beates not, or beates unevenly,
Whose voice, the *Bell*, doth rattle, or grow dumbe,
Or idle,'as men, which to their last houres come,

108 securely'have] securely,'have *1633 uncorrected*   110 the'abridgment] the
abridgment *1633*   hath.] hath, *1633 uncorrected*   114 the'equinoctiall] the equinoctiall
1633   117 Where ... where *TCD, Dob, O'F*: When ... when *1633, C 57, H 49, Gr*
118 then,] then *1633 corrected*   can] can, *1633*   121 that, *C 57, H 49, TCD (no comma)*:
it *1633, Dob, O'F, Gr*   125 irreligions] irrelegions *1633*   126 agues,] agues; *1633*
130 tell] sett *Dob, O'F*   133 *hand* gets] *hands* get *1633, O'F*   134 Soule ... *spring*]
Soule ... spring 1633

If these clockes be not wound, or be wound still,
Or be not set, or set at every will;   140
So, youth is easiest to destruction,
If then wee follow all, or follow none;
Yet, as in great clocks, which in steeples chime,
Plac'd to informe whole townes, to'imploy their time,
An error doth more harme, being generall,   145
When, small clocks faults, only'on the wearer fall;
So worke the faults of age, on which the eye
Of children, servants, or the State relie.
Why wouldst not thou then, which hadst such a soule,
A clock so true, as might the Sunne controule,   150
And daily hadst from him, who gave it thee,
Instructions, such as it could never be
Disorder'd, stay here, as a generall
And great Sun-dyall, to have set us All?
O why wouldst thou be any instrument   155
To this unnaturall course, or why consent
To this, not miracle, but Prodigie,
That where the ebbs, longer then flowings be,
Vertue, whose flood did with thy youth begin,
Should so much faster ebb out, then flow in?   160
Though her flood were blowne in, by thy first breath,
All is at once sunke in the whirle-poole death.
Which word I would not name, but that I see
Death, else a desert, growne a Court by thee.
Now I grow sure, that if a man would have   165
Good companie, his entry is a grave.
Mee thinkes all Cities, now, but Anthills bee,
Where, when the severall labourers I see,
For children, house, provision, taking paine,
They'are all but Ants, carrying eggs, straw, and grain; 170
And Church-yards are our cities, unto which
The most repaire, that are in goodnesse rich.

141 is] bee *TCD, Dob, O'F*   146 fall;] fall. *1633*   153 Disorder'd] Disordered
1633   158 where *Σ*: when *1633, C 57, Gr*   159–61 did . . . her flood] *omit C 57,*
H 49   161 were] was *1633, C 57, Gr*   165 grow] am *TCD, Dob, O'F*
169 provision] Provision *1633*   170 and] or *TCD, Dob, O'F*   172 that] who
TCD, Dob: w^ch *O'F*

There is the best concourse, and confluence,
There are the holy suburbs, and from thence
Begins Gods City, New Jerusalem,   175
Which doth extend her utmost gates to them.
At that gate then Triumphant soule, dost thou
Begin thy Triumph; But since lawes allow
That at the Triumph day, the people may,
All that they will, 'gainst the Triumpher say,   180
Let me here use that freedome, and expresse
My griefe, though not to make thy Triumph lesse.
By law, to Triumphs none admitted bee,
Till they as Magistrates get victorie;
Though then to thy force, all youthes foes did yield,   185
Yet till fit time had brought thee to that field,
To which thy ranke in this state destin'd thee,
That there thy counsailes might get victorie,
And so in that capacitie remove
All jealousies, 'twixt Prince and subjects love,   190
Thou could'st no title, to this triumph have,
Thou didst intrude on death, usurp'dst a grave.
Then (though victoriously) thou'hadst fought as yet
But with thine owne affections, with the heate
Of youths desires, and colds of ignorance,   195
But till thou should'st successefully advance
Thine armes 'gainst forraine enemies, which are
Both Envy,'and acclamations popular,
(For, both these engines equally defeate,
Though by a divers Mine, those which are great,)   200
Till then thy War was but a civill War,
For which to Triumph, none admitted are.
No more are they, who though with good successe,
In a defensive war, their power expresse;

    176 them.] them; *1633*   183 Triumphs] triumph *TCD, Dob, O'F*   184 victorie;]
victorie, *1633*   189 remove] remove, *1633 uncorrected*   190 jealousies,] jealousies
1633 corrected   192 usurp'dst *Σ*: usurp'st *1633, C 57*: usurpe *O'F*   193 Then *Σ*:
That *1633, C 57*: When (*corr. to* Then) *Dob*   thou'hadst] thou hadst *1633*   196 suc-
cessefully] successively *TCD, Dob, O'F (b.c.)*   198 Envy,'and] Envy, and *1633*   accla-
mations *Σ*: acclamation *1633*   202 are.] are; *1633*   204 expresse;] expresse. *1633*

Before men triumph, the dominion   205
Must be *enlarg'd*, and not *preserv'd* alone;
Why should'st thou then, whose battailes were to win
Thy selfe, from those straits nature put thee in,
And to deliver up to God that state,
Of which he gave thee the vicariate,   210
(Which is thy soule and body) as intire
As he, who takes endeavours, doth require,
But didst not stay, t'enlarge his kingdome too,
By making others, what thou didst, to doe;
Why shouldst thou Triumph now, when Heav'n no more
Hath got, by getting thee, then 't had before?   216
For, Heav'n and thou, even when thou livedst here,
Of one another in possession were.
But this from Triumph most disables thee,
That, that place which is conquered, must bee   220
Left safe from present warre, and likely doubt
Of imminent commotions to breake out:
And hath he left us so? or can it bee
His territory was no more but Hee?
No, we were all his charge, the Diocis   225
Of ev'ry'exemplar man, the whole world is,
And he was joyned in commission
With Tutelar Angels, sent to every one.
But though this freedome to upbraid, and chide
Him who Triumph'd, were lawfull, it was ty'd   230
With this, that it might never reference have
Unto the Senate, who this triumph gave;
Men might at Pompey jeast, but they might not
At that authoritie, by which he got
Leave to Triumph, before, by age, he might;   235
So, though, triumphant soule, I dare to write,
Mov'd with a reverentiall anger, thus,
That thou so earely wouldst abandon us;

Yet am I farre from daring to dispute
With that great soveraigntie, whose absolute   240
Prerogative hath thus dispens'd for thee,
'Gainst natures lawes, which just impugners bee
Of early triumphs; And I (though with paine)
Lessen our losse, to magnifie thy gaine
Of triumph, when I say, It was more fit,   245
That all men should lacke thee, then thou lack it.
Though then in our time, be not suffered
That testimonie of love, unto the dead,
To die with them, and in their graves be hid,
As Saxon wives, and French soldurii did;   250
And though in no degree I can expresse
Griefe in great Alexanders great excesse,
Who at his friends death, made whole townes devest
Their walls and bullwarks which became them best:
Doe not, faire soule, this sacrifice refuse,   255
That in thy grave I doe interre my Muse,
Who, by my griefe, great as thy worth, being cast
Behind hand, yet hath spoke, and spoke her last.

An Hymne to the Saints, and to Marquesse Hamylton

WHETHER that soule which now comes up to you
     Fill any former ranke or make a new;
Whether it take a name nam'd there before,
Or be a name it selfe, and *order* more
Then was in heaven till now; (for may not hee   5
Bee so, if every severall Angell bee
A *kind* alone?) what ever order grow

---

239 am I Σ: I am *1633*, C *57*, Gr   241 for Σ: with *1633*, *Dob*, *O'F*, *Gr*   247
time] times *TCD*, *Dob*, *O'F*   250 soldurii Σ: soldarii *1633*   251 expresse]
expresse, *1633*

An Hymne etc. *1633*. *MSS.*: TC, O'F. *Title from 1633*: A Hymne . . . *MSS.*
1, 3 Whether] Whither *1633*   2 new;] new, *1633*   6–7 so, . . . alone?] so?
. . . alone; *1633*   7 what] What *1633*

Greater by him in heaven, wee doe not so;
One of your orders growes by his accesse;
But, by his losse grow all our *orders* lesse;   10
The name of *Father*, *Master*, *Friend*, the name
Of *Subject* and of *Prince*, in one are lame;
Faire mirth is dampt, and conversation black,
The *Household* widdow'd, and the *Garter* slack;
The *Chappell* wants an eare, *Councell* a tongue;   15
Story, a theame; and *Musicke* lacks a song;
Blest *order* that hath him, the losse of him
Gangreend all *Orders* here; all lost a limbe.
Never made body such hast to confesse
What a soule was; All former comelinesse   20
Fled, in a minute, when the soule was gone,
And, having lost that beauty, would have none;
So fell our *Monasteries*, in an instant growne
Not to lesse houses, but, to heapes of stone;
So sent this body that faire forme it wore,   25
Unto the spheare of formes, and doth (before
His soule shall fill up his sepulchrall stone,)
Anticipate a Resurrection;
For, as in his fame, now, his soule is here,
So, in the forme thereof his bodie's there.   30
And if, faire soule, not with first *Innocents*
Thy station be, but with the *Pœnitents*,
(And, who shall dare to aske then when I am
Dy'd scarlet in the blood of that pure Lambe,
Whether that colour, which is scarlet then,   35
Were black or white before in eyes of men?)
When thou rememb'rest what sins thou didst finde
Amongst those many friends now left behinde,
And seest such sinners as they are, with thee
Got thither by repentance, let it bee   40
Thy wish to wish all there, to wish them cleane;
Wish *him* a *David*, her a *Magdalen*.

14 *Household . . . Garter*] household . . . garter *1633*   18 Gangreend] Gangred *1633*
22 none;] none, *1633*   23 an *MSS.*: one *1633*, *Gr*   30 there.] there; *1633*
36 eyes] yᵉ eyes *TCC*: th'eyes *O'F*   40 let] Let *1633*

EPITAPHS AND INSCRIPTIONS

Epitaph for Elizabeth Drury

Quo pergas, viator, non habes.
Ad Gades omnium venisti, etiam et ad tuas:
hic jaces, si probus es, ipse;
ipsa etenim hic jacet probitas,
Elizabetha,   5
cui,
cum, ut, in pulchritudine, et innocentia
angelos aemulata strenue fuerat, id et in hoc praestare nisa est
ut sine sexu degeret;
ideoque corpus intactum, qua factum est integritate,   10
(Paradisum sine serpente,)
Deo reddere voluit,
Quae nec adeo aulae splendoribus allicefacta, ut a semet exularet,
nec adeo sibimet coenobium facta, ut se societati denegaret,
nec ob corporis, fortunaeve dotes, minus in animo dotata,   15
nec ob linguarum peritiam, minus taciturna,
Vitam, mortemve nec pertaesa, nec insectata,
sine remis, sine remoris,
Deum ductorem sequta
hunc portum post XV fere annos assequta,   20
Rob. Druri Eq. Aur: et Anna uxor,
unica filia, itaque et ipso parentum nomine spoliati,
hoc monumentum extruendo,
filiae suae (eheu deperditae) aliquantilla praesentia,
luctuosissimae suae orbitati blandiuntur;   25
Secessit
Anni Aetat: XV^i mense X, et sui Jesu CIƆIƆCX.

Epitaph for Sir Robert Drury

Roberti Druri
quo vix alter eius ordinis maioribus maioribus ortus
cum nec ephoebos excesserat,
nec vestem de paterna morte lugubrem exuerat,
Equit: Aur: honore (nec id domi,   5
sed obsidione Rhotomagensi) Anno 1591 insigniti,
quem
et bellicae expeditiones
et exterae peregrinationes
et aulicae occupationes,   10
satis, (ipsa invidia, qua saepe tactus, fractus nunquam,
teste) instruxerant
tam ad exercitus ducendos,
quam ad legationes peragendas
aut res civiles pertractandas,
iam Anno suo 40: et sui Iesu 1615   15
anima summa constantia, eaque Christiana, Deo tradita,
bonorum bona parte pauperibus
v. ante febrem, qua correptus annis (idque perenniter) erogata
corpus, olim Spiritus Sancti templum,
animae postliminio reddendum   20
terrae postliminio reddi,
hoc loco curavit
Anna uxor

nec infaecunda nec mater tamen
Dorotheae et Elizabethae filiarum orba   25
illustri familia Bacon oriunda,
cui unice, hoc dedit Deus stirpi,
ut pater et filius, eodem munere, eoque summo, fungerentur
Nicolao patre Sigilli Custode
Francisco filio Cancellario   30
Etiam
officio, erga defunctum pie, pie functa,
hoc quod restat, saxi spatium
quae de ipsa dicenda erunt, inserendis,
(ita velit Deus, ita velint illi,)   35
posteris reliquit.

Epitaph for Ann Donne

Annae

Georgij	⎰More de	⎰Filiae
Robertj	⎱Lothesley	⎱Soror:
Willelmj	Equit:	Nept:
Christophorj	Aurat:	Pronept:

Foeminae lectissimae, dilectissimaeque;
Coniugi charissimae, castissimaeque;
Matri piissimae, indulgentissimaeque;
xv annis in coniugio transactis,
vii post xii^m partum (quorum vii superstant) dies
Immani febre correptae,
(Quod hoc saxum farj iussit
Ipse, prae dolore Infans)
Maritus (miserrimum dictu) olim charae charus
Cineribus cineres spondet suos
Nouo matrimonio (annuat Deus) hoc loco sociandos
Johannes Donne
Sacr: Theolog: profess:
Secessit
Anno xxxiii° Aetat: suae et sui Jesu
CIƆ DC xvii°
Avg: xv.

Inscription in a Bible presented to Lincoln's Inn

In Bibliotheca Hospit⟨i⟩j Lincoln: London:
Celeberrimi, in Urbe, in Orbe,
Juris Municipalis Professorum, Colleg⟨i⟩j,
Reponi voluit, (petit potius)
Haec Sex, in uniuersas Scripturas, Volumina,   5
Sacrae Theologiae Professor
Serenissimo Munificentissimo
REGI IACOBO
A Sacris
IOANNES DONNE,   10
Qui huc, in prima iuuentute, ad perdiscendas leges, missus,
Ad alia, tam studia, quam negotia, et peregrinationes deflectens,
Inter quae tamen nunquam studia Theologica intermiserat,
Post multos annos, agente Spiritu Sancto, suadente Rege,
Ad Ordines Sacros evectus,   15
Munere suo, frequenter et strenue hoc loco concionandi
Per quinque annos functus,
Novi Sacelli primis Saxis sua manu positis
Et ultimis fere paratis,
Ad Decanatum Ecclesiae Cathedr: S. Pauli, London: 20
A Rege (cui benedicat Dominus)
Migrare iussus est
Anno L° Aetat: Suae, et sui IESU
CIƆ IƆC XXI.

Inscription in the 'Album Amicorum' of Michael Corvinus

In propria venit, nec sui eum receperunt. Jo. i. 11
  quod enim de Christo dictum, de omni Christiano
    dicere licet;
         Omnia enim uestra sunt. 1 Cor: 3. 22.
Annuat Deus Opt: Max: ut apud omnes, hanc inveniat   5
Communionem Sanctorum, vir iste Ornatissimus Doctissimusque
Michael Corvinus Hungar^{is}, quam ei in aedibus
Paulinis, suisque, London: offert spondetque
       Joannes Donne: ibidem Decanus.
          Sept: 27. 1623.   10

Epitaph for Himself

Ioannes Donne
Sac: Theol: profess:
post varia studia,
quibus ab annis tenerrimis
fideliter nec infoeliciter incubuit,   5
instinctu, et impulsu Spiritus Sancti,
monitu, et hortatu Regis Iacobi,
Ordines Sacros amplexus
Anno sui Jesu 1614, et Suae Aetat. 42,
Decanatu   10
hujus Ecclesiae indutus
27° Novemb. 1621,
exutus morte
ultimo die Martii, Anno 1631,
Hic licet in occiduo cinere,   15
Aspicit eum cujus Nomen est Oriens.

ELEGIES UPON THE AUTHOR

To the Memorie of my Ever Desired Friend
Dr Donne

To have liv'd eminent, in a degree
    Beyond our lofty'st flights, that is, like Thee,
Or t'have had too much merit, is not safe;
For, such excesses finde no Epitaph.
At common graves we have Poetique eyes   5
Can melt themselves in easie Elegies;
Each quill can drop his tributary verse,
And pin it, with the Hatchments, to the Hearse:
But at Thine, Poeme, or Inscription
(Rich soule of wit, and language) we have none.   10
Indeed a silence does that tombe befit,
Where is no Herald left to blazon it.
Widow'd invention justly doth forbeare
To come abroad, knowing Thou art not here,
Late her great Patron; Whose Prerogative   15
Maintain'd, and cloth'd her so, as none alive
Must now presume, to keepe her at thy rate,
Though he the Indies for her dowre estate.
Or else that awfull fire, which once did burne
In thy cleare Braine, now falne into thy Urne   20
Lives there, to fright rude Empiricks from thence,
Which might prophane thee by their Ignorance.
Who ever writes of Thee, and in a stile
Unworthy such a Theme, does but revile
Thy precious Dust, and wake a learned Spirit   25
Which may revenge his Rapes upon thy Merit.
For, all a low pitch't phansie can devise,
Will prove, at best, but Hallow'd Injuries.
    Thou, like the dying Swanne, didst lately sing
Thy Mournfull Dirge, in audience of the King;   30
When pale lookes, and faint accents of thy breath,

Elegies etc. Text of the first twelve elegies from 1633. To the Memorie etc. *Also in*
Deaths Duell, *1632*   6 Elegies;] Elegies, *1633*   8 with] like *1633*

Presented so, to life, that peece of death,
That it was fear'd, and prophesi'd by all,
Thou thither cam'st to preach thy Funerall.
O! had'st Thou in an Elegiacke Knell   35
Rung out unto the world thine owne farewell,
And in thy High Victorious Numbers beate
The solemne measure of thy griev'd Retreat;
Thou might'st the Poets service now have mist
As well, as then thou did'st prevent the Priest;   40
And never to the world beholding bee
So much, as for an Epitaph for thee.
    I doe not like the office. Nor is't fit
Thou, who did'st lend our Age such summes of wit,
Should'st now re-borrow from her bankrupt Mine,   45
That Ore to Bury Thee, which once was Thine.
Rather still leave us in thy debt; And know
(Exalted Soule) more glory 't is to owe
Unto thy Hearse, what we can never pay,
Then, with embased Coine those Rites defray.   50
    Commit we then Thee to Thy selfe: Nor blame
Our drooping loves, which thus to thy owne Fame
Leave Thee Executour. Since, but thine owne,
No pen could doe Thee Justice, nor Bayes Crowne
Thy vast desert; Save that, wee nothing can   55
Depute, to be thy Ashes Guardian.
    So Jewellers no Art, or Metall trust
    To forme the Diamond, but the Diamonds dust.
                                                                H. K.

To the deceased Author,
Upon the Promiscuous printing of his Poems,
the Looser sort, with the Religious

WHEN thy *Loose* raptures, *Donne*, shall meet with Those
                That doe confine
            Tuning, unto the Duller line,
        And sing not, but in *Sanctified Prose*;
            How will they, with sharper eyes,   5
        The *Fore-skinne* of thy phansie circumcise?

And feare, *thy wantonnesse* should now, begin
Example, that hath ceased to be *Sin*?

And that *Feare* fannes their *Heat*; while knowing eyes
        Will not admire   10
        At this *Strange Fire*,
    That here is *mingled with thy Sacrifice*:
    But dare reade even thy *Wanton Story*,
      As thy *Confession*, not thy *Glory*.
And will so envie *Both* to future times,   15
That they would buy thy *Goodnesse*, with thy *Crimes*.
                  Tho: Browne.

On the death of Dr Donne

I CANNOT blame those men, that knew thee well,
   Yet dare not helpe the world, to ring thy knell
In tunefull *Elegies*; there's not language knowne
Fit for thy mention, but 't was first thy owne;
The *Epitaphs* thou writst, have so bereft   5
Our tongue of wit, there is not phansie left
Enough to weepe thee; what henceforth we see
Of Art or Nature, must result from thee.
There may perchance some busie gathering friend
Steale from thy owne workes, and that, varied, lend,   10
Which thou bestow'st on others, to thy Hearse,
And so thou shalt live still in thine owne verse;
Hee that shall venture farther, may commit
A pitied errour, shew his zeale, not wit.
Fate hath done mankinde wrong; vertue may aime   15
Reward of conscience, never can, of fame,
Since her great trumpet's broke, could onely give
Faith to the world, command it to beleeve;
   Hee then must write, that would define thy parts:
Here lyes the best Divinitie, All the Arts.   20
                  Edw. Hyde.

On the death etc. *Also in* Deaths Duell, *1632*   2 world,] world *1632*   3 *Elegies*;]
Elegies. *1632*   4 't was] was *1632*   4, 10 thy] thine *1632*   6 tongue . . . there
is not] pens . . . ther's not one *1632*   7 thee;] thee, *1632*   8 or] and *1632*   10 that,
. . . lend,] that varied lend *1632*   11 Which . . . others,] (Which . . . bestowd'st . . .
others) *1632*   Hearse,] hearse; *1632*   12 verse;] verse. *1632*   13 shall . . .
farther] will . . . further *1632*   16 can,] can *1632*   18 beleeve;] beleeve. *1632*
19 would] world *1633*   parts :] parts *1632*   *Poem unsigned in 1632*

On Doctor Donne

By Dr C. B. of O.

Hᴇᴇ that would write an Epitaph for thee,
      And do it well, must first beginne to be
Such as thou wert; for, none can truly know
Thy worth, thy life, but he that hath liv'd so;
He must have wit to spare, and to hurle downe: 5
Enough, to keepe the gallants of the towne.
He must have learning plenty; both the Lawes,
Civill, and Common, to judge any cause;
Divinity great store, above the rest;
Not of the last Edition, but the best.   10
Hee must have language, travaile, all the Arts;
Judgement to use; or else he wants thy parts.
He must have friends the highest, able to do;
Such as *Mecænas*, and *Augustus* too.
He must have such a sicknesse, such a death;   15
Or else his vaine descriptions come beneath;
    Who then shall write an Epitaph for thee,
    He must be dead first, let'it alone for mee.

An Elegie upon the Incomparable Dr Donne

Aʟʟ is not well when such a one as I
      Dare peepe abroad, and write an *Elegie*;
When smaller *Starres* appeare, and give their light,
Phoebus is gone to bed: Were it not night,
And the world witlesse now that DONNE is dead,   5
You sooner should have broke, then seene my head.
Dead did I say? Forgive this *Injury*
I doe him, and his worthes *Infinity*,
To say he is but dead; I dare averre
It better may be term'd a *Massacre*,   10
Then *Sleepe* or *Death*; See how the *Muses* mourne
Upon their oaten *Reeds*, and from his *Urne*
    Threaten the World with this *Calamity*,
    They shall have *Ballads*, but no *Poetry*.

On Doctor etc.   5 spare,] spare *1633*

Language lyes speechlesse; and *Divinity*,   15
Lost such a *Trump* as even to *Extasie*
Could charme the Soule, and had an *Influence*
To teach best *judgements*, and please dullest *Sense*.
The *Court*, the *Church*, the *Universitie*,
Lost *Chaplaine*, *Deane*, and *Doctor*, All these, Three.   20
   It was his *Merit*, that his *Funerall*
   Could cause a losse so *great* and *generall*.

If there be any Spirit can answer give
Of such as hence depart, to such as live:
Speake, Doth his body there vermiculate,   25
Crumble to dust, and feele the lawes of Fate?
Me thinkes, *Corruption*, *Wormes*, what else is foule
Should spare the *Temple* of so faire a *Soule*.
I could beleeve they doe; but that I know
What inconvenience might hereafter grow: 30
   Succeeding ages would *Idolatrize*,
   And as his *Numbers*, so his *Reliques* prize.

If that Philosopher, which did avow
The world to be but Motes, was living now:
He would affirme that th'*Atomes* of his mould   35
Were they in severall bodies blended, would
Produce new worlds of *Travellers*, *Divines*,
Of *Linguists*, *Poets*: sith these severall *lines*
In him concentred were, and flowing thence
Might fill againe the worlds *Circumference*.   40
I could beleeve this too; and yet my faith
Not want a *President*: The *Phoenix* hath
(And such was He) a power to animate
Her ashes, and herselfe perpetuate.
But, busie Soule, thou dost not well to pry   45
Into these Secrets; *Griefe*, and *Jealousie*,
The more they know, the further still advance,
And finde no way so safe as *Ignorance*.
Let this suffice thee, that his *Soule* which flew
A pitch of all admir'd, known but of few,   50

(Save those of purer mould) is now translated
From Earth to Heavên, and there *Constellated*.
For, if each *Priest* of God shine as a *Starre*,
His *Glory* is as his *Gifts*, 'bove others farre.

                              Hen. Valentine.

An Elegie upon Dr Donne

I s *Donne*, great *Donne* deceas'd? then England say
     Thou'hast lost a man where language chose to stay
And shew it's gracefull power. I would not praise
That and his vast wit (which in these vaine dayes
Make many proud) but as they serv'd to unlock   5
That Cabinet, his minde: where such a stock
Of knowledge was repos'd, as all lament
(Or should) this generall cause of discontent.
     And I rejoyce I am not so severe,
But (as I write a line) to weepe a teare   10
For his decease; Such sad extremities
May make such men as I write *Elegies*.
     And wonder not; for, when a generall losse
Falls on a nation, and they slight the crosse,
God hath rais'd *Prophets* to awaken them   15
From stupifaction; witnesse my milde pen,
Not us'd to upbraid the world, though now it must
Freely and boldly, for, the cause is just.
     Dull age, Oh I would spare thee, but th'art worse,
Thou art not onely dull, but hast a curse   20
Of black ingratitude; if not, couldst thou
Part with *miraculous Donne*, and make no vow
For thee and thine, successively to pay
A sad remembrance to his dying day?
     Did his youth scatter *Poetrie*, wherein   25
Was all Philosophie? Was every sinne,
Character'd in his *Satyres*? made so foule
That some have fear'd their shapes, and kept their soule
Freer by reading verse? Did he give *dayes*
Past marble monuments, to those, whose praise   30
He would perpetuate? Did hee (I feare
The dull will doubt:) these at his twentieth yeare?

But, more matur'd: Did his full soule conceive,
And in harmonious-holy-numbers weave
A *Crowne of sacred sonets*, fit to adorne   *La Corona.*   35
A dying Martyrs brow: or, to be worne
On that blest head of *Mary Magdalen*:
After she wip'd Christs feet, but not till then?
Did hee (fit for such penitents as shee
And hee to use) leave us a *Litany*?   40
Which all devout men love, and sure, it shall,
As times grow better, grow more classicall.
Did he write *Hymnes*, for piety and wit
Equall to those great grave *Prudentius* writ?
Spake he all *Languages*? knew he all *Lawes*?   45
The grounds and use of *Physicke*; but because
'Twas mercenary wav'd it? Went to see
That blessed place of *Christs nativity*?
Did he returne and preach him? preach him so
As none but hee did, or could do? They know   50
(Such as were blest to heare him know) 'tis truth.
Did he confirme thy age? convert thy youth?
Did he these wonders? And is this deare losse
Mourn'd by so few? (few for so great a crosse.)
But sure the silent are ambitious all   55
To be *Close Mourners* at his Funerall;
If not; In common pitty they forbare
By repetitions to renew our care;
Or, knowing, grief conceiv'd, conceal'd, consumes
Man irreparably, (as poyson'd fumes   60
Do waste the braine) make silence a safe way
To'inlarge the Soule from these walls, mud and clay,
(Materialls of this body) to remaine
With *Donne* in heaven, where no promiscuous paine
Lessens the joy wee have, for, with *him*, all   65
Are satisfyed with *joyes essentiall*.
My thoughts, Dwell on this *Joy*, and do not call
Griefe backe, by thinking of his Funerall;
Forget he lov'd mee; Waste not my sad yeares;
(Which haste to *Davids* seventy, fill'd with feares   70
And sorrow for his death;) Forget his parts,

35 *Crowne*] *Crowme 1633*   70 seventy,] seventy) *1633*

Which finde a living grave in good mens hearts;
And, (for, my first is daily paid for sinne)
Forget to pay my second sigh for him:
Forget his powerfull preaching; and forget   75
I am his *Convert*. Oh my frailtie! let
My flesh be no more heard, it will obtrude
This lethargie: so should my gratitude,
My vowes of gratitude should so be broke;
Which can no more be, then *Donnes* vertues spoke   80
By any but himselfe; for which cause, I
   Write no *Encomium*, but an *Elegie*.
               Iz. Wa.

An Elegie upon the Death of the
Deane of Pauls, Dr John Donne

By Mr Tho. Carie

CAN we not force from widdowed Poetry,
   Now thou art dead (Great DONNE) one Elegie
To crowne thy Hearse? Why yet dare we not trust
'Though with unkneaded dowe-bak't prose thy dust,
Such as the uncisor'd Churchman from the flower   5
Of fading Rhetorique, short liv'd as his houre,
Dry as the sand that measures it, should lay
Upon thy Ashes, on the funerall day?
Have we no voice, no tune? Did'st thou dispense
Through all our language, both the words and sense?   10
'Tis a sad truth; The Pulpit may her plaine,
And sober Christian precepts still retaine,
Doctrines it may, and wholesome Uses frame,
Grave Homilies, and Lectures, But the flame
Of thy brave Soule, (that shot such heat and light,   15
As burnt our earth, and made our darknesse bright,
Committed holy Rapes upon our Will,
Did through the eye the melting heart distill;
And the deepe knowledge of darke truths so teach,
As sense might judge, what phansie could not reach;)   20

An Elegie etc.   15-20 (that ... reach;)] that ... reach; *1633*

Must be desir'd for ever. So the fire,
That fills with spirit and heat the Delphique quire,
Which kindled first by thy Promethean breath,
Glow'd here a while, lies quench't now in thy death;
The Muses garden with Pedantique weedes   25
O'rspred, was purg'd by thee; The lazie seeds
Of servile imitation throwne away;
And fresh invention planted, Thou didst pay
The debts of our penurious bankrupt age;
Licentious thefts, that make poëtique rage   30
A Mimique fury, when our soules must bee
Possest, or with Anacreons Extasie,
Or Pindars, not their owne; The subtle cheat
Of slie Exchanges, and the jugling feat
Of two-edg'd words, or whatsoever wrong   35
By ours was done the Greeke, or Latine tongue,
Thou hast redeem'd, and open'd Us a Mine
Of rich and pregnant phansie, drawne a line
Of masculine expression, which had good
Old Orpheus seene, Or all the ancient Brood   40
Our superstitious fooles admire, and hold
Their lead more precious, then thy burnish't Gold,
Thou hadst beene their Exchequer, and no more
They each in others dust, had rak'd for Ore.
Thou shalt yield no precedence, but of time,   45
And the blinde fate of language, whose tun'd chime
More charmes the outward sense; Yet thou maist claime
From so great disadvantage greater fame,
Since to the awe of thy imperious wit
Our stubborne language bends, made only fit   50
With her tough-thick-rib'd hoopes to gird about
Thy Giant phansie, which had prov'd too stout
For their soft melting Phrases. As in time
They had the start, so did they cull the prime
Buds of invention many a hundred yeare,   55
And left the rifled fields, besides the feare
To touch their Harvest, yet from those bare lands
Of what is purely thine, thy only hands
(And that thy smallest worke) have gleaned more
Then all those times, and tongues could reape before;   60

But thou art gone, and thy strict lawes will be
Too hard for Libertines in Poetrie.
They will repeale the goodly exil'd traine
Of gods and goddesses, which in thy just raigne
Were banish'd nobler Poems, now, with these   65
The silenc'd tales o'th'Metamorphoses
Shall stuffe their lines, and swell the windy Page,
Till Verse refin'd by thee, in this last Age,
Turne ballad rime, Or those old Idolls bee
Ador'd againe, with new apostasie;   70
    Oh, pardon mee, that breake with untun'd verse
The reverend silence that attends thy herse,
Whose awfull solemne murmures were to thee
More then these faint lines, A loud Elegie,
That did proclaime in a dumbe eloquence   75
The death of all the Arts, whose influence
Growne feeble, in these panting numbers lies
Gasping short winded Accents, and so dies:
So doth the swiftly turning wheele not stand
In th'instant we withdraw the moving hand,   80
But some small time maintaine a faint weake course
By vertue of the first impulsive force:
And so whil'st I cast on thy funerall pile
Thy crowne of Bayes, Oh, let it crack a while,
And spit disdaine, till the devouring flashes   85
Suck all the moysture up, then turne to ashes.
    I will not draw the envy to engrosse
All thy perfections, or weepe all our losse;
Those are too numerous for an Elegie,
And this too great, to be express'd by mee.   90
Though every pen should share a distinct part,
Yet art thou Theme enough to tyre all Art;
Let others carve the rest, it shall suffice
I on thy Tombe this Epitaph incise.

Here lies a King, that rul'd as hee thought fit   95
The universall Monarchy of wit;
Here lie two Flamens, and both those, the best,
Apollo's first, at last, the true Gods Priest.

61, 71, 87 *No paragraph in 1633*

An Elegie on Dr Donne

By Sir Lucius Carie

POETS attend, the Elegie I sing
   Both of a doubly-named Priest, and King:
In stead of Coates, and Pennons, bring your Verse,
For you must bee chiefe mourners at his Hearse,
A Tombe your Muse must to his Fame supply,   5
No other Monuments can never die;
And as he was a two-fold Priest; in youth,
Apollo's; afterwards, the voice of Truth,
Gods Conduit-pipe for grace, who chose him for
His extraordinary Embassador,   10
So let his Liegiers with the Poets joyne,
Both having shares, both must in griefe combine:
Whil'st Johnson forceth with his Elegie
Teares from a griefe-unknowing Scythians eye,
(Like Moses at whose stroke the waters gusht   15
From forth the Rock, and like a Torrent rusht.)
Let Lawd his funerall Sermon preach, and shew
Those vertues, dull eyes were not apt to know,
Nor leave that Piercing Theme, till it appeares
To be goodfriday, by the Churches Teares;   20
Yet make not griefe too long oppresse our Powers,
Least that his funerall Sermon should prove ours.
Nor yet forget that heavenly Eloquence,
With which he did the bread of life dispense,
Preacher and Orator discharg'd both parts   25
With pleasure for our sense, health for our hearts,
And the first such (Though a long studied Art
Tell us our soule is all in every part,)
None was so marble, but whil'st him he heares,
His Soule so long dwelt only in his eares.   30
And from thence (with the fiercenesse of a flood
Bearing downe vice) victual'd with that blest food
Their hearts; His seed in none could faile to grow,
Fertile he found them all, or made them so:
No Druggist of the Soule bestow'd on all   35
So Catholiquely a curing Cordiall.

Nor only in the Pulpit dwelt his store,
His words work'd much, but his example more,
That preach't on worky dayes; His Poetrie
It selfe was oftentimes divinity,   40
Those Anthemes (almost second Psalmes) he writ
To make us know the Crosse, and value it,
(Although we owe that reverence to that name
Wee should not need warmth from an under flame.)
Creates a fire in us, so neare extreme   45
That we would die, for, and upon this theme.
Next, his so pious Litany, which none can
But count Divine, except a Puritan,
And that but for the name, nor this, nor those
Want any thing of Sermons, but the prose.   50
   Experience makes us see, that many a one
Owes to his Countrey his Religion;
And in another, would as strongly grow,
Had but his Nurse and Mother taught him so,
Not hee the ballast on his Judgement hung;   55
Nor did his preconceit doe either wrong;
He labour'd to exclude what ever sinne
By time or carelessenesse had entred in;
Winnow'd the chaffe from wheat, but yet was loath
A too hot zeale should force him, burne them both;   60
Nor would allow of that so ignorant gall,
Which to save blotting often would blot all;
Nor did those barbarous opinions owne,
To thinke the Organs sinne, and faction, none;
Nor was there expectation to gaine grace   65
From forth his Sermons only, but his face;
So Primitive a looke, such gravitie
With humblenesse, and both with Pietie;
So milde was Moses countenance, when he prai'd
For them whose Satanisme his power gainsaid;   70
And such his gravitie, when all Gods band
Receiv'd his word (through him) at second hand,
Which joyn'd, did flames of more devotion move
Then ever Argive Hellens could of love.

Now to conclude, I must my reason bring,   75
Wherefore I call'd him in his title King,
That Kingdome the Philosophers beleev'd
To excell Alexanders, nor were griev'd
By feare of losse (that being such a Prey
No stronger then ones selfe can force away)   80
The Kingdome of ones selfe, this he enjoy'd,
And his authoritie so well employ'd,
That never any could before become
So Great a Monarch, in so small a roome;
He conquer'd rebell passions, rul'd them so,   85
As under-spheares by the first Mover goe,
Banish't so farre their working, that we can
But know he had some, for we knew him man.
Then let his last excuse his first extremes,
His age saw visions, though his youth dream'd dreames.   90

On Dr Donnes Death

By Mr Mayne of Christ-Church in Oxford

WHO shall presume to mourn thee, *Donne*, unlesse
        He could his teares in thy expressions dresse,
And teach his griefe that reverence of thy Hearse,
To weepe lines, learned, as thy Anniverse,
A Poëme of that worth, whose every teare   5
Deserves the title of a severall yeare.
Indeed so farre above its Reader, good,
That wee are thought wits, when 'tis understood,
There that blest maid to die, who now should grieve?
After thy sorrow, 'twere her losse to live;   10
And her faire vertues in anothers line,
Would faintly dawn, which are made Saints in thine.
Hadst thou beene shallower, and not writ so high,
Or left some new way for our pennes, or eye,
To shed a funerall teare, perchance thy Tombe   15
Had not beene speechlesse, or our Muses dumbe;

But now wee dare not write, but must conceale
Thy Epitaph, lest we be thought to steale,
For, who hath read thee, and discernes thy worth,
That will not say, thy carelesse houres brought forth   20
Fancies beyond our studies, and thy play
Was happier, then our serious time of day?
So learned was thy chance; thy haste had wit,
And matter from thy pen flow'd rashly fit,
What was thy recreation turnes our braine,   25
Our rack and palenesse, is thy weakest straine.
And when we most come neere thee, 'tis our blisse
To imitate thee, where thou dost amisse.
Here light your muse, you that do onely thinke,
And write, and are just Poëts, as you drinke,   30
In whose weake fancies wit doth ebbe and flow,
Just as your recknings rise; that wee may know
In your whole carriage of your worke, that here
This flash you wrote in Wine, and this in Beere,
This is to tap your Muse, which running long   35
Writes flat, and takes our eare not halfe so strong;
Poore Suburbe wits, who, if you want your cup,
Or if a Lord recover, are blowne up.
Could you but reach this height, you should not need
To make, each meale, a project ere you feed,   40
Nor walke in reliques, clothes so old and bare,
As if left off to you from *Ennius* were,
Nor should your love, in verse, call Mistresse, those,
Who are mine hostesse, or your whores in prose;
From this Muse learne to Court, whose power could move
A Cloystred coldnesse, or a Vestall love,   46
And would convey such errands to their eare,
That Ladies knew no oddes to grant and heare;
　　But I do wrong thee, *Donne*, and this low praise
Is written onely for thy yonger dayes.   50
I am not growne up, for thy riper parts,
Then should I praise thee, through the Tongues, and Arts,
And have that deepe Divinity, to know,
What mysteries did from thy preaching flow,

49 *No paragraph in 1633*

Who with thy words could charme thy audience,   55
That at thy sermons, eare was all our sense;
Yet have I seene thee in the pulpit stand,
Where wee might take notes, from thy looke, and hand;
And from thy speaking action beare away
More Sermon, then some teachers use to say.   60
Such was thy carriage, and thy gesture such,
As could divide the heart, and conscience touch.
Thy motion did confute, and wee might see
An errour vanquish'd by delivery.
Not like our Sonnes of Zeale, who to reforme   65
Their hearers, fiercely at the Pulpit storme,
And beate the cushion into worse estate,
Then if they did conclude it reprobate,
Who can out pray the glasse, then lay about
Till all Predestination be runne out.   70
And from the point such tedious uses draw,
Their repetitions would make Gospell, Law.
No, In such temper would thy Sermons flow,
So well did Doctrine, and thy language show,
And had that holy feare, as, hearing thee,   75
The Court would mend, and a good Christian bee.
And Ladies though unhansome, out of grace,
Would heare thee, in their unbought lookes, and face.
    More I could write, but let this crowne thine Urne,
Wee cannot hope the like, till thou returne.   80

Upon Mr J. Donne, and his Poems

W HO dares say thou art dead, when he doth see
    (Unburied yet) this living part of thee?
This part that to thy beeing gives fresh flame,
And though th'art *Donne*, yet will preserve thy name.
Thy flesh (whose channels left their crimsen hew,   5
And whey-like ranne at last in a pale blew)
May shew thee mortall, a dead palsie may
Seise on't, and quickly turne it into clay;

79 *No paragraph in 1633*

Which like the Indian earth, shall rise refin'd:
But this great Spirit thou hast left behinde,   10
This Soule of Verse (in it's first pure estate)
Shall live, for all the World to imitate,
But not come neer, for in thy Fancies flight
Thou dost not stoope unto the vulgar sight,
But, hovering highly in the aire of Wit,   15
Hold'st such a pitch, that few can follow it;
Admire they may. Each object that the Spring
(Or a more piercing influence) doth bring
T'adorne Earths face, thou sweetly did'st contrive
To beauties elements, and thence derive   20
Unspotted Lillies white; which thou did'st set
Hand in hand, with the veine-like Violet,
Making them soft, and warme, and by thy power,
Could'st give both life, and sense, unto a flower.
The Cheries thou hast made to speake, will bee   25
Sweeter unto the taste, then from the tree.
And (spight of winter stormes) amidst the snow
Thou oft hast made the blushing Rose to grow.
The Sea-nimphs, that the watry cavernes keepe,
Have sent their Pearles and Rubies from the deepe   30
To deck thy love, and plac'd by thee, they drew
More lustre to them, then where first they grew.
All minerals (that Earths full wombe doth hold
Promiscuously) thou couldst convert to gold,
And with thy flaming raptures so refine,   35
That it was much more pure then in the Mine.
The lights that guild the night, if thou did'st say,
They looke like eyes, those did out-shine the day;
For there would be more vertue in such spells,
Then in Meridians, or crosse Parallels: 40
What ever was of worth in this great Frame,
That Art could comprehend, or Wit could name,
It was thy theme for Beauty; thou didst see,
Woman, was this faire Worlds Epitomie.
Thy nimble *Satyres* too, and every straine   45
(With nervy strength) that issued from thy brain,
Will lose the glory of their owne cleare bayes,
If they admit of any others praise.

But thy diviner Poëms (whose cleare fire
Purges all drosse away) shall by a Quire   50
Of Cherubims, with heavenly Notes be set
(Where flesh and blood could ne'r attaine to yet)
There purest Spirits sing such sacred Layes,
In Panegyrique Alleluiaes.

                                                    Arth. Wilson.

In Memory of Doctor Donne

By Mr R. B.

*D*ONNE dead? 'Tis here reported true, though I
    Ne'r yet so much desir'd to heare a lye,
'Tis too too true, for so wee finde it still,
Good newes are often false, but seldome, ill:
But must poore fame tell us his fatall day,   5
And shall we know his death, the common way,
Mee thinkes some Comet bright should have foretold
The death of such a man, for though of old
'Tis held, that Comets Princes death foretell,
Why should not his, have needed one as well?   10
Who was the Prince of wits, 'mongst whom he reign'd,
High as a Prince, and as great State maintain'd?
Yet wants he not his signe, for wee have seene
A dearth, the like to which hath never beene,
Treading on harvests heeles, which doth presage   15
The death of wit and learning, which this age
Shall finde, now he is gone; for though there bee
Much graine in shew, none brought it forth as he,
Or men are misers; or if true want raises
The dearth, then more that dearth *Donnes* plenty praises. 20
Of learning, languages, of eloquence,
And Poësie, (past ravishing of sense,)
He had a magazine, wherein such store
Was laid up, as might hundreds serve of poore.
    But he is gone, O how will his desire   25
Torture all those that warm'd them by his fire?
Mee thinkes I see him in the pulpit standing,
Not eares, or eyes, but all mens hearts commanding,

Where wee that heard him, to our selves did faine
Golden Chrysostome was alive againe;   30
And never were we weari'd, till we saw
His houre (and but an houre) to end did draw.
How did he shame the doctrine-men, and use,
With helps to boot, for men to beare th'abuse
Of their tir'd patience, and endure th'expence   35
Of time, O spent in hearkning to non-sense,
With markes also, enough whereby to know,
The speaker is a zealous dunce, or so.
'Tis true, they quitted him, to their poore power,
They humm'd against him; And with face most sowre   40
Call'd him a strong lin'd man, a Macaroon,
And no way fit to speake to clouted shoone,
As fine words [truly] as you would desire,
But [verily,] but a bad edifier.
Thus did these beetles slight in him that good,   45
They could not see, and much lesse understood.
But we may say, when we compare the stuffe
Both brought; He was a candle, they the snuffe.
Well, Wisedome's of her children justifi'd,
Let therefore these poore fellowes stand aside;   50
Nor, though of learning he deserv'd so highly,
Would I his booke should save him; Rather slily
I should advise his Clergie not to pray,
Though of the learn'dst sort; Me thinkes that they
Of the same trade, are Judges not so fit,   55
There's no such emulation as of wit.
Of such, the Envy might as much perchance
Wrong him, and more, then th'others ignorance.
It was his Fate (I know't) to be envy'd
As much by Clerkes, as lay men magnifi'd;   60
And why? but 'cause he came late in the day,
And yet his Penny earn'd, and had as they.
No more of this, least some should say, that I
Am strai'd to Satyre, meaning Elegie.
No, no, had DONNE need to be judg'd or try'd,   65
A Jury I would summon on his side,
That had no sides, nor factions, past the touch
Of all exceptions, freed from Passion, such

As nor to feare nor flatter, e'r were bred,
These would I bring, though called from the dead: 70
Southampton, Hambleton, Pembrooke, Dorsets Earles,
Huntingdon, Bedfords Countesses (the Pearles
Once of each sexe.) If these suffice not, I
Ten *decem tales* have of Standers by:
All which, for DONNE, would such a verdict give,   75
As can belong to none, that now doth live.
    But what doe I? A diminution 'tis
To speake of him in verse, so short of his,
Whereof he was the master; All indeed
Compar'd with him, pip'd on an Oaten reed.   80
O that you had but one 'mongst all your brothers
Could write for him, as he hath done for others:
(Poets I speake to) When I see't, I'll say,
My eye-sight betters, as my yeares decay,
Meane time a quarrell I shall ever have   85
Against these doughty keepers from the grave,
Who use, it seemes their old Authoritie,
When (Verses men immortall make) they cry:
Which had it been a Recipe true tri'd,
Probatum esset, DONNE had never dy'd.   90
    For mee, if e'r I had least sparke at all
Of that which they Poetique fire doe call,
Here I confesse it fetched from his hearth,
Which is gone out, now he is gone to earth.
This only a poore flash, a lightning is   95
Before my Muses death, as after his.
Farewell (faire soule) and deigne receive from mee
This Type of that devotion I owe thee,
From whom (while living) as by voice and penne
I learned more, then from a thousand men: 100
So by thy death, am of one doubt releas'd,
And now beleeve that miracles are ceas'd.

Epitaph

HEERE *lies Deane Donne*; Enough; Those words alone
    Shew him as fully, as if all the stone
His Church of Pauls contains, were through inscrib'd   105
Or all the walkers there, to speake him, brib'd.

None can mistake him, for one such as Hee
DONNE, Deane, or Man, more none shall ever see.
Not man? No, though unto a Sunne each eye
Were turn'd, the whole earth so to overspie.   110
A bold brave word; Yet such brave Spirits as knew
His Spirit, will say, it is lesse bold then true.

Epitaph upon Dr Donne

By Endy: Porter

THIS decent Urne a sad inscription weares,
   Of *Donnes* departure from us, to the spheares;
And the dumbe stone with silence seemes to tell
The changes of this life, wherein is well
Exprest, A cause to make all joy to cease,   5
And never let our sorrowes more take ease;
For now it is impossible to finde
One fraught with vertues, to inrich a minde;
But why should death, with a promiscuous hand
At one rude stroke impoverish a land?   10
Thou strict Attorney, unto stricter Fate,
Didst thou confiscate his life out of hate
To his rare Parts? Or didst thou throw thy dart,
With envious hand, at some Plebeyan heart;
And he with pious vertue stept betweene   15
To save that stroke, and so was kill'd unseene
By thee? O 'twas his goodnesse so to doe,
Which humane kindnesse never reacht unto.
Thus the hard lawes of death were satisfi'd,
And he left us like Orphan friends, and di'de.   20
Now from the Pulpit to the peoples eares,
Whose speech shall send repentant sighes, and teares?
Or tell mee, if a purer Virgin die,
Who shall hereafter write her Elegie?
Poets be silent, let your numbers sleepe,   25
For he is gone that did all phansie keepe;
Time hath no Soule, but his exalted verse;
Which with amazements, we may now reherse.

In Obitum Venerabilis Viri Iohannis Donne,

Sacrae Theologiae Doctoris, Ecclesiae Cathedralis Divi *Pauli*,
nuper Decani; Illi honoris, tibi (multum mihi colende Vir)
observantiae ergo Haec ego.

CONQUERAR? ignavoque sequar tua funera planctu?
    Sed lachrimae clausistis iter: nec muta querelas
Lingua potest proferre pias: ignoscite manes
Defuncti, et tacito sinite indulgere dolori.
    Sed scelus est tacuisse: cadent in maesta liturae   5
Verba. Tuis (docta umbra) tuis haec accipe jussis
Caepta, nec officii contemnens pignora nostri
Aversare tuâ non dignum laude Poëtam.
    O si Pythagorae non vanum dogma fuisset:
Inque meum â vestro migraret pectore pectus   10
Musa, repentinos tua nosceret urna furores.
Sed frustra, heu frustra haec votis puerilibus opto:
Tecum abiit, summoque sedens jam monte Thalia
Ridet anhelantes, Parnassi et culmina vates
Desperare jubet. Verum hâc nolente coactos   15
Scribimus audaces numeros, et flebile carmen
Scribimus (ô soli qui te dilexit) habendum.
    Siccine perpetuus liventia lumina somnus
Clausit? et immerito merguntur funere virtus?
Et pietas? et quae poterant fecisse beatum,   20
Caetera, sed nec te poterant servare beatum.
    Quo mihi doctrinam? quorsum impallescere chartis
Nocturnis juvat? et totidem olfecisse lucernas?
Decolor et longos studiis deperdere Soles
Vt prius aggredior, longamque arcessere famam.   25
Omnia sed frustra: mihi dum cunctisque minatur
Exitium crudele et inexorabile fatum.
    Nam post te sperare nihil decet: hoc mihi restat
Vt moriar, tenues fugiatque obscurus in auras
Spiritus: ô doctis saltem si cognitus umbris.   30
Illic te (venerande) iterum, (venerande) videbo.
Et dulces audire sonós, et verba diserti

In Obitum etc. *Text of this and the next two Elegies from 1635*   10 pectore] pectore,
1635   21 beatum.] beatum *1635*   23 olfecisse] olfecissë *1635*   25 arcessere
Gr : accessere *1635*   26–7 mihi . . . Exitium] mihi, . . . Exitium, *1635*

Oris, et aeternas dabitur mihi carpere voces.
Quêis ferus infernae tacuisset Ianitor aulae
Auditis: Nilusque minus strepuisset: Arion   35
Cederet, et sylvas qui post se traxerat Orpheus.
Eloquio sic ille viros, sic ille movere
Voce feros potuit: quis enim tam barbarus? aut tam
Facundis nimis infestus non motus ut illo
Hortante, et blando victus sermone sileret?   40
    Sic oculos, sic ille manus, sic ora ferebat,
Singula sic decuere senem, sic omnia. Vidi,
Audivi et stupui quoties orator in Aede
Paulina stetit, et mira gravitate levantes
Corda, oculosque viros tenuit: dum Nestoris ille   45
Fudit verba (omni quanto mage dulcia melle?)
Nunc habet attonitos, pandit mysteria plebi
Non concessa prius nondum intellecta: revolvunt
Mirantes, tacitique arrectis auribus astant.
    Mutatis mox ille modo, formaque loquendi   50
Tristia pertractat: fatumque et flebile mortis
Tempus, et in cineres redeunt quod corpora primos.
Tunc gemitum cunctos dare, tunc lugere videres,
Forsitan â lachrymis aliquis non temperat, atque
Ex oculis largum stillat rorem; aetheris illo   55
Sic pater audito voluit succumbere turbam,
Affectusque ciere suos, et ponere notae
Vocis ad arbitrium, divinae oracula mentis
Dum narrat, rostrisque potens dominatur in altis.
    Quo feror? audaci et forsan pietate nocenti   60
In nimia ignoscas vati, qui vatibus olim
Egregium decus, et tanto excellentior unus
Omnibus; inferior quanto est, et pessimus, impar
Laudibus hisce, tibi qui nunc facit ista Poëta.
Et quo nos canimus? cur haec tibi sacra? Poëtae   65
Desinite: en fati certus, sibi voce canorâ
Inferias praemisit olor, cum Carolus Albâ
(Vltima volventem et Cycnaeâ voce loquentem)
Nuper eum, turba et magnatum audiret in Aulâ.
    Tunc Rex, tunc Proceres, Clerus, tunc astitit illi   70
Aula frequens. Solâ nunc in tellure recumbit,

38 Voce feros] Voceferos *1635*

Vermibus esca, pio malint nisi parcere: quidni
Incipiant et amare famem? Metuere Leones
Sic olim, sacrosque artus violare Prophetae
Bellua non ausa est quàmquam jejuna, sitimque   75
Optaret nimis humano satiare cruore.
    At non haec de te sperabimus; omnia carpit
Praedator vermis: nec talis contigit illi
Praeda diu; forsan metrico pede serpet ab inde:
Vescere, et exhausto satia te sanguine. Iam nos   80
Adsumus; et post te cupiet quis vivere? Post te
Quis volet, aut poterit? nam post te vivere mors est.
    Et tamen ingratas ignavi ducimus auras:
Sustinet et tibi lingua vale, vale dicere: parce
Non festinanti aeternum requiescere turbae.   85
Ipsa satis properat quae nescit Parca morari,
Nunc urgere colum, trahere atque occare videmus.
Quin rursus (Venerande) Vale, vale: ordine nos te
Quo Deus, et quo dura volet natura sequemur.
    Depositum interea lapides servate fideles.   90
Faelices illâ quêis Aedis parte locari
Quâ jacet iste datur. Forsan lapis inde loquetur,
Parturietque viro plenus testantia luctus
Verba: et carminibus quae *Donni* suggeret illi
Spiritus, insolitos testari voce calores   95
Incipiet: (non sic Pyrrhâ jactante calebat.)
    Mole sub hâc tegitur quicquid mortale relictum est
De tanto mortale viro. Qui praefuit Aedi huic,
Formosi pecoris pastor, formosior ipse.
Ite igitur, dignisque illum celebrate loquelis,   100
Et quae demuntur vitae date tempora famae.
      Indignus tantorum meritorum Praeco, virtutum
      tuarum cultor religiosissimus,
                    Daniel Darnelly.

79 inde:] inde *1635*   86 Parca morari,] parca morari *1635*   88 rursus] rusus
1635   96 Incipiet:... calebat.] Incipiet ... calebat *1635*

Elegie on D. D.

Now, by one yeare, time and our frailtie have
    Lessened our first confusion, since the Grave
Clos'd thy deare Ashes, and the teares which flow
In these, have no springs, but of solid woe:
Or they are drops, which cold amazement froze   5
At thy decease, and will not thaw in Prose:
All streames of Verse which shall lament that day,
Doe truly to the Ocean tribute pay;
But they have lost their saltnesse, which the eye
In recompence of wit, strives to supply: 10
Passions excesse for thee wee need not feare,
Since first by thee our passions hallowed were;
Thou mad'st our sorrowes, which before had bin
Onely for the Successe, sorrowes for sinne,
We owe thee all those teares, now thou art dead,   15
Which we shed not, which for our selves we shed.
Nor didst thou onely consecrate our teares,
Give a religious tincture to our feares;
But even our joyes had learn'd an innocence,
Thou didst from gladnesse separate offence: 20
All mindes at once suckt grace from thee, as where
(The curse revok'd) the Nations had one eare.
Pious dissector: thy one houre did treate
The thousand mazes of the hearts deceipt;
Thou didst pursue our lov'd and subtill sinne,   25
Through all the foldings wee had wrapt it in,
And in thine owne large minde finding the way
By which our selves we from our selves convey,
Didst in us, narrow models, know the same
Angles, though darker, in our meaner frame.   30
How short of praise in this? My Muse, alas,
Climbes weakly to that truth which none can passe,
Hee that writes best, may onely hope to leave
A Character of all he could conceive
But none of thee, and with mee must confesse,   35
That fansie findes some checke, from an excesse
Of merit most, of nothing, it hath spun,
And truth, as reasons task and theame, doth shunne.

She makes a fairer flight in emptinesse,
Than when a bodied truth doth her oppresse.   40
Reason againe denies her scales, because
Hers are but scales, shee judges by the lawes
Of weake comparison, thy vertue sleights
Her feeble Beame, and her unequall Weights.
What prodigie of wit and pietie   45
Hath she else knowne, by which to measure thee?
Great soule: we can no more the worthinesse
Of what you were, then what you are, expresse.

Sidney Godolphin.

On Dr John Donne, late Deane of S. Paules, London

LONG since this taske of teares from you was due,
    Long since, ô Poëts, he did die to you,
Or left you dead, when wit and he tooke flight
On divine winges, and soard out of your sight.
Preachers, 'tis you must weep; The wit he taught   5
You doe enjoy; the Rebels which he brought
From ancient discord, Giants faculties,
And now no more religions enemies;
Honest to knowing, unto vertuous sweet,
Witty to good, and learned to discreet,   10
He reconcil'd, and bid the Usurper goe;
Dulnesse to vice, religion ought to flow;
He kept his loves, but not his objects; wit
Hee did not banish, but transplanted it,
Taught it his place and use, and brought it home   15
To Pietie, which it doth best become;
He shew'd us how for sinnes we ought to sigh,
And how to sing Christs Epithalamy:
The Altars had his fires, and there hee spoke
Incense of loves, and fansies holy smoake: 20
Religion thus enrich'd, the people train'd,
And God from dull vice had the fashion gain'd.

The first effects sprung in the giddy minde
Of flashy youth, and thirst of woman-kinde,
By colours lead, and drawne to a pursuit,   25
Now once againe by beautie of the fruit,
As if their longings too must set us free,
And tempt us now to the commanded tree.
Tell me, had ever pleasure such a dresse,
Have you knowne crimes so shap'd? or lovelinesse   30
Such as his lips did cloth religion in?
Had not reproofe a beauty passing sinne?
Corrupted nature sorrow'd when she stood
So neare the danger of becomming good,
And wish'd our so inconstant eares exempt   35
From piety that had such power to tempt:
Did not his sacred flattery beguile
Man to amendment? The law, taught to smile,
Pension'd our vanitie, and man grew well
Through the same frailtie by which he fell.   40
O the sick state of man, health doth not please
Our tasts, but in the shape of the disease.
Thriftlesse is charitie, coward patience,
Justice is cruell, mercy want of sense.
What meanes our Nature to barre vertue place,   45
If shee doe come in her owne cloathes and face?
Is good a pill, we dare not chaw to know?
Sense the soules servant, doth it keep us so
As we might starve for good, unlesse it first
Doe leave a pawne of relish in the gust?   50
Or have we to salvation no tie
At all, but that of our infirmitie?
Who treats with us must our affections move
To th'good we flie by those sweets which we love,
Must seeke our palats, and with their delight   55
To gaine our deeds, must bribe our appetite.
These traines he knew, and laying nets to save,
Temptingly sugred all the health hee gave.
     But, where is now that chime? that harmony
Hath left the world, now the loud organ may   60

23, 59 *No paragraph in 1635*

Appeare, the better voyce is fled to have
A thousand times the sweetnesse which it gave.
I cannot say how many thousand spirits
The single happinesse this soule inherits,
Damnes in the other world, soules whom no crosse   65
O'th sense afflicts, but onely of the losse,
Whom ignorance would halfe save, all whose paine
Is not in what they feele, but others gaine,
Selfe executing wretched spirits, who
Carrying their guilt, transport their envy too: 70
But those high joyes which his wits youngest flame
Would hurt to chuse, shall not we hurt to name?
Verse statues are all robbers, all we make
Of monument, thus doth not give but take
As Sailes which Seamen to a forewinde fit,   75
By a resistance, goe along with it,
So pens grow while they lessen fame so left;
A weake assistance is a kinde of theft.
Who hath not love to ground his teares upon,
Must weep here if he have ambition.
                    J. Chudleigh.

COMMENTARY

Note on Versification

DONNE's verse is regularly syllabic, but involves much use of elision and synalœpha. Syllables which are assimilated are not necessarily unpronounced, but they are not counted metrically and are 'like grace-notes in music', which do not disturb the time (Gardner, *Divine Poems*, p. 54). The copy in Donne's handwriting of the verse letter 'To the Lady Carey and Mrs. Essex Rich' (discovered in 1970) confirms that he used elision marks, as might be deduced from their appearance in the *Anniversaries* and the 'Elegy on Prince Henry' (printed from copies written out by Donne). He did not, however, use them consistently, judging by their appearance in the holograph verse letter. This contains more marks than occur in the text of the poem in *1633* but fewer than complete consistency would demand. The printer of the *Anniversaries* apparently tried merely to reproduce (with what degree of success is uncertain) those he found in the copy that Donne sent him. It has been necessary to add elision marks in eight places in *The First Anniversary*, one in 'A Funeral Elegy', and fifteen in *The Second Anniversary*. In this I have been guided by the practice of the editor of *1633*, who was prepared to supply elision marks, not only in obvious places, but also where elision cannot, strictly speaking, take place: for example, 'If'the', 'The Storm', l. 40; 'Lethe'that', 'To Mr. I. L.' ('Of that short Roll of friends'), l. 6. Although considerable care was taken in *1633*, however, an elision mark was not supplied in every place where one was needed, and in the first line of 'Elegy on the Lady Markham' the editor added a mark erroneously. In l. 46 of the 'Elegy upon the Death of Mistress Bulstrode' the placing of the elision mark is perhaps dubious, but I have let it stand.

The holograph of the verse letter to Lady Carey and her sister also shows that Donne used contraction marks. The printer of the *Anniversaries*, either because he overlooked marks in Donne's copy, or because Donne himself had failed to add them, left a number of inconsistencies in his indication of contractions; and I have made six in *The First Anniversary* and fifteen in *The Second Anniversary*. The printers of the 'Elegy on Prince Henry' and *1633* were more, but not wholly, consistent in using contraction marks.

The holograph confirms (as the manuscripts and early editions suggest) that Donne did not indicate when an unstressed medial syllable was to be suppressed. His alertness to the movement of colloquial speech is shown by the great liberties he takes here, and he relies on his reader to sense the proper rhythm. Such word-endings as '-ion', '-ial', for instance, are sometimes treated as monosyllabic, sometimes as disyllabic. In *The Second Anniversary* 'ingredients' has three syllables in l. 124, but four in l. 266; 'essentiall' counts as four syllables in l. 384, but as three in l. 443.

In the poems in this volume Donne's practice is less free than in others of his verses. He allows himself the usual liberty in English syllabic verse of an extra weak final syllable. There are, however, no examples of a defective first foot (except, possibly, in the Somerset 'Epithalamion', l. 129), or of a defective foot creating a strong pause in the middle of a line. Fairly frequently, however, Donne allows an extra light syllable before a medial pause; and in these cases I have extended the practice in *1633* of inserting an elision mark.

The editor of *1633* also took trouble over the indenting and arrangement of lines in poems written in stanzas to draw attention to line-length and rhyme scheme. He was not, however, thorough-going or consistent, and in the Epithalamions I have felt free to make what I hope is a satisfactory compromise among the claims of rhyme, length of line, and the look of the poem on the page. I have not followed the example of *1611* in indenting alternate lines of couplets to make them resemble 'elegiacs' in 'A Funeral Elegy', or the similar arrangement in *1633* in the induction to the Somerset 'Epithalamion', the funeral elegy on Lady Markham, and in both of those on Mistress Bulstrode (and in Arthur Wilson's elegy on Donne himself).

EPITHALAMIONS

Epithalamion made at Lincolnes Inne (p. 3)

MSS.: Group II (*A 18, N, TCC, TCD*); *DC* (ll. 1–72); Group III (*Dob, Lut, O'F, S 96*); *W*; *O2, P; B.*
Miscellanies: Brit. Lib. MS. *Add. 34744; EH; Grey.*

Readings of *1633* have been discarded in ll. 23, 26, 49, 55, 59, 60, and 62. The printer was following his Group II manuscript, which led him into error in ll. 49, 55, and 59; he misprinted or misread his copy in ll. 60 and 62; in l. 26 both these conditions seem to have operated; and in l. 23 the editor tried to 'correct' the text, with or without the aid of a Group III manuscript, in which the same solution was arrived at. My text differs from Grierson's in ll. 55 and 62, where he follows *1633*; and in l. 57, where I retain a reading in *1633* which he rejected.

In *W* the poem is entitled simply 'Epithalamion'; *1633* follows the Group II title; otherwise the title is 'Epithalamion on a Citizen' (except in *O2, P*, where it is said to celebrate 'the La: Eliz:', being confused with the poem next printed here). Possibly, the poem was first called 'Epithalamion' (as in *W*), and after the other two epithalamions were composed Donne added the words 'made at Lincolnes Inne' to distinguish it from them.

The information that the epithalamion was 'made at Lincoln's Inn' seems in any case to derive from one of Donne's own copies of the poem, to which the text in Group II and *1633* is probably, therefore, more directly related than that in other manuscripts, except that in *W*. That the poem is early is suggested by its inclusion in the first part of *W*, in which no poem (with one explicable exception) appears that can be dated after 1598. Grierson noted that in this epithalamion Donne is closer to Spenser than in any of his other poems, and Professor D. Novarr is right, I think, in further suggesting that the poem was inspired by Spenser's 'Epithalamion' (published in 1595), and that it is not necessary to suppose that it was written for an actual wedding ('Donne's "Epithalamion made at Lincoln's Inn": Context and Date', *R.E.S.*, N.S. vii, 1956). It is likely that the poem was composed soon after Spenser's appeared; Donne was, as far as we know, still a member of the Inn in 1595, though he does not appear in the Inn records as a student after the end of 1594, and his employment of a servant in July 1595 (Bald, p. 77) might indicate that he had only recently set up an establishment elsewhere. That the poem was written 'at Lincoln's Inn' does not, however, necessarily imply that it was written *for* the Inn; and Professor Novarr's suggestion that it was composed for a mock-wedding that formed part of midsummer revels at Lincoln's Inn in 1595 is, I think, untenable. There is no evidence that revels were held there at any time other than the Christmas season. For a discussion of Professor Novarr's contention that the poem is a parody of Spenser's, see Heather D. Ousby, 'Donne's "Epithalamion . . .".: an Alternative Interpretation', *S.E.L.* xvi (1976).

l. 1. Cf. 'His golden beame upon the hils doth spred', Spenser, *Epithalamion*, l. 20.

l. 6. *other you*: the bridegroom. Love makes two persons one (l. 39), and one person two. Cf. 'To the Lady Bedford' ('You that are shee and you'), ll. 1–4; and the Hymn to Hymen (ll. 3–6) at the end of Chapman's *Masque of the Middle Temple* . . . for Princess Elizabeth's marriage.

meet: are due to meet.

l. 12. *perfection*. For the idea that a woman is 'imperfect' and does not achieve complete womanhood until her union with a man, cf. 'The Primrose' and notes (pp. 220–1) in Gardner, *Elegies etc.*; *Twelfth Night*, II. iv. 39–40: 'alas, that they are so; To die, even when they to perfection grow!'; and *The Problemes of Aristotle* (Edinburgh, 1595, sig. H2): 'the nature of women is unperfect'; 'as the matter dooth covet a forme or perfection, so doth a woman the male'.

Donne's refrain is echoed by Jonson in the epithalamions in *Hymenaei* (ll. 473, 532, etc.) and *The Haddington Masque* (ll. 379, 390, etc.).

l. 14. *Mines*: sources of wealth (cf. l. 16). The word also had a bawdy sense, as in *Othello*, IV. ii. 79–80.
furnish'd: well supplied.

l. 16. *Angels*: gold coins (i.e. their dowries). Cf. 'The Bracelet', ll. 9 ff.

l. 17. *devise*: inventive fancy, ingenuity (*O.E.D.*, 'device', sb. 1).

l. 18. *grow due*: are becoming imminent (they too will soon marry).

l. 19. *Conceitedly*: 'fancifully, whimsically, in the manner of a conceit' (*O.E.D.*, adv. 2).

l. 22. *Flora*: goddess of flowers and spring in ancient Rome, whose festival, for five days from 28 April, was celebrated with much licentiousness.
Inde: India, the land of gorgeous clothes and of gems.

l. 26. *Sonnes of these Senators wealths deep oceans*: 'Suns/Sons of these Senators' wealth's deep oceans.' The congested syntax has caused difficulty for the writers of the manuscript copies. 'Sonnes', and especially 'sonns', is easily misread as 'some', as, presumably, in *1633* or the Group II manuscript which the printer was following.
The 'Patricians', young men accompanying the bridegroom, are sons of the wealthy aldermen, officials, or merchants of the City, who are referred to by Donne in his first Paul's Cross sermon (*Sermons*, i. 208) as '*Senators of London*'. Their 'oceans' of wealth are, and will be, sucked up by these 'sons' or 'suns', to be poured out in lavish spending. Cf. 'The Storm', ll. 43–4: 'it rain'd more / Then if the Sunne had drunke the sea before'.

l. 29. *fellowships*: Societies, sc. the Inns of Court.
one: a member of one.

l. 30. *Hermaphrodits*: creatures combining opposite qualities in one nature; here, equally devoted to study and amusements.

l. 31. *shine*. The subjects of the verb are arranged in anti-climax, and refer to City, Court, and Country, a familiar trio in Donne, e.g. in the letter 'To Sir Henry Wotton' ('Sir, more then kisses').
Temple. In the 'Roman' context (cf. 'Patricians', 'Senators', 'two-leav'd gates') the Temple here and in l. 37 might be any fane; but it could, as the main or a punning meaning, refer to the chapel of the Inner and Middle Temples, a church closely associated with the Inns of Court.

l. 34. *Except my sight faile*, etc. If he can believe his eyes, there is a 'sober virgin' still to be found in the City, and the bridegroom is not improving his fortunes by marrying a rich widow.

l. 37. *two-leav'd*: Latin *biforis*. Cf. Spenser, *Epithalamion*, l. 204: 'Open the temple gates unto my love'.

l. 39. *mystically*: a reference to the analogy made in the marriage service, between marriage and the 'mystical union that is betwixt Christ and His Church'.

l. 40. *hunger-starved wombe*: a phrase coarsely relevant to the bride (carrying on the bawdy sense of 'Temple' and 'two-leav'd'), though primarily referring to the vaults in, or crypt beneath, the church, which will swell with the buried bodies of the couple and their parents (l. 42).

l. 41. *bodies . . . tombe*. Cf. ll. 4–5; the thought reaches an appropriate final development in ll. 79–80. Cf. Sidney, *Arcadia*, 'The Third Eclogues', i. ll. 31–2: 'Let one time (but long first) close up their daies, / One grave their bodies seaze' (*Poems*, ed. W. A. Ringler (1962), p. 92).

l. 43. *elder claimes*: previous claims on the love of either partner.

l. 46. *All waies*: both 'all ways' (in every way) and 'always'.

l. 50. *for they*: because they.

l. 52. *jollities*. This word, used by Spenser in *Epithalamion*, l. 245, is found elsewhere in Donne's verse only in the Palatine 'Epithalamion', l. 32.

l. 57. *will*. Grierson followed *W* in reading 'nill' against the edition and all other manuscripts (except *B*, where 'not' is inserted after 'will'). I regard the reading of *W* as a copyist's error, or a 'correction' anticipating Grierson's, who conjectured 'nill' before he found the reading in *W*.

The midsummer sun is blazing in the eastern hemisphere and appears to be standing still. But shadows have moved from west to east, and the sun has passed its zenith (cf. 'A Lecture upon the Shadow'). Whereas in winter he hastens to the west, in summer he dallies, reining in his steeds; but once he has begun his descent into the western hemisphere he will go quickly. See J. V. Hagopian, 'Some Cruxes in Donne's Poetry', *N. and Q.* ccii (1957), p. 501, who points out the pause at the end of l. 57 and the quickening of the tempo, when 'restraint' is removed, in l. 58.

l. 61. *amorous evening starre*: Venus.

l. 64. *Musicians*: four syllables.

l. 70. *feasts*: cf. 'sweets', l. 51.

l. 71. *turne*: return (from the marriage bed).

ll. 74–5. *altar . . . sacrifice*. The metaphor is resumed in ll. 89–90.

ll. 81–3. *but able . . . I am*. Donne is using the scholastic distinction between 'in potentia' and 'in actu', deriving from Aristotle's discussion in *Metaph.* 1046^a–1052^a, e.g. 'the actuality is also better and more valuable than the good potency' (1051^{a}9). Similarly Aquinas: 'according to the Philosopher, better than every power is its act. For form is better than matter; and action than active power, since it is its end' (*S. T.* I^a pars, q. xxv. art. 1).

She has now fully achieved the state which was hitherto only a potentiality or 'ability' in her.

l. 90. *embowell*: 'disembowel', as applied to the priest's role; as applied to the bridegroom's, the sense is that given in *O.E.D.* II. 3, which cites: 'all was embowelled, and enwombed in the waters' (*Sermons*, ix. 99).

l. 93. *This Sun*: applied to the bride, as in the Palatine 'Epithalamion', l. 85, and the Somerset 'Epithalamion', ll. 144–5: reversing the usual identification, as in Ps. xix. 4–5: 'the sun which is as a bridegroom'.

l. 95. *had no maime.* She was a virgin (l. 33).

An Epithalamion, Or Mariage Song on the Lady Elizabeth, and Count Palatine being married on St. Valentines Day
(p. 6)

MSS.: Group I (*C 57, D, H 49, Lec, SP*); Group II (*N, TCD*); probably in *DC* on missing quire; Group III (*Dob, Lut, O'F, S 96*); *O2, P; A 25, C* (ll. 1, 15–28); *D 17, JC; B.*
Miscellanies: *Hd, HK 2;* Brit. Lib. MS. *Harleian 3511;* Bodleian MSS. *Eng. Poet. e. 37* (ll. 1–70, 85–112), *Rawl. Poet. 117* (2), *142* (extracts), *160.*

The MSS. not represented in the apparatus offer no other variations in the title of the poem. I agree with Grierson in rejecting readings of *1633* in ll. 46, 56, and 94; but I also read against *1633* in ll. 37 and 83.

Princess Elizabeth, only daughter of James I, was married to Frederick, Elector Palatine, on St. Valentine's Day, 14 February 1613. The wedding was accompanied by lavish festivities, including masques by Francis Beaumont, George Chapman, and Thomas Campion. Grierson quotes from Arthur Wilson's account:

> In *February* following, the Prince *Palatine*, and that lovely *Princess*, the Lady *Elizabeth*, were married, on Bishop *Valentines* Day, in all the *Pomp* and *Glory* that so much *Grandure* could express. Her *Vestments* were white, the *Emblem* of *Innocency*; her *hair* dishevil'd, hanging down her back at length, an *Ornament* of *Virginity*; a Crown of pure Gold upon her *head*, the *Cognizance* of *Majesty*, being all over beset with pretious *gems*, shining like a *Constellation* [cf. ll. 34–9]; her *Train* supported by Twelve young *Ladies* in *white Garments*, so adorned with *Jewels*, that her *Passage* looked like a milky way. She was led to Church by her Brother Prince *Charles*, and the Earl of *Northampton*; the Young *Batchelor* on the right hand, and the Old on the left. (*The History of Great Britain*, 1653, p. 64.)

For a full account of the nuptials see Carola Oman, *Elizabeth of Bohemia* (London, 1938), especially pp. 74–94. John Chamberlain remarks on the splendour of the wedding finery: 'The Lady Wotton had a gowne that cost fifty pound a yard the embroidering. . . . The Viscount Rochester, the Lord Hayes, and the Lord Dingwell were exceding rich and costly but above all they speake of the erle of Dorset, but this extreem cost and riches makes us all poore' (*Letters*, ed. N. E. McClure (1939), i. 424–5).

Princess Elizabeth, born in 1596, had been educated by Lord and Lady Harington, parents of Lucy, Countess of Bedford. They accompanied her to Heidelberg after the wedding, but Lord Harington died on his way home, and Lady Harington soon afterwards. Donne seems to have had a genuine regard for the Princess, and his interest was doubtless increased by her associations with the parents of his patroness. Later he preached before her and her husband (*Sermons*, ii, no. 12) during his visit to Heidelberg in 1619 as chaplain to Lord Hay, then Viscount Doncaster. He sent her copies of his *Devotions* (1624) and *The First Sermon preached to King Charles* (1625) with covering letters, to which the Princess, then Queen of Bohemia, in exile, sent replies (Gosse, ii. 205–6, 233–4). She and her husband had become Queen and King of Bohemia in 1619, but their reign was brief and they lost their dominion. Frederick died in exile in 1632, and Elizabeth ('the Winter Queen') moved to England in 1661, where she died in the following year. She called forth from Sir Henry Wotton his lyric 'Ye meaner beauties of the night'. Epithalamions for her marriage were written by George Wither, Thomas Heywood, Henry Peacham, John Taylor the Water Poet, and others. It may be, as Bald suggests (*Donne and the Drurys*, pp. 102–3, 122), that a further reason for the composition of Donne's epithalamion was 'to offset the bad impression created by Sir Robert Drury's indiscretion in criticizing the Elector Palatine'.

ll. 1–16. Grierson notes the general resemblance of this passage to Chaucer's *Parlement of Foules*, ll. 309 ff.

l. 1. *Bishop Valentine*. One of two saints named Valentine whose feast day was 14 February was a martyred Bishop of Terni.

l. 2. *All the Aire is thy Diocis*. The traditional belief that birds mate on St. Valentine's Day suggested that St. Valentine had charge of the air in which they fly.

l. 7. *The Sparrow that neglects his life for love*. The lechery of the sparrow was proverbial; its shortness of life was supposed to be due to its lustfulness. Cf. 'The Progress of the Soul', ll. 193–211, and notes in Milgate, *Satires etc.*, pp. 180–1.

l. 8. *stomacher*: waistcoat.

l. 9. *speed*: achieve success. Black was supposed to be a forbidding and ill-omened colour; but under St. Valentine's care differences between ugly and beautiful birds do not count.

l. 10. *Halcyon*: the kingfisher, suggesting brightness because of its plumage.

l. 11. *sped*: 'successfully accommodated'; cf. 'speed', l. 9.

l. 14. *Old Valentine.* Cf. Jonson, *A Tale of a Tub*, I. i. 1, 'old Bishop *Valentine*'. Lines 1–7 of Jonson's play borrow extensively from this stanza.

l. 18. *two Phoenixes.* Only one phoenix was supposed to exist at a time; it reproduced itself by setting itself afire ('enflaming') and rising again from its ashes (cf. ll. 25–6).

ll. 20–2. *what the Arke . . . Did not containe.* Since Noah was commanded to take into the Ark 'two of every sort' of every living thing (Gen. vi. 19–20, vii. 9), the phoenix, being unique, could not have been 'contained' in the Ark. It was, however, a problem for Biblical commentators how the phoenix survived the Flood. Pererius (*Comment. et Disput. in Genesim*, 1601, ii. 466–7) discusses the matter and concludes that if the phoenix existed 'nullus fuit in arca Noë Phoenix'; if it did not survive the Flood, it was renewed by a special act of creation. See D. C. Allen, 'Donne's Phoenix', *M.L.N.* lxii (1947), 340–2.

l. 27. *courage*: desire, 'sexual vigour and inclination' (*O.E.D.*, sb. I. 3. e); as in l. 97.

l. 29. *frustrate*: 'render ineffectual' (*O.E.D.* v. I. 2); i.e. by anticipating and outshining the sun's rising (cf. l. 85).

l. 31. *from thine eye.* Cf.:

> And as the sun, which is the heart of the universe, sends out from its orbit its light, and through its light its own strength to lower things; so the heart . . . pours spirits through the whole body, and through them sparks of light through the various single parts, but especially through the eyes. . . . [The eye] throws missiles of its own light into near-by eyes. (*Marsilio Ficino's Commentary on Plato's Symposium*, trans. S. R. Jayne, U. of Missouri Studies, xix. 1 (1944), p. 222.)

Of the six powers of the soul pertaining to cognition, reason is assigned to supreme divinity, 'sight to fire' (ibid., p. 165).

ll. 37–8. *by this blazing, signifie*, etc. Comets were thought to presage the death of a prince (or some other notable disaster); cf. *Julius Caesar*, II. ii. 30–1:

> When beggars die there are no comets seen:
> The heavens themselves blaze forth the death of princes.

l. 39. *new starre.* See note (p. 143) to *The First Anniversary*, ll. 259–60.

l. 42. *all men date Records.* The most notable new star was that which led the Wise Men to Bethlehem at Christ's nativity, from which event, in the Christian world, records are dated (in years A.D.).

this thy Valentine. This phrase (which troubled the scribe of *JC* and the compiler of *1669*, who have 'this day, Valentine') seems to mean simply 'this thy Valentine's day, the day on which you married'.

ll. 45–50. I follow Grierson in strengthening the stop after 'growe' (l. 46), as in most MSS. The punctuation in *1633* comes from its Group I MS., which resembled *C* 57 and *Lec.* The clause 'Since separation . . . can disunite' clearly belongs to what follows, and explains l. 50.

Robert Gould borrowed from this stanza in stanza ii of his 'Mirrilla and Amynta: A Hymeneal Pindaric Poem . . .', published in his *Works*, 1709; stanza v of the same poem is based on the 'Epithalamion made at Lincoln's Inn'. See *English Epithalamies*, ed. R. H. Case (1896), pp. xlii, 178.

l. 46. *growe.* Grierson rightly rejected the reading 'goe' in *1633*, which was an error in the Group I MS. used by the editor. Both words, 'Meeting' and 'growes' in l. 44 are thus echoed in ll. 45–6 ('meet', 'growe').

l. 52. *his way*: the sacrament of marriage (as distinct from their love for each other and their sexual union).

l. 56. *or.* The reading of *1633* ('O') seems to be an inept emendation by the editor, who did not follow the thought. 'Bishop Valentine has paired them; the Bishop in church has united them; the consummation is their own act' (Grierson).

l. 62. *procession*: four syllables.

l. 67. *masquers*: guests taking part in the wedding-masque, probably that by Thomas Campion, performed on the night of the wedding (*The Lorde's Mask*). M. Novak suggests that ll. 67 ff. of Donne's poem were influenced by the last song in Campion's masque ('The cocks alreadie crow', etc.) (*N. and Q.* cc (1955), pp. 471–2).

  too late. The reading of *1633* and Group I is supported in *JC* and *S 96*. The omission of 'too' in other MSS. seems to have been due to independent sophistication for the sake of the metre.

l. 75. *nicely*: carefully, meticulously.

l. 84. *eve*: the time of preparation for a festival, usually the day before it.

l. 85. *Here lyes a shee Sunne*, etc. The sexes usually assigned to sun and moon are reversed, to emphasize the point; the two interchange their natures (l. 87). Cf. the Somerset 'Epithalamion', ll. 120–5.

l. 86. *the best light to his Spheare.* Like the sun, the main source of light in the heavens, which gives its light to the moon.

l. 94. *acquittances*: '*Acquitance*, is a discharge in writing of a summe of money, or other duitie which ought to be payed or done' (J. Rastell, *The Exposition of . . . Termes of the Lawes*, 1609, f. 11r).

ll. 95–6. *let fall . . . liberall*: lose no opportunity to bestow such joys on each other.

l. 98. *turtles*: turtle-doves, types of conjugal affection and constancy (*O.E.D.*), hence of 'truth' (l. 97). Cf. Tilley, T 624, 'As true as a Turtle to her mate'. *sparrows*: types of sexual vigour, hence of 'courage'.

l. 100. *Nature againe restored is.* It was 'natural' that there should be only one phoenix (that was its essential nature).

l. 104. *Satyres.* Satyrs, half men, half beasts, given to wine and lascivious revelry throughout the night.

ll. 104–5. *will stay Waiting.* It was customary to serenade the bride and groom on the morning after their marriage. Chambers cites Cotgrave's statement that the song sung on these occasions was called the *Hunt's Up*.

l. 105. *let out day.* Day does not break till their eyes open and illumine the earth. Cf. l. 29, and the note to l. 31 above.

l. 108. *at which side*: that is, of the curtained four-poster bed in which they are lying (l. 110).

l. 111. *try'd*: tested, proved.

   after nine. Ten o'clock was the usual hour for the first 'public' appearance of members of the fashionable world; cf. 'Satire IV', l. 175.

l. 112. *enlarge*: extend, prolong.

Epithalamion at the Marriage of the Earl of Somerset (p. 10)

MSS.: Group I (*C 57, D, H 49, Lec, SP*); Group II (*A 18, N, TCC, TCD*); Group III (*Dob* [ll. 1–225], *Lut, O'F, S 96*); *B* (ll. 1–225).
Miscellanies: *A 23, Grey, Hd* (ll. 1–170), *HK 1* (ll. 1–170); U. of Edinburgh Library MS. *Laing iii. 436* (stanza ix only); *Rosenbach 1083/16* (extracts).

I have adapted the general title from Group II and *L 74*. The other MSS. begin with the word 'Eclogue' and have only the sub-title and introductory prose 'setting', except that *HK 1* begins 'Alophanes finding Idios'.

The reading of *1633* has been abandoned (as by Grierson) in ll. 12, 29, 34, 57, 61, 126, 128, 129, and 145; in addition I have rejected a reading in l. 222 and have adopted a different form of the verb in l. 183.

Robert Ker, or Carr, knighted in 1607, created Viscount Rochester in 1611 and Earl of Somerset in 1613, came with James I from Scotland, and was the King's chief favourite and the most powerful nobleman at Court until his disgrace in 1616. He formed a liaison with Frances Howard (daughter of Thomas Howard, Earl of Suffolk), who in 1606 had married the youthful Earl of Essex (later the Parliamentary general). After a long suit, a decree of nullity of this marriage was granted to her, and almost at once she married Rochester, on 26 December 1613. For an account of the affair and its aftermath, see E. Le Comte, *The Notorious Lady Essex* (1969), and for Donne's association with Rochester see Bald, pp. 272–4, 289–94.

Donne had cultivated the favourite, and was willing to assist in defending the divorce of the Countess (though there is no evidence that he did so). On 19 January 1614 he wrote (? to Sir Henry Goodyer):

> some appearances have been here, of some treatise concerning this Nullity, which are said to proceed from *Geneva*, but are beleeved to have been done within doors, by encouragements of some whose names I will not commit to this letter. My poor study having lyen that way, it may prove possible, that my weak assistance may be of use in this matter, in a more serious fashion, then an Epithalamion. This made me therefore abstinent in that kinde; yet by my troth, I think I shall not scape. I deprehend in my self more then an alacrity, a vehemency to do service to that company; and so, I may finde reason to make rime (*Letters*, pp. 180–1; cf. p. 270).

The epithalamion was at length written and sent through Sir Robert Ker, the 'Eclogue' being added in apology for its not having been offered until some weeks after the wedding. Donne's hopes that the poem would have a favourable effect in advancing his claims upon a position at Court are somewhat disingenuously reflected in ll. 99–100, 235. He was by no means the only poet to compose a tribute to the bride and groom; Thomas Middleton presented his *Masque of Cupids*, Jonson wrote his *Challenge at the Tilt* and *Irish Masque*; and other masques were prepared by Thomas Campion and Francis Bacon. Jonson's verses 'To the most Noble and above his Titles Robert, Earle of Somerset, sent to him on his wedding-day' were pasted in Somerset's copy of Jonson's *Works* (1640): see *N. and Q.*, 1st ser. v (1852), 193–4. Chapman composed his unfortunate *Andromeda Liberata* for the occasion.

Grierson convincingly suggested that, in the 'Eclogue', 'Idios' represents Donne himself, 'the private man, who holds no place at Court'; 'Allophanes' (meaning 'with another sound', hence 'sounding like another') is the man 'who seems like another, who bears the same name as he'—that is, Donne's friend, Sir Robert Ker, who was a kinsman and protégé, as well as the namesake, of Somerset, the bridegroom.

In the prose introduction, the last phrase 'his absence thence', though preserved only in C 57, Lec, and 1633 (D and S 96 have 'his absence then'), is clearly right, since Donne missed the wedding celebrations because of illness (*Letters*, pp. 201, 180; Bald, pp. 278–9); cf. l. 39.

l. 5. *that courage*: 'Natures instinct'.

l. 8. *freeze*: frieze, a coarse woollen cloth, with a pun on 'freeze'.

l. 14. *in Lent*: not in this Christmas season.

ll. 15–19. I have punctuated so as to bring out the sense. It is not the sun that brings spring to the Court, but Somerset's loyal zeal and his love for his bride, both springing from the 'light' of the Prince's favour.

ll. 21–2. *that early light*, etc. God created light first ('early') and the sun and moon on the fourth day (Gen. i. 3, 14–19). See note (p. 139) on *The First Anniversary*, l. 202.

l. 24. *Natures*. James I now appears as a sort of Creator; his 'creation' of noblemen bestows on them (by 'favour') more elevated 'natures', as well as names (in the peerage) and wealth. 'God made light first, that his other works might appear' (*Sermons*, ii. 240).

ll. 25–9. Cf. l. 31 of the preceding poem, and note.

l. 27. *prevent*: exceed (*O.E.D.* v. 3. b). The bride's eyes assume some of the Creator's power in producing the firmament of fixed stars.

l. 34. *plotts*: a 'plot' is a piece of ground, 'area' (as in 'The Progress of the Soul', l. 129), hence a 'place' (cf. the reading of *1633*); but also, a 'conspiracy'.
  fire without light. This property of hell, well known from *Paradise Lost*, i. 63 ('No light, but rather darkness visible'), is mentioned by Donne in a passage quoted by Grierson: 'Fool, saies Christ, this night they will fetch away thy soul; . . . he hath no light but lightnings, a sodain flash of horror first, and then he goes into fire without light . . . this dark fire' (*Sermons*, ii. 239–40).

l. 36. *artificiall*: by contrast to the warmth of loyal gratitude engendered by the natural 'light' of the King's favour.
  heat. Cf. 'Obsequies to the Lord Harington', l. 125.

l. 37. *disgest*: part, disperse.

l. 40. *dispos'd*: open, or receptive in attitude, to spiritual truth. Cf. *The Second Anniversary*, l. 154, and note, p. 160.

l. 43. *full*: amply supplied with all he needs.

ll. 44–9. The 'correspondence' between the King in the State and God in the universe emerges in l. 22, and is further developed from l. 40. The argument is that God can enlarge the capacities of men to understand their blessings and know more of His glory as their blessings increase. Idios is able to share in festivities at Court, though absent from it, because the King has a similar power to enlarge his understanding of what it is like to be there.

l. 44. *patterne*. God provides a 'paradigm' or analogy of the King's status, and a 'model' for the exercise of kingly power. Cf. *Sermons*, iv. 240–1, viii. 115–17.

l. 48. *reclus'd*. This is the earliest example of the use of this word given in *O.E.D.*, but Donne had already used it in 'To the Countess of Bedford' ('You have refin'd mee'), l. 17.

ll. 50–2. Man, the microcosm, is an epitome of the universe (the macrocosm); his heart is an epitome of God's book of creatures. Cf. 'O man, which art said to be the Epilogue, and *compendium* of all this world, and the *Hymen* and Matrimoniall knot of Eternal and Mortall things, whom one [Pico della Mirandola] says to be *all Creatures*' (Simpson, *Essays*, p. 30). Cf. 'Obsequies to the Lord Harington', l. 110. For the Book of Creatures see W. Schleiner, *The Imagery of John Donne's Sermons* (Providence, 1970), pp. 94–103.

l. 53. *So is the Country of Courts.* The country is an epitome of Courts.

sweet peace. A reference to James I's peace-making foreign policy. Cf. 'Elegy on Prince Henry', ll. 32–8.

l. 54. *one common soule.* Peace is in the soul of the King which 'animates' all his 'State' (ll. 41–2), country and Court alike.

l. 56. *fantastique:* one given to fancies or wild notions (*O.E.D.* B. 1).

l. 57. *East-Indian.* The word 'East' is dropped from *1633*, but the MSS. are obviously right. Spices came from the East Indies, precious metals from the West.

l. 58. *amber in thy taste.* 'Amber' is ambergris, used in cooking for its scent and flavour. Grierson cites *Paradise Regained,* ii. 344, 'Grisamber-steamed'; and Beaumont and Fletcher, *The Custom of the Country,* iii. 2 (*Works,* ed. A. Glover (1905), i. 334): 'Be sure / The wines be lusty, . . . / And amber'd all.' *O.E.D.* (sb. 1) notes that William Harrison, in his *Description of England,* speaks of the 'induing' of fruits with 'the savour of muske, ambre . . .'.

ll. 61–4. All metals were thought to strive and to alter towards the perfection of gold, provided that their elements were suitably arranged, and they were sufficiently near the surface of the earth to feel the influence of the sun. See note, p. 179, on 'Elegy on the Lady Markham', ll. 23–5, and cf. *Paradise Lost,* iii. 583–6, 606–12, vi. 478–81.

l. 64. *heaven gild it with his eye:* (*a*) the rays of the sun ('eye of heaven' in 'The Progress of the Soul', l. 11) change it to gold; (*b*) the King raises 'well dispos'd' subjects, near enough to the Court, to nobility.

l. 66. *tinctures:* purifying and ennobling forces. The 'tincture' was a spiritual quality in a substance, specifically in gold; through mortification and regeneration, or 'ripening', gold could be refined into a tincture, which had the power to change other metals to itself.

l. 69. *unbeguile:* undeceive.

l. 72. *abroad:* away from home.

to honest actions come: act honestly; and (if 'honest' is taken to mean 'honourable') rise to a place of honour in the performance of state duties.

l. 75. *history:* history book.

l. 76. *affections:* desires, feelings, motives. Contrast 'disaffected'.

l. 77. *and that, that Kings are just:* 'shows that the affections of that King are just', i.e. justly directed upon those he chooses as his confidants (ll. 89–90).

l. 78. *no levity to trust:* neither frivolous nor foolish to trust others.

l. 83. *in him:* in anyone he favours; for example, Somerset. All share in the favour shown to any particular person, since the favours that he, in his turn, can then bestow are directed to virtue to which they all aspire.

l. 84. *pretend*: lay claim, make pretension, aspire.

l. 85. *Thou hast no such*, etc. 'You have no history book that describes such a Court; yet here all the time was a Court like this; and even more, it contained an earnest lover', etc.

l. 86. *earnest lover*: a lover in earnest, a true lover.

wise then, and before: wise in love (where many men are foolish), and before he became a lover. The wisdom that earned him the King's confidence is shown equally in his love and marriage. The compliment reverses the proverb (Tilley, L 558) used by Herrick in 'To Silvia to Wed': 'No man at one time can be wise and love'. Cf. Erasmus, *Adagia* 476 E: 'Amare et sapere vix Deo conceditur'; and, '*sapere et amare*, to be wise and to love, which perchance never met before nor since, are met in this text' (*Sermons*, i. 238).

l. 87. *sued Livery*. 'Land held by feudal tenure lapsed to the lord at the death of a tenant, until it was ascertained if the heir was of age; if so he took possession at once, on payment of a year's profits, known as *primer seisin*; if not, the estate remained in the lord's hands, as his guardian, until he became so, when he could claim *livery*, or *delivery*, *of wardship*, by suing for a writ of *ouster le main* and paying half a year's profits' (Chambers). In Donne's day this law applied specifically to tenants of the King (see J. Cowell, *The Interpreter*, 1607, s.v. 'Liverie', SS 3ʳ).

Cupid is no longer a minor but a grown man, and can now enter and take possession of the heart of a statesman. Love claims its rightful and lasting place in Somerset's breast, which had hitherto held only the confidences of the King.

l. 91. *lost*: by being absent from such a Court.

l. 92. *therefore*: for this reason.

l. 96. *no Grace to say*: no thanks to utter.

l. 97. *I scap'd not*. Cf. 'I think I shall not scape', in the letter quoted in the introductory note above.

l. 101. *dead, and buried*: the social condition of those in the country away from the Court.

Epithalamion. I have added this title from the Group I MSS.; it was presumably in the printer's copy, and was omitted, probably by accident.

l. 107. *five dayes*: referring to the date of the marriage, 26 December.

l. 110. *largest circle*: at the summer solstice, when the sun appears to be at the highest point of its supposed orbit.

l. 111. *The passage of the West or East*: the North-West passage for ships round the north of the American continent, and the presumed passage to the north of Russia to the East Indies.

l. 113. *Promethean*. Prometheus stole fire from Olympus and gave it to man.

After l. 115. Equality of Persons. Rochester was raised to the Earldom of Somerset just before the marriage, so that he would be equal in rank to his bride.

l. 121. *maid*: i.e. if judged for his beauty. The word could, however, hardly fail to recall the fact that the plea for the Countess's divorce from the Earl of Essex was that she forcedly remained a virgin. She was married with her hair hanging 'untrimmed' in curls to her waist—the mark of a virgin bride.

l. 123. *scornes unjust opinion*. The marriage caused considerable scandal, which Donne ascribes to envy (l. 124).

l. 126. *both th'enflaming eyes*. This is the reading of all MSS. except *C 57*, *Lec*, and presumably the printer's Group I manuscript. That the omission of 'both' is an error is shown by the fact that though the metre is disturbed, the contraction mark is retained. The singular 'eye' in *C 57*, *Lec*, and *1633*, to match 'heart', indicates that the meaning was misunderstood. Donne has spoken of the Bride's 'inflaming eyes' in l. 115, and now identifies the lovers completely, so that 'both the eyes of both are lit with the same flame, both their hearts kindled at the same fire' (Grierson); their hearts are one. Cf. ll. 223–5.

l. 127. *divorce*. In the circumstances, a rather daring use of the word.

l. 129. *Yet let*. Though most MSS. omit 'Yet', its presence in *Lut*, *O'F*, and the copy (*A 23*) in Goodyer's hand suggests that the word is not a sophistication. As Grierson says, 'Yet' improves both the sense and the metre. Its similarity to 'let' could lead to the dropping of 'Yet' independently by different scribes.

l. 131. *prevent'st*: anticipatest. Rising before sunrise on the wedding-day seems to have been customary; cf. the preceding epithalamion, l. 29.

l. 133. 'Having confided to the care of the King.'

ll. 134–5. *reinvest Them*: reclothe yourself in them (as in clothes 'laid downe'); i.e. take up your responsibilities again.

l. 135. *forward*: eager (*O.E.D.*, adj. 6).

l. 136. *doth the like impart*: kindles a similar fire in you.

l. 142. *Pouder*. Powdering the hair had only recently become fashionable; brides usually powdered their hair for their wedding-day. Professor A. J. Smith (*John Donne—The Complete English Poems*, 1971) cites Webster, *The White Devil*, v. iii. 117–18: 'Her hair is sprinkled with arras powder, / That makes her look as if she had sinned in the pastry.'

l. 145. *meant for Phoebus, would'st be Phaëton*. She is meant to play the part of the sun, but without some subduing of the radiance of her hair she would scorch those who looked on her. Phaeton, son of Phoebus (Helios) the sun-god, was allowed to drive the chariot of the sun for one day, but drove so recklessly that he scorched the earth and nearly set it on fire.

l. 147. *so quencht*: the fire in your eyes thus quenched.

l. 149. *Thus*: by the powder in her hair (l. 142) and more especially by the tear of joy.
    our infirmitie: in not being able to look straight at the sun without being blinded.

l. 150. *Who can the Sun in water see*: we who can look at the sun reflected in water (as at the bride's eyes 'in' her tears). In *The Republic* 514 ff., Plato suggests that a 'prisoner' taken from the cave eventually, after being able to see reflections in the water, 'would be able to look at the sun and observe its nature, not its appearances in water or on alien material, but the very sun itself in its own place' (trans. A. D. Lindsay). Dryden borrows Donne's image in *Eleanora*, ll. 135–9:

> For how can Mortal Eyes sustain Immortal Light!
> But as the Sun in Water we can bear,
> Yet not the Sun, but his Reflection there,
> So let us view her here, in what she was;
> And take her Image, in this watry Glass.

l. 154. *fruits of wormes and dust*: silk and gold (l. 151).

l. 156. *not so pure, as their spheares*. Plotinus speaks of 'the peculiar excellence of the body constituting the stars, a material so pure, so entirely the noblest' (*Enneads*, II. 1. 4). Though usually thought to be of the same substance, the spheres in which the stars were fixed, and in which they rotated, were purer (less 'mixed') in composition, the crystalline sphere especially so. 'We take a Star to be the thickest, and so the impurest, and ignoblest part of that sphear; and yet, by the illustration of the Sun, it becomes a glorious star' (*Sermons*, iv. 83).

l. 157. *stoope*: might condescend.

ll. 157–9. Though she deigns to show herself to us in a way accommodated to our limited perceptions, her full glory is conveyed through her eyes to form the image of her imprinted on Somerset's heart. Cf. the Elegy, 'His Picture', l. 2.

l. 160. *Easts*. Somerset and his bride are both suns, and each rises in his or her proper quarter to meet at the church.

ll. 162–5. 'Cipres' can mean crepe cloth; or the tree, whose foliage can also be thought of as a veil (l. 164). I have not found any reference to this optical illusion in writers on optics or elsewhere. In *Biathanatos*, p. 154, Donne refers to Pliny's account (*Nat. Hist.* ii. 31) of the sighting of several suns at an angle to the real sun 'either at sunrise or sunset'.

The 'vaile' refers to the limitations of the onlookers' power of vision which cause them to see the bridal couple as two distinct beings.

ll. 166–7.   *The Church Triumphant made this match before,*
                  And now the Militant doth strive no more;

The Church Triumphant is invoked because marriages are 'made by God in heaven' (*Sermons*, iii. 249); the efforts of the Church Militant on earth are no longer needed, because it has completed its work by uniting the couple. There had, however, been 'strife' in the Church on earth in respect of the Countess's nullity suit. In the special Court of Delegates commissioned by the King to consider her petition for divorce, Archbishop Abbot and John King, Bishop of London, with three out of five doctors of law, gave judgement against the divorce, but they were outvoted seven against five by other Bishops and two doctors of law who judged in favour.

l. 171. *payre of Swans*. Swans were emblems of purity, as in Spenser's *Prothalamion*.

interbring: bring to each other. This use of the verb is the only example recorded in *O.E.D.*, s.v. 'inter-'; the word is possibly a coinage of Donne's own. For his fondness for compounds beginning with 'inter-' (e.g. 'inter-inanimates') see Z. R. Sullens, *Neologisms in Donne's English Poems* (Rome, 1964).

l. 172. *never sing*. Swans were thought to sing only once, at the time of their death. Cf. *The First Anniversary*, ll. 407–8.

l. 173. *grounds of*: reasons for; until all their wishes are fulfilled.

ll. 177–8. May there live here till the end of the world heirs from this King to take thanks, heirs from you to give thanks.

l. 179. *Nature and grace doe all, and nothing Art*: 'may this mutual relation owe everything to nature and grace, the goodness of your descendants, the grace of the king, nothing to art, to policy and flattery' (Grierson).

l. 180. *overthwart*: obstruct.

l. 181. *West . . . North*: fading . . . coldness. Cf. 'The Good-Morrow', l. 18: 'Without sharpe North, without declining West'.

l. 182. *over-blest*. The compound word is not recorded in *O.E.D.* The festivities are too lavish, delaying the consummation of the marriage. Cf. the Palatine 'Epithalamion', stanza v.

ll. 186–9. *And were the doctrine new*, etc. The idea that the earth rotated was first proposed by Aristarchus of Samos (and was therefore hardly 'new'), and was revived as part of the theory of Copernicus. The popular objection to the notion was that if the earth 'moved', one would not be able to jump up, and land in the same place—an objection to which Copernicus made a careful reply. Here, as C. M. Coffin suggests, Donne is light-heartedly giving 'the traditional reason why the earth does not move as an explanation of its motion' (*John Donne and the New Philosophy*, New York, 1938, p. 113).

l. 190. *part*: depart.

l. 191. *masks*: for the eyes, as well as the masques (entertainments) in which the guests danced.

l. 192. *Center*: a focus, or still point, i.e., rest, to the unified heart of the couple. The image is of the centre of the planetary system; cf. 'The Sun Rising', l. 30: 'This bed thy center is, these walls, thy sphere.'

l. 200. *point*: of time (*O.E.D.*, sb. 7), rather than of place (point of the compass).

doe not set so: the moon (the bride) would set before the sun (bridegroom). Even if they rose at the same hour that morning, the bride (as was customary) may go to bed first.

ll. 204–5. *As he that sees a starre fall . . . findes a gellie.* The word 'jelly' was 'applied to the alga *Nostoc*, which appears as a jelly-like mass on dry soil after rain, and was popularly supposed to be the remains of a fallen "star" or meteor' (*O.E.D.*, 'jelly', 2. b). I have not found an earlier reference to this piece of folk-lore. Suckling refers to it in 'Farewell to Love', ll. 11–15. Grierson quotes Dryden, Dedication to *The Spanish Friar* ('when I had taken up what I supposed a fallen star, I found I had been cozened with a jelly; nothing but a cold, dull mass, which glittered no longer than it was a-shooting'), and Nathanael Lee's *Oedipus*, II. i, *Dramatick Works* (1734), i. 28 ('The shooting Stars end all in purple Gellies, / And *Chaos* is at Hand').

l. 211. *clothes*: sc. of the soul; 'this muddy vesture of decay' (*The Merchant of Venice*, v. i. 64).

ll. 215–16.   *Now, as in Tullias tombe, one lampe burnt cleare,*
              Unchang'd for fifteene hundred yeare,

There are many references in the sixteenth and seventeenth centuries to the story that during the papacy of Paul III (1534–49) an ancient tomb on the Appian Way had been opened, in which were found the body of a beautiful girl, perfectly preserved, and a lamp still burning. At the touch of the air, the body crumbled to dust, and the lamp was extinguished. The tomb bore the inscription 'Tulliolae filiae meae', and the body was identified as that of Tullia (or Tulliola), the daughter of Cicero (not his sister, as Sir Thomas Browne says in *Vulgar Errors*, iii. 21). 'The belief is supposed to have arisen from the taking fire of pent-up gases at the moment of opening' (Grosart). The story was well known, but Donne would have found it in the work by Guido Panciroli which he certainly read (see notes to 'Elegy on the Lady Markham'), *Rerum Memorabilium* . . . , 1599, in the chapter 'De Oleo Combustibili'; see note to 'The Undertaking' in Gardner, *Elegies etc.*, p. 180.

They had a precious composition for *lamps*, amongst the *ancients*, reserved especially for *Tombes*, which kept light for many hundreds of yeares; we have had *in our age* experience, in some casuall openings of ancient vaults, of finding such lights, as were kindled, (as appeared by their inscriptions) *fifteen* or *sixteen hundred* yeares before; but, as soon as that light comes to our light, it vanishes (*Sermons*, iii. 357).

l. 219. *aspire*: try to rise upwards.

ll. 219-20. *Fire . . . turnes all to fire*. This common idea was attacked by J. C. Scaliger (*Exercitationes . . .* , p. 69).

l. 222. *none of them is fuell, but fire too*. Neither (and no part) of them is fuel to the other's fire; both (and every part) of them is also fire; hence neither can reduce the other to ashes.

l. 223. *bonfire*: a fire lit in celebration of a festive occasion (e.g. a marriage).

l. 230. *of all*: shared by all.

l. 235. *Such Altars*: the King, or Somerset himself, to whom Donne's friend Sir Robert Ker had access.

THE ANNIVERSARIES

The text is based on the first edition of each poem: that of 'To the Praise of the Dead, and the Anatomy', 'An Anatomy of the World', and 'A Funeral Elegy' on the text of *An Anatomy of the World*, 1611; that of *The Second Anniversary* and 'The Harbinger to the Progress' on the edition of 1612. The readings of an errata slip (correcting errors in both *Anniversaries*) found in one surviving copy of *1612* have been adopted. The marginal notes added to both poems in *1612* (which gave the title *The First Anniversary* to 'An Anatomy of the World') are included as very probably added on Donne's instructions. The text given here differs, therefore, considerably from Grierson's, which was based on the text in the *Poems* of 1633. He was also, of course, not aware of the existence of the errata slip, first noted in 1946.

Grierson recognized that *1633* took its text of the *Anniversaries* from the edition of 1625, many of whose errors it corrected. He thought that the fact that its corrections often restored the readings of earlier editions showed that its editor had consulted them, and his high opinion of the authority of *1633* led him to accept its corrections although they conflicted with the readings of the first edition. Proof that the editor of *1633* did not consult earlier editions, that his agreements with them are random and coincidental, and that his independent readings are mere guesses at possible sense, can be seen from the apparatus, which gives a complete collation of all substantive variants in the sequence of editions: *1611, 1612, 1621, 1625, 1633*. It will be seen that where *1633* agrees in its correction of *1625* either with the first editions or with the errata slip the correction is obvious and one that any careful editor would make. Further proof is given, as was pointed out by Manley, by *The Second Anniversary*, l. 96, where the misprint 'pach'd' (*1625*) for 'parch'd' (*1611–1621*) was corrected to 'patch'd'.

The text here agrees substantially with Manley's, which was based on the first editions corrected by the errata slip, the differences being in the treatment of accidentals (see Textual Introduction, pp. lvii–lxi).

For information on the occasion, dates, and publication of the poems, and on Donne's relations with the Drurys and with Joseph Hall (see the General Introduction, pp. xxix–xxxii).

The title 'Anniversaries' is Donne's own. He so describes the poems in a letter to George Garrard (*Letters*, p. 238; also p. 255); and it was presumably on his instructions that in *1612* 'The First Anniversarie' and 'The Second Anniversarie' were placed at the top of the title-pages of 'An Anatomy of the World' and 'Of the Progress of the Soul' respectively, and were used on alternate pages of the respective poems as running-titles. J. C. Scaliger (*Poetices*, 1581, pp. 425–6) describes two sorts of 'epitaph', the 'epitaphium recens' which concerned a recent death, and the 'epitaphium anniversarium' which commemorated a death at yearly intervals; epitaphs of the latter type included all the usual topics of the genre, except expressions of grief ('Nemo enim iam annum bienniumve defunctum deflet'). In ecclesiastical use, the word 'anniversary' was used for the days of annual commemoration of saints or martyrs, and other '*Holy dayes . . . Anniversaries*' (*Sermons*, iv. 368). George Puttenham, however, seems to indicate a greater flexibility in the intervals of writing epitaphs: 'the lamenting of deathes was chiefly at the very burialls of the dead, also at monethes mindes and longer times, by custome continued yearely' (*The Arte of English Poesie*, ed. G. D. Willcock and A. Walker, p. 48). As Manley points out, Claudio in *Much Ado About Nothing*, v. iii. 1–23, hangs an epitaph on the tomb of Hero and concludes: 'Now, unto thy bones good night. / Yearly will I do this rite.'

'A Funeral Elegy' was apparently the poem corresponding to the relatively brief epitaph assumed to be spoken over, or affixed to, the 'tomb' of the dead girl (l. 1); 'An Anatomy of the World', since it contains expressions of grief, can be described as an 'anniversary' only loosely, being rather a more elaborate epitaph, composed in the indefinite period after the girl's death suggested by Puttenham; and only 'The Progress of the Soul' is strictly an 'anniversary', devoid of expressions of grief (cf. l. 66), fulfilling the promise made in *The First Anniversary*, ll. 447–51.

THE FIRST ANNIVERSARIE (p. 20)

An 'anatomy' was the dissection of a corpse (cf. 'Love's Exchange', l. 42, and 'Upon Mr. Thomas Coryate's *Crudities*', l. 54); but it also meant, figuratively, a systematic analysis or satiric exposure (as in Stubbes's *Anatomie of Abuses* and Nashe's *Anatomie of Absurditie*). Cf. 'Solomons Anatomy, and cutting up of the world' (*Sermons*, iii. 51).

To the Praise of the Dead, and the Anatomy

For the attribution of this poem to Joseph Hall, see the General Introduction, pp. xxx–xxxi.

l. 3. *No evill wants his good*: some good comes out of every calamity. Cf. *Henry V*, iv. i. 4: 'There is some soul of goodness in things evil.'

l. 5. *state*: estate (to which the heirs succeed); *O.E.D.* I. I. e.

l. 9. *informe*: be to it as a soul (the 'form' of the body, which gives it life and characteristic quality); *O.E.D.* II. Cf. *The First Anniversary*, 'An Anatomy', l. 36 and note.

l. 14. *relate*: (*a*) tell; (*b*) present, portray as in a painting (l. 18); (*c*) hand down to future generations.

l. 15. *nephews*: descendants (*O.E.D.*, sb. 4).

ll. 25–6. Cf. Ovid, *Amores* I. xv. 39–40 (Manley):

> Pascitur in vivis Livor: post fata quiescit,
> Cum suus ex merito quemque tuetur honor.

ll. 27–30. Cf. Sparrow, *Devotions*, p. 36: 'some *Nations*, (the *Egiptians* in particular) built themselves better *tombs*, then *houses*, because they were to dwell *longer* in them'. Diodorus Siculus, I. 51, contrasts the humble houses of the Egyptians with the zeal they lavished on burials (because the dead spend eternity in Hades). The idea became a commonplace; Manley cites, e.g., L. C. Rhodiginus (*Lectionum Antiquarum libri...*, Lyon, 1560, ii. 506) and Alexander ab Alexandro (*Genialium Dierum libri sex*, Paris, 1539, f. 139), who also says that the Egyptians lived in huts of stone or wattle. Hall probably adds 'clay' (l. 28) as appropriate to the mortal body.

l. 32. *thus*: thus thanked.

l. 38. *the Quire of Saints and Seraphim*. Only a virtuous soul with her degree of 'grace' (l. 34) would rank with the seraphim, the highest order of angels. Aquinas, citing Luke xx. 36 ('they are equal unto the angels'), says that 'by the gift of grace men can merit glory in such a degree as to be equal to the angels, in each of the angelic grades; and this implies that men are taken up into the orders of angels' (*S.T.* Iᵃ pars, q. cviii, art. 8); he quotes St. Augustine, *De Civ. Dei*, xii. 9. Cf. *Sermons*, ii. 342, iv. 184–5, etc.

l. 44. *burden*: (*a*) refrain, repeated chorus; (*b*) wearisome load.

l. 48. *ditty... note*: words... music. *O.E.D.*, 'ditty', sb. 3, cites *As You Like It*, v. iii. 33–4: 'there was no great matter in the ditty, yet the note was very untuneable.'

An Anatomy of the World (p. 22)

l. 1. *rich*: Manley quotes:

Riches is the Metaphor, in which, the Holy Ghost hath delighted to expresse God and Heaven to us; *Despise not the riches of his goodnesse*, sayes the Apostle; And againe, *O the depth of the riches of his wisdome* [Rom. ii. 4; xi. 33]; And so, after, *The unsearchable riches of Christ*; And for the consummation of all, *The riches of his Glory* [Eph. iii. 8, 16]. Gods goodnesse towards us in generall, our Religion in the way, his Grace here, his Glory hereafter, are all represented to us in Riches (*Sermons*, vi. 303–4).

her Heaven: the place prepared for her in heaven (John xiv. 2); the heaven for which she is fitted. Cf. 'An Hymn to the Saints, and to Marquess Hamilton', l. 2, and note (p. 210).

l. 2. *celebrate*: proclaim, honour, extol; and also to remember with solemn rites (*O.E.D.* 3, 4). But 'this is truly to glorifie God in his Saints, to sanctifie our selves in their examples; To celebrate them, is to imitate them' (*Sermons*, x. 190; cited by Manley); and so 'by Deedes praise' virtue (cf. ll. 18, 78).

who know they'have one: who are aware that they have a soul, and responsibilities towards it.

l. 4. *see, and Judge, and follow.* These actions correspond to the three faculties of the rational soul: memory, understanding, and will. Manley cites:

As God, one *God* created us, so wee have a soul, *one soul*, that represents, and is some image of that one God; As the three Persons of the *Trinity* created us, so we have, in our one soul, a *threefold impression* of that image, and, as Saint *Bernard* calls it, *A trinity from the Trinity* [Migne, *P.L.* clxxxiv. 546–7], in those *three faculties* of the soul, the *Understanding*, the *Will*, and the *Memory* (*Sermons*, ii. 72–3; cf. iii. 145, 154, v. 149).

l. 6. *In-mate*: a (temporary) lodger, guest. Cf. the lines of Hadrian translated by Donne in *Ignatius his Conclave* (Healy, p. 5), 'My little wandring sportful Soule, Ghest, and Companion of my body'; 'thou hast a poor guest, an Inmate, a sojourner, within these mudwals, this corrupt body of thine' (*Sermons*, ii. 215; cf. vi. 350); and 'The Anniversary', l. 18.

ll. 7–8. *Queene . . . progresse . . . standing house.* Donne extends the metaphor of the soul as a prince in the body ('The Ecstasy', l. 68; 'The Progress of the Soul', l. 334); a 'progress' is a royal ceremonial journey within the kingdom, a 'standing house' the royal palace or place of permanent residence (as in *Sermons*, ii. 221, vii. 137, viii. 84).

l. 9. *attend*: await.

l. 10. *a part both of the Quire, and Song*: both a singer of praise and part of what is praised in the song. Cf. 'To the Praise of the Dead, and the Anatomy', ll. 35–44.

l. 11. *earth-quake*. Donne here establishes a basic 'conceit' of the poem, developed from the correspondence of the macrocosm to the microcosm (or 'little world' of man; cf. *Sermons*, vii. 272). In the death of Elizabeth Drury the world's body has lost its soul or animating principle; but the severance of soul and body in a man at death corresponds to an earthquake in the macrocosm.

languished: wasted away and died.

l. 12. *in a common Bath of teares it bled*: bathed in tears (of grief shared by all), it bled from its 'wound' (l. 25)—all the more because a bath of tears would be warm.

l. 13. *vitall spirits*. For the spirits in the human blood, see 'Obsequies to the Lord Harington', l. 63, and note (p. 200). 'The vital spirite is conteyned in the harte, and is caried to the partes of the bodye, to cause naturall heate. It is engendred of inspiration, and of exhalation, or outbreathinge of bloode' (De Vigo, *The Most Excellent Workes of Chirurgerye*, 1543, glossary, s.v. 'Vital spirites'). Bleeding would dissipate them, and life would gradually become extinct.

l. 14. *perplexed*: (*a*) complicated, intricate; (*b*) causing perplexity, puzzling. The 'doubt' is whether her death (loss) will be more than repaid by the 'gaine' in our endeavouring to be good, so that we might see her again in heaven.

l. 19. *consumption*: a devitalizing disease that 'consumes' the body. Cf. 'Wastfull consumptions', 'Elegy on Mrs. Bulstrode', l. 28.

l. 20. *it joy'd, it mournd*: rejoiced at the prospect of seeing her in heaven, bewailed her loss (alternately, as in the 'fits' of fever).

l. 21. *Agues physicke are*. Manley cites: 'A Cramp is a violent shrinking of sinewes. . . . If feavers come upon this shrinking, that is best remedie' (*Batman upon Bartholome*, 1582, f. 91); 'in Cramps which are contortions of the Sinewes, or in Tetars, which are rigors and stiffenesses in the Muscles, wee may procure to our selfe a fever to thaw them, or we may procure them in a burning feaver, to condense and attemper our bloud againe' (*Biathanatos*, p. 171). Both Donne and Batman cite Hippocrates, *Aphorisms* (iv. 57).

ll. 23–4. *mistak'st thy selfe to bee Well*. After the wasting of the body and thinning of the blood (the world's first 'grief' at her death), a 'fever' (of alternate joy and mourning) ensued, which the world mistakenly thought to be curative, so that no more 'care' was needed.

l. 24. *in a Letargee*: at the point of death. Cf. 'A Valediction: of my Name in the Window', l. 63: 'Neere death inflicts this lethargie.' The disease was characterized (ll. 28–31) by loss of sense, speech, and memory (even of one's name and identity). So, too, 'There are spirituall Lethargies, that make a man forget his name; forget that he was a Christian, and what belongs to that duty. God knows what forgetfulnesse may possesse thee upon thy death-bed, and freeze thee there' (*Sermons*, v. 386; cf. iii. 56).

l. 30. *speechlesse*: 'as in bodily, so in spirituall diseases, it is a desperate state, to be speechlesse' (*Sermons*, v. 233).

l. 31. *hast forgot thy name*. Cf. 'thy last sickness, which may be a Lethargy in which thou mayest forget thine own name' (*Sermons*, ii. 239).

ll. 31–2. The world has lost its identity in losing her; in surviving her it has lasted beyond ('o'repast') its own death. Manley cites: 'Thou pursuest the works of the flesh, and hast none . . . ; Dissolution and putrefaction is gone over thee alive; Thou hast over liv'd thine own death, and art become thine own ghost, and thine own hell' (*Sermons*, ii. 83).

l. 35. *unnam'd*. The world would not then have had any identity, for 'names are to instruct us, and express natures and essences. This *Adam* was able to do' (Simpson, *Essays*, p. 23); 'All creatures were brought to *Adam*, and, because he understood the natures of all those creatures, he gave them names accordingly' (*Sermons*, ix. 256); 'with the result that their natures were apprehended as soon as their names were uttered' (Philo Judaeus, *De Opificio*, lii; Loeb ed. of his *Works*, i. 119). The power of the name is especially associated in folk beliefs with baptism (ll. 33–5). In this case it was 'her name' that defined the world's nature (l. 37); her name is the world's name (l. 38) forgotten in the present 'lethargy'; and the poet's 'celebration' will thus to some degree revive the world's memory of its name, and hence of its nature and living identity.

l. 36. *Palace*. A variation of the traditional idea of the soul as a prince ('Queene', l. 7) in the prison of the body (from Plato, *Phaedo* 82). She performed as a 'world-soul' the functions of the soul in the microcosm of man. The soul is the 'forme' of the body (Aristotle, *De Anima* 414ª4–19; Aquinas, *S.T.* Iª pars. q. lxxvi, art. 1; q. cx, art. 1), giving it cohesion and individuality ('frame') as well as life (l. 37); cf. *Sermons*, vii. 108–9.

ll. 39–42. She has been dead some months but, she being dead, all reckoning of times is over; nevertheless she has been a long time away and yet nobody offers to tell us what it is we have lost.

l. 40. *determined*: ended, ceased (*O.E.D.*, ppl.a.1).

l. 47. *thaw*: melting, loosening, 'disintegration'.

l. 48. *example*: precedent (*O.E.D.* 5), as well as pattern. In interpreting a law, the appeal to precedents can influence the judgement as powerfully as the law itself.

l. 49. *faithfully compact*: securely hold together.

l. 50. *resolv'd*: dissolved.

l. 51. *some*: to some extent.

l. 56. *putrified*. Cf. ll. 436–42.

l. 57. *Thy' ntrinsique Balme*. Cf. notes (pp. 183, 200) to 'Elegy on Mrs. Bulstrode', l. 10, and 'Obsequies to the Lord Harington', l. 101. 'Something that hath some proportion and analogy to this Balsamum of the body, there is in the soule of man too: The soule hath *Nardum suam*, her Spikenard . . . , a naturall disposition to Morall goodnesse' (*Sermons*, v. 348; cf. vii. 108–9). The hyperbole here seems to be that the world's life can 'never be renew'd' because there is no vitalizing quality 'like' hers.

l. 59. *trie*: attempt to work out, test.

l. 64. *discovered*: uncovered, revealed.

l. 68. *inanimate*: act as a soul (*anima*) to. The earliest use of the verb recorded in *O.E.D.* is in *Pseudo-Martyr*, p. 172.

l. 73. *shut in all day*: enclosed all light, away from our eyes. She is a sun now set, but our memory of her is the twilight (l. 74).

ll. 75–7. The sun was thought to have the power to breed new life out of carcasses and of mud. The commonplace begins in Aristotle, *Physics* 194^{b}14; cf. *Hamlet*, II. ii. 180–1.

l. 75. *carcasse*. Cf. 'A Fever', ll. 9–10: 'if, when thou, the worlds soule, goest, It stay, 'tis but thy carkasse then'.

free. The 'new creatures' are free from the corruption of the carcass out of which they were bred.

l. 76. *a new world*. Identified in ll. 82–4 as 'A paradise within thee' (*Paradise Lost*, xii. 587). Manley cites: 'that man, who hath taken hold of God, . . . is no field, but a garden, a Garden of Gods planting, a Paradise in which grow all things good to eate, and good to see, (spirituall refection, and spirituall recreation too) and all things good to cure' (*Sermons*, ix. 51–2).

ll. 77–8. The 'forme', not the 'matter', gives things their 'nature' and identity (Aristotle, *Physics* 193). Her virtue is unrealized unless we practise it in our lives.

l. 79. *thus Elemented*: composed of such materials.

l. 81. *assum'd*: taken up (chosen, elevated).

ll. 82–4. It was a problem whether in Eden there were useless or harmful plants, and poisonous snakes. Most commentators thought that all the plants were useful and that no plant or animal in Eden was harmful until after the Fall; agreeing with Basil, *De Paradiso*, iii. 7 (Migne, *P.G.* xxx. 67). The 'forraine Serpent' is Satan, who tempted man to 'poison' his soul by sin; cf. 'Elegy on the Lady Markham', ll. 13–14, and note, p. 178. Cf.:

the earth itself feels its curse. In the first place, it does not bring forth the good things it would have produced if man had not fallen. In the second place, it produces many harmful plants, which it would not have produced, such as darnel, wild oats, weeds, nettles, thorns, thistles [Gen. iii. 18]. Add to these the poisons, the injurious vermin, and whatever else there is of this kind. All these were brought in through sin (Luther, *Lectures on Genesis*, trans. G. V. Schick; *Works*, St. Louis, 1958, ed. J. Pelikan, i. 204).

l. 82. *weedlesse*. This is the earliest example of the use of the word in *O.E.D.*

l. 84. *forraine*: coming from outside; and with a nature 'foreign' to the bliss of Eden.

l. 85. *outward stormes the strongest breake*. This has the air of a common saying, but I have not found it elsewhere. The meaning seems to be that troubles from outside burst upon us with greater force than troubles arising from within us ('home-borne', l. 80).

l. 89. *due temper*: balanced judgement, proper discretion.

ll. 91 ff. The ideas in the following lines are founded upon traditional common-places concerning the decay of the world. The ancient ideas of the decline from the golden age (from Hesiod) and the decline of the world (e.g. Lucretius, *De Rerum Natura*, ii. 1105 ff.) were first developed at length in Christian terms, and attributed to man's sin, by St. Cyprian (Migne, *P.L.* iv. 561-4, 623) in what Donne calls 'a contemplation that the whole frame of the world' is 'decayed and languished' (*Biathanatos*, p. 215); in this poem Donne touches on many of the points which Cyprian makes. Later Fathers repeated and elaborated upon Cyprian's statements, and in the forty years before *The First Anniversary* the subject was often treated by English writers; e.g. by Henry Cuffe in *The Differences of the Ages of Mans Life* (1607), of which Donne owned a copy (Keynes, L 56), and which I sometimes cite below. Notable later examples will be found in Raleigh's *History of the World*, 1614 (Preface, and I. v. 5), and Godfrey Goodman's *The Fall of Man* (1616). The conventional arguments for the decay of the world, however, came under attack, and a good account of the ensuing controversy is given by V. Harris, *All Coherence Gone* (Chicago, 1949). See also M. Macklem, *An Anatomy of the World* (Minnesota, 1958), and Lewalski, pp. 185-8, 229-31. Citing Cyprian, Donne says:

As the world is the whole frame of the world, God hath put into it a reproofe, a rebuke, lest it should seem eternall, which is, a sensible decay and age in the whole frame of the world, and every piece thereof. The seasons of the yeare irregular and distempered; the Sun fainter, and languishing; men lesse in stature, and shorter-lived. No addition, but only every yeare, new sorts, new species of wormes, and flies, and sicknesses, which argue more and more putrefaction of which they are engendred (*Sermons*, vi. 323).

l. 91. *There is no health*. Cf. Ps. xxxviii. 3: 'There is no soundness in my flesh' ('Non est sanitas in carne mea' *V.*). Preaching on the text, Donne says: 'God created man in health, but health continued but a *few hours*, and sicknesse hath had the Dominion 6000 years. . . . And no sicknesse can be worse, then that which is intended here, for it is all over, *Non sanitas, no soundnesse*, no health in any part' (*Sermons*, ii. 79–80; cited by Manley); cf. *Letters*, p. 30.

l. 92. *neutralitee*: 'the Physicians Rule, that the best state of Mans body is but a *Neutrality*, neither well nor ill, but *Nulla sanitas*, a state of true and exquisit health, say they, no man hath [l. 94]' (*Sermons*, ii. 80; cf. v. 352). The idea is documented by D. C. Allen, 'John Donne's Knowledge of Renaissance Medicine', *J.E.G.P.* xlii, 1943, p. 327.

ll. 95–8. Manley cites:

What miserable revolutions and changes, what downfals, what break-necks, and precipitations may we justly think our selves ordained to, if we consider, that in our comming into this world out of our mothers womb, we doe not make account that a childe comes right, except it come with the head forward, and thereby prefigure that headlong falling into calamities which it must suffer after? (*Sermons*, vi. 333; cf. v. 171).

That a child is normally born head foremost is stated by Fernelius, *Universa Medicina* (Hanover, 1610, p. 174), and implied by Nashe, who says that those named 'Agrippae', like Marcus Agrippa, are so called 'beeing preposterously borne with their feete forward' (*Anatomie of Absurditie*, *Works*, ed. R. B. McKerrow, i. 36–7).

ruinous . . . precipitation. 'Ruinous' has its root meaning, 'rushing headlong forward'. Similarly, 'precipitation' (from *praeceps*, *prae* + *caput*) includes the sense 'head-first'.

l. 99. *witty*: cunning.

l. 102. *reliefe . . . languishment.* Eve, created as a 'help meet for' Adam ('ei adjutorium', Gen. ii. 18 *V*), became the cause of man's 'languishing' (susceptibility to death) because she brought about original sin. Cf. 'lest otherwise she prove *in Ruinam*, who was given *in Adjutorium*' (*Sermons*, ii. 345).

l. 103. *were to*: created for.

l. 104. *accessory . . . principall.* They are still helpers, but only helpers, in good purposes; in evil they are principals. Donne is using a distinction made in Common Law: 'Accessory: . . . most commonly and notoriously . . . signifieth a man that is guiltie of a fellonious offence, not principally, but by participation: as by commandement, advice, or concealement' (John Cowell, *The Interpreter*, 1607; cited by Manley).

ll. 105–7. Cf. 'The Progress of the Soul', ll. 91–4:

> Man all at once was there by woman slaine,
> And one by one we'are here slaine o'er againe
> By them. The mother poison'd the well-head,
> The daughters here corrupt us . . .

The orthodox doctrine of the Church was that Adam's sin brought about the Fall (Rom. v. 12; 1 Cor. xv. 21–2; cf. *Sermons*, iv. 148); but here Donne's authority is Ecclesiasticus xxv. 24: 'Of the woman came the beginning of sin, and through her we all die.'

l. 109. *profusely*: wastefully (Lat. *profundere*, 'pour out, squander'); the first use of the word recorded in *O.E.D.* is Burton's in 1621.

l. 110. *We kill our selves, to propagate*. The idea that the act of coition devitalizes by expending 'radical moisture' derives from Aristotle, *De Longitudine et Brevitate Vitae* 466ᵇ. Cf. 'Farewell to Love', ll. 24-5.

l. 111. *doe not that*. We in fact produce offspring who are less than men.

l. 114. *Joynt tenants*. 'Jointenants be where two men come to any lands and tenements by one joint title' (J. Rastell, *An Exposition of . . . Termes of the Lawes*, 1609, f. 120). Neither the sun nor man could have sole ownership of the world till the other died; hence the apparent striving to 'survive' longer. Cf. l. 26.

l. 115. *Stag, and Raven, and the long-liv'd tree*. Cf. 'the naturall man hath life more abundantly [in Gen. ii. 7] then any other creature, (howsoever Oakes, and Crowes, and Harts may bee said to out-live him) because he hath a life after this life' (*Sermons*, ix. 149). Pliny says that Hesiod (in a work now lost) 'fictitiously, as I think, assigns nine of our lifetimes to the crow, four times a crow's life to stags, three times a stag's to ravens, and for the rest in a more fictitious style in the case of the phoenix and the nymphs' (*Nat. Hist.* vii. 48, Loeb ed. ii. 609; cited by Cuffe, p. 87). Similarly Ausonius, *Eclogue V*, 1-8 (Loeb ed. i. 173-4), who adds the tree ('Nymphae Hamadryades quarum longissima vita est'). Manley cites Jean Bodin's opinion that the tree was a palm; others agreed with Donne that it was an oak.

l. 116. *minoritee*: youth.

ll. 118-20. Donne is using a commonplace; as does Cuffe (pp. 88-9), who refers to the ancient source in Josephus:

Again, alike for their merits and to promote the utility of their discoveries in astronomy and geometry, God would accord [the first men] a longer life; for they could have predicted nothing with certainty had they not lived for 600 years, that being the complete period of the great year (*Antiquities*, I. iii. 9; Loeb ed. iv. 51).

l. 120. *observation plaine*. 'Observation' (*O.E.D.* 6), the taking of the altitude of a heavenly body. 'Plaine' = fully.

l. 122. *Mans grouth confes'd, and recompenc'd the meat*: man's physical stature bore witness to the quality of the food, and increased by as much as he ate of it. The general belief was that the food of the Patriarchs was better than that available in later ages (this point is made by Josephus, *Antiquities*, I. iii. 9); partly because of the curse on the land in Gen. iii. 17-18, and partly because of the effects of the Flood upon the soil. So Raleigh, *History of the World*, I. v. 5; Cuffe (p. 88); *Sermons*, vii. 145.

ll. 125–6. The fact that man, of all the creatures, alone walks fully upright was an ancient commonplace of speculation, from Plato, *Timaeus* 90ᵃ. Cf. Cicero, *De Legibus* I. ix. 26 ('solum hominem erexit ad caeli quasi cognationis domiciliique pristini conspectum excitavit'); St. Augustine, Migne, *P.L.* xlii. 999 ('ad caelestia naturaliter erectum est'); and the problem attributed to Aristotle, answered in part by the opinion that man alone has his face lifted towards heaven because he 'is ordayned unto the kingdome of Heaven, and . . . because that despising worldly and earthly things, he ought to contemplate on heavenly things' (*The Problemes of Aristotle*, Edinburgh, 1595, A4ʳ). Cf. *Paradise Lost*, vii. 506–16, and:

Wee attribute but one priviledge and advantage to Mans body, above other moving creatures, that he is not as others, groveling, but of an erect, of an upright form, naturally built, and disposed to the contemplation of *Heaven*. Indeed it is a thankfull forme, and recompences that *soule*, which gives it, with carrying that soule so many foot higher, towards *heaven* (Sparrow, *Devotions*, p. 10, cited by Manley; cf. Simpson, *Essays*, p. 30; *Sermons*, iii. 105, vii. 243).

l. 128. *Methusalem.* Methuselah lived 969 years (Gen. v. 27).

l. 130. *new made.* The reading of *1611*, re-established against 'true' (in *1612*) by the errata slip in at least some copies of *1612*, is clearly right. There would be no need to test a clock made 'true'; a 'new' clock might (as Grierson suggested, defending 'true', *T.L.S.*, 20 July 1946) show its defects early, but this is Donne's point—modern men would not even live long enough to find out how accurate it was.

l. 134. *three lives.* The deluded peasant strives to secure a lease 'for three lives', sharing the popular misconception that this will give him security of tenure for three generations (or perhaps ninety-nine years). But a 'lease for three lives' (*O.E.D.*, 'life', sb. II. 8. b) was made to three persons, to remain in force during the life of the longest liver of the three; hence the peasant's expectation in fact dwindles to one miserable (modern) lifetime.

l. 141. *so equall to him.* Early Christian commentators on the Bible were much interested in the giants mentioned in Gen. vi. 4; Deut. ii. 11, 20; 1 Sam. xvii. 4 (Goliath); and Judith xvi. 7. Large bones found in excavations had already suggested to the ancients (e.g. Pliny, *Nat. Hist.* vii. 16; Aulus Gellius, *Noct. Att.* iii. 10) that the physical stature of men had continually diminished. Further evidence was discovered in the Christian era (cf. St. Augustine, *De Civ. Dei*, xv. 9), and the topic became a regular part of discussions of the decay of the earth. There is a full account of later evidence for the decline in the size of men in *Variarum Lectionum, seu Miscellaneorum Libri IIII* (Venice, 1564, ff. 13–28) by Hieronymus Magius (whom Donne names in *Devotions*, p. 91). See D. C. Allen, 'Donne among the Giants', *M.L.N.* lxi (1946).

ll. 142–3. 'Naturall men will write of lands of Pygmies, and of lands of

Giants; . . . But yet advisedly they do not beleeve, (at least confidently they do not know) that there are such Giants, or such Pygmies . . . in the world' (*Sermons*, ix. 100–1, cited by Manley). Most opinions followed Strabo's (XVII. ii. 1), that accounts of pygmies were fables.

ll. 145–6. *Onely death addes t'our length*, etc. The anonymous annotator of the 1621 edition of the *Anniversaries* in the Bodleian Library (Tanner 876) glosses the line: 'For ye same Person (wn *layd out*) seems longer, than alive on his legs he did.'

l. 147. *were light*: would be of little moment.

ll. 148–9. *chang'd to gold Their silver*. As Manley notes, a metaphor from alchemy (gold was also denser than silver); and also a reference to the ages of the world (the Patriarchs lived in the silver age, Adam in the golden).

ll. 149–50. *dispos'd into lesse glas, Spirits*: by distilling or subliming a substance, reducing its bulk so that it could be contained in a smaller vessel, but retaining its 'spirit' or essential quality.

l. 150. *vertue*: potency, the excelling qualities of our fathers; also, goodness.

l. 151. *w'are not retir'd, but dampt*. Grosart is right, I think, in taking 'retir'd' as meaning 'contracted, shrunk' (*O.E.D.*, ppl. a. 5. b), and suggesting that Donne has in mind a worm or snail that can 'retire' itself into an apparently smaller bulk without losing its nature or quality. 'Dampt' usually means 'stifled, stupefied, deadened'. The earliest example in *O.E.D.* ('damp', vb. 5) of the sense 'moisten, wet' is dated 1671; but Grosart may be correct in thinking that the sense is defined by l. 153: modern men are shrunken like damp wool, the threads cramped and distorted; Donne opposes this to the genuine high quality of cloth closely woven from the start.

l. 154. *bedwarfed*. This is the earliest example of the use of the word given in *O.E.D.*

l. 156. *Of nothing he made us*. Cf. Aquinas, *S.T.* Ia pars, q. xlv, art. 1, 2. 'Creatio est constitutio substantiae ex nihilo. E nihilo, inquam, ut est terminus, non ut est materia' (J. C. Scaliger, *Exercitationes* . . . , p. 39).

Men are 'the Children of *Adam*, the child of durt, the child of Nothing. Yea, our souls, which we magnify so much, . . . is a veryer upstart then our body, being but of the first head, and immediately made of Nothing: . . . it is impossible that any man should wish himself Nothing: . . . Nothing was not a pre-existent matter, nor mother of this All, but onely a limitation when any thing began to be' (Simpson, *Essays*, pp. 30–1).

l. 158. *so soone as hee*: in as short a time as God in the creation.

ll. 159–60. Influenza, which soon became known as the 'new disease', reached England in epidemic proportions in 1612; Donne probably suffered from it himself while in Paris, a few months after writing this poem (Bald, p. 250). The most dreaded of the new diseases, however, was syphilis, which overran

Europe in the fifteenth century. It was the subject of a book of which Donne owned a copy (Keynes, L 157), G. Rondelet's *Le traicté de Verole* (Bordeaux, 1576), which begins: 'Tous ceux qui ont tracte la verole confessent qu c'est une nouvelle maladie' (p. 3). The 'warre' men wage with themselves applies to a disease that spread by deliberate indulgence in sexual licence. The 'new phisicke' (a more destructive weapon) is that of Paracelsus, who, in *Ignatius his Conclave* (Healy, p. 21), is made to say that he brought all orthodox medicine into such contempt 'that that kind of phisick is almost lost; This also was ever my principal purpose, that no certaine new Art, nor fixed rules might be established, but that al remedies might be dangerously drawne from my uncertaine, ragged, and unperfect experiments, in triall whereof, how many men have beene made carkases?'; he lived, he continues, in 'those times which did abound with paradoxicall, & unusuall diseases, of all which, the pox, which then began to rage, was almost the center and sinke.' In *Biathanatos*, as Manley shows, Donne collects scattered remarks of Paracelsus (and in this poem turns them against him):

as *Paracelsus* says, of that foule contagious disease [syphilis] which then had invaded mankind in a few places, and since overflown in all, that for punishment of generall licentiousnes, God first inflicted that disease, and when the disease would not reduce us, he sent a second worse affliction, which was ignorant, and torturing Physitians (p. 215).

l. 161. *Vice-Emperor*. Man became God's deputy on earth when he was given 'dominion' over the creatures (Gen. i. 26, 28).

ll. 162-6. Cf. 'The properties, the qualities of every Creature, are in man; the Essence, the Existence of every Creature is for man; so man is every Creature' (*Sermons*, iv. 104); see note (p. 119) to ll. 50-2 of the Somerset 'Epithalamion'.

l. 172. *allow*: even if one could give.

ll. 173-4. *depart With*: part with, lose.

ll. 175-6. Most abstract nouns in Greek and Latin, including the names of virtues, are of the feminine gender.

l. 178. *Allay*: alloy.

l. 180. *poysonous tincture*. Cf. 'The poysonous tincture of Originall sinne' ('To Sir Edward Herbert, at Juliers', l. 20). In alchemy the 'tincture' was wholly beneficial as the purifying spiritual principle in a substance, or as medicine. Donne's use of the term is paradoxical. Cf. *The Second Anniversary*, ll. 163-8, 258, and the Somerset 'Epithalamion', l. 66.

the stayne of Eve. Cf. ll. 105-7, and note. 'Stayne' plays on a related meaning of 'tincture': dye or colouring.

ll. 187-8. *feed ... on ... Religion*. Manley cites:

Now, as the end of all bodily eating, is Assimilation, that after all other concoctions, that meat may be made *Idem corpus*, the same body that I am; so the end of all spirituall eating, is Assimilation too, That after all Hearing, and all Receiving, I may be made *Idem spiritus cum Domino*, the same spirit, that my God is' (*Sermons*, vi. 223; cf. vii. 280–1).

l. 187. *feed (not banquet)*: make it your daily sustenance, not an occasional indulgence.

l. 190. *Be more then man*. Cf. Samuel Daniel, 'To the Countess of Cumberland': 'unlesse above himselfe he can / Erect himselfe, how poore a thing is man' (*Poems and a Defence of Rhyme*, ed. A. C. Sprague (1950), p. 114). The thought is from Seneca, *Quaestiones Naturales*, i, preface. Donne had in his library a copy of J. Wilde's edition of *Augustanus. De Formica*, 1615 (Keynes, L 192).

ll. 192–6. *almost created lame*, etc. The book of Genesis does not mention the creation of the angels; they were, however, created before the world, and the rebellious angels must have fallen at once (Aquinas, *S.T.* Iᵃ pars, q. lxiii, art. 6). The gloss on Gen. i. 3, 'Let there be light', states that this creative act included the angels (from St. Augustine, Migne, *P.L.* xxxiv. 269). The sin (lameness) of disobedience therefore followed very closely on the first act of creation, and 'almost' coincided with it. See note to *The Second Anniversary*, l. 446 (pp. 173–4), and cf.:

We know that light is Gods eldest childe, his first borne of all Creatures; and it is ordinarily received, that the Angels are twins with the light, made then when light was made. And then the first act, that these Angels that fell, did, was an act of Pride. . . . So early, so primary a sin is Pride, as that it was the first act of the first of Creatures (*Sermons*, ii. 294; cited by Manley).

l. 194. *the best*. Cf. 'To Sir Henry Wotton' ('Sir, more then kisses'), ll. 39–40: 'For in best understandings, sinne beganne, / Angels sinn'd first'. Cf. *Sermons*, ii. 170, viii. 126, ix. 372–6.

l. 197. *And turn'd her braines*. Angels are purely intellectual beings; 'Est vero dogma fidei, saltem in eo sensu angelos esse, quod in rerum natura sunt substantiae quaedam intellectuales creatae nobilitate excedentes humanam naturam' (L. Molina, *Comment. in Primam Divi Thomae Partem*, 1592, ii, col. 1572). Donne regards them as the world's brains, unbalanced by their fall.

l. 200. *curst in the curse of man*. Cf. the curse in Gen. iii. 14, 17–18; and *Paradise Lost*, x. 707–15.

l. 202. *That evening was beginning of the day*. Biblical commentators found great difficulty in interpreting Gen. i. 5, 'And the evening and the morning were the first day', the sun and moon not having yet been created. Pererius (*Comment. et Disput. in Genesim*, 1601, pp. 33–7) assembles, without resolving, the differing opinions. Manley cites the Pseudo-Bede and others who identified the first evening as the darkness of man's sin. Donne, following Aquinas (*S.T.* Iᵃ pars, q. lxiii, art. 5), identifies the darkness with the sin of the angels, whose immediate fall produced an evening almost as soon as light itself ('day') came into being.

l. 203. *now the Springs and Sommers.* The deterioration of the seasons after the Fall is a complaint as old as St. Cyprian. Cf. 'we playnlie perceyve al things dayly to waxe woorse and woorse, and decrease in their vertue. The aire is oftentimes corrupt, sometime with untimely showres, sometime with unprofitable drinesse, now with too much cold, now with extreame heate. The fruitfulnes of the feilde is not such as it hath been aforetime' (Shelton a Geveren, *Of the Ende of this Worlde*, trans. T. Rogers, 1577, f. 7ᵛ).

l. 204. *sonnes of women after fifty.* Pliny says that a woman does not bear children after the age of fifty (*Nat. Hist.* vii. 14).

l. 205. *Philosophy*: natural philosophy. Burton's 'Digression of Air', *Anatomy*, part. 2, sect. 2, mem. 3, gives a lively account of the modern 'doubt'.

l. 206. *The Element of fire is quite put out.* It was believed from ancient times that beneath the moon there were four spheres of the elements earth, water, air, and 'The element of the fire which is next to the Spheare of the Moone' (*M. Blundevile his Exercises*, 1597, ff. 138, 182; so Pererius, p. 26; J. C. Scaliger, *Exercitationes* . . . , p. 49). The notion of an elemental region of fire was attacked by Jerome Cardan (*De Subtilitate*, 1560, pp. 30, 64). Donne refers to one of his arguments (itself suggested by Aristotle's account of the four elements, *Meteor.* 382ª): 'Against the popular opinion of the Spheare, or Element of Fire, some new Philosophers have made this an argument, that it is improbable, and impertinent, to admit an Element that produceth no Creatures' (*Sermons*, vii. 184; cf. ix. 230–1; both passages cited by Manley). Kepler, building on the work of Tycho Brahe, had disproved the existence of the sphere of fire by noting the absence of refraction of stellar light. See C. M. Coffin, *John Donne and the New Philosophy* (N.Y., 1938), pp. 166–74, and cf. *The Second Anniversary*, ll. 193–4.

l. 207. *The Sunne is lost, and th'earth.* Donne refers to the controversy aroused by the theories of Copernicus, Tycho Brahe, Kepler, etc., about the relative roles of the sun and the earth in the movements of the universe in space. Cf. *Ignatius his Conclave* (Healy, pp. 13–15); 'To the Countess of Bedford' ('T'have written then'), ll. 37–8; and *Sermons*, vi. 265, vii. 271.

l. 209. *this world's spent.* John Dove is typical of the general chorus: the world 'is not onely in the staggering and declining age, but, which exceedeth dotage, at the very upshot, and like a sicke man which lyeth at deaths doore, ready to breath out the laste ghaspe' (*Sermon . . . at Pauls Crosse the 3 of November*, 1594, f. A3ʳ).

l. 211. *new.* Recent discoveries of astronomers, and especially of Galileo with the aid of the telescope, revived ancient speculations concerning a '*pluralitie of worlds*' (Sparrow, *Devotions*, p. 23) inhabited, it might be, by beings like man. Burton (*Anatomy*, ii. 54–6) names many of those who, in their respective ages, supported the notion. In the previous two centuries Nicholas de Cusa,

Giordano Bruno, and Campanella were the chief advocates of the theory; Kepler and Tycho Brahe gave limited approval to it. Cf. *Sermons*, iii. 225, ix. 47, and see M. H. Nicolson, *Science and Imagination* (Ithaca, N.Y., 1956), pp. 53–6, 103–5.

Donne satirically attributes the astronomers' zeal to discover new worlds to their recognition that this one is nearing its end. Only Galileo had discovered new 'Planets' (l. 210)—the moons of Jupiter; Kepler thought that there were probably other planets to be discovered. See C. M. Coffin, *John Donne and the New Philosophy*, pp. 132–4.

l. 212. *crumbled out againe t'his Atomis*. The analogy with the microcosm continues. Paracelsus says that man's death leads to his dissolution, and the 'first seeds' (or 'first matter') are separated out from him (*Hermetic and Alchemical Writings*, trans. A. E. Waite (1894), i. 161–2). Similarly, the world is disintegrating into the original chaos ('againe'), separating out into the minimal particles of matter (called by Epicurus 'atoms'), which elsewhere remind Donne of grains of sand.

ll. 212–18. Cf. 'To the Countess of Salisbury', ll. 9–21, which reads in part:

> All the worlds frame being crumbled into sand,
> Where every man thinks by himselfe to stand,
> Integritie, friendship, and confidence,
> (Ciments of greatnes) being vapor'd hence,
> And narrow man being fill'd with little shares . . .

l. 217. *a Phoenix*. Only one existed at a time. To be unique is to be unrelated to any order.

l. 220. *reunion*. The first use of the word recorded in *O.E.D.* 1 is that in *Pseudo-Martyr*, p. 23.

l. 221. *Magnetique force*. As C. M. Coffin pointed out (*John Donne and the New Philosophy*, pp. 84–7), the reference here is to William Gilbert's *De Magnete*, which Donne cites in *Essays in Divinity* (Simpson, p. 34). Gilbert proved that the earth was a magnet, having a 'vigour' or power (which he calls 'coition') 'innate and diffused through all her inward parts', 'that concord without which the universe would go to pieces, that analogy, namely, of the perfect and homogeneous spheres of the universe to the whole, and a mutual concurrence of the principal forces in them tending to soundness, continuity, position, direction and to unity' (Gilbert Club translation, 1900, pp. 212, 67–8). He also calls this force a 'form'; Donne takes it that 'She' was the 'form' or soul of the world (cf. note to l. 36). 'Magnetic' is not recorded in *O.E.D.* before 1621.

l. 224. *every sort of men*: not only mariners.

l. 225. *voyage in this worlds Sea*. Cf. 'A Funeral Elegy, to L. C.', l. 14, 'rigg'd a soule for heavens discoverie'. On Donne's use of the image, see E. M. Simpson, 'Two Notes on Donne' (ii. 'Donne the Seafarer'), *R.E.S.*, N.S.

xvi (1965), and D. C. Allen, 'Donne and the Ship Metaphor', *M.L.N.* lxxvi (1961).

l. 226. *compasse.* The image develops from that of 'Magnetique force' (l. 221). The inventions of the magnetic compass, of gunpowder and printing, were usually thought to be the only sound contributions to man's knowledge since the time of the Ancients. The main recent study of this question had been Guido Panciroli's *Nova Reperta,* mentioned by Donne in *The Courtier's Library,* Item 17, and Healy, *Ignatius his Conclave,* p. 65; see note to 'Elegy on the Lady Markham', ll. 20–1 (pp. 178–9).

l. 229. *Steward to Fate.* She dispensed faithfully to the world, as God's servant, what God had willed. Cf. 'A Funeral Elegy', ll. 91–6.

l. 230. *Guilt:* gilded (cf. 'gold', l. 233).

the West Indies, . . . the East. Cf. 'Eastward . . . the land of Perfumes and Spices; . . . Westward . . . the land of Gold, and of Mynes' (*Tobie Mathew Collection,* p. 305). She gave their essential quality to both.

l. 234. *single money:* small change. Manley cites: 'Hath [God] changed his blessings unto me into single mony? Hath he made me rich by half pence and farthings . . .?' (*Sermons,* iii. 345).

ll. 240–6. Donne is describing the third stage of 'Hectique fever' (*febris hectica*). Fernelius, *Universa Medicina* (1577; ed. of 1610, p. 260) says: 'Tertius hecticae gradus est, quum absumpta carnosa substantia, calor ille febrilis et immanis primigenium humidum manifeste depopulatur.' This apparently authoritative description is quoted by Forestus, *Observationes et Curationes Medicinales* (Frankfurt, 1602, p. 109a). Cf. *Batman upon Bartholome,* 1582, ff. 98b–99b; *Sermons,* iii. 365. In the third stage the patient was beyond help.

l. 247. *subtilst:* most attenuated and refined. Donne is probably thinking of the 'spirits' in the blood, dried out by fever (which in the world is the result of age and decay).

l. 250. *Beauty, that's colour, and proportion.* 'Shape' or 'proportion', and 'colour' are the attributes of beauty in Xenophon, *Memorabilia,* iii. 10; similarly St. Augustine, *De Civ. Dei,* xxii. 19. Aquinas quotes Pseudo-Dionysius's opinion that God is said to be beautiful as being the cause of the harmony and clarity of the universe; 'from which we may gather that beauty results from the concurrence of clarity of colour and due proportion' (*S.T.* IIa pars, II, q. cxlv, art. 2). In his classic summary, however, he says: 'For beauty includes three conditions, *integrity* or *perfection . . .;* due *proportion* or *harmony;* and lastly, *brightness,* or *clarity,* whence things are called beautiful which have a bright colour' (Ia pars, q. xxxix, art. 8). As S. L. Hynes points out ('Donne and Aquinas', *M.L.R.* xlviii, 1953), the poem follows Aquinas's terms in order; the world lacks integrity or perfection ('out of joynt', 'lame', l. 192; 'all in pieces', l. 213; etc.), proportion (ll. 252, 277, 285, etc.), and colour (ll. 340–1). Donne interprets 'claritas' in an obvious sense as the liveliness and 'glow' of colour in a young, healthy body (contrast 'how wan a Ghost', l. 370). Cf. Spenser, 'An Hymn of Beauty', ll. 64–98.

l. 255. *Eccentrique parts.* It was anciently believed that the motions of the fixed stars were perfectly circular (Plato, *Timaeus* 36 C), only circular motion being continuous and eternal (Aristotle, *De Caelo* 269ᵇ, 286ᵇ–287ᵃ). The heavenly spheres in which the stars and planets were fixed were thought to revolve on the same 'centre' (ll. 275–6), earth itself. The changes in the brightness of stars and certain planets (e.g. Mars, Jupiter, Saturn) and their apparently irregular movements, however, caused Ptolemy to postulate that the centres of their orbits did not in fact coincide, but moved in relation to the earth (i.e. were 'eccentric'). 'Parts' may suggest another refinement of Ptolemy to account geometrically for movements of planets which did not describe a perfect circle or 'cycle': the idea that the paths of such planets were traced in an epicycle centred on the theoretical circumference of their orbit. Cf. *Paradise Lost*, viii. 82–4: 'gird the sphere With centric and eccentric scribbled o'er, Cycle and epicycle.'

l. 256. *downe-right*: running straight up and down.

   overthwarts: transverse lines. The criss-cross lines on charts of the heavens seem actually to throw the heavens out of 'proportion'. Cf. the use of 'engrave' in 'Obsequies to the Lord Harington', l. 112; and ll. 278–81 below.

l. 257. *pure*: circular. 'Motio circularis . . . expressissima imago est verae foelicitatis. . . . In orbem non moventur nisi immortalia et incorrupta corpora', etc. (Pico della Mirandola, *Commentationes*, 1495, Diiiᵛ).

l. 258. *eight and fortie sheeres.* Ptolemy, in the tables (adapted from Hipparchus's catalogue of stars) given in his *Almagest*, vii–viii, divided the stars into forty-eight constellations. 'Sheeres' (*O.E.D.*, 'share', 4) = 'portions'. The lines which 'tear the Firmament' are those on maps of the heavens (l. 256). Manley quotes Gregor Reisch, *Margarita Philosophica*: 'Ex his firmamenti stellis astrologorum nonnulli imaginum quarundam lineamenta imaginati sunt: non tamen credendum eas in coelo realiter actu existere, aut coloribus tincta qualibus depinguntur, sed ab effectibus et situ earum, et colores et nomina ipsis indiderunt' (Basle, 1535, p. 551).

ll. 259–60. *there arise New starres.* It was believed from ancient times that the heavens above the sphere of the moon were without alteration, generation, or corruption (cf. 'unchangeable firmament', 'A Fever', l. 24). Tycho Brahe's faith in the old doctrine was shaken by his observation of a new star in the constellation of Cassiopeia in 1572. In 1600 Kepler discovered one in the constellation of Cygnus or the Swan, and in 1604 one in that of the Serpent. In 1610 Galileo, in *Sidereus Nuncius*, revealed the existence of the four moons of Jupiter and the constitution of the Milky Way as of innumerable fixed stars. Cf. *Biathanatos*, p. 146.

l. 260. *old do vanish*. In Tycho Brahe's catalogue of the stars, only 777 of the 1022 listed by Hipparchus were retained. See C. M. Coffin, *John Donne and the New Philosophy*, pp. 127–35. The confusion ('disproportion') of the heavens is matched by the confused ideas of the astronomers.

ll. 263–77. The Zodiac was the name given to a belt of the heavenly sphere extending eight or nine degrees on each side of the ecliptic, within which the apparent movements of the sun, moon, and planets were supposed to take place. It was divided into twelve equal parts (each with its own 'sign' and named after a constellation) through which the sun passed once a year; the 'Crab' (Cancer) and the 'Goat' (Capricornus) were those in which the sun appeared at the summer and winter solstices respectively (in the northern hemisphere), when the sun reached its maximum declination and began to move 'backe' towards its other solsticial position. The solsticial points were called 'tropics'; but in saying that the tropics 'fetter' the sun, Donne is probably also thinking of the lines on maps representing the tropics of Cancer and Capricorn, north and south of the equator and parallel to it, 'under' the solsticial positions of the sun. Cf. 'Obsequies to the Lord Harington', l. 111. If they did not restrain the sun, it might extend the obliquity of its ecliptic and appear over 'eyther Pole' in turn. The sun's constant endeavour to exercise its 'freedom' is alleged as the reason why it cannot 'perfit a Circle' (l. 269).

l. 268. Not only does the sun imperceptibly change the obliquity of its course each day, but also each year it crosses the equator at a point a little further ahead, owing to the 'precession of the equinoxes' (due to a slow movement of the earth upon its axis).

l. 274. *falne nearer us*. Ptolemy calculated the distance of the sun from the earth as 1210 semidiameters of the earth, but later mathematicians (beginning with Albategnius in A.D. 880) had estimated the distance progressively as being less; from which largely accidental circumstance it was deduced by many Renaissance thinkers that the sun was apparently approaching the earth. Some, however, rejected this conclusion: 'Solis corpus longe propius nos esse, quam quantum ab antiquis scriptum sit: ita ut in ipsa deferentis corpulentia locum mutasse videatur: vel ipsa scripta spongiis, vel ipsa authores scuticis sunt castigandi' (J. C. Scaliger, *Exercitationes* . . . , pp. 342–3, cited by Manley). Cf. 'To the Countess of Huntingdon' ('Man to Gods image'), ll. 17–18; Spenser, *The Faerie Queene*, proem to bk. V, stanzas 4–8.

l. 278. *Meridians, and Parallels*: lines representing celestial longitude and latitude, analogous to those on maps of the earth.

l. 280. *his owne*: caught in his 'net'; but they become like horses (ll. 283–4), tamed and controlled, though at times recalcitrant.

l. 284. *diversly*: in different ways, to a different degree.

l. 285. *keepes the earth her round proportion still?* It was traditionally believed that the earth was 'Created . . . round' (*Paradise Lost*, ii. 832); since God saw that it was 'good' (Gen. i. 10), it must have had the perfect form of a circle or sphere. Christian commentators attributed the irregularities of the earth's surface to the effects of the Flood, and hence of man's sin. Pererius, summarizing previous opinion, *Comment. et Disput. in Genesim*, 1601, rejects the idea 'fuisse terram ante diluvium totam aequabiliter rotundam, nulla celsiorum humiliorumque locorum inaequalitate; post diluvium autem hanc quam in terra cernimus montium et vallium distinctionem extitisse' (p. 47). Those who supported the idea of the original perfect roundness of the earth emphasized the relatively small heights of mountains and depths of the sea (e.g. Cleomedes, cited by Manley, *De Mundo*, Basle, 1585, p. 155); cf. *Sermons*, v. 282–3.

l. 286. *Tenarif*. The Pico de Teide, the mountain on the Island of Teneriffe, rises to 12,172 feet. Grierson quotes Burton: 'The pike of Teneriffe how high it is? 70 miles? or 50, as Patricius holds? or 9, as Snellius demonstrates in his *Eratosthenes*?' (*Anatomy*, ii. 37.) But the peak was a standard example. The instructor in W. Cunningham's *The Cosmographical Glasse* (1559) defends the perfect roundness of the earth against the following objection: 'It semeth sufficient to credit th'Earth not to be round, if we consider the greate deepe valleis, that are in it . . .: but moste of all, the hougie and hie Mountaines, and Hilles: Of whiche, some of them are supposed to be 60. miles in height. As the Hille in th'Iland Teneriffa'; but these, says the instructor, are like mere 'Pittes and holes of a rough polished Gunstone' (ff. 47–8).

ll. 289–91. *Whales being strooke*, etc. After trying in vain to free itself from the hook, says Aldrovandus (cited by Manley), the whale plunges to the depths of the sea: 'acerrimis doloribus affecta, in pelagi profundum demergitur. . . . Cum autem pervenit ad imam maris sedem, defatigata quiescit, ingentes fluctus anhelans' (*De Piscibus*, 1613, p. 673).

l. 294. *Antipodies*: 'the inhabitantes whiche be directly under us (the Geographers name them Antipodes)' (W. Cunningham, *The Cosmographical Glasse*, 1559, ff. 21, 70). The root meaning is 'with feet opposite to ours'; cf. *Sermons*, iv. 59, vii. 245.

ll. 295–8. *Vault infernall*, etc. Grierson and Manley cite:

one Author, who is afraid of admitting too great a hollownesse in the Earth, lest then the Earth might not be said to be solid, pronounces that Hell cannot possibly be above three thousand miles in compasse, (and then one of the torments of Hell will be the throng, for their bodies must be there, in their dimensions, as well as their soules) (*Sermons*, vii. 137; cf. Simpson, *Essays*, p. 36).

In both places there is a marginal reference to Sebastian Munster (*Cosmographia Universalis*, Basle, 1572, pp. 11–12) on hell: 'Est quidem magna caverna, capax tot millium corporum humanorum damnatorum, sed quae nihil est, ut diximus collata ad terram, etiamsi, longitudine et latitudine atque altitudine duo aut tria millia contineat Germanicorum miliariorum.' Others reduced the size of hell even more; cf. Burton, *Anatomy*, ii. 42.

l. 300. *Are these*: can these properly be described as.

warts, and pock-holes: the results of disease in the world being anatomized. Cf. Simpson, *Essays*: Earth's 'hills, though they erect their heads beyond the Country of Meteors, . . . are but as warts upon her face: And her vaults, and caverns, . . . are but as so many wrinkles, and pock-holes' (p. 36). Cleomedes (see note to l. 285) says that from the tip of the highest mountain to the lowest depth of the sea the distance is 30 stadia: 'Triginta autem stadia ad plus octoginta milia rationem nullam habent; quod non aliter se habet, si pulvisculus in pila esset. Atque tubercula, quae sunt in pilulis platanorum, non prohibent, quin sunt pilulae, quamquam illa ad totam pilularum magnitudinem maiorem rationem habent quam curvaturae maris et montium exsuperantiae ad totam terrae magnitudinem.'

ll. 311–12. *that Ancient*. The precise reference cannot be identified. Grosart and Chambers suggested that the 'Ancient' was Pythagoras; Norton (Grolier), that it was Simmias in Plato's *Phaedo* 85 E–86 D; Grierson, that it was Aristoxenus because Cicero says that he held the soul to be a harmony of the body (*Tusc. Disput.* i. 10) analogous to the harmony of the lyre; cf. Burton, *Anatomy*, part. i, sec. 1, mem. 2, subsec. 9 (i. 162), and Aristotle, *De Anima* 407[b]. Grierson also points out, however, that Hippocrates (*Regimen*, I. viii) and Galen thought (like Plato's Simmias) that the soul was a harmony of the bodily elements or humours, and that l. 321 gives weight to the medical meaning here.

l. 312. *at next*. The expression was rare at this date. As Grierson points out, *O.E.D.* cites no example later than 1449.

l. 314. *Resultances*. Donne's use of the word here is quoted as an example in *O.E.D.*, sb. 3: 'something which issues, proceeds, or emanates from another thing.' 'She is the harmony from which proceeds that harmony of our bodies which is their soul' (Grierson).

l. 316. *As to our eyes, the formes from objects flow*. This was the usual theory of vision in Donne's time, explained by Aristotle (*De Sensu et Sensibili*, 437[a]–438[b]): rays emitted by objects imprint the forms of the objects on the mind through the eyes. So *Batman upon Bartholome*, 1582, f. 389[b].

ll. 317–18. *those great Doctors*, etc. '*Francis George* in his *Harmony* sayes, That after he had curiously observed, that *the Ark of Noah*, and *our body* had the same proportion and correspondency in their parts, he was angry, when he found after, that S[t] *Augustine* had found out that before' (Simpson,

Essays, p. 32). Augustine describes the Ark as a type of the Church, made in the proportions of the human body which Christ assumed to rescue us from the flood of sin: 'Nam et mensurae ipsae longitudinis, altitudinis, latitudinis eius, significant corpus humanum, in cuius veritate ad homines praenuntiatus est venturus, et venit' (*De Civ. Dei*, xv. 26). Another 'Doctor', St. Ambrose (Migne, *P.L.* xiv. 387–8), as Manley notes, though taking the measurements of the Ark as a 'type' of the human body, allegorizes it as the 'just' man surrounded by an ocean of sin.

ll. 319–22. Cf. 'To Sir Edward Herbert, at Juliers', ll. 1–2: 'Man is a lumpe, where all beasts kneaded bee, Wisdome makes him an Arke where all agree' (cf. *Sermons*, iii. 184). The commonplace, as Manley notes, derives from St. Ambrose, *De Noe et Arca*, ix (Migne, *P.L.* xiv. 374); the just man achieves inner harmony and peace by controlling his irrational passions and the senses: 'Quis est justus in nobis, nisi mentis vigor qui intra istam arcam includit omne animantium genus, quod est super terram.' Cf. Pererius, *Comment. et Disput. in Genesim* (1601), p. 448; and see D. C. Allen, *The Legend of Noah* (Urbana, Ill., 1949), pp. 77, 148.

ll. 327–8. Cf. *Sermons*, iii. 48, ll. 41–4.

l. 335. *most men be such*, etc. Cf. Simpson, *Essays*: 'since most men are such, as most men think they be' (p. 38); Manley cites:

for the most part, most men are such, as most men take them to be; *Neminem omnes, nemo omnes fefellit*; All the world never joyned to deceive one man, nor was ever any one man able to deceive all the world. *Contemptu famae contemnuntur & virtutes*, was so well said by *Tacitus*, as it is pity S. *Augustine* said it not, They that neglect the good opinion of others, neglect those vertues that should produce that good opinion (*Sermons*, viii. 323; cf. vii. 250).

l. 337. *good, and well*: virtue, and 'fitness' (l. 333) of conduct.

l. 338. *Wicked . . . indiscreet.* Discretion is the ability to show the discrimination between good and evil in our daily conduct; it is 'the mother of all vertues' (*Sermons*, v. 199; the phrase is St. Bernard's); the deacons in Acts vi. 3 were 'full of Religion towards God, and full of such wisedome as might advance it towards men; full of zeale, and full of knowledge; full of truth, and full of discretion too' (*Sermons*, iv. 287). Not to show the Christian virtues in one's conduct is almost as bad as being 'wicked', i.e. not possessing them.

ll. 343–4. *a compassionate Turcoyse*, etc. The turquoise was supposed to gain or lose in lustre in sympathy with its wearer's state of health. In a standard work on gems, as Manley notes, Anselmus Boethius de Boot tells of a ring his father gave him which had lost its lustre and colour, but which, after he had worn it for some months, regained its former appearance: 'Mutatio coloris naturaliter fieri potest. . . . Animadverti, cum icteritia vel obstructionibus laborassem, et iam corpus sudoribus transpirabile ac bene constitutum esset, meam turcoidem pulchriorem esse, ita ut mihi valetudinis index sit' (*Gemmarum et Lapidum Historia*, Hanover, 1609, pp. 135–6). Cf. Jonson's *Sejanus*, I. i. 37–8: 'And true, as turkise in the deare lords ring, Looke well, or ill with him.' Grierson (ii. 273) quotes an apparent borrowing of Donne's lines by Sir Francis Kynaston (*Minor Poets of the Caroline Period*, ed. G. E. B. Saintsbury, ii. 161); J. Swan, *Speculum Mundi* (1635), p. 296, misquotes Donne's couplet.

l. 345. *gold fals sicke being stung with Mercury*. The reference is to gold amalgam made by combining gold with quicksilver (mercury), which is paler in colour and less valuable than gold. 'Stung' is a metaphor from the bite of a poisonous creature (in alchemy, the 'serpens mercurialis'). Pliny says (*Nat. Hist.* xxxiii. 32) that quicksilver acts as a poison on everything and that gold is the only thing which it attracts to itself. Cf. Scaliger, *Exercitationes . . .*, p. 323 (noted by Manley): 'Aurum metallorum rex est; Argentum vivum tyrannus . . . quia caetera omnia absumit. Plinius in vicesimo nono ita scribit: Auro liquescenti si Gallinae carnes admisceantur, ab illis rapi. Itaque auri venenum esse.'

l. 352. *his various Rainbow*. Donne seems to deny the existence of the rainbow before the Deluge, after which God told Noah that He would set the rainbow in the sky as a token of their covenant (Gen. ix. 11–17). In *Essays in Divinity* (Simpson, p. 89) Donne quotes St. Chrysostom as implying that the rainbow did not exist before the Flood (Migne, *P.G.* liii. 254–9); most commentators, however, thought that it did, but was not then the sign of the Divine Covenant (e.g. G. Reisch, *Margarita Philosophica*, 1535, p. 798; Pererius, *Comment. et Disput. in Genesim*, 1601, p. 525).

l. 353. *Sight is the noblest sense*: 'so much the Noblest of all the senses' (*Sermons*, viii. 221; cited by Manley). The idea was a commonplace; cf. Aquinas, *S. T.* Iᵃ pars, q. lxvii, art. 1: 'the noblest and most trustworthy of the senses'.

l. 354. *Sight hath onely color to feed on*: 'for onely colour is the object of sight' (*Biathanatos*, p. 154; cited by Manley). The theory is Aristotle's: 'Whatever is visible is colour and colour is what lies upon what is in its own nature visible' (*De Anima* 418ᵃ); 'we may define colour as the limit of the Translucent in a determinately bounded body' (*De Sensu et Sensibili* 439ᵇ); cf. *Sermons*, vii. 344. The latter idea probably suggested l. 366, and less directly *The Second Anniversary*, ll. 243–6.

ll. 357–8. *Our blushing redde*, etc. Manley cites:

[God] made us all of earth, and all of red earth. Our earth was red, even when it was in Gods hands: a rednesse that amounts to a shamefastnesse, to a blushing at our own infirmities, is imprinted in us, by Gods hand. . . . But that redness, which we have contracted from bloud shed by our selves, the bloud of our own souls, by sinne, was not upon us, when we were in the hands of God. . . . Our sinnes are our owne, and our destruction is from our selves. . . . We have dyed our selves in sinnes, as red as Scarlet (*Sermons*, ix. 64–6; cf. ii. 78–9, 200, x. 197).

The Hebrew words for 'Adam' and 'red, blush' are the same when written without vowel points, and almost indistinguishable even with the points. For 'Adam' as 'red earth' cf. 'A Litany', l. 7.

ll. 365-6. *miraculous, Being all color, all Diaphanous.* The 'miracle' is that she should simultaneously be wholly both transparency and colour. Only the spiritual light of God, the 'true light' of Christ (cf. *Sermons*, iii. 354-5), is all transparency, uncoloured by the dross of earth, and of sin; yet spiritual light is the source of all colour, shining through the material. The terms are Aristotle's; Manley cites Aquinas's *Comment. in Aristotelis De Anima*, ii. 14: the transparent spiritual light 'has no intrinsic colour to make it visible of itself' and is 'other than the light that is sense-perceived'; colour is 'a kind of light somehow dimmed by admixture of opaque matter'.

l. 380. *The father, or the mother barren is.* The father is traditionally the sky, the mother the earth; upon their union life and growth depend. Cf. Lucretius, *De Rerum Natura*, ii. 991-8; 'To Mr. Tilman after he had taken orders', ll. 51-2. The end of the world is very near, says John Dove:

For, nature beginneth generally to intermitte her wonted course, the mother elements of the world ... do loose their qualities and naturall vigor ..., the starres and planets of Heaven wax dimme and olde ... our mother the earth ... is out of hart, waxeth barren and dead ... the herbes and symples which are appointed for medcines for mans body, have almost loste their virtue and man himselfe ... is of lower stature, lesse strength, shorter life ..., so that there is a general decay of nature (*A Sermon ... at Pauls Crosse the 3. of November 1594*, Sig. C7-8).

l. 382. *balmy*: probably suggesting the balsam or balm in living things, which preserves and heals (l. 57, and note). Cf. 'A Nocturnal upon St. Lucy's Day', ll. 5-6: 'The world's whole sap is sunke: / The generall balme th'hydroptique earth hath drunk.'

ll. 387-8. *Th'Ayre showes such Meteors*, etc. In Donne's time 'meteor' was still the name for phenomena in the 'sphere' of the air or atmosphere (wind, rain, snow, lightning, dew, etc.). Notable events, especially disasters, were supposed to be foretold by unusual meteorological disturbances (cf. *Julius Caesar*, I. iii). The decay of the world was thought to be producing an increasing number of prodigies and monstrosities in the atmosphere (cf. Burton, *Anatomy*, ii. 48).

ll. 389. *new wormes*: worms or maggots produced from the decaying carcass of the world (cf. ll. 75-7). Manley quotes Renaissance statements to the effect that snakes (also called 'wormes') were bred out of corruption; there is also, as Grierson suggested, a probable reference to 'new' species of serpents, etc., discovered in Africa and America.

l. 390. *Th'Egyptian Mages.* In Exod. vii. 10-12, Aaron 'cast down his rod before Pharaoh, ... and it became a serpent'; 'the magicians of Egypt, they also did in like manner with their enchantments. For they cast down every man his rod, and they became serpents'.

l. 391. *Artist*: a practitioner of occult arts; an astrologer, or an alchemist.

ll. 391–6. *bring Heaven hither*, etc. The reference is to medical cures made by controlling the influence of the stars. Manley quotes:

> As to cure diseases by touch, or by charme, (both which one excellent Chirurgian, and one excellent philosopher, are of opinion may be done, because what vertue soever the heavens infuse into any creature, man, who is Al, is capable of, and being borne when that vertue is exacted, may receive a like impression, or may give it to a word, or character made at that instant, if he can understand the time) though these, I say be forbidden by divers Lawes, out of a Just prejudice that vulgar owners of such a vertue, would mis-imploy, it, yet none mislikes that the Kings of *England* and *France*, should cure one sicknesse [the 'King's evil'] by such meanes (*Biathanatos*, pp. 216–17).

The 'Chirurgian' is identified by a marginal note as Paracelsus, who, as Manley notes, urged modern doctors to rediscover these curative arts, known to the ancient Medes and Persians. Donne's point here, however, is that the arts are irretrievably lost because of the declining influence of the stars (l. 378) and the weakening of man's intellectual powers and of his sense of moral responsibility. The 'excellent philosopher' is identified as Petrus Pomponatius.

l. 392. *constellate*: work out, and use the power of, a favourable constellation of stars for. *O.E.D.* dates Donne's use of 'constellate' here to 1631, the first example given dating from 1621. Cf., however, Nashe: 'to constellate it and plannet it so portentously' (*Works*, ed. R. B. McKerrow, iii. 83).

l. 396. *correspondence*: the interchange between earth and heaven (cf. 'trafique', l. 400); *O.E.D.*, sb. 5.

l. 399. *commerce*: accented on the second syllable.

l. 400. *Embarr'd*: stopped, forbidden.

l. 404. *Ashes too, are medicinall*. Pliny gives many examples of the use of ashes in medicines (*Nat. Hist.* xxxii, etc.), as do the ancient and Renaissance medical writers. The 'virtue' of the substance remained after the purifying effect of fire. Cf. D. C. Allen, 'John Donne and Renaissance Medicine', *J.E.G.P.* xlii (1943), p. 340.

l. 405. *vertue*: both innate goodness, and power to influence (cf. ll. 411–12).

ll. 407–8. *one dying Swan, To sing*. Swans were traditionally thought to sing only once, at the point of death.

ll. 409–12. *Serpents poison*, etc. Cf. 'some poisons, and some medicines, hurt not, nor profit, except the creature in which they reside, contribute their lively activitie, and vigor' (*Letters*, p. 107; similarly *Pseudo-Martyr*, pp. 140–1). None of the medical writers to whom Donne refers by name mentions this point, and it has not been exactly paralleled elsewhere. Donne may be thinking of the making of theriaca or mithridate (cf. *The Second Anniversary*, l. 127, and note, p. 159), and the conditions in which the venom which was one of the ingredients would be harmful to the patient. 'Tales igitur transeunte in mortuas etiam veneno, carnem habent ad theriacae compositionem aptam. Quaedam enim sunt quae cum morte venenum amittunt, ut rabidi canes scorpiique: quaedam servant, ut viperae: neque enim aliter prodesse possent carnes earum in theriaca, si omnino expertes fierent veneni . . . [In viperis] potentia venenum manet, ob vehementem siccitatem, ut securè tractare mortuas possis, non edere . . .' (Cardan, *De Subtilitate*, 1560, p. 278).

ll. 417–18. *transubstantiate . . . guilded.* The contrast is between changing the whole substance to gold, and covering it with a film or coating of gold. Cf. 'To the Countess of Huntingdon' ('Man to Gods image'), ll. 25–6: virtue 'guilded us: But you are gold . . . ; she . . . transubstantiates you'.

l. 418. *states*: people of all kinds and stations in life.

ll. 421–2. 'Some people have some restraint and crave no more than Kings should give them' (Manley).

l. 426. *Iron, and rusty too.* It was a commonplace in accounts of the decay of the world that it had sunk from the Golden Age through the Silver and Brass Ages to the last (Iron) Age. Cf. 'Satire V', ll. 35–7: 'O Age of rusty iron! . . .'

l. 436. *to have read*: to have itself expounded.

l. 440. *were punctuall*: were to discuss it in detail, point by point.

l. 456. *concoction*: refining, purifying (alchemically); as in 'The Ecstasy', ll. 27–8. Manley cites:

> Precious stones are first *drops of the dew* of heaven, and then refined by the sunne of heaven. When by long lying they have exhal'd, and evaporated, and breathed out all their grosse matter, and received another concoction from the sunne, then they become precious in the eye, and estimation of men (*Sermons*, iii. 372; cf. i. 272).

l. 460. *fit for Chronicle, not verse*: because 'In this present case there is so much truth as it defeats all Poetry' (Donne's letter accompanying the Hamilton 'Hymn'; see p. 209 below).

ll. 461–6. God spoke to Moses and Joshua for the 'last' time before Moses died and the Israelites entered the Promised Land, commanding them to write the song which He gave them; and Moses taught the people the song (Deut. xxxi. 19, xxxii. 1–43). The idea that the reason for presenting God's message in the form of a song was to ensure its being remembered (l. 466) and not 'let fall' from their minds (l. 464) originates, as Manley notes, from St. John Chrysostom (Migne, *P.G.* lvi. 57). Cf. Simpson, *Essays*, p. 92. That the song was a summary of the Law (as distinct from the new covenant in

Christ) was the standard gloss: 'when God had given all the Law, he provided, as himself sayes, a safer way, which was to give them a heavenly Song of his owne making: for that Song, he sayes there, he was sure they would remember' (*Sermons*, ii. 171; cf. iv. 179–80, *Biathanatos*, p. 159; and see Lewalski, pp. 236–40).

l. 467. *in due measure*: with proper reverence; and in verse (appropriately, following the example of God's own song).

l. 469. *incomprehensiblenesse*. She cannot be confined within limits ('emprison', l. 470); she is not fully knowable.

l. 474. *fame*: 'which is a mean Nature between' body and soul (Simpson, *Essays*, p. 38). Cf. 'An Hymn to the Saints, and to Marquess Hamilton', ll. 29–30.

A Funerall Elegie (p. 35)

ll. 1–2. The lines suggest the opening of an epitaph to be spoken over the grave, or pinned to the funeral 'hearse'. ''Tis lost' = it is labour lost.

l. 2. *chest*. See Donne's 'Epitaph for Elizabeth Drury' and notes (pp. 76, 211). The Drurys provided an elaborate marble tomb for their daughter.

l. 4. *Priz'd*: appraised, compared in value.

Chrysolite. Jerome Cardan says that chrysolite, the topaz of the ancients, shines without equal (*De Subtilitate*, 1560, p. 200).

l. 5. *Pearles, and Rubies*: the white and pink of her complexion. Cf. *The First Anniversary*, ll. 361–2.

l. 8. *escurials*. The Escorial was completed by Philip II of Spain in 1584 as a magnificent palace and mausoleum, incorporating a church, a library and art collection, a college, and a monastery. Cf. 'To the Countess of Bedford' ('You have refin'd mee'), l. 48.

ll. 9–10. Cf. *The First Anniversary*, ll. 469–70.

l. 18. *house*: her body, the tabernacle of the Holy Ghost. Cf. 2 Cor. v. 4, vi. 16; 2 Pet. i. 13–14.

ll. 21–7. For the commonplace that the members of the human body 'correspond' to classes and occupations in the 'body-politic', see E. M. W. Tillyard, *The Elizabethan World Picture* (1943), pp. 88–91.

l. 27. *fine spirits*: people like her, who enable society to work harmoniously, as attenuated breaths (cf. *spiritus*) of air enable an organist to produce harmonies, and as the 'spirits' in the blood enable the soul to work harmoniously through the parts of the body.

tune and set: an obsolete phrase meaning 'set in tune'; 'set' is used in *O.E.D.*, sense 26. c.

l. 28. *Organ*: referring to the world as analogous to the human 'organism', and also to the creation (including human society) as a musical instrument. Cf. 'Obsequies to the Lord Harington', ll. 1–4, and notes (pp. 197–8).

l. 29. *Wonder and love*. Cf. 'A Valediction: of the Book', ll. 28–9: 'all Divinity Is love or wonder.'

l. 40. *then*: when reassembled.

ll. 41–4. *the Affrique Niger*, etc. In Donne's time the River Niger was identi-fied, wholly or in part, with the upper waters of the Nile, flowing partly above, partly below, the ground. Most accounts consisted, as Manley notes, of various interpretations of Pliny's (*Nat. Hist.* v. 10): the Nile begins in western Mauritania and flows eastward, twice disappearing underground, until it leaps out in a fountain, 'ut verisimile est, illo quem Nigrum vocavere'.

l. 50. *An Angell made a Throne, or Cherubin*. Angels are the lowest of the nine heavenly orders (on which see note, p. 184, on 'Elegy on Mrs. Bulstrode', l. 20); only the seraphim are above the cherubim and thrones.

l. 51. *We lose by't*: because, as Manley suggests, angels alone are involved with human affairs (Aquinas, *S.T.* I^a pars, q. cxii, art. 2; q. cxiii, art. 3); cherubim and thrones contemplate or serve God.

l. 56. *last fires*: which will end the world.

l. 61. *through-light*: translucent. *enroule*: enwrap (*O.E.D.* II. 7). Cf. *The Second Anniversary*, ll. 244–6, and Dryden, 'The Monument of a Fair Maiden Lady', ll. 7–18.

ll. 63–4. Men who had not the courage to do more confined themselves to admiration of her; others of more worth dared to desire her.

l. 65. *emulate*: vie with each other (*O.E.D.*, vb. 3).

ll. 67–70. For the 'new starres' (the 'new eyes' of heaven), cf. *The First Anniversary*, ll. 259–60, and note (p. 143); and, for similar complimentary uses of the idea, the 'Palatine' Epithalamion, ll. 39–40, and 'To the Countess of Huntingdon' ('Man to Gods image'), ll. 5–16. The new star of 1572 was invisible by the end of March 1574; that of 1600 soon disappeared; that of 1604 'went out' by March 1606. The astronomers argued (without agree-ment) whether the 'place' of the new stars was in the atmosphere below the moon, or in the ether above it, or in the eighth sphere (of the 'fixed' stars). See C. M. Coffin, *John Donne and the New Philosophy*, pp. 124–30.

l. 68. *Artist*: 'astronomer', but with a disparaging suggestion of charlatanry (cf. *The First Anniversary*, l. 391).

l. 71. *peece*. Cf. 'peeces', l. 28.

l. 72. *no bodies else, nor shee*: no man's wife, nor (as a human being alive on earth) herself.

ll. 73–4. *a Lampe of Balsamum*, etc. Cf. '*Constantine* ordained, that upon this [Christmas] day, the Church should burne no Oyle, but Balsamum in her Lamps' (*Sermons*, ix. 152). As Manley notes, the ancient record of Constantine the Great's founding and furnishing of churches states that in several of them balsam was used in lamps (at Easter, for instance, in the basilica which he built in Rome). Cf. Migne, *P.L.* cxxvii. 1515–24, and viii. 804. In the latter place a note by Severinus Binnius refers to a similar lavishness on the part of the Emperor Heliogabalus, recorded by Lampridius (*Heliogabalus*, xxiv. 1). Balsam, an aromatic resin, was costly; Pliny says that in the time of Alexander the Great it was worth more than twice its weight in silver (*Nat. Hist.* xii. 54). Dryden paraphrases Donne's lines in *Eleanora*, ll. 301–4.

ll. 75–6. White is the colour of virginity. If she had survived to marry, though marriage is not sinful she would have lost this 'white integrity'. Dryden borrows Donne's couplet in 'The Monument of a Fair Maiden Lady', ll. 19–20.

l. 80. *opium*: i.e. a brief sleep.

l. 81. *could not, nor could chuse to die*: could not die eternally, being virtuous; and her virtue would make it impossible for her to wish to die.

l. 82. *Extasie*. Manley cites:

> I will finde out another death, *mortem raptus*, a death of rapture, and of extasie, that death which S. *Paul* died more then once [2 Cor. xii. 1–4; Acts ix], The death which S. *Gregory* speaks of, *Divina contemplatio quoddam sepulchrum animae*, The contemplation of God, and heaven, is a kinde of buriall, and Sepulchre, and rest of the soule (*Sermons*, ii. 210).

If the soul 'stands apart' from the body for 'too long', the body will die. It was prolonged contemplation of God, not choice, that brought about her death.

l. 92. *infer*: confer, put into her own hands (*O.E.D.*, vb. 1. b).

l. 94. She used the 'liberty' Fate gave her only to the extent of dying, as far as she has died (i.e. as far as earthly life is concerned).

l. 96. *Fellow-Commissioner*. Cf. 'Great Destiny the Commissary of God' ('The Progress of the Soul', l. 31). Destiny is envisaged as the agent of God's providential will. Though she, too, was fitted to be such an agent, she humbly used her power only to die.

l. 101. *that booke*: mentioned in ll. 84–90.

l. 104. *rise*. Her example is a general deed of gift from which spring virtuous deeds which are her legacies to the world.

l. 106. *play*: impersonate, imitate (like actors); i.e. show her virtue in their actions. For 'well' and 'good', cf. *The First Anniversary*, l. 337.

THE SECOND ANNIVERSARIE (p. 39)

The Harbinger to the Progres

For Joseph Hall's authorship of this poem, see the General Introduction, pp. xxx–xxxi. In the title, a 'harbinger' (*O.E.D.* 3) is one that goes before and announces the approach of someone; but, by the pun (ll. 27–8, 34) on 'royal progress' and the title of Donne's poem, Hall exploits the more restricted meaning (*O.E.D.* 2): an officer of the Court going ahead of the monarch to prepare lodgings etc. for his approach.

l. 6. *The worlds last day, thy glories full degree*: the general resurrection, when even bodies will be glorified, and the saved will enter fully into eternal bliss. Cf. ll. 491–4 below.

l. 7. *ore-lookest*: lookest down upon (from her place in heaven).

l. 8. *in their place, and yet still moved.* The stars (as distinct from the planets) are fixed in their sphere (the eighth in the Ptolemaic system), which itself, however, moves around the earth.

l. 16. *Journals*: records of the events of your daily life, or of your daily journeys (*O.E.D.*, 'journal', B. 4, 7).

l. 23. *raught*: reached.

l. 27. *Hy*: a spelling found occasionally elsewhere in Hall's verse (see A. Davenport's edition of his *Poems*, p. 275).

ll. 27–8, 34. The pun on 'progress' was originally Donne's own; cf. *The First Anniversary*, ll. 7–8.

l. 36. *Laura*: adored and praised in verse by Petrarch.

ll. 39–40. It was a matter of debate whether the separated souls of the dead knew what happened on earth. As Manley notes, Augustine thought that they did not (Migne, *P.L.* xl. 604–5), Gregory that they did (ibid. lxxv. 999); Aquinas eventually agreed with Gregory (*S.T.* Iᵃ pars, q. lxxxix, art. 8).

Of the Progres of the Soule (p. 41)

l. 2. *an everlastingnesse.* Ironic: for 'heaven and earth shall pass away' (Matt. xxiv. 35).

l. 4. She gave light not only to the earth but also to the sun itself.

l. 7. *strooke*: lowered.

ll. 9–18. Grierson (ii. 273) suggests as a source of this simile Lucretius, *De Rerum Natura*, iii. 642–56.

ll. 19–20. *Or as a Lute*, etc. An anonymous untitled poem in Brit. Lib. MS. *Harl.* 6918 begins:

> The Lute, saith high sould Donne, thus rings
> Even her owne knell with her owne strings.

The phenomenon was ominous: 'I knew it boded no good lucke, that all my Lute-strings crack't last night of their owne accord' (Barten Holyday, *Technogamia*, 1618, IV. vi. 907–8, ed. Sr. M. J. C. Cavanagh, 1942, p. 91).

l. 22. *there is motion in corruption*. Cf. 'That *body* which . . . is mouldring, and crumbling into lesse, and lesse dust, and so hath some *motion*, though no *life*' (*Sermons*, viii. 92).

ll. 23–4. The book of Genesis (i. 5, 8, 13) names three 'days' before the creation of the sun on the fourth (vv. 16–19). There was much, though inconclusive, discussion of how there could be days without the sun (e.g. Pererius, *Comment. et Disput. in Genesim*, 1601, pp. 33–7). Cf. *The First Anniversary*, l. 202.

l. 27. *of Lethe flood*: a new Deluge which, like Lethe, the river in Hades, produces forgetfulness.

l. 29. *Reserve*: store (*O.E.D.*, sb. 3. b; the earliest example is dated 1644).

ll. 34–5. *be unto my Muse a Father*: 'act as a fecundating force upon my poetic powers'; and so allow the poet to compose further 'anniversary' poems.

l. 42. *but vanish, and not die*. Donne considers several times in the *Sermons* (especially in vi, no. 2) what is to happen to those who are alive on the Day of Judgement. Manley cites:

> Taking then this Text for a probleme, *Quis homo*, *What man lives, and shall not see Death?* [Ps. lxxxix. 48] we answer, It may be that those Men, whom Christ shal find upon the earth alive, at his returne to Judge the World, shall dye then, and it may be they shall but be changed, and not dye (*Sermons*, ii. 204). Cf. 1 Cor. xv. 51.

ll. 43–4. *These Hymns thy issue*, etc. The poems of praise which are her progeny may multiply 'and sound in men's ears, quickening in them virtue and religion, till they are drowned in the greater music of God's *Venite*' (Grierson). The 'great Venite' is that of the Day of Judgement: 'Then shall the King say unto them on his right hand, Come, ye blessed of my Father ['Venite, benedicti Patris mei' *V*], inherit the kingdom prepared for you from the foundation of the world' (Matt. xxv. 34). Cf. *Sermons*, ii. 249.

l. 46. *safe-sealing Bowle*. 'Sealing' is obviously misprinted in *1612*. The 'Bowle' is the cup, in Protestant churches given to the laity at the Communion. In the *Sermons* Donne very frequently refers to the sacraments as 'seals'; 'safe' refers to the 'salvation' to which the sacraments are a means ('the sealing of my Pardon', *Sermons*, v. 318). 'It was a *seal* upon a *seal*, a seal of *confirmation*, it was a *sacrament* upon a *sacrament*, when in instituting the *sacrament* of his *body and his bloud*, Christ presented it so, *Doe this in re-membrance of me'* (ibid. ii. 73–4). In the context, as Manley notes, the phrase also suggests Rev. vii. 3–8: 'till we have sealed the servants of our God in their foreheads . . . '.

l. 47. *goe*: i.e. from the body; for at 'that time' (l. 45) the blessed will not 'thirst any more'; the Lamb 'shall lead them unto living fountains of waters' (Rev. vii. 16–17).

l. 48. *Hydropique*: dropsical (*O.E.D.*, 'hydropical', 1), and hence (2) having an insatiable thirst like a dropsical person. The use of the metaphor (for a spiritual thirst) is familiar in European poetry from the twelfth century (see E. R. Curtius, *European Literature and the Latin Middle Ages*, tr. W. R. Trask, 1953, pp. 280–1). Donne's alteration of the spelling in the errata slip shows that he cared about the correct form, and preferred it to that often used, 'hydroptique' (in which 't' is inserted on a false analogy with 'epileptic'). Elsewhere in his work (e.g. in 'Obsequies to the Lord Harington', l. 126) the spelling should probably be changed to 'hydropique'. See R. Bozanich, 'Donne and Ecclesiastes', *Pubns. Mod. Lang. Assocn. of America*, xc (1975), 270–6.

l. 53. *try . . . forth*: test thoroughly.

ll. 56–9. It was a traditional commonplace that worms are witless, insensitive and forgetful: 'Nullum Vermibus ingenium, nulla memoria . . . Unde est quod quidam Vermes obliviosos esse dixerint' (U. Aldrovandus, *De Animalibus Insectis*, 1602, p. 641, cited by Manley). Cf. ll. 117–18.

l. 56. *that*: which that.

l. 63. *Alacrity*: liveliness and positiveness of outlook: a virtue which Donne often advocates in his sermons and elsewhere, e.g. in *Letters*, pp. 46–7.

l. 66. *congratulate*: 'rejoice with' (Lat. *congratulari*).

l. 70. *Some Figure of the Golden times*: some image of the Golden Age of the world: i.e. in Christian terms, of the time before the Fall; in pagan mythology, of the age when Astraea, goddess of justice, dwelt on earth. Astraea left the earth because it was 'unfit, To be staid in' (ll. 73–4). For Donne's use of suggestions from this myth, see Marjorie H. Nicolson, *The Breaking of the Circle* (rev. ed. 1960), pp. 92–6.

l. 72. *the forme*: i.e. the soul. See note (p. 131) to *The First Anniversary*, l. 36.

l. 75. *tried*: tested. The metaphor is from testing the purity of metals by heating. Cf. 'the fire shall try every man's work of what sort it is' (1 Cor. iii. 13; cf. 1 Pet. i. 7).

l. 78. *enspheard*: held, as in a sphere (like that in which the stars were fixed). This is the earliest example of the word in *O.E.D.*

ll. 79–80. *the South controll . . . the Star-full Northern Pole*: the southern heavens surpass, in the multitude of stars, the northern. 'We say that the *Firmament* is full of *starres*, as though it were equally full; but we know, that there are more *stars* under the *Northerne*, then under the *Southern Pole*' (Sparrow, *Devotions*, p. 74, cited by Manley). Cf. Pererius, *Comment. et Disput. in Genesim* (1601), p. 99: 'stellae . . . quae sunt ultra tropicum Capricorni versus antarcticum polum, quae sane perpaucae sunt'.

l. 82. *fragmentary*. The first example of the adjective in *O.E.D.*, in a letter of Donne, is dated 1611; the use of the word here is dated 1631.

   rubbidge: rubbish.

ll. 85–6. *. . . outward roome*. Cf. 'this world and the next world, are not, to the pure in heart, two houses, but two roomes' (*Sermons*, vii. 340; cf. iv. 63).

ll. 91–2. *Division*: the dividing of the soul from the body; and in music a melody made up of a run of short notes (considered as the dividing of longer notes). 'Broken' refers both to the breath of the dying person, and to 'breaking': musical figuration, or the ornamenting of a line of melody with rapid notes.

ll. 97–8. *Anger thine Ague . . . Thy Physicke*. Cf. 'men thinke, that Agues physicke are', *The First Anniversary*, 'An Anatomy', l. 21; see note, p. 130.

l. 98. *slacknesse*: mildness.

l. 101. *to the Triumphant Church, cals thee*. Cf. 'we enter into the *Triumphant Church* by the sound of *Bells*, (for we *enter* when we *die*)' (Sparrow, *Devotions*, p. 94).

l. 102. *Sergeants*: officers of law charged with the arrest of offenders, here of debtors (*O.E.D.* 4); cf. l. 372.

l. 103. *for Legacies they thrust*. They crowd around the death-bed like rapacious heirs.

l. 118. *insensibly*: without their being aware of it.

l. 120. *but a saint Lucies night*. St. Lucy's Day was 13 December, popularly considered to be the shortest day, the winter solstice (actually 12 December in the Julian calendar); the night of 12–13 December is probably that referred to here as the longest night. Yet, as Grierson says, long as it seems, 'it too passes, is only a night. Death is a long sleep, yet a sleep from which we shall awaken'. As in Ps. xc. 4, a period which seems long, 'as a watch in the night', is short.

l. 122. *that shee*: that lady.

ll. 123–6. *whose Complexion was so even*, etc. 'The four humours were so equally tempered in her that neither the anxiety of friends nor the skill of doctors could have predicted which humour would overpower the others and so cause her death: so far were all the humours from excess or defect in her.'

All 'mixed' or compound substances under the sphere of the moon were thought to be prone to dissolution because they lacked an equal 'temper' of their constituents (cf. Aquinas, *S.T.* Iᵃ pars, q. lxxv, art. 6). Cf. 'The Good-morrow', l. 19: 'What ever dyes, was not mixt equally.' A 'just' (l. 127) or perfectly balanced 'complexion' of 'Elements and Humors' (l. 135) would produce perfect health in the body—a condition (except in her case) never attainable (cf. *The First Anniversary*, ll. 89–94, and notes). Fernelius discusses the matter at some length, e.g.: 'Id quasi iustitiae ritu temperatum omnino est quod generis sui decoram illam et consentaneam aequabilitatem est adeptum, qua tanquam numeris omnibus et partibus absolutum, salubriter, integre et naturae suae congruenter se gerit, omnibusque muniis, ad quae natura sua ducitur, incorrupte fungitur. . . . Atque eius potissimum hominis qui optimi sit habitus, quique omnium iudicio temperatus, si non omnino, at certe quasi iustitia quadam censeatur' (*Universa Medicina*, 1610, pp. 64–6). She, however, seemed to have this incorruptible perfection.

l. 127. *Mithridate*: an antidote, especially against poisons, supposed to have been discovered by King Mithridates VI of Pontus. It was made of many ingredients; Pliny (*Nat. Hist.* xxix. 8) mentions a recipe using fifty-four substances (cf. xxiii. 77). Cf. 'To the Countess of Bedford' ('Reason is our Soules left hand'), ll. 25–8.

just: perfectly blended.

l. 130. *all were*: all the parts were best.

ll. 131–4. Everyone knows that quantities (geometrical figures; *O.E.D.* II. 12) are made up of lines, and lines of points; but nobody can divide a line into points, which have position but no magnitude, or break up a figure into lines, which are only limits having length but no breadth.

l. 137. *wonne*: won over, persuaded.

l. 138. *Sunne*. The sun, being above the sphere of the moon and made of 'unmixed' celestial matter, is not subject to change or dissolution (so Ficino, *Liber de Sole*, xiii; *Opera*, 1576, i. 975). Cf. note to ll. 123–6.

ll. 139–40. *and make a spirit feare*, etc. Spirits, being simple beings composed of one pure substance, cannot therefore be divided. Manley cites Plato, *Phaedo* 78–80, Cicero, *Tusc. Disput.* I. xxix. 71, and Aquinas, *S.T.* Iᵃ pars, q. lxxv, art. 6 (on the indivisibility of the soul); see also Aquinas, Iᵃ pars, q. l, art. 5, who proves the same quality in angels.

l. 142. *unstable*: unsteady, because irregular.

ll. 143–6. *such a Chaine, as Fate emploies*, etc. The 'aurea catena Homeri' (*Iliad*, viii. 19), allegorized in the Renaissance as the inevitable sequence of cause and effect. See E. R. Curtius, *European Literature and the Latin Middle Ages*, tr. W. R. Trask, p. 110; and cf. the 'Elegy on Prince Henry', ll. 71–6.

l. 146. *Accident*: both (1) a chance occurrence, mishap, and (2) any event (respectively, *O.E.D.* I. 1. b, c, and I. 1. a). As Manley points out, since this is the chain of Fate, the 'fast' sequence of 'events' can never allow 'mishaps', or occurrences not linked in the inevitable chain of cause and effect.

l. 147. *meat*: food.

l. 150. *Title*: legal 'right' (l. 155), his 'plea' for obtaining which is his faith. Cf. Rom. v. 1–2.

l. 151. *pretend*: claim by law (*O.E.D.* I. 2).

l. 152. *Heaven was content to suffer violence*. 'And from the days of John the Baptist until now the kingdom of heaven suffereth violence, and the violent take it by force' (Matt. xi. 12).

l. 154. *For they'are in Heaven on Earth*, etc. Cf. 'the Joy, and the sense of Salvation, which the pure in heart have here, is not a joy severed from the Joy of Heaven, but a Joy that begins in us here, and continues, and accompanies us thither' (*Sermons*, vii. 340; cf. vi. 235–6, vii. 71, viii. 108).

l. 155. *he had right, and power, and Place*: three valid claims to a piece of land or property—a justified legal claim, power to assert his title, and the right of long possession. He cannot, however, enter fully into possession of heaven till he dies.

l. 158. *sinke*: sewer, cesspool.

ll. 160–2. *those two soules*, etc. In Aristotle's theory of the threefold soul, *De Anima* ii. 413^b–415^a (adopted by Aquinas, *S.T.* I^a pars, q. lxxvi, art. 3), the vegetative and sensible souls were thought to exist in man before the rational soul was infused into him; the third (rational) soul transcended and subsumed (or, as Donne suggests here, consumed) the powers of the other two. Cf. 'To the Countess of Bedford' ('Honour is so sublime perfection'), ll. 34–6, 'To the Countess of Salisbury', ll. 51–6, and Sparrow, *Devotions*, p. 105. Manley cites:

First, in a naturall man wee conceive there is a soule of vegetation and of growth; and secondly, a soule of motion and of sense; and then thirdly, a soule of reason and understanding, an immortall soule. And the two first soules of vegetation, and of sense, wee conceive to arise out of the temperament, and good disposition of the substance of which that man is made, they arise out of man himselfe; But the last soule, the perfect and immortall soule, that is immediatly infused by God (*Sermons*, iii. 85); our immortall soule when it comes, swallowes up the other soules of vegetation, and of sense, which were in us before (ibid. ii. 358; cf. viii. 221).

l. 163. *obnoxious*: liable to be hurt, vulnerable (*O.E.D.* I. c); four syllables. Cf. *Letters*, p. 19: 'I am not obnoxious to that law' and *Paradise Lost*, ix. 170–1: 'obnoxious first or last To basest things'. Contrast 'unobnoxious', 'Elegy on the Lady Markham', l. 35.

ll. 164–7. *poison . . . Infect thee with originall sinne.* Cf. 'the purest Soule becomes stain'd and corrupt with sinne, as soone as it touches the body' (*Pseudo-Martyr*, p. 31, also p. 247); 'To Sir Edward Herbert', ll. 19–20; 'To the Countess of Bedford' ('T'have written then'), ll. 59–60. The orthodox doctrine was that 'if the soule were not infected, the body shoulde not be stained therewith' (*The French Academy*, 1594, II. lxxxi, p. 492; lxxxvi, p. 519; cf. St. Augustine, *De Civ. Dei*, xiv. 3). The difficulty for those who believed that each rational soul was a new creation was that God could not be supposed to make something already evil. Donne's solution, held consistently in the sermons, as Manley points out, was that original sin is derived, not from the body or the soul alone, but from the union of the two. See *Sermons*, ii. 58–9, v. 172, etc.

l. 165. *curded milke.* Manley quotes Job x. 9–10: 'thou hast made me as the clay; and wilt thou bring me into dust again? Hast thou not poured me out as milk, and curdled me like cheese?'
unlittered: as yet unborn; not recorded in this sense in *O.E.D.*

l. 169. *Anchorit*: hermit, recluse (who remained in one place).

l. 170. *fixt to'a Pillar, or a Grave.* Of the 'Stylites', or pillar-saints, the best-known is Simeon the Elder (born *c*. A.D. 390), of Syria, who began pillaring at increasing heights in A.D. 423 and died on his pillar *c*. 460. An order of stylites developed in and around Syria, including Simeon the Younger, who died in 596, aged over seventy. St. Baradatos, a Syrian hermit (*c*. A.D. 460), lived for many years cramped in a hole in the ground, with an inadequate wooden shelter over him (Theodoret, *Relig. Hist.* xxvii; Migne, *P.G.* lxxxii. 1483–6; noted by P. Legouis, *Donne: Poèmes choisis*, Paris, 1955, p. 216).

l. 171. *Bedded and Bath'd*, etc. The basis of the comparison of the state of these hermits with that of the unborn child is explained by Manley, who cites H. Fabricius, *De Formato Foetu* (Venice, 1600, pp. 128–38), and quotes:

L'enfant estant au ventre de sa mere, commence à uriner soudain que toutes ses parties sont formées, par le conduit de l'Umbilic nommé *Urachus*, mais aux derniers mois, prochains de sa nativité, ledit *Urachus* se ferme, comme avons dit, & alors l'enfant masle urine par la verge, la femelle par le col de la vessie. Cette urine se conserve avec les autres excremens, à sçavoir, la sueur, & les serositez, & autres superfluitez du sang menstruel, qui servent pour supporter plus facilement l'enfant nageant en icelles . . . (A. Paré, *Œuvres*, Lyon, 1641, p. 595).

Coleridge copied this line into a notebook in 1803 (*Notebooks*, ed. K. Coburn, i, 1957, no. 1787).

l. 173. *how poore a prison.* The idea of the soul as a prisoner in the body derives from Plato, *Phaedo* 82, and Ps. cxlii. 7: 'Bring my soul out of prison.' Cf. ll. 221, 249, below, and the Holy Sonnet, 'Oh my blacke Soule!', ll. 5–8.

l. 174. *After*: after birth.

l. 175. *when 'twas growne to most*: when the body was fully grown.
  Inne. Cf. *The First Anniversary*, l. 6, and note (p. 128), and 'The Progress of the Soul', l. 181.

  As W. M. Lebans notes (*E.L.H.* xxxix, 1972), this passage uses many of the commonplaces of classical 'consolations' (the soul as a lodger in the contemptible body, defiled by the flesh; the body under threat of sickness and age; the enfranchisement of the soul by death), as in Plutarch, *Consol. ad Apollonium*; Seneca, *Consol. ad Marciam*.

l. 181. *Peece*: firearm.

l. 182. *his owne*: free to act on its own.

ll. 183–4. Cf. Sir John Davies, *Nosce Teipsum* (1599), *Poems*, ed. R. Kreuger and R. Nemser (1975), p. 65:

> For though the *Soule* doe seeme her grave to beare,
>   And in this world is almost buried quick;
>   We have no cause the bodies death to feare,
>   For when the shell is broke, out comes a chick.

Donne in his turn might have influenced Carew in his lines on Lady Mary Wentworth, ll. 4–6 (*Poems*, ed. R. Dunlap, p. 56):

> . . . the soule grew so fast within,
>   It broke the outward shell of sinne,
>   And so was hatch'd a Cherubin.

ll. 188 ff. Probably in 1610 Donne adopted the belief, to which he held consistently thereafter, that at the moment of death the soul of the virtuous Christian goes immediately to heaven and shares the full vision of God; see Gardner, *Divine Poems*, pp. xliii–xlvii, 114–17. Manley cites:

my soule, as soone as it is out of my body, is in Heaven, and does not stay for the possession of Heaven, nor for the fruition of the sight of God, till it be ascended through ayre, and fire, and Moone, and Sun, and Planets, and Firmament, to that place which we conceive to be Heaven, but without the thousandth part of a minutes stop, as soone as it issues, is in a glorious light, which is Heaven (*Sermons*, vii. 71).

l. 190. *Meteors*: phenomena of the lower region of the air (wind, rain, snow, etc.).

l. 192. *intense*: dense, because intensely cold. 'The middle Region is extreame cold' (*M. Blundevile his Exercises*, 1597, f. 181ᵛ). Cf. 'The Storm', l. 14: 'th'ayres middle marble roome'; *Sermons*, vi. 308.

l. 193. *th'Element of fire*. Cf. *The First Anniversary*, l. 206, and note (p. 140).

l. 195. *baits not*: does not stop for rest and refreshment.
  trie: discover, determine (*O.E.D.* 5).

l. 196. *that new world*. Cf. note (p. 140) to *The First Anniversary*, l. 211.

ll. 197–204. The sequence of the spheres of the planets (I. A. Shapiro, *T.L.S.*, 3 July 1937, p. 492) is that proposed by Tycho Brahe, in which the positions of Venus and Mercury are the reverse of those which they occupied in the traditional Ptolemaic system. The 'new Philosophy' was casting doubt on the old theories (*The First Anniversary*, ll. 205 ff.). But, as Manley says, the point here is that such things do not matter to the ascending soul; 'Little know we, how little a way a soule hath to goe to heaven, when it departs from the body; Whether it must passe locally, through Moone, and Sun, and Firmament, . . . I know not, I dispute not, I inquire not' (*Sermons*, vii. 383).

ll. 197–8. *Venus*, etc. Cf. Donne's Problem, 'Why is Venus-star multinominous, called both *Hesperus* and *Vesper*' (Keynes, *Paradoxes and Problems*, pp. 54–5). They are two names for her when she appears as the evening-star.

l. 199. *Argus . . . Mercury.* Ovid (*Metam.* i. 622–721) tells how Juno, after Io had been changed into a heifer by Jupiter, stationed Argus (who had a hundred eyes) to guard Io; Mercury charmed all Argus's eyes to sleep with a flute and a magic wand, and then slew him. 'Mercury' here is both the messenger of the gods and the planet.

l. 200. *growne all Ey.* Freed of the defective organs of the bodily senses, the soul perceives directly and completely, as if it were wholly an eye. Cf. 'When [the body] is once illuminated with the beames of the holy Ghost, it is presently turn'd into all Eye, all Spirit, all Light' (A. Stafford, *The Femall Glory*, 1635, p. 202); and Dryden's imitation of Donne in *Eleonora*:

> O happy soul! if thou canst view from high
> Where thou art all intelligence, all eye (ll. 340–1).

(For Dryden's imitations of the *Anniversaries*, see Lewalski, pp. 342–55.)

l. 204. *his father*: Saturn.

l. 208. *undistinguish'd*: too fast for her to notice the spheres separately.

l. 211. *Pith*: spinal cord. Cf. 'The Funeral', ll. 9–11.

ll. 214–15. *third birth*, etc. Manley cites:

> There are in this man, this Christian, *Tres nativitates*, sayes S. *Gregory*, three births; one, *Per generationem*, so we are borne of our naturall mother; one *Per regenerationem*, so we are borne of our spirituall Mother, the Church, by Baptisme; and a third, *Per Resurrectionem*, and so we are borne of the generall Mother of us all, when the earth shall be delivered, not of twins, but of millions . . . in the Resurrection (*Sermons*, vi. 134–5).

Here, however, the 'third birth' is the moment of death itself, when the redeemed soul has the sight of God (cf. note to ll. 188 ff. above). For Donne the general resurrection is another occasion, when the soul is rejoined to the glorified body.

l. 219. *long-short*: covering a great distance in a short time.

ll. 221–4. This is one of many passages adapted by Prince Henry's chaplain, Daniel Price, in his memorial sermons on the Prince; see Lewalski, pp. 312–16.

l. 226. *prefer*: raise, for comparison (*O.E.D.* I. 1. e).

l. 228. *The Westerne treasure*, etc. Cf. *The First Anniversary*, l. 230, and note (p. 142) and 'The Sun Rising', ll. 17–18.

l. 229. *unknowen*: two syllables.

l. 232. *in her some one part*: in any single part of her.

l. 233. *riches is*. For the singular after 'riches', cf., for example, *Sermons*, vi. 303, vii. 254; cf. Middle English 'richesse'.

ll. 235–40. *did first betroth The Tutelar Angels*, etc. Cf. 'Obsequies to the Lord Harington', l. 228, and note. Medieval theologians extended the idea, Donne thought, to absurd excesses (though they at least had the support of Dan. x. 13, where a guardian angel is assigned to the kingdom of the Persians; cf. *Sermons*, iii. 217). 'And it is as imperfect which is taught by that religion wch is most accommodate to sense. . . . That all mankinde hath one protecting Angel; all Christians one other, all English one other, all of one Corporation and every civill coagulation or society one other; and every man one other' (*Letters*, p. 43). Similarly:

if [the Pope] could come to a true and reall exercise of all that power which they attribute to him, I doubt not, but that *Angell*, which hath so long served in the place of being the particular *Assistant* in the *Conclave*, (for, since they affoord a particular *Tutelar Angell* to everie *Colledge* and *Corporation*, And *to the race of Flyes and of Fleas, and of Ants*, since they allowe such an *Angell to every Infidell Kingdome, yea to Antichrist, yea to Hell it selfe*, it were verie unequall to denie one to this place,) This *Angell*, I say, would be glad of the roome, and become a Suiter to the *holy Ghost*, to name him in the next *Conclave* (*Pseudo-Martyr*, pp. 248–9; the marginal reference to Andreas Victorellus, *De Angelorum Custodia*, 1605, indicates a pertinent passage, quoted by Manley).

ll. 241–3. *Gold, . . . the'Electrum . . . Many degrees of that*. Electrum is an amalgam of four parts of gold to a fifth part of silver; it shines more brightly than silver, and has the property of detecting poisons (Pliny, *Nat. Hist.* xxxiii. 23; Cardan, *De Subtilitate*, 1560, pp. 183–4; cf. *Sermons*, iii. 300). 'Her body, then, is not pure gold, but an alloy in which are many degrees of gold' (Grierson). For Paracelsus, electrum is a substance midway between ore and metal, neither perfect nor imperfect, but moving towards perfection (*The Hermetic and Alchemical Writings of . . . Paracelsus*, ed. A. E. Waite, 1894, ii. 364, noted by Grierson).

l. 244. *sight*: appearance.

ll. 244–6. *her pure and eloquent blood*, etc. These lines were quoted or imitated by Nathanael Lee, *Theodosius* (1680), Dedication; Dryden, 'The Monument of a Fair Maiden Lady who dy'd at Bath' (1700), ll. 10–18; Steele, *Spectator*, i (1712), no. 41; and Fielding, *Tom Jones* (1749), ii. 11 (Keynes, pp. 299–306).

Patrick Cruttwell (*The Shakespearean Moment*, London, 1954, pp. 87-8, 104) notes resemblances to Donne's lines in Marvell's 'To his Coy Mistress', ll. 35-6, and in *The Winter's Tale*, IV. iv. 147-8, 159-60.

l. 247. *largely*: bounteously.

l. 249. *Our prisons prison*: the prison of our bodies, which are the prisons of the soul (cf. l. 173, and note). 'If it be liberty to be delivered out of this bodie, what is the body but a prison?' (*The French Academie*, 1594, p. 756).

l. 251. *roome*: dwelling-place (changed from earth to heaven); cf. l. 156.

l. 252. *Tombe*. For the body as the soul's tomb, cf. Plato, *Phaedrus*, 250; *Gorgias*, 493; and 'The Anniversary', l. 20.

l. 254. *what do'st thou know?* Cf. Cicero, *Prior Academics*, II (Lucullus), xxiii. 73-4: 'Metrodorus the Chian, at the beginning of his book about Nature says: "I say we do not know whether we know anything or whether we know nothing, nor do we either know or not know anything about the very statement just made, or whether anything exists or nothing." . . . So many dialogues have been written at length which place it beyond question that Socrates held knowledge to be impossible. He made only one exception "that he knew himself to know nothing" ' (*The Academics of Cicero*, trans. J. S. Reid, 1880, p. 60; cf. *Sermons*, vii. 260).

l. 255. *know'st thy selfe so little*, etc. 'How little we know our selves, which is the end of all knowledge' (*Sermons*, viii. 107). Cf. Montaigne, 'An Apology of Raymond Sebond' (*Essays*, ii. 12): 'If man know not himselfe, how can hee know his functions and forces?' (trans. Florio, ed. W. E. Henley, ii. 279). Donne remarks that Adam named every creature (Gen. ii. 19) except himself, and 'it may be by some perhaps argued, that he understood himselfe lesse then he did other creatures' (*Sermons*, ix. 256).

l. 256. *did'st die*: incurred the penalty of death due to original sin.

l. 257. *at first cam'st in*: whether by 'traduction' from your parents, or by 'infusion' by God. Donne often refers to the subject (e.g. *Letters*, pp. 16-18).

l. 258. *the poyson of mans sin*. Luther calls sin 'this poison of Satan' with which we are 'infected'; 'we are born from unclean seed [cf. l. 158] and . . . from the very nature of the seed we acquire ignorance of God . . . and similar grave faults' etc. (*On Genesis*; *Works*, St. Louis, 1958, i. 163, 166).

ll. 259-60. As Manley notes, there was a lively controversy about proofs of the immortality of the soul in the early Renaissance. Most thinkers came to agree with Petrus Pomponatius: 'animam esse immortalem est articulus fidei' (*De Immortalitate Animae*, Leyden, 1534, pp. 144-5, cited by Manley): an article of faith, not the subject of reasoning.

l. 262. *bend*: condescend.

l. 263. *To know thy body.* Cf. 'We know nothing of our own bodies: as to the situation of each organ, and the functions of each part we are quite in the dark. . . . Have we any sufficient knowledge of the structure of the nerves, or of the veins? Do we understand what the mind is, or where it is, or in fine whether there is such a thing . . . and, whatever it is, whether it is a perishable thing or immortal. Much indeed is alleged on both sides of these questions' (Cicero, *Prior Academics*, II. xxxix. 122–4; trans. J. S. Reid, pp. 80–1).

l. 265. *Fire, and other Elements.* The traditional medicine of Galen was based on the theory that man's body was made of the four elements, earth, air, fire, and water. Cf. note (p. 140) to *The First Anniversary*, l. 206; and *Letters*, pp. 13–15.

l. 266. *new ingredients*: sulphur, mercury, and salt. These three 'elements' were proposed, instead of Galen's four, by the Benedictine monk, Basil Valentine, who wrote in the second half of the fifteenth century. His theory was adopted by Paracelsus. See M. Foster, *Lectures on the History of Physiology* (Cambridge, 1901), pp. 124–5.

l. 268. *lay*: wager.

ll. 271–2. Though the occurrence of stones in the bladder, and the origin of mucus (l. 273) occasioned no notable controversy, the passage of blood from one ventricle to the other was the subject of much discussion. See D. C. Allen, 'John Donne's Knowledge of Renaissance Medicine', *J.E.G.P.* xlii, at p. 331. Vesalius (1543), following Galen, says: 'The septum of the ventricles, composed . . . of the thickest substance of the heart, abounds on each side with little pits impressed in it. Of these pits, none, so far at least as can be perceived by the senses, penetrate through from the right into the left ventricle, so that we are driven to wonder at the handiwork of the Almighty, by means of which the blood sweats from the right into the left ventricle through passages which escape human vision' (trans. by Foster, *Lectures on the History of Physiology*, p. 14). Donne returns to the subject in *Sermons*, iii. 235–6, where he seems to show an acquaintance with Harvey's unpublished lectures (G. L. Keynes, *The Life of William Harvey*, 1966, pp. 121–2).

l. 275. Cf. Marvell, *Fleckno*, ll. 98–9: 'there can no Body pass Except by penetration hither'; and 'An Horatian Ode', ll. 41–2: 'Nature that hateth emptiness, Allows of penetration less'.

ll. 275–6. *piercing of substances.* As Grierson notes (ii. 273), the penetration of one substance by another was a Stoic doctrine, opposed to Aristotle's theory of mixture of substances (what we should call chemical combination) which stated that, though the qualities of the substances combined to produce a new quality, the substances themselves remained juxtaposed; he refers to Plotinus's discussion of the matter in *Enneads*, ii. 7.

ll. 277–8. *many' opinions . . . Of Nailes and Haires.* It was a matter of controversy whether nails and hair are to be classed as skin, bones, organs of the body, or merely waste products (excrements) and not properly parts of the body at all. Fernelius, for instance, has no doubt that they are 'excrementi' (*Universa Medicina*, 1610, p. 44). Cf. *Sermons*, iv. 160; viii. 177.

l. 282. Cf. Simpson, *Essays*: 'Man, who (like his own eye) sees all but himself, in his opinion, but so dimly, that there are marked an hundred differences in mens Writings concerning an *Ant*' (p. 14); and the note (p. 139) to *The First Anniversary*, l. 190.

l. 284. *Catechismes and Alphabets*: the rudiments of knowledge.

l. 285. *unconcerning*: trivial (the earliest example cited in *O.E.D.*).

l. 288. 'Why is the bloud red?' is one of the problems attributed to Aristotle (*The Problemes of Aristotle*, Edinburgh, 1575, E5ᵛ).

ll. 290–9. In *Tusc. Disput.* i. 43–5, Cicero says that nothing is swifter than the soul's movement as it surmounts the atmosphere and reaches its natural habitation among the stars (cf. ll. 179–219); freed from bodily desires and limitations, the eye of the mind can pierce to the truth (l. 200). He goes on to speak of the senses as the medium of knowledge on earth, but as clogged by their earthly weaknesses: 'cum autem nihil erit praeter animum, nulla res obiecta impediet quo minus percipiat quale quidque sit' (i. 46–7; also § 75). Similarly Plutarch, *Consol. ad Apollonium*, 108 B, C: 'if we are ever going to have any pure knowledge, we must divest ourselves of the body, and with the soul itself "observe the realities"' (*Moralia*, Loeb ed. ii. 141).

l. 290. *forme*: state, condition (*O.E.D.*, sb. 5. b). P. Legouis (*Donne: Poèmes choisis*, p. 217) suggests that the 'forme' is a school class (*O.E.D.* 6. b) using 'Catechismes and Alphabets' (l. 284; cf. 'Pedantery', l. 291, 'taught', l. 292, and 'schoole', l. 301).

l. 291. *Pedantery*: accented on the second syllable. This is the earliest example quoted in *O.E.D.* (though Sidney had used 'pedanteria' in 1581).

l. 292. *taught by sense, and Fantasy?* The most widely accepted opinion (based upon Aristotle, *De Anima* iii) was that we do not know the world outside us immediately, but that our different senses carry impressions to a part of the mind called the fantasy, which makes a synthetic image of the object perceived called a phantasm; 'our intellect understands material things by abstracting from the phantasms' (Aquinas, *S.T.* Iᵃ pars, q. lxxxv, art. 1; see also q. lxxv, art. 6; q. lxxxiv, art. 7; q. lxxxvi, art. 1). Ficino discusses the matter in *Theologia Platonica*, ix (*Opera*, Basle, 1576, i. 204). Cf. *Sermons*, vii. 334.

l. 293. *spectacles*: artificial means of seeing (mirrors, telescopes, etc.); as we might say, 'distorting lenses'.

l. 294. *watch-towre*: an emblem of the mind, from ancient classical and Biblical sources. Cf. Plato, *Timaeus* 70 A; *Republic* 560 B; Isaiah xxi. 5–8; Hab. ii. 1–2. The commonplace is further documented by D. C. Allen, *The Harmonious Vision* (Baltimore, 1954), pp. 17–18. Cf. *The Faerie Queene*, II. ix. 44–58.

l. 297. *Laberinths*. First recorded in this meaning (*O.E.D.* 3) in 1696. Cf. Chapman, 'Hymnus in Noctem', l. 23 (*Poems*, ed. P. B. Bartlett, 1962, p. 20): 'breake the labyrinth of everie eare'.

l. 298. *circuit, or collections*: roundabout methods, or inferences.

l. 299. *it*: heaven itself. Manley quotes:

As he that fears God, fears nothing else, so, he that sees God, sees every thing else: when we shall see God, *Sicuti est*, as he is, we shall see all things *Sicuti sunt*, as they are; for that's their Essence, as they conduce to his glory. We shall be no more deluded with outward appearances: for, when this sight, which we intend here comes, there will be no delusory thing to be seen. All that we have made as though we saw, in this world, will be vanished, and I shall see nothing but God, and what is in him (*Sermons*, iii. 111–12).

ll. 301–20. As Manley points out, Donne is working with the familiar image, 'the book of the mind': man's mind is a book inscribed with the wisdom and art of God. See Curtius, *European Literature and the Latin Middle Ages*, tr. W. R. Trask, pp. 320–1. Her virtue enabled her to know essential truth on earth as she now does in heaven; we, however, could understand it only as we studied her example.

l. 302. *full*: fully instructed.

l. 308. *aye*: always. The spelling of *1612–21*, 'aie', is a common variant; it was corrupted to 'are' in *1625*; and the editor of *1633*, using *1625* as copy, emended to 'all'.

l. 315. *waite*: weight.

ll. 316–17. *over-fraite . . . Ballast*: overload and so cause to sink, as distinct from 'ballasting'—loading a vessel just enough to keep it steady on an even keel. Cf. 'Air and Angels', ll. 15–18.

l. 324. *conversation*: society (*O.E.D.* 2, 5).

l. 325. *wilt thou Converse*: i.e. on earth.

ll. 331–2. *no things bee So like as Courts*. Manley cites: 'no things are liker one another, then *Court* and *Court*, the same ambitions, the same underminings in one Court as in another' (*Sermons*, iii. 123).

ll. 335–6. *poysons affect Chiefly the cheefest parts*. Cardan, *De Venenis*, I. xv (published as part of *In Septem Aphorismorum Hippocrates particulas commentaria*, Basle, 1564, col. 896), refers to Galen, *De Locis Affectis*, i. 7, as his authority for the following: 'vim illam qua sentimus, à cerebro, ut solis lumen diffundi ac permeare statim per nervos ipsos, atque ad extrema usque, unde etiam ab extremis ipsis statim ad ipsum principium remeat. Atque idem de veneno ipso dicendum est. receptum enim per cavitates ipsorum nervorum solita in naturae eorum, transgreditur ad prima principia, maximéque cerebrum'; though, he adds, some poisons first affect the liver, the heart, etc.

l. 337. *Nailes, and Haires, yea excrements.* Cardan (see previous note), ii. xiii, col. 968, says of those dead by poisoning: 'ungues nigri post mortem . . . capilli qui sponte decidunt' (citing Galen, *De Locis Affectis*, vi. 5). The nails and hair were thought by many to be excrements of the body; see ll. 277–8, and note. Manley quotes Raphael Volaterranus: 'Inter excrementa pili quoque connumerantur, & ungues' (*Commentariorum Urbanarum Libri xxxviii*, Basle, 1559, p. 581); and Thomas Nashe, *The Unfortunate Traveller* (*Works*, ed. R. B. McKerrow, rev. F. P. Wilson (1958), ii. 227, 230).

l. 338. *will.* The misprint 'wise' in *1612* (corrected in the errata-slip) was preserved in the edition of *1625*, used by the printer of *1633*; the reading 'lyes' in *1633* is an example of the fairly skilful editing shown throughout that volume.

ll. 339–58. Donne's hierarchy (the Blessed Virgin, Patriarchs, Prophets, Apostles, Martyrs, Virgins) follows the order of the Catholic Litany of the Saints and of Cranmer's Litany of 1544. He omits the Angels after Mary, having referred to them in l. 340, and the Confessors before the Virgins; and others (Doctors, Bishops, etc.) found in the Roman Litany but not included by Cranmer. Cf. 'A Litany', v–xiv, and see the note in Gardner, *Divine Poems*, pp. 83–4.

l. 339. *new eare*: i.e. the spiritual 'ear'; cf. 'growne all Ey', l. 200.

l. 342. *Joy in not being that, which men have said.* Theologians (who are merely men) have put forward the opinion that the Virgin Mary was free of original sin; but in fact she rejoices in not being free of it, but in having won her honoured place in Heaven by her goodness. (The doctrine of the Immaculate Conception was not a dogma of the Roman Church until 1854.) Cf. 'A Litany', l. 40, and the note in Gardner, *Divine Poems*, p. 84; Manley quotes:

He came into the world; it is not *in mundam*, into so clean a woman as had no sin at all, none contracted from her Parents, no original sin; for so Christ had placed his favours and his honors ill, if he had favoured her most who had no need of him: to dye for all the world, and not for his mother, or to dye for her, when she needed not that hell, is a strange imagination: she was not without sin; for then why should she have died? for even a natural death in all that come by natural generation, is of sin (*Sermons*, i. 307; cf. vi. 183).

ll. 343–4. Grierson quotes St. Augustine (Migne, *P.L.* xl. 398): 'Beatior ergo Maria percipiendo fidem Christi, quam concipiendo carnem Christi'. Augustine goes on to quote Luke xi. 27–8:
said unto him, Blessed is the womb

hast sucked. But he said, Yea rather, blessed are they that hear the word of God, and keep it.'

l. 344. *her interest, of mother-hood*: any special claim she might have as being Christ's mother.

ll. 345–6. *Patriarckes, which did longer sit*, etc. The time from the Creation to the birth of Christ was longer than that from His birth to the present day.

l. 350. *All the Sunnes course.* They went to all parts of the earth, preaching the gospel to all nations, thus bringing a greater light with them than the sun's.

ll. 351–2. *Martyrs, who did calmely bleed . . . dew to their seed.* A variation of the proverb (originating in Tertullian, *Apologeticus*, ch. 50), 'the blood of the martyrs was the seed of the Church'; quoted in *Biathanatos*, p. 63; cf. *Sermons*, i. 157, 162. Donne uses another variation in *Pseudo-Martyr*: 'The blood of the Martyres was the milke which nourished the Primitive Church, in her infancy' (p. 6).

l. 354. *joyntenants.* Cf. *The First Anniversary*, l. 114, and note (p. 135); here, 'fellow-owners and joint lodgers'.

l. 355. *his Temple*: their bodies; 'your body is the temple of the Holy Ghost' (1 Cor. vi. 19; cf. iii. 16–17).

l. 360. *royalties*: the prerogatives (l. 373) of a sovereign. These are listed (ll. 361–74) in turn: to make war and conclude peace, to administer justice, to exert unquestioned authority, to dispense pardon, to coin money, to grant protection against legal arrest. These points look like a selection from such a discussion as that of Petrus Gregorius Tholosanus, *De Republica* (Lyon, 1609), bk. ix, ch. i ('De potestate regia'), pp. 264–76.

l. 364. *together kisse.* Cf. 'Mercy and truth are met together; righteousness and peace have kissed each other' (Ps. lxxxv. 10).

l. 369. *impressions*: (1) imprints of the sovereign's head stamped on coins (giving the metal its value); (2) the acts that influenced our conduct for good.

l. 371. *protections.* 'Protection . . . is used for an exemption, or an immunitie given by the King to a person against suites in lawe, or other vexations upon reasonable causes him thereunto mooving, which I take to be a braunch of his prerogative' (J. Cowell, *The Interpreter*, 1607, s.v. 'Protection'; cited by Manley). Donne is thinking especially of the King's granting of immunity from arrest. His extravagant friend, Sir Henry Goodyer, for many years staved off his creditors by obtaining royal protections of this kind (Bald, pp. 494–5).

l. 374. *state.* In the previous fifteen lines Donne has been working with the familiar 'correspondence' of the individual human being to the 'body-politic'. Cf. 'Every Christian is a state, a common-wealth to *himselfe*, and in him, the *Scripture* is his *law*, and the *conscience* is his *Judge*' (*Sermons*, iv. 216).

ll. 374–5. *religion Made her a Church.* Cf. 'Every man is a little *Church*' (*Sermons*, iv. 194; cf. iv. 84, viii. 184); 'every man hath *a Church* in himselfe' (ibid. vii. 403).

l. 382. *accidentall joyes in Heaven doe grow.* The essential joy of heaven is the sight of God; accidental joys (the conversation of the saints, joy in the repentance of sinners, etc.), unlike the essential joy, increase. Her presence in heaven is an accidental joy; but she herself possesses the unchanging essential joy. Manley cites:

> The blessednesse of heaven it selfe, Salvation, and the fruits of Paradise . . . have yet got no other name in the subtilty of the Schools, nor in the fulnesse of the Scriptures, but to be called the joys of heaven; Essentiall blessednesse is called so, *Enter into thy Masters joy*, that is, into the Kingdome of heaven; and accidentall happinesse added to that essentiall happinesse is called so too: There is joy in heaven at the conversion of a sinner (*Sermons*, iii. 339).

ll. 385–6. 'An accessorie shal be punished, and that have judgement of life and member, as well as the principal which bid the felonie: but such an accessory shal never be put to that till the principal be attaint or convict, or bee outlawed thereupon' (J. Rastell, *An Exposition of . . . Termes of the Lawes*, 1609, fol. 7ʳ). There is a pun on 'tried', as it applies both to a legal trial, and to the 'testing' or 'proving' of the sources of joy.

ll. 387–9. Cf. 'In this world we enjoy nothing; enjoying presumes perpetuity; and here, all things are fluid, transitory: There I shall enjoy, and possesse for ever, God himself . . .' (*Sermons*, ix. 128).

l. 391. *couse'ned cose'nor*: deceived deceiver.

ll. 391–400. Cf. Montaigne's argument that we are not the same persons today as we were yesterday; and that since we have no permanent existence, our identity is not fixed: 'what admitteth alterations, continueth not the same: and if it be not one selfe same, then it is not' ('An Apology of Raymond Sebond', *Essays*, II. xii; trans. Florio, ed. Henley, ii. 331).

ll. 395–6. *although the river keep the name*, etc. The famous illustration used by Heraclitus. Cf. 'Obsequies to the Lord Harington', ll. 47–52.

l. 398. *That saint, nor Pilgrime*: in Petrarchan convention, the beloved lady, and her lover. Grierson quotes *Romeo and Juliet*, I. v. 95–7, where Juliet says:

> Good pilgrim, you do wrong your hand too much
> Which mannerly devotion shows in this;
> For saints have hands that pilgrims' hands do touch.

l. 400. *howrely in inconstancee.* Cf. 'Woman's Constancy', ll. 2–5.

l. 401. *pretence unto*: claim upon.

ll. 401–5. When God was alone, He was without honour, since honour is not an intrinsic quality but depends on the attitude of others. Cf. 'To the Countess of Bedford' ('Honour is so sublime perfection'), ll. 1–3, and:

[God] is content to receive his Honour from us, (for although all cause of Honour be eternally inherent in himselfe, yet that Act proceeds from us, and of that Honour, which is *in Honorante*, he could have none, til he had made Creatures to exhibit it) (Simpson, *Essays*, p. 54; cited by Manley).

l. 406. *that, to his hands, man might grow more fit*: that man might (1) become more fittingly the product of the hands of his Creator, and (2) grow in virtue so as to become the instrument of God's purposes. As Manley points out, it was generally held that Adam would have increased in goodness if he had not fallen. Cf. *Sermons*, vii. 108; Aquinas, *S.T.* I^a pars, q. cii, art. 4; *Paradise Lost*, v. 493–503.

ll. 407–9. Cf. 'To the Countess of Bedford' ('Honour is so sublime perfection'), ll. 7–9:

> . . . from low persons doth all honour flow;
> Kings, whom they would have honour'd, to us show,
> And but *direct* our honour, not *bestow*.

l. 409. *that*: for the repeated conjunction, 'since' (like French *que*).

l. 412. *casuall*: accidental, inessential, depending on chance and change.

l. 414. *arrest*: give rest or security to (*O.E.D.* 3, but used transitively).

l. 415. *a worse*: a worse course.

l. 416. *Thinke*: a subjunctive, 'should think', 'might think'.

ll. 417–22. Manley cites:

Men have considered usefully the incongruity of building the towre of Babel, in this, That to have erected a Towre that should have carried that height that they intended in that, the whole body of the earth, the whole Globe, and substance thereof would not have served for a basis, for a foundation to that Towre. If all the timber of all the forests in the world, all the quarries of stones, all the mines of Lead and Iron had beene laid together, nay if all the earth and sea had beene petrified, and made one stone, all would not have served for a basis, for a foundation of that Towre; from whence then must they have had their materials for all the superedifications? (*Sermons*, viii. 322–3).

No direct source is known for this argument (see D. C. Allen, 'John Donne and the Tower of Babel', *M.L.N.* lxiv, 1949). Pererius quotes Philo Judaeus' refutation (*De Conf. Linguarum*, ii. 5) of those who doubted the Biblical story because 'etiam si universae terrae partes superstruerentur fundamento modico, ut in unius columnae formam attollerentur, longissimo tamen intervallo distarent a sphaera aetherea' (*Comment. et Disput. in Genesim*, 1601, i. 588 ff.).

l. 418. *for that effect*: to achieve their purpose, which was to build a tower 'whose top may reach unto heaven' (Gen. xi. 4).

l. 421. *this Center*: the earth.

ll. 425–8. As Manley notes, Cicero speaks of the deification of 'Amor, Dolus, Morbus, Labor, Invidentia, Fatum, Senectus, Mors, Tenebrae, Miseria, Querella, Gratia, Fraus, Pertinacia, Parcae, Hesperides, Somnia', and says that 'perniciosis . . . rebus non modo nomen deorum tribueretur, sed etiam sacra constituerentur. Febris enim fanum in Palatio et Orbonae ad aedem Larum et aram Malae Fortunae Esquiliis consecratam videmus' (*De Deorum Natura*, III. xvii. 44; xxv. 63). Cf. *Sermons*, iii. 83, vi. 308. Juvenal adds the onion (*Sat.* xv. 9–11). Tertullian speaks of the worship of human traits and of 'bulbi' as gods (*Ad Nationes* ii, Migne, *P.L.* i. 587–607); Donne cites this passage in Simpson, *Essays*, p. 22; Sparrow, *Devotions*, p. 43; and *Sermons*, ix. 125.

l. 426. *Rods*: chastenings, punishments.

l. 432. *thrust*: crowd, throng.

l. 435. *thy first pitch*: (1) the height of the human soul before the Fall; with a suggestion of the 'pitch' or point to which a hawk soars before 'stooping' on its prey; (2) the point (centre) from which one describes or 'pitches' a circle (*O.E.D.*, sb. III. 10); (3) the musical 'pitch' of the soul attuned to God ('first pitch' = 'perfect harmony').

l. 436. *lines which circles doe containe*: diameters.

l. 439. *Double*: an imperative.

l. 440. *All will not serve.* Even if you do all in your power to think of heaven, it will not be enough. One cannot on earth even think about the essential joy of heaven.

l. 441. *it*: the sight of God. Only those who have actually seen God fully can conceive ('thinke') what the sight of God is; it is both the 'object' seen and the power of understanding ('wit') that enables the soul to see it. Cf. Aquinas's argument that, since God alone belongs to His own subsistent being, 'to know self-subsistent being is natural to the divine intellect alone; and this is beyond the natural power of any created intellect. . . . Therefore the created intellect cannot see the essence of God, unless God by His grace unites Himself to the created intellect, as an object made intelligible to it' (*S.T.* Iª pars, q. xii, art. 4; noted by Manley). This is based on Aristotle, *Metaph.* 1075ª: 'Since, then, thought and the object of thought are not different in the case of things that have not matter, the divine thought and its object will be the same, i.e. the thinking will be one with the object of its thought' (trans. W. D. Ross). Cf. *Sermons*, vii. 344–6. On 'the sight of God' see *Sermons*, vi. 234–6.

l. 446. *Had th'Angels once look'd on him, they had stood.* As Manley notes, at the first moment of their creation some of the angels looked at once to their Creator and 'stood' (did not fall); others, however, looked at their own natures and became proudly absorbed in themselves: 'when there was nothing but God and themselves, they fell in love with themselves, and neglected

God, and so fell *in aeternum*, for ever' (*Sermons*, iii. 254; cf. viii. 361, x. 180); they never 'enjoyd The sight of God' (ll. 440–1). Cf. Augustine, *De Genesi ad Litteram*, iv. 29–32 (Migne, *P.L.* xxxiv. 311–17); Aquinas, *S.T.* Iª pars, q. lxiii, arts. 5–6.

l. 447. *To fill the place of one of them, or more*. Cf. note (p. 128) to 'To the Praise of the Dead, and the Anatomy', l. 38.

l. 449. *Here*: 'on earth'. The capital might be authentic, matching those in 'Heaven' and 'Earth', l. 439.

   so much essentiall joye. Cf. *The First Anniversary*, ll. 433–4.

l. 450. *distract*: undo, disperse, spoil (*O.E.D.* v. 2. b).

l. 453. *in any naturall Stone, or Tree*: that is, in the Book of the Creatures, in which some part of God's nature is revealed.

l. 456. *reparation*: good repair (*O.E.D.* 2).

l. 457. *decay*: the principle of death, brought in by Original Sin. If Adam had not sinned, the image of God would have remained unsullied in the hearts of men. See Lewalski, pp. 112–41.

ll. 459–62. Marriage pre-contracts, or betrothals, cannot be relied on, but God's promises are sure. She resisted temptations to break faith through her knowledge that God is wholly to be trusted; and she is now with Him in heaven. The word 'solicited' (l. 459) has sexual overtones.

l. 462. *Betroth'd*: as a virgin.

l. 463. *Whose twilights were more cleare*, etc. Cf. *The First Anniversary*, ll. 73–4.

l. 464. *Who dreamt devoutlier, then most use to pray*. Manley cites: 'those Saints of God who have their Heaven upon earth, doe praise him in the night: according to that of S. *Jerome, Sanctis ipse somnus, oratio* [Migne, *P.L.* xxii. 421]; and that of S. *Basil, Etiam somnia Sanctorum preces sunt* [cf. Migne, *P.G.* xxxi. 243–6, xxxii. 1239]; That holy men doe praise God, and pray to God in their sleep, and in their dreames' (*Sermons*, viii. 53; cf. ii. 227, viii. 202, x. 220).

   use to: are accustomed to.

l. 466. *more capacitee*: i.e. to receive grace. Cf. ll. 440–5.

l. 470. *as our joyes admit*: in so far as we are capable of joy on earth.

ll. 471–2. Even if this world could give us essential joys, heaven's accidental joys would far surpass them, for in heaven even accidental, or 'casuall', joys are lasting (ll. 487–8).

l. 473. *casuall*: not essential, 'accidents' in the philosophical sense; but also '(subject to) chance'.

l. 475. *swell thee*: i.e. with pride.

l. 477. *Redresse*: remedy, relief.

l. 479. *Apostem*: imposthume, deep-seated abscess. Manley quotes: 'A Pos-
tume is gathered of superfluitie of humours in some member, and maketh
rotting and swelling. . . . [The humours] be received in the hollowness of
members, and ther boyle and putrifie, and as paast set in an oven, and dryed
by fire, receiveth a manner crusting . . . so the humour gathered, by heat
boyleth and maketh a manner crust ['bag', l. 481] above, under the which
crust rotted humor is hidde, and swelleth: and such a swellyng is called
Apostema' (*Batman upon Bartholome*, 1582, f. 110b).

l. 480. *rest*: residue.

l. 481. *bag*: the sac containing the fluid (*O.E.D.*, sb. III. 11).

l. 482. *aye*: always. What has so far always been a matter of chance is likely
to continue to be so.

l. 483. *What should the Nature change?* What could possibly change the nature
(of casual joys into certain joy)?

l. 486. *that it can away*: that it is equally able to leave us.

l. 488. *accidentall things*: those joys in Heaven (e.g. those mentioned in ll.
489–96) which are different from, and additional to, the essential joy of the
sight of God.

l. 496. *Degrees of grouth.* Cf. 'the glory of the next world, is not in the measure
of that glory, but in the measure of my capacity; it is not that I shall have as
much as any soule hath, but that I shall have as much as my soul can
receive; it is not in an equality with the rest, but in a fulnesse in myself'
(*Sermons*, vi. 335; cf. Aquinas, *S.T.*, Supp., q. xciii, art. 3).

ll. 498–9. *he that names degree, Doth injure her*: anyone who tries to describe
her status in heaven (i.e. to specify the extent of her virtue, and blessedness)
would only disparage her.

ll. 499–500. The materials of which she is made make her a being of a
superior order; it demeans her to call her the 'best' of an inferior order of
beings.

ll. 501–6. *such a body*, etc. The passage is developed from ll. 221–47.

l. 503. *Made better*: i.e. by being glorified for its reunion with the soul at
the general resurrection (ll. 491–4).

l. 504. *full, on both sides written Rols*: rolls of parchment written all over on
both sides. Oddly enough, Donne's name appears, as Dean of St. Paul's, on
such a roll, listing the members of the court of High Commission (P.R.O.,
C/66/2352 (4)).

ll. 507–8. *making full perfection grow*, etc. Already perfect in goodness and joy,
she grows to an even fuller perfection; she adds to the perfection of a circle,
while keeping it a circle (the symbol of perfection), though it was already
perfect before.

l. 508. *Peeces*: augments. Cf. *Antony and Cleopatra*, I. v. 45–6: 'I will piece Her opulent throne with kingdoms'.

l. 509. *Long'd for*: i.e. by heaven itself. As Grierson notes, in Dante's *Vita Nuova*, xix, the angels and saints ask God that they might have Beatrice with them in heaven (e.g. 'Madonna è desiata in sommo cielo', Canzone Prima, l. 48).

l. 510. *gives addition*. In heaven each rejoices in the good of others as well as in his own.

l. 511. *Here*: France, where Donne stayed with Sir Robert Drury from the end of November 1611 until mid April 1612 (Bald, pp. 245–57). Cf. 'A Letter to the Lady Carey, and Mrs. Essex Rich, from Amiens', ll. 1–9.

ll. 511–12. *mis-devotion frames*, etc. Cf. 'Trust not in flesh, but in spirituall things, That wee neither bend our hopes downeward, to infernall spirits, to seeke help in Witches; nor mis-carry it upward, to seeke it in Saints, or Angels, but fix it in him, . . . our blessed, and gracious, and powerfull God' (*Sermons*, vi. 295–6; cf. viii. 113).

ll. 514–15. *what lawes of poetry admit*, etc.: invocations, in poetry of the muses and pagan deities, in Roman Catholicism of the saints.

l. 517. *Could any Saint provoke that appetite*: if any saint could prompt in him the desire to invoke a saint instead of God Himself, it would be she (l. 518).

l. 518. *a French convertite*: a convert to Catholicism. Irony is added to the word here, and in 'A Letter to the Lady Carey . . .', l. 7, since in French *converti* was a name given to beggars who made a profession of their change of religion in order to extract alms from passers-by (*Larousse du XIXᵉ siècle*); they would be very free in their invocations of saints.

l. 519. *wouldst not*: wouldst not countenance this 'mis-devotion'.

l. 521. *stampe*: impression.

ll. 527–8. The poet is the herald blowing the trumpet before the reading of a royal proclamation. The priests in Num. x. 2–3, 10, were to blow their silver trumpets, at whose voice the people came together. See Lewalski, pp. 277–80; and cf. 'To the Countess of Huntingdon' ('Man to Gods image'), ll. 69–70: 'I was your Prophet . . . [am] now your Chaplaine, God in you to praise.'

EPICEDES AND OBSEQUIES

Elegie on the Lady Marckham (p. 57)

MSS.: Group I (*C 57, D, H 49, Lec, SP*); *H 40*; Group II (*A 18, N, TCC, TCD*); *L 74*; *DC* (ll. 45–62); Group III (*Dob, Lut, O'F, S 96*); *Cy, O 2, P; A 25, C, D 17, JC; B, O 1.*

Miscellanies: *Grey, Hd, Hol, La, S 962 TCD* (2), *Wed, Wel*; Brit. Lib. MSS. *Add. 30982, 19268* (ll. 43–6); University of Edinburgh, Halliwell–Phillips Colln., MS. *401* (ll. 17–20, 41–4, 53–62); National Library of Scotland, *Hawthornden MS. VIII* (ll. 15–16, 59–60).

The titles in the MSS. and most of the miscellanies are the same as, or similar to, those given in the apparatus; the poem is untitled in *B*. Ll. 44–5 are omitted from *1633*, and I take the accidents from *1635*; otherwise I reject readings of *1633* in ll. 6, 9, 12, 42, 58, and 62. My text differs from Grierson's in ll. 9, 42, and 62, where he retains the *1633* reading, and in l. 11, where he does not.

Bridget, the daughter of Sir James Harington (younger brother of John, first Baron Harington of Exton), married in 1598 Sir Anthony Markham of Sedgebrook, Nottinghamshire. She was a first cousin of Lucy, Countess of Bedford (daughter of the first Baron Harington), and was one of the Ladies of the Queen's Bedchamber. Sir Anthony Markham died on 10 December 1604, and his widow became (if she was not already) a close friend of the Countess. She died at Twickenham Park (the Countess's estate) on 4 May 1609, aged 30. On her monument at Twickenham church it is said that she was 'inclytae Luciae, Comitissae de Bedford sanguine (quod satis) sed et amicitia propin-quissima'. Francis Beaumont's elegy upon her (beginning 'As unthrifts grieve in straw for their pawn'd beds') occurs fairly frequently in MS. collections, sometimes ascribed to Donne. In *HK 2, H 40*, and *RP 31* there is the following anonymous epitaph upon her (*H 40*, fol. 252ʳ):

> A mayde, a wief, shee liv'd, a wydowe, dyed,
> her virtue through all womans state was varyed,
> the wydowe, bodye, which this vayle doth hide
> keepes in, expecting to be highlie marryed,
> when that great bridegroome from the clouds shall call
> and joyne, each to his owne, himselfe to all.

(In *HK 2* the poem is entitled simply 'Epitaph'.)

l. 1. *death the Ocean*. L. C. Rhodiginus says that water 'figuram mortis ostendit' (*Lectionum Antiquarum libri . . .*, 1560, ii. 337). 'Death comes to us in the name, and notion of waters too, in the Scriptures' (*Sermons*, ix. 107).

l. 3. *as yet*: since we are still alive.

l. 5. *pretend*: *O.E.D.*, vb. 12, 'stretch forward'; reach at, threaten.

ll. 7–8. *land waters . . . waters, then, above our firmament*. The little 'World' (l. 1) of man has 'waters' (tears) corresponding to the two kinds of waters in the macrocosm: those that flow through and from the 'land', and the 'seas above the firmament'. The location of the waters above the firmament (Gen. i. 7, 9) puzzled commentators. Aquinas says that if by 'firmament' is meant the firmament of fixed stars these waters, being incorruptible, must be of a different kind from those on earth; if by 'firmament' is meant the dense upper

part of the air, the waters are the vapours of which rain is formed (*S.T.* Iᵃ
pars, q. lxviii, art. 2; similarly Pererius, *Comment. et Disput. in Genesim*, 1601,
pp. 37–46). Donne's conceit is favoured by the former interpretation. Cf.

> God made the Firmament, which he called Heaven, after it had divided the waters:
> After we have distinguished our teares, naturall from spirituall, worldly from
> heavenly, then there is a Firmament established in us, then there is a heaven
> opened to us (*Sermons*, iv. 340); The water of Heaven, teares for offending thy God,
> are better then teares for worldly losses (ibid. viii. 201).

l. 7. *passion*: suffering (as in l. 16).
   vent: flow out (*O.E.D.*, vb. II. 11).

l. 11. Cf. 'there be good teares and bad teares, teares that wash away sin,
and teares that are sin'; 'To mourne . . . imoderately for the death of any
that is passed out of this world, is not the right use of teares'; 'Thy first
teares must be to God for sin' (*Sermons*, iv. 340–2; cf. vi. 290).

In those grieving for Lady Markham, tears of contrition are confused with
tears for worldly losses, and are tainted with the saltiness of the 'Ocean' of
death; thus their spiritual life is invaded by griefs which belong to man's
'lower parts'. (The pre-Christian statement of the thought is represented in
Plutarch, *Consol. ad Apollonium*, xxiv: *Moralia*, Loeb ed. ii. 173–5; cf. ii. 161.)

l. 12. *Gods Noe*: God's promise to Noah (Gen. ix. 11, 15) that 'the waters
shall no more become a flood to destroy all flesh'.

With Grierson, I reject the reading 'the world' in *1633* and some manu-
scripts. It is 'our world', the microcosm of man, that is in question; another
flood could not, after God's promise, occur in the physical world. The scribe
of *Cy* recognizes the point in his wording of the line: 'Wee after Gods mercy
drowne our soules again.'

ll. 13–14. Cf.

> *nec seipso, homo, nisi perniciose uti potest* . . . we have no interest in our selves, no power
> to doe any thing of, or with our selves, but to our destruction. Miserable man! a
> Toad is a bag of Poyson, and a Spider is a blister of Poyson, and yet a Toad and a
> Spider cannot poyson themselves; Man hath a dram of poyson, originall-Sin, in an
> invisible corner, we know not where, and he cannot choose but poyson himselfe
> and all his actions with that (*Sermons*, i. 293).

l. 19. *embroderd workes*: delicate and intricate patterns; 'workes' as in 'needle-
work' (*O.E.D.*, 'work', sb. 16).

ll. 21–2. *As men of China*, etc. Grierson quotes Sir Thomas Browne, who
himself quotes a work with which Donne was familiar, Guido Panciroli's
Nova Reperta, sive Rerum Memorabilium, Part II of which appeared in 1602,
with annotations by Heinrich Salmuth. In the chapter *De Porcellanis*, Panciroli
says of 'Porcellanae': 'sunt autem massa quaedam, et gypso, ovo trito, puta-
mina locustae marinae, & aliis speciebus composita: quae si probè stipata &

densata fuerit, sub terra in locum aliquem secretiorum reconditur. Atque ibi octoginta annos manet recondita' (p. 141). Salmuth corrects Panciroli, and quotes more recent authority to the effect that porcelain was made of clay (pp. 142–3). Cf. R. N. Ringler, 'Donne's Specular Stone', *M.L.R.* lx (1965), at p. 338.

ll. 23–8. The alchemical image is a development of those used by Donne in 'Resurrection, imperfect', ll. 9–16, in the Eclogue prefixed to the Somerset 'Epithalamion', ll. 61–4, and in 'Epitaph on Himself', ll. 11–14; it is discussed by E. H. Duncan, 'Donne's Alchemical Figures', *E.L.H.* ix (1942), at p. 267.

   The alchemists held that, by 'dying' (through mortification by fire or by putrefaction) into its first elements, a substance might achieve regeneration or transmutation into a better form. Metals and gems (like all substances) strive towards the perfection of gold, and were thought to change gradually over long periods, through the influence of the sun and the condensation of mercury and sulphur vapours among the stones, into gold. Gold itself could be refined by the same processes into a 'tincture', 'quintessence' or 'Elixar' (l. 28), which is the spiritual principle or 'soul' of gold, and is capable of transmuting baser substances to gold by being infused into them. Lady Markham's grave is like a 'limbecke' (alembic, refining vessel), in which her flesh (already equal in substance to the most precious earthly substances) will be transmuted by its 'soul' (which is 'her soule', l. 25) into a quintessential substance. This 'Elixar' will be used by God at the Last Day to change all earthly flesh into the substance of men's heavenly bodies: 'for there Bodies are purer, then best Soules are here' ('Elegy on Mrs. Bulstrode', ll. 47–8).

l. 24. *Mines*: precious metals, including gold (*O.E.D.*, sb. 1. b).

ll. 26–7. *last fire Annuls this world*: foretold in Mal. iv. 1; 2 Pet. iii. 7–12.

l. 28. *this All*: the physical universe, as in 'The Progress of the Soul', l. 27, and the 'Elegy on Mrs. Bulstrode', l. 26.

l. 29. *They say, the sea*, etc. The commonplace is used by Donne elsewhere: 'the Sea gaines in one place, what it loses in another' (*Sermons*, x. 67). It derives ultimately from Lucan, *De Bello Civili*, i. 409–11. John Ray collects it (in the form given to it by Burton, *Anatomy*, 2. 2. 3) in *Miscellaneous Discourse concerning the Dissolution and Changes of the World* (1692), p. 159: 'What the sea takes away in one place it adds in another.' The opening conceit of the poem is extended to the relations of the 'two deaths' (ll. 30 ff.).

ll. 31–2. Our soul, though subject to spiritual death by sin, is freed from the body by the 'younger' (physical) death which sin brought as its consequence. Paradoxically, the 'elder' death, the spiritual death of the unrepentant sinner, is called in Rev. ii. 11, xxi. 8 'the second death'. 'It is appointed unto men once to die' (Heb. ix. 27), and, 'since the promise of a Messiah, there is no Law, no Decree, by which any man must necessarily die twice; a Temporal

[= 'carnall', l. 30] death, and a Spiritual death too. It is not the Man, but the Sinner, that dies the second death' (*Sermons*, i. 232). Cf. *Sermons*, iv. 55; '*La Corona*', vi ('Resurrection'), l. 7; St. Augustine, *De Civ. Dei*, xiii. 2, xx. 6.

l. 33. 'Both deaths perish when the just die, for carnal death has no power over the soul, and spiritual death has no power over the good' (Grolier).

attempt: try to subdue (*O.E.D.*, vb. 9), with the suggestion of attempted rape (cf. l. 38).

l. 34. *trophies*: the signs of the triumph of 'the just' over both kinds of death.

l. 35. *unobnoxious*: not exposed, not liable (to harm) (*O.E.D.* i; this is the earliest example cited), as in *Paradise Lost*, vi. 404–5: 'unobnoxious to be pained / By wound'.

l. 36. *to death*: to the point of being subject to spiritual death: 'mortally'.

l. 37. *not loth*: Cf. 'it is a rebellious thing not to be content to die . . .; to harbour a disobedient loathnesse all the way, or to entertain it at last, argues but an irreligious ignorance' (*Sermons*, iv. 53).

l. 38. *So hath she this*, etc. In being willing to die because she is assured of eternal life ('this'), and in having been unwilling to sin ('that'), she overcomes 'both deaths'.

virginity: spiritual innocence and purity. 'Virgo' is allegorized by Rabanus Maurus as 'anima sancta', 'mens prava' (Migne, *P.L.* cxii. 1080). Cf. 'A Litany', ll. 107–8:

> Divorce thou sinne in us, or bid it die,
> And call chast widowhead Virginitie.

ll. 39–40. In St. Augustine's terms (e.g. *Enchiridion*, xxx) God's grace gave her the ability not to sin (the inability to sin being reserved for the just in heaven, *De Civ. Dei*, xxii. 30); grace also helped her to win victory over sin by repentance (*De Civ. Dei*, xxi. 16). Cf. *Sermons*, vi. 335; and 'To the Countess of Bedford' ('Reason is our Soules left hand'), l. 28.

l. 41. *Of what small spots pure white complaines!* Cf. Tilley, S781, 'A spot is most seen upon the finest cloth'; quoting Francis Thynne, *Emblemes and Epigrames*: 'Since finest white doth soonest take all staines' (ed. F. J. Furnival, E.E.T.S., lxiv, 1876, p. 19).

l. 42. *poyson breaks a christall glasse*. Crystal glass was made in Venice; glass with an infusion of clay, made in Florence, was called porcelain. Sir Thomas Browne remarks that 'though it be said that poyson will break a Venice glass, yet have we not met with any of that nature' (*Vulgar Errors*, VII. xvii. 3; *Works*, ed. Keynes, 1964, ii. 536). In reply, Alexander Ross asserts that 'Such is the venome of some Spiders that they will crack a *Venice* glass, as I have seen; and *Scaliger* doth witnesse the same however the Doctor denies it' (*Arcana Microcosmi*, 1651, II. iv. 2, p. 211). J. C. Scaliger says: 'Negant veneno posse infici: disrumpi enim' (*Exercitationes* . . ., xcii. 327–8). Panciroli (see note to ii. 21–2), in his chapter 'De Porcellanis' ascribes to porcelain vases 'haec virtus . . ., quodsi venenosum quidipsio immissum sit, ilicò rumpantur'; Salmuth comments on this idea, and then turns to the subject of crystalline glasses, emphasizing their fragility (pp. 144–60).

In extensive 'Observations' added to an anonymous translation of A. Neri's *L'arte vitraria*, we read that 'in the finest Glasses, wherein the salt is most purified, and in a greater proportion of salt to the sand, you shall find that such Glasses standing long in subterraneous and moist places will fall to pieces, the union of the salt and sand decaying. And this is the reason of that saying, that *Venice* Glasses will break with poison, which is true of some Mineral, but not of Vegetable or animal poyson' (*The Art of Glass*, 1662, pp. 211–12).

l. 44. *All, sinners be.* 'For all have sinned' (Rom. iii. 23).

l. 45. *rarifie.* I have preferred the Group II reading to the 'rectifye' of Groups I and III. That Lady Markham's conscience was 'rectified' has already been established in the preceding lines. 'Rarifie' continues the alchemical imagery from ll. 23–8 and agrees better than 'rectifye' with 'extreme' (l. 46). It could easily be misread by scribes expecting a phrase like the familiar 'rectified conscience'. 'Rarifie' = refine, purify (*O.E.D.*, 'rarefy', 2).

ll. 46–8. *extreme truth lack'd little of a lye*, etc. Her moral sense was so refined that she came close to falsifying the degree of her faults: calling her sins of omission sins of commission ('acts'), and accusing herself of sins when they may have been rightly so called only in different circumstances.

ll. 49–52. *As* Moses *Cherubines*, etc. The reference is to the winged cherubim on the Ark of the Covenant, Exod. xxv. 18–20. Aquinas says that angels are able to move instantly from place to place (*S. T.* Iᵃ pars, q. liii, art. 3). This power would seem to make it unnecessary for them to have wings; similarly, it seemed unnecessary that Lady Markham, already in heaven as she lived a life of virtue on earth, should in addition shed tears of repentance in order to fit herself for heaven. Problems concerning the wings of angels (e.g. in Isa. vi. 2, Ps. xviii. 10, Rev. iv. 8) were frequently discussed; for instance in Salmuth's commentary in the work of Panciroli (p. 58) mentioned in the note to ll. 21–2 above.

l. 51. *already'in heaven.* Cf. *The Second Anniversary*, l. 154: 'For they'are in Heaven on Earth, who Heavens workes do.'

l. 52. To mount, as ordinary men must, by tears of contrition.

l. 54. *vaine hast.* Though death was hasty in taking her (as a young woman), her virtue made his efforts vain.

l. 55. *even*: unvarying (in virtue).

l. 56. *good in all her titles*: worthy of her reputation ('fit for us'); having secure entitlement to salvation ('fit . . . for God'; cf. *The Second Anniversary*, ll. 149–50).

l. 57. *forward*: presumptuous (*O.E.D.* a. 8).

l. 58. *women can no parts of friendship bee*. Plato (*Laws* 837 B) says that friendship is the love of 'the like in virtue to the like, and the equal to the equal'. It became a commonplace in Neo-Platonic writers that women were therefore incapable of so lofty a relationship. Grierson quotes from the essay attributed to Montaigne 'Of Presumption' (ii. 17); in Florio's translation: 'this thrice-sacred amitie, whereunto we read not, her sexe could yet attaine' (ed. W. E. Henley, 1892, ii. 398). W. M. Lebans (*R.E.S.*, N.S. xxiii, 1972) cites the essay 'Of friendship', I. xxvii: 'the ordinary sufficiency of women, cannot answer this conference and communication . . . nor seeme their mindes strong enough to endure the pulling of a knot so hard, so fast, and durable' (ed. cit. i. 200).

l. 62. *tryumphs*. Ironic: Death's triumph is false, for it is the 'just' who have the 'trophies' (l. 34) of the encounter.

Elegie on M^ris Boulstred (p. 59)

MSS.: Group I (*C 57, D, H 49, Lec, SP*); *H 40*; Group II (*A 18, N, TCC, TCD*); *L 74*; *DC*; Group III (*Dob, Lut, O'F, S 96*); *Cy, O 2, P*; *A 25, C* (extracts); *B, S, O 1*.
Miscellanies: *HN, La, S 962, Wed, Wel*; Brit. Lib. MSS. *Add. 30982, 19268* (ll. 5–6, 46–52, 73–4); Nat. Lib. of Scotland, *Hawthornden MS. VIII* (ll. 35–40, 46–8).

The poem is untitled in *B* and *S 962*; the other MSS. associate the poem with the death of Mistress Bulstrode, the variations in title being unimportant.

With Grierson, I reject a reading of *1633* in l. 74, but retain a reading of *1633* which he rejects, in l. 27. For the relation of this elegy to that beginning 'Death be not proud', see Appendix B.

'Cecill Bulstrode, my wife's sister, gentlewoman to queen An, ordinarye of her bedchamber, dyed at Twitnam, in Middlesex, the erl of Bedford's house, 4 August 1609' (*The Liber Famelicus of Sir James Whitelocke*, Camden Soc., 1858, p. 18). She was Cecilia, daughter of Edward Bulstrode, of Hedgerley Bulstrode, Bucks., and was baptized at Beaconsfield on 12 February 1584. She was a close friend of her kinswoman, the Countess of Bedford, at whose house, Twickenham Park, she died. The parish register of Twickenham church states that she was buried on 6 August 1609 'out of the parke'. Ben Jonson read to Drummond 'Verses on the Pucelle of the Court Mistriss Boulstred [*Underwood*, xlix], whose Epitaph Done made' (Jonson, *Works*, i. 135), and remarked that the poem 'was stollen out of his pocket by a Gentleman who drank him drousie & given Mistress Boulstraid, which brought him great displeasur' (ibid. i. 150). In the epigram Jonson implies that she had been twice engaged to be married and had broken off both engagements, and says that she composed verses which she circulated among the Court wits. A remark of Donne's in a letter to George Garrard seems to suggest that Sir Thomas Roe had been her lover (*Letters*, p. 39); and Sir John Roe's 'Elegie to Mᵣⁱˢ Boulstred: 1602' (Grierson, i. 410–11) has been taken to imply the same of him (Bald, pp. 177–9). During her last illness, Donne wrote to Sir Henry Goodyer:

> I fear earnestly that Mistress *Bolstrod* will not escape that sickness in which she labours at this time. I sent this morning to aske of her passage of this night; and the return is, that she is as I left her yesternight, and then by the strength of her understanding, and voyce, (proportionally to her fashion, which was ever remisse) by the eavennesse and life of her pulse, and by her temper, I could allow her long life, and impute all her sicknesse to her minde. But the History of her sicknesse, makes me justly fear, that she will scarce last so long, as that you when you receive this letter, may do her any good office, in praying for her; for she hath not for many days received so much as a preserved Barbery, but it returnes, and all accompanied with a Fever, the mother, and an extream ill spleen (*Letters*, pp. 215–16).

The title of Sir Edward Herbert's memorial poem, 'Epitaph. *Caecil. Boulstr.* quae post languescentem morbum non sine inquietudine spiritus & conscientiae obiit' (*Poems*, ed. G. C. Moore Smith, pp. 20–1), conveys the same impression of a troubled mind and a protracted illness. Ben Jonson wrote an epitaph upon her at George Garrard's request (*Works*, viii. 371–2), and it is a fair inference that Donne's letter to Garrard mentioned above, with its promise to send a tribute 'in the memory of that good Gentlewoman', is in answer to a similar request made to him. That Donne and Jonson should both have abandoned the censoriousness of their earlier comments on the 'remisse' Mistress Bulstrode, and the tenor of Herbert's verses upon her, lend plausibility to the suggestion by Jonson's editors (xi. 88) that she had made a deathbed repentance.

Donne's elegy is placed in the context of earlier English poems in this genre by A. L. Bennett, 'The Principal Rhetorical Conventions in the Renaissance Personal Elegy', *S.P.* li (1954). Browning could quote the poem at will (A. L. Lowe, 'Browning and Donne', *N. and Q.* cxcviii, 1953, pp. 491–2).

l. 1. *I recant.* The poem is possibly a palinode, withdrawing the scorn of death in the Holy Sonnet, 'Death be not proud'; see Appendix B.

l. 2. *slip'd*: fallen carelessly from my lips.

l. 8. *his bloody,' or plaguy, or sterv'd jawes*: war, plague, and famine, a Biblical trio of causes of death. Cf. Ezek. xiv. 21; Rev. vi. 8.

l. 10. *Eating the best first, well preserv'd to last.* The traditional idea that 'the good die young' is elaborated by a suggestion of the preservative 'balsam' which, according to Paracelsus (*Hermetic and Alchemical Writings*, trans. A. E. Waite, ii. 69–74), kept the body healthy and counteracted poisons. It was most active in the young, who were thus apparently well fitted to 'last', but it was exhausted by age and, as Donne suggests, by sin: 'We are so far from that naturall Balsamum, as that we have a naturall poyson in us, Originall sin' (*Sermons*, vi. 116).

The reading 'fruite' may be an authentic variant, clarifying the reference to the cates and dainties (including preserved fruit) served in the early dessert course at banquets.

l. 13. *sinkes*. The *O.E.D.* gives no examples of 'sink' vb. as meaning 'sink into'.

l. 15. *Roes of living sand*: Cf. 'A female fishes sandie Roe', 'The Progress of the Soul', l. 223.

l. 16. *spunge*: dry up as with a sponge. Unless fish died, their numerous spawn would form land made of 'sandy' roes.

l. 17. *rounds*: encompasses (*O.E.D.*, vb. II. 9); i.e. attacks all its inhabitants.

l. 18. *organique*: musically sounding, like organs.

l. 20. *the heavenly hierarchie*. There are nine orders of angels, first classified by the Pseudo-Dionysius, *De Coelesti Hierarchia*.

ll. 21–2.
> *death, how cam'st thou in?*
> *And how without Creation didst begin?*

Cf. God did not make death, saies the Wiseman [Wisd. of Sol. i. 13], And therefore S. *Augustine* makes a reasonable prayer to God, *Ne permittas Domine quod non fecisti, dominari Creaturae quam fecisti*; Suffer not O Lord, death, whom thou didst not make, to have dominion over me whom thou didst. Whence then came death? The same Wiseman [ii. 24] hath shewed us the father, Through envy of the devill, came death into the world; and a wiser then he, the holy Ghost himselfe hath shewed us the Mother, *By sin came death into the world* [Rom. v. 12] (*Sermons*, iv. 54).

ll. 23–4. Death, 'the last enemy that shall be destroyed' (1 Cor. xv. 26), has seen the end of the Four Monarchies (Babylon, Persia, Greece, and Rome), and will see the end of Antichrist, the great opponent of Christ and his kingdom (Dan. xii. 7; Rev. xiii. 11–17) who, after the Fifth Monarchy or Millenium (Christ's thousand-year reign on earth), will appear before the end of the world, to be destroyed by Christ Himself (Isa. xi. 4).

l. 26. *this All*: the created universe, as in 'Elegy on the Lady Markham', l. 28.

l. 27. *births*: a 'degree' of death because the act of coition was thought to shorten life (cf. *The First Anniversary*, l. 110); and, further, 'Doth not man die even in his birth? The breaking of prison is death, and what is our birth, but a breaking of prison?' (*Sermons*, iv. 52). Cf. St. Augustine, *De Civ. Dei*, xiii. 10, 13; Seneca, *Consol. ad Marciam*, x. 5 ('mors enim illi denunciata nascenti est').

life. '*Quotidiè morimur, et tamen nos esse aeternos putamus*, sayes S. *Hierome*

[Migne, *P.L.* xxii. 602]; We die every day [1 Cor. xv. 31], and we die all the day long' (*Sermons*, iv. 52; cf. p. 46). Similarly Seneca, *Consol. ad Marciam*, xi. 3–4, xxi. 6.

vices. 'Our sinnes are our owne, and our destruction is from our selves' (*Sermons*, ix. 65). Cf. Rom. vii. 5; *The First Anniversary*, ll. 155–8; Sparrow, *Devotions*, pp. 68–9.

vertues: a degree of death because of self-sacrifice, the mortification of the flesh, the war against the world and the devil. Cf. *Sermons*, iv. 48.

The thought in this passage is a Christianized version of a commonplace in elegiac writing which is at least as old as Plutarch, *Consol. ad Apollonium*, 104 (*Moralia*, Loeb ed. ii. 121); see W. M. Lebans, *R.E.S.*, N.S. xxiii, 1972.

l. 29. *our bellowes weare, and breath*. Cf. 'death is in nature but *Expiratio*, a breathing out, and we do that every minute' (*Sermons*, iv. 53). 'Weare' = 'wear out'.

ll. 31 ff. On a blank leaf at the back of his copy of *1633* (Victoria and Albert Museum, D. 25. D. 15) Alexander Dyce has written of these lines, 'A grand passage'.

l. 32. *reclaim'd*: 'Reclaim' was the technical term for recalling a hawk from its flight (*O.E.D.*, vb. I. a), and also the technical and legal term for taming wild creatures (especially hawks) to obedience (*O.E.D.* 3. a).

l. 34. *Reserve but few*. 'Many be called, but few chosen', Matt. xx. 16; cf. vii. 14; Luke xiii. 23–4. 'Reserve' (*O.E.D.*, vb. trans.) has several meanings appropriate here: 2. 'retain as one's own'; 6. b, 'set apart for some destiny or end'; 7. 'save from death'; 9. 'preserve what is liable to decay', etc. The 'few' are the redeemed.

l. 36. *not ours, nor thine own*: for she is now entirely in God's possession.

ll. 37–40. The common idea 'overthrown by the blow' of death (ll. 35–6) develops into a conceit. Mistress Bulstrode was a castle of which the 'fort' (her body) was the abode of the King and Captain of her being (her soul). Death, without hope of capturing her virtuous soul, made his assault on her body (the 'lower roome'), which had the dignity and beauty of a Court serving the King (her soul). Even her body is ultimately beyond death's reach, for it will be glorified at the general resurrection (cf. 'Elegy on the Lady Markham', ll. 25–7).

l. 37. *more*: than death could assail. Her virtue put her beyond his reach.

l. 38. *offer'd at*: *O.E.D.*, 'offer', v. 5. c, 'make an attempt upon'.

l. 40. *mist*: *O.E.D.*, 'miss (of)', v. V. 23. c, 'fail to seize or capture'.

l. 45. *a separation, no divorce*. Cf.:

God married the Body and Soule in the Creation, and man divorced the Body and Soule by death through sinne, in his fall. . . . But because God hath made the band of Marriage indissoluble but by death, farther then man can die, this divorce cannot fall upon man; . . . For, though they be separated *à Thoro & Mensa*, from Bed and Board, they are not divorced; Though the soule be at the *Table of the Lambe*, in Glory, and the body but at the table of *the Serpent, in dust*; . . . yet they are not divorced; they shall returne to one another againe, in an inseparable re-union in the Resurrection (*Sermons*, vii. 257–8; similarly, vi. 71–2).

l. 46. *usher up*: act as usher for, announce.

l. 48. *Bodies are purer*, etc. The glorified body, after the resurrection, 'shall be like a soule, like a spirit, like an Angel of light, in all endowments that glory it selfe can make that body capable of, that body remaining still a true body' (*Sermons*, vii. 254; cf. ii. 82). Cf. 1 Cor. xv. 42–5, 52–3; 'Elegy on the Lady Markham', ll. 23–8, and note; Aquinas, *S.T.* IIIᵃ pars, Supp. q. lxxxv, art. 1.

ll. 49–50. *her virtues did outgoe Her yeares.* For this commonplace of Consolation, Bennett cites as ancient sources Cicero, *14th Philippic*, xii; *De Senectute*, xix ('Breve enim tempus aetatis satis est longum ad bene honesteque vivendum.'). Cf. also Plutarch, *Consol. ad Apollonium*, 117. D; Seneca, *Consol. ad Marciam*, xxiv. 1.

l. 50. *do so*: act in this manner ('kill her young').

l. 51. *to thy losse*: 'to your own disadvantage', because, by dying young, Mistress Bulstrode avoided the sins of a longer life, and the effect of these upon others (ll. 51–68).

ll. 51–2. Beauty and wit are likely to seduce others into sin and to cost them dearly; must Death forgo this opportunity of increasing the number of his victims?

ll. 53–66. The phrasing hints at possible scandal; and perhaps at a deathbed repentance of which society was ignorant or sceptical. See introductory comments.

l. 54. *every age a diverse sinne pursueth.* Cf. 'Obsequies to the Lord Harington', ll. 71, 121–9. 'Our *youth* is *hungry and thirsty*, after those *sinnes*, which our *infancy knew not*; And our *age* is *sory* and *angry*, that it *cannot pursue* those *sinnes* which our *youth* did' (*Sermons*, x. 234; cf. iv. 137). 'Cursus est certus aetatis et una via naturae eaque simplex, suaque cuique parti aetatis tempestivitas est data' (Cicero, *De Senectute*, x. 33).

l. 55. *taken better hold*: on her soul, by allowing her more opportunity to sin.

l. 56. *Shortly, ambitious; covetous, when old.* Cf. 'when thy heats of youth are not overcome, but burnt out, then thy middle age chooses ambition, and thy old age chooses covetousness' (*Sermons*, ii. 245). Covetousness as the sin of old age is mentioned by Plutarch, *Moralia* 786 B; Terence, *Adelphoe*, ll. 832–3. Cicero adds the sin of youth: 'ut petulantia, ut libido magis est adulescentium quam senum'; '[senes] etiam avari' (*De Senectute*, xi. 36, xviii).

65); cf. *2 Henry IV*, I. ii. 217–19. Ambition as the sin of middle age is a further addition to the general idea.

l. 58. *once*: 'in time', 'some day' (*O.E.D.*, adv. B. 5).

l. 61. *persever'd*: accented on the second syllable.

ll. 63–4. *faine To sociablenesse, a name profane*: pretend that her love of company should be called by the name of a sin (? promiscuity), or by a name that profanes her. 'Sociablenesse' has five syllables.

l. 67. *crost*: 'thwarted'.

l. 68. *triumph*: cf. 'Elegy on the Lady Markham', ll. 61–2.

army: the qualities (e.g. beauty and wit, l. 52) which, had she lived longer, might have served as instruments for death's further conquests.

l. 70. *immoderate griefe*. Cf. 'Elegy on the Lady Markham', ll. 7–16, and notes.

l. 72. *due*: merited, proper (*O.E.D.*, adj. 1. 5b); an obligation.

such: such as she was. Tears for one's unworthiness are not 'immoderate'.

l. 73. Her death must cost her small company of intimates at least some tears.

l. 74. *chaine*. Though the circle of people linked in friendship is broken on earth by her death, it will be completely made up again in heaven.

Elegie upon the Death of Mistress Boulstred (p. 61)

MSS.: Group II (*A 18, N, TCC, TCD*): *L 74*; Group III (*Lut, O'F, S 96*); *Cy, O 2, P*; *B, S, O 1*.

Miscellanies: *Grey, H 40, HK 1, HN, RP 31, S 962*; Brit. Lib. MS. *Add. 19268* (extracts); Nat. Lib. of Scotland, *Hawthornden MS. VIII*; Folger Lib. MS. *V. a. 162* (extracts).

This elegy is untitled in *HN* and *K*, but the other MSS. describe the poem as having been written on the death of Mistress Bulstrode. In *1633* the poem follows the lyrics, with the title 'Elegie'. The addition of the word '*Death*' to the title in *1635* seems to have no authority, and is in any case inappropriate since the subject of the poem is Sorrow. I have adopted the title given in Group II (and, with unimportant variations, in nearly all other MSS.).

The poem is not included in the Group I collection, and the compiler of *1633* took his text from the Group II MS. also available to him. My text differs from *1633* in ll. 21, 48, and 58, and from Grierson's in ll. 48 and 58.

For Cecilia Bulstrode, see introductory note to the preceding elegy; and for the connection of this poem with the elegy 'Death be not proud', see Appendix B.

l. 2. *great sorrow cannot speake*. Proverbial: 'Small sorrows speak, great ones are silent' (Tilley, S 664).

l. 4. *Griefe weares, and lessens, that tears breath affords.* 'Grief wears out, and diminishes that affords tears breath (gives utterance to tears).' I take 'griefe' as subject of 'affords', 'breath' as direct, and 'tears' as indirect, object of the verb; and 'breath' in the sense (*O.E.D.*, sb. 9) 'utterance, speech'. As great sorrow is speechless, so it also cannot find expression in sighs and tears.

l. 7. *estate*: state, condition.

l. 8. *sense*: feeling (*O.E.D.*, sb. I. 8).

l. 9. *Sorrow*, etc.: cf. Gen. iii. 16, 'I will greatly multiply thy sorrow and thy conception: in sorrow thou shalt bring forth children'.

l. 10. After the passing of the 'foure Monarchies' (cf. 'Elegy on Mrs. Bulstrode', l. 24, and note), the Fifth will be the establishment of Christ's kingdom on earth (Dan. ii. 44; Luke xxi. 27; Rev. i. 7). Sorrow will be associated with the signs of its coming: Matt. xxiv. 6 ff., e.g. 'All these are the beginning of sorrows' (*v.* 8); 'then shall be great tribulation' (*v.* 21); 'then shall all the tribes of the earth mourn' (*v.* 30).

ll. 15–16. 'Was it not enough that through sickness you took possession of her body but you had to destroy what you had already ruined?'

l. 16. *undone*: ruined (*O.E.D.* II. 8).

l. 17. *there*: within her.

l. 18. *All . . . that . . . flies.* For a singular verb following a plural subject, see Abbott, *Shakespearian Grammar*, § 333.

l. 21. *Saphirine.* 'Sapphirus', is allegorized as 'claritas angelorum' by Rabanus Maurus (Migne, *P.L.* cxii. 1044).

ll. 23–4. The fragility of crystal, and of Miss Bulstrode's person, is due, not to weakness, but to the purity of their substance.

l. 24. *Christall Ordinance.* The alchemist's arrangement of his vessels of fine glass for his experiments (presumably, *O.E.D.*, 'ordinance', 2).

l. 26. *end*: purpose. The aim of conquest is to subdue people, not to kill them off or to treat them so harshly that they rebel. Cf. 'The Prohibition', ll. 13–15.

l. 27. *to rebell*: against sorrow, since those who knew her when she was 'well' (good) now know her to be 'better' (in heaven).

ll. 33–4.   *For of all morall vertues she was all,*
                       The Ethicks speake of vertues Cardinall.

She embodied all the moral virtues in the degree of perfection advocated by ethical writings on the cardinal virtues.

Ethicks: works entitled *Ethics* or dealing with moral questions.

vertues Cardinall: prudence, justice, temperance, and fortitude. For their use as conventional topics in earlier English elegies, see A. L. Bennett, *S.P* li (1954), at pp. 114–16.

ll. 35-6. The cherubim placed at the entrance to Eden in Gen. iii. 24 are here allegorized as grace. They are, however, usually taken to signify 'charitas' by which the Christian can attain to the Tree of Life: so St. Augustine (Migne, *P.L.* xxxiv. 215) and St. Bernard ('Plenitudo ergo scientiae Cherubim, et plenitudo legis charitas'; Migne, *P.L.* clxxxiv. 184).

l. 38. *consumption*: often used by Donne to mean 'the process of dying' (*O.E.D.* I. 3), as in 'Elegy on Mrs. Bulstrode', l. 28.

l. 40. *him and his lawes above.* 'Some of us' might have been tempted to set ourselves above God's laws and therefore above Him (in loving her more than Him), like Adam in his disobedience in tasting the fruit of the Tree of Knowledge (Gen. ii. 17).

l. 44. *Wee' had had a Saint, have now a holiday*: we should have had a saint on earth, and now, having a saint in heaven, have a feast-day to celebrate. No MS. has the reading of *1633* (though 'have' has been inserted in *O'F* from the edition), which may be an editorial 'correction'. It is difficult to believe, however, that Donne wrote the line as it stands in the MSS.

ll. 45-6. *that strange bush*, etc.: the burning bush in Exod. iii. 2.

l. 46. *Religion*: four syllables.

l. 48. *what we turne to feasts, she turned to pray.* Grierson read *'feast'* and *'pray'*, taking them as imperatives. 'Feast', however, seems to be an error in *1633*, since no MS. has the singular. 'Pray' is used in the sense of 'prayer' (*O.E.D.*, sb.). What are generally celebrated as 'festal days' Mistress Bulstrode made days of prayer.

l. 50. *last*: be eternal.

l. 51. That 'Angels did hand her up' is probably suggested by Luke xvi. 22: 'the beggar died, and was carried by the angels into Abraham's bosom'.

l. 52. *order*: the seraphim, the highest order of angels, who stand 'nearest God' (l. 51) and attend on Him. Aquinas concludes that most of the angels who fell were of the lowest orders (*S.T.* Iᵃ pars, q. lxiii, art. 9), but Donne follows the tradition that the words addressed to the cherub in Ezek. xxviii. 12-19 were spoken 'ipsi angelo, qui primus est conditus' (Gregory, Migne, *P.L.* lxxvi. 1250). In *Paradise Lost* the fallen angels are of the highest two orders (e.g., i. 324, 'Cherub and seraph').

l. 55. *beautiousnesse.* Not recorded in *O.E.D.* till 1855.

l. 58. *will be* Lemnia. The 'a' of *1633* (inserted from the edition by the 'second corrector' of *O'F*) appears in none of the MSS., and seems to be an editorial 'correction'. The accent is on the second syllable of '*Lemnia*'.

Terra Lemnia, according to Pliny, *Nat. Hist.* xxxv. 14, was a red clay found in Lemnos, thought to be a remedy for poisons and snakebite, and hence used in antidotes (so Galen, *De Antidotis*, ii; J. C. Scaliger, *Exercitationes* . . . , xciii. 328; etc.). Among alchemists, however, the name was given to an essential ingredient of the philosophers' stone, helping the process of transmuting base to precious metals; cf. *The Hermetic Museum*, ed. A. E. Waite (1893), ii. 262 (Grolier). The earth will act as *terra Lemnia* upon the crystal of Miss Bulstrode's pure body (cf. ll. 21–4) and change it to diamond (ll. 59–60).

ll. 58–60. *the tree . . . Shall be tooke up spruce.* The ordinary wood of her coffin will also be transmuted. W. M. Lebans suggests that the early examples, s.v. 'spruce', in *O.E.D.* seem to indicate that it was rare, exotic, and valuable in Donne's time.

l. 62. *Stoicks.* The Stoic claimed to be unmoved by passion. The word, perhaps, harks back to 'Ethicks', l. 34.

Elegie on Prince Henry (p. 63)

MSS.: Group II (*N*, *TCD*); *DC* (ll. 1–87); Group III (*Lut*, *O'F*); *Cy*. (In *D*, a Group I MS., the title has been written and a space left for the poem.)
Miscellanies: Brit. Lib. MS. *Add. 27407*; Bodleian Library, MS. *Rawl. Poet. 26.*

The elegy was first printed in the third edition (dated 1613) of *Lachrymae Lachrymarum, or The Spirit of Tears distilled from the untimely Death of the Incomparable Prince Panaretus*, by Joshua Sylvester. Sylvester's poem is followed by verses in Latin, Italian, and English by Joseph Hall and others, and then by a separate title page: *Sundry Funerall Elegies . . . Composed by severall Authors.* This in turn is followed by an address 'To the Several Authors of these surrepted Elegies' by Humphrey Lownes, the printer; it is ostensibly an apology for the unauthorized publication of the poems, but seems mainly to have been designed to protect the reputation of the authors as gentleman amateurs. Sylvester himself had special reason to lament the death of Prince Henry, who had been his patron since 1608; he apparently thought that he had a responsibility as a spokesman for the general grief. The writers of the added 'sundry funeral elegies', apart from Donne, were George Garrard, Sir Peter Osborne, Hugh Holland, Sir William Cornwallis, Sir Edward Herbert, Sir Henry Goodyer, and Henry Burton. Most of the authors were friends of Donne, and some were closely associated with the Prince (Sylvester himself was a Groom of the Chamber of the Prince, Hall one of his chaplains, and Burton a member of his household). See Bald, pp. 268–9; E. C. Wilson, *Prince Henry and English Literature* (Ithaca, N.Y., 1946), pp. 123–71; and L. Parsons, 'Prince Henry . . . as a Patron of Literature', *M.L.R.* xlvii (1952). Whatever reluctance (if any) Donne felt in 'descending' to publish his verses, since he allowed their publication, and since the poem was presumably printed from his own MS., the edition of 1613 must serve as a copy-text. I have, however, abandoned Sylvester's hysterical typography, with its liberal and indiscriminate use of italic and upper case letters.

The MS. copies seem to descend from another source than 1613, probably from a copy of the poem kept by Donne himself. The editor of 1633 used a text in this tradition found in his Group II MS., not that in 1613. Where 1613 and the MS. tradition disagree, since in each case there is the possibility of inaccuracies in the transmission of what Donne wrote, the editor must use his discretion. I have, however, departed from the readings of 1613 only in ll. 71 and 73; my text differs from Grierson's (which follows 1633) in twelve places.

I adopt the title as it appears in 1633 and O'F. That prefixed to the poem by Sylvester ('Elegie upon the Untimely Death of the Incomparable Prince, Henry') was given to all the other poems added in 1613, and derives from Sylvester's own title-page; it obviously has no authority.

Henry Frederick, Prince of Wales, elder son of James I, was born on 19 February 1594, and died of typhoid at St. James's Palace on 6 November 1612 (he was buried on 7 December). He was a youth of great ability and promise, and was very popular with his father's subjects; his death caused a profound shock, and called forth an unprecedented number of elegies (see J. P. Edmonds, 'Elegies and other Tracts issued on the Death of Prince Henry', *Pubns. of the Edinburgh Bibliographical Soc.* vi (1906), 141–58).

Ben Jonson remarked to Drummond that Donne had told him that 'he wrott that Epitaph on Prince Henry Look to me Fath to match Sir Ed: Herbert in obscurenesse' (*Works*, i. 136); this may have been true, or Jonson may have offered a disparaging jest which Drummond reported as fact.

A full account of the poem was given by Ruth C. Wallerstein, *Studies in Seventeenth-Century Poetic* (Madison, Wis., 1950, especially at pp. 68–95). She pointed out that the structure of the poem resembles that of Donne's sermons (or, as he often called them, 'meditations'; cf. l. 18, 'contemplation'; l. 86, 'considering God'): the first line is his 'text', which is 'divided' (ll. 2–24); each 'part' of the division is then 'proved' (Faith, ll. 25–62; Reason, 63–82); and the poem concludes with an 'application', including a partial resolution of the spiritual problem in terms of 'love' (l. 88) and in a prayer already foreshadowed in the 'text'.

ll. 1–20. Donne's opening conceit of the orbit of man's mind having two 'centres' may have been suggested by Kepler's discovery of the elliptical orbit of the planets, the first law of planetary motion propounded in *Astronomia Nova* (1609); geometrically, an ellipse has two foci ('centres'). See R. I. Scott, 'Donne and Kepler', *N. and Q.* cciv (1959), 208–9.

Donne calls on Faith (Reason, it is implied, is of no avail), and then on God because Faith is also at a loss. Both Faith and Reason are shaken by this conclusive event ('period'). Reason is the centre of 'weight'—that is, its sphere is things measurable; Faith is the centre of 'greatnesses'—that is, of things immeasurable. The province of Reason, the natural world, is a perfect circle in which the radii flow into the centre from points, equally distant from the centre, on the circumference; in other words, the natural world is completely knowable. But infinite matters ('enormous greatnesses', that is things of immense, or immeasurable magnitude) such as the Being of God, His 'place' (if He is 'everywhere' He can have no 'place'), His providence, or the problem of what happens to the soul at death, cannot be brought into relation (are 'disproportionate') or included in a circle (are 'angular'). These things, but for Faith, would have no centre (be 'eccentrique'). But not all such matters find their centre ('strike') on Faith alone, nor do they strike in the same way on all men. For Reason, exerted to its utmost ('put t'her best extension') almost reaches to matters of Faith and thus almost makes both circles, of Knowledge of the world and of Knowledge of Divine things, concentric. We never approached so near this happy state as in contemplating the Prince we have lost. Our belief in man's capacity and our rational deductions from the Prince's behaviour supported each other: both Faith and Reason looked confidently to what he would do.

Donne always affirms that both Faith and Reason are necessary to religion; 'that religion is certainly best, which is reasonablest' (*Letters*, p. 43). 'Mysteries of Religion are not the less believ'd and embrac'd by Faith, because they are presented, and induc'd, and apprehended by Reason' (*Sermons*, i. 169). 'A Regenerate man is not made of Faith alone, but of Faith and Reason' (ibid. vi. 175). See T. G. Sherwood, 'Reason in Donne's Sermons', *E.L.H.* xxxix (1972).

l. 1. *Look to*: 'have a care for' (*O.E.D.*, vb. 21. d); sustain. Jonson parodies the line in *The Staple of Newes* (1626): 'Look to me, wit, and look to my wit, Land' (1. i. 3).

l. 7. *Quotidian things*: things that surround us in 'everyday' experience.

l. 11. *God's essence*. Cf. 'so doth Faith, as soon as our hearts are touched with it, direct and inform us in that great search of the discovery of Gods Essence, and the new *Hierusalem*, which Reason durst not attempt' (Simpson, *Essays*, p. 20).

l. 21. *movings of the centre*: earthquakes.

ll. 26-8. His reputation put neighbouring states into a trance, so that they saw no reason for action until he revealed his own intentions. In an 'ecstasy' the soul wakes but the person sleeps (is in a trance); neighbouring states could not wake and become active until the Prince himself acted.

l. 29. Such princes as tried to win him as an ally.

l. 30. *torpedo*: the numb-fish, cramp-fish, or electric ray, which caused cramp or numbness when touched. Cf. 'To Sir Henry Wotton' ('Sir, more then kisses'), l. 18.

l. 31. *And others studies.* Elliptical: 'and who was the subject of others' studies'.

bent: disposed or trained. Other princes carefully observed the direction his policies tended to follow.

The comma after 'bent' 'opens' the sentence, after a series of relative clauses, so that the principal clause continues from 'hee', l. 25.

ll. 33–4. The soul was 'tied' to the body in the 'subtile knot, which makes us man' ('The Ecstasy', l. 64) by the 'animal spirit' in the blood; this spirit 'conveyed' the functions originated by the soul to all parts of the body. 'It is called animal bycause it is the first instrument of the soule, whych the latines call animam' (De Vigo, *The Most Excellent Workes of Chirurgerye*, London, 1543, Glossary). Cf. the Harington 'Obsequies', ll. 46, 63–6, and note (p. 200).

Through the 'correspondence' of the human body to the 'body-politic', Donne represents Prince Henry as the force that would extend and make operative throughout Christendom ('through Christianitie') the peace-making policies of his father, James I ('This soule of peace'), to which Donne refers in *Sermons*, i. 218, iii. 80, vii. 166.

ll. 35–8. The earthly peace Henry would bring would be an emblem, or 'type', of the Kingdom of Heaven under the reign of Christ, the Prince of Peace, when the earth has passed away. Since the end of the world (the 'last dayes', l. 40) was generally thought to be near (cf. *The First Anniversary*, l. 209), it was also a tenet of Faith that the peace which Prince Henry would establish would last until ('overtake') the millenium (Rev. xx; xxi. 1–4).

l. 41. *but from his aspect and exercise*: merely because of the Prince's bearing and pursuits. Grosart points out that Prince Henry's liking for all martial exercises 'hardly betokened him a peaceful follower of his peace-loving father'. He was also the hope of many Englishmen who thought that England should be more active in the defence of Protestantism in Europe (Grierson).

l. 42. *rumors of warrs*: echoing Christ's words in reply to the disciples' inquiry, 'what shall be the sign of thy coming, and of the end of the world?': 'And ye shall hear of wars and rumours of wars: . . . but the end is not yet' (Matt. xxiv. 3, 6).

l. 44. *Still stay*: remain on earth, the last days being not yet.

vexe our great-grand-mother, dust. Our parents were descended from our common grandparents, Adam and Eve, who were the children of dust (Gen. ii. 7, i. 27). Dust was the 'mother' (matter) on which the 'Father' (Creator) imposed form and life. We must remain alive (l. 53), and trouble the dust of the earth with our pursuits.

ll. 45–6. *his store Of plagues*: like those inflicted, for example, on the Egyptians (Exod. vii ff.) and on Job.

ll. 45–54. Has God expended on us the full tally of woes, and only now is unwilling to add a further woe, that of our death (the curse on Adam, Gen.

ii. 17, iii. 19), which would much relieve our misery at the loss of the Prince? Just as the earth, the lowest of all things, would be ambitious if it desired only to fall further, so God knows that our desire for death is only a scheme for relieving the misery of our mourning. Thus we live on, but the only signs we can give of living are our cries of woe.

Donne extends the usual idea about the mandrake, a plant which was thought to groan or shriek when pulled from the ground.

ll. 55–8. 'What might he not have achieved if he had grown to maturity and fulfilled his creative potentialities, since now even in bodily decay he is able to continue some living quality in us? For grief gives some life to mortal men and is, indeed, all that vitalizes the material world.' The lines are related to the basic 'conceit' of *The First Anniversary*.

'Generation' seems to refer to a kind of 'fruitfulness' that goes beyond the begetting of heirs: a quality of creativeness, of engendering valuable things. Cf. '*Propagation* is the truest Image and nearest representation of eternity' (Simpson, *Essays*, p. 69).

ll. 59–61. 'If grief could ascend to heaven, the choir of angels, forgetting their new joy at the Prince's arrival, would desire, with grief at seeing him in heaven, that he had stayed below on earth.' Their grief would be for the plight of mankind, bereft of the Prince.

l. 62. *they foreknowe*. According to Aquinas, angels understand the causes of things, and God's revelation, more universally and distinctly than men, and so can foreknow events, though they fall short of God's eternity by which He can see things in a way embracing all time, and beyond (*S. T.* Iᵃ pars, q. lvii, art. 3).

l. 63. *faster*: more secure.

l. 64. *not men*: because deprived of the full powers of human understanding by the Prince's death.

l. 66. *With causes*: our link with the notion of, or our ability to perceive, causation.

to us: belonging to us. We are bereft of Reason.

ll. 67–8. *if all the substances were spent . . . accident.* Aristotle opposed substances (the basic essential natures of things) to accidents (their variable properties). If there were no 'substances' it would be folly to investigate 'accidents', because the latter term has meaning only in relation to substances. Reason (ll. 69–70) disappears with the Prince—the only substance upon which Reason could operate.

ll. 71–6. *If Fate have such a chaine*, etc. Donne is referring to the chain in Homer, which was interpreted by Renaissance Neoplatonists and some other thinkers as representing the chain of natural cause and effect. Cf. *The Second Anniversary*, ll. 143–4, and note (p. 159).

The reading 'Faith' for 'Fate' in 1613 seems to be an easily made printer's error. As Mr. John Sparrow pointed out (London Mercury, xx (1929), pp. 93–7), Reason is our ability to perceive causal connections; Reason is not itself a chain of causes. Nor does Faith 'have', or indeed require, such a chain; Faith could accommodate an extra miraculous event (ll. 73–4) without difficulty. But Reason cannot do so; it is at a loss in dealing with miraculous events (l. 76) in terms of cause and effect, and is even more helpless when by the Prince's death a link in the chain of causation is removed. It is Fate, not Faith, whose secure linking of cause and effect has hitherto enabled men to 'knowe' (l. 24) by Reason.

l. 73. *steal in*: insert stealthily (unexpectedly and mysteriously).

l. 75. *At a much deader fault*. The metaphor concerns hunting-dogs; 'dead' is used as in the phrase 'a dead scent'; 'to be at a fault' (O.E.D., 'fault', sb. 8) means 'to lose or be off a scent or track' of the quarry. Reason's 'bafflement' is 'even greater'.

ll. 77–9. 'But now, for us to come busily proving that we have no reason would be a proof that in fact we did have a remnant of reason. So would appropriate grief.'

l. 80. *wee are dead*: because we have lost the peculiarly human faculty of reason and cannot grieve for him in appropriate measure (ll. 81–2).

l. 82. *excuse*: for not declaring our griefs.

l. 84. *think him, as hee is hee*: think of (envisage) him as he really is.

l. 85. *bayting*: pause on a journey for rest and refreshment. Cf. The Second Anniversary, l. 195.
   mid-period: halfway stop.

ll. 86–7. *Yet (no dishonor) I can reach him*, etc. Without dishonouring him, I can claim to contemplate him because he shared with ordinary men the emotion of love.

l. 89. *since I live*: with the limited understanding given to men in this life.

l. 90. *That shee-intelligence which mov'd this sphear*. The relation of a spiritual principle to the more material thing it inspires and controls is often expressed by Donne in the image of an angelic Intelligence controlling one of the spheres in which the heavenly bodies were fixed. The compound 'she-intelligence' is not recorded in O.E.D.

l. 91. *I pardon fate my life*: I forgive fate for forcing me to remain alive.

l. 92. I follow 1633 in placing a comma after 'shee'. 'Conscience' means 'inward knowledge' and 'that' is understood before 'thou': 'whoever you are who have the noble inner knowledge that you are she I speak of, I conjure you . . .'. Prince Henry had shown little interest in any of the noble ladies with whom matches were proposed for him; Donne is imagining a lady whom the Prince might have loved.

l. 93. *charmes*: spells, words of love's incantations.

l. 95. *soules you sigh'd*. The common idea that the soul is breathed out in sighs arose because *psyche* and *anima* mean both 'breath' and 'soul'. Cf. the song 'Sweetest love, I do not goe', ll. 25–6.

l. 96. *you wish I knew your historie*: you will wish that I knew you and the story of your love (so that I might celebrate both).

ll. 97–8. 'In order that, to something like the degree to which each of you was a heaven to the other, I might in singing your merits be like an angel singing praises (cf. l. 59) in heaven.'

Obsequies to the Lord Harrington (p. 66)

MSS.: Group I (*C 57, D, H 49, Lec, SP*); Group II (*N, TCD*); *DC* (ll. 109–258); Group III (*Dob, Lut, O'F, S 96*); *A 25, C, D 17, JC; B, S, O1* (ll. 1–248). Miscellanies: *HK 1*; Bodleian MS. *Eng. Poet. e. 14*.

The text in *1633* was taken from a Group I MS., which was occasionally in error. My text differs from Grierson's in ll. 7, 11, 35, 117, 121, 158, 224, 239, and 241; and from *1633* in these places and also in ll. 53, 102, 133, 192, 193, 198, and 250. The titles to the poem given in the MSS. are the same as, or unimportant variations of, those given in the apparatus.

In *1633* and several MSS. the poem is preceded by a letter 'To the Countesse of Bedford'. The letter is, however, omitted from Groups I and II, *DC*, *S 96*, and *Eng. Poet. e. 14*; in *A 25* it occurs separately forty leaves after the poem with a note, 'This was sent wth ye Elegie of the Lorde Harrington'. I print from *1633* (in which the reading 'nobles brothers' in some copies was corrected during printing), repairing its omission of the words 'it are yours . . . evidences concerning':

To the Countesse of Bedford
Madame,
I have learn'd by those lawes wherein I am a little conversant, that hee which bestowes any cost upon the dead, obliges him which is dead, but not the heire; I do not therefore send this paper to your Ladyship, that you should thanke mee for it, or think that I thanke you in it; your favours and benefits to mee are so much above my merits, that they are even above my gratitude, if that were to be judged by words which must expresse it: But, Madame, since your noble brothers fortune being yours, the evidences also concerning it are yours, so his vertue being yours, the evidences concerning that belong also to you, of which by your acceptance this may be one peece, in which quality I humbly present it, and as a testimony how intirely your familie possesseth
                    Your Ladiships most humble, and thankfull servant
                                                        John Donne.

Sir John Harington, 2nd Baron Harington of Exton, Lady Bedford's bro-
ther, 'the most compleat yong gentleman of his age that this kingdom could
afford for religion, learning, and courteous behaviour' (Sir James Whitelocke,
Liber Famelicus, p. 39), was born in 1592 and died of smallpox on 27 February
1614. His father, also Sir John, the 1st Baron, had died in August 1613 at
Worms when he was returning home after escorting the Princess Elizabeth
and her husband to Heidelberg. The young heir had been educated at Sidney
Sussex College, Cambridge. He was a close friend of Prince Henry, and when
he visited Venice in 1609 he was presented to the Doge as one who would be
influential in England when Henry should succeed to the throne. Sir Henry
Wotton, who met him then, wrote: 'He is learned in philosophy, has Latin
and Greek to perfection, is handsome, well-made as any man could be, at
least among us' (L. Pearsall Smith, *Life and Letters of Wotton*, i. 441 n.). Lord
Harington died at his sister's house at Twickenham Park; the funeral sermon
was preached on 31 March 1614 by Richard Stock and published as *The
Churches Lamentation for the losse of the Godly* (1614), with verses by, among
others, Sir Thomas Roe. Stock speaks of Harington's learning and high
abilities, and makes it clear that the religious life of the young nobleman was
devout and methodical (pp. 61–94); this is confirmed by Thomas Fuller,
Worthies of England (1662), s.v. 'Warwickshire' (p. 130). Donne's poem
reflects Harington's interest in learning and religion; it arises out of a genuine
regard for its subject and for the Countess, whose double bereavement
in the space of six months was accompanied by other misfortunes (Bald,
pp. 275–6).

The writing of the poem for a patron, however, did not preclude a further
motive, which was thought not incompatible with genuine sympathy. Lord
Harington bequeathed two-thirds of his fortune to the Countess (see P.
Thomson, *M.L.R.* xliv, 1949), a fact to which Donne makes reference in the
letter printed above. Donne was hopeful that his 'Obsequies' would receive
acknowledgement from the Countess, as indeed they did; but in a letter to
Goodyer (*Letters*, pp. 218–20) he makes clear his bitter disappointment at
the scale of his reward (cf. Bald, pp. 296–7).

ll. 1–2. *all soules bee . . . harmony*. Cf. *The First Anniversary*, ll. 311–12: 'that
Ancient . . . who thought soules made / Of Harmony', and note, p. 146.
J. C. Scaliger (*Exercitationes . . .*, p. 994) speaks of the idea that 'Anima est
harmonia' as 'exploded'.

l. 2. *when thou wast infused*. The soul is 'thou', that which gave Harington his
individuality. Donne frequently refers to the problem whether the soul of an
infant was infused into the body directly by God, or propagated from the
parents; 'the opinion of infusion from God, and of a new creation . . . is now
the more common opinion' (*Letters*, p. 17). Cf. *Sermons*, i. 157, iii. 85, ix.
213–4, etc.

l. 3. *did'st continue so*: by a religious and virtuous life. 'What an Organe hath that man tuned, how hath he brought all things in the world to a Consort, and what a blessed Anthem doth he sing to that Organe, that is at peace with God' (*Sermons*, x. 131). Cf. 'A Litany', ll. 200–1: 'A sinner is more musique, when he prayes, / Then spheares, or Angels praises be.' In his funeral sermon, Stock says that Harington 'tuned his best instrument, his heart' by prayer (p. 78).

ll. 3–4. *beare A part*: sing a part in the universal harmony. 'Is the world a great and harmonious Organ, where all parts are play'd, and all play parts; and must thou only sit idle and hear it?' (*Sermons*, i. 207).

l. 4. *Gods great organ, this whole Spheare.* 'Heaven and earth are as a musical Instrument'; 'God does (as it were) play upon this Organ in his administration and providence by naturall means and instruments' (*Sermons*, iii. 59, i. 290).

l. 6. *pervious*: offering a way or passage, passable (*O.E.D.* a. 1).

l. 12. *unapparell*: divest of clothing; here, of the clothing (or limitations) of the flesh. The word appealed to Coleridge, who notes in 1803 'Mismotion' (l. 132) / 'to unapparel' (*Notebooks*, ed. K. Coburn, i, 1957, no. 1786). Cf. 'devest', l. 16.

l. 13. *soft extasie*: easy way to perceive spiritual truth, while his mind 'stands apart' from his body.

l. 15. *midnight*. 'Man *sees* best in the *light*, but *meditates* best in the *darke*; . . . to behold him so, as to fixe upon him in meditation, God benights us, or eclipses us, or casts a cloud of medicinall afflictions, and wholsome corrections upon us . . . ; and so in our afflictions we stand, and looke upon God, and we behold him' (*Sermons*, iv. 174).

l. 19. *Subject to change*: at the Last Trumpet, when 'the dead shall be raised incorruptible, and we shall be changed' (1 Cor. xv. 52).

l. 23. *sad*: sober, serious.

l. 26. *that Sunne*: the spiritual illumination caused by contemplating Harington.

l. 30. *hardest*: most difficult to contemplate.

l. 31. *glasse*: mirror (that reflects to Harington, 'glorified' in heaven, all that 'concerns' him).

ll. 31–2. Cf. 'Our seeinge of God hereafter is the blessednes we hope for, and our comfort in the way to that, is, that he sees us . . . He sees as God and therefore he allwayes sawe all' (*Sermons*, ii. 150; cf. iv. 87, vii. 341–2).

l. 34. *these mirrors of thy wayes, and end*: these mirrors which are your Christian living and your partaking of heavenly bliss; for 'the glory of God shines through godly men' (*Sermons*, vii. 238; cf. iii. 374). Calvin says that an 'elected' person in whom God's image is (partly) restored 'doeth represent the wisdome, righteousnesse and goodnesse of God as it were in a loking glasse' (*Institutes*, III. xvii; *Commentary . . . upon . . . Colossians*, tr. R. V[aux], 1581, p. 68; cited by Lewalski, pp. 128–9).

ll. 35–6. Cf. 'Here, in this world, we see God *per speculum*, says the Apostle [I Cor. xiii. 12], by reflection, upon a glasse. . . . As he that fears God, fears nothing else, so, he that sees God, sees every thing else: when we shall see God, *Sicuti est* [I John iii. 2], as he is, we shall see all things *Sicuti sunt*, as they are' (*Sermons*, iii. 111; cf. iv. 73). Cf. 2 Cor. iii. 18.

ll. 37–9. *Yet are the trunkes . . . Deeds of good men.* An inversion: 'the deeds of good men are the telescopes . . .'. 'Who but Donne', asks Dr. Johnson (quoting ll. 35–40), 'would have thought that a good man is a telescope?' (*Life of Cowley*.)

l. 37. *trunkes*: *O.E.D.*, 'trunk', sb. 14, 'perspective trunk, telescope'. Donne had read of the telescope in Galileo's *Sidereus Nuncius* (1610), to which he refers in *Ignatius his Conclave* (Healy, pp. 7, 81); he calls the telescope 'Optick glasses' in *Sermons*, iii. 210. Cf. 'To Mr. Tilman after he had taken orders', ll. 45–6.

derive: *O.E.D.* v. 4: convey, impart, pass on.

l. 41. *affirme*: give a firm stand to (from the root sense, Lat. 'affirmare').

l. 43. *fluid vertue cannot be look'd on.* Virtue 'flows' through every part of our lives: 'For vertue is even, and continuall, and the same. . . . Vice and her fruits may be seen, because they are thick bodies, but not vertue, which is all light' (*Letters*, p. 97).

ll. 53–5. Cf.:

Does this trouble thee, says Justin Martyr [Migne, *P.G.* vi. 1478], . . . *Quod homo à piscibus, et piscis ab homine comeditur*, that one man is devoured by a fish, and then another man that eats the flesh of that fish, eats, and becomes the other man? *Id nec hominem resolvit in piscem, nec piscem in hominem*, that first man did not become that fish that eate him, nor that fish become that second man, that eate it; *sed utriusque resolutio fit in elementa*, both that man, and that fish are resolved into their owne elements, of which they were made at first (*Sermons*, iii. 96–7; cf. iv. 326–7, vi. 156).

ll. 55–6. Cf.

In the generall resurrection upon naturall death, God shall work upon this dispersion of our scattered dust . . . ; where mans buried flesh hath brought forth grasse, and that grasse fed beasts, and those beasts fed men, and those men fed other men, God that knowes in which Boxe of his Cabinet all this seed Pearle lies, in what corner of the world every atome, every graine of every mans dust sleeps, shall recollect that dust, and then recompact that body, and then re-inanimate that man, and that is the accomplishment of all (*Sermons*, vii. 115).

l. 57. *of all those*: from the knowledge of all those.

l. 61. *discontinue*: make discontinuous, 'separate' (*O.E.D.* v. I. 4).

l. 63. *spirits*. 'A spirite is a subtile, fyne, aerye, and cleare substaunce, produced
of the thynnest, and fynest parte of bloode, that vertue, and strength maye
be caried from the principal parte to *the* rest' (De Vigo, *The Most Excellent
Workes of Chirurgerye*, 1543, Glossary). Cf. *Sermons*, ii. 261–2, vi. 128.

l. 64. *nam'd*. For the process of naming as a division of the one ('simple', l.
66) into the many, cf. *Paradise Lost*, vii. 535–6 ('no place Is yet distinct by
name').

ll. 67–8. *a point and one . . . entirer*. 'Everywhere the one is indivisible either
in quantity or in kind. Now that which is indivisible in quantity is called a
unit if it is not divisible in any dimension and is without position, a point
if it is not divisible in any dimension and has position' (Aristotle, *Metaphysics*
1016^b).

l. 69. *told*: counted one by one.

l. 73. A variation on the elegiac commonplace in 'Elegy upon the Death of
Mistress Bulstrode', ll. 33–4.

l. 74. *thrust*: crowd together, throng (*O.E.D.* B. I. 3).

l. 80. *long breath'd*: 'long-winded'.

ll. 85–6. *repaire To*: make his way to, visit (*O.E.D.* v^1. 1).

ll. 87–90. *this Angell in an instant, knowes*. Angels apprehend by instantaneous
intuition (Aquinas, *S.T.* I^a pars, q. liv, art. 4; q. lviii, arts. 3, 4), which Donne
interprets here as a rapid process of perception or 'thinking' ('thoughts', l.
91); this we (ll. 91–2) misinterpret as a mental process of a different order.

l. 93. *perfect*: skilled. Cf. 'a man can remember when he began to *spell*, but
not when he began to *reade perfectly*' (*Sermons*, iv. 149).

l. 95. *distinctly*: separately (cf. l. 61).

l. 99. *in that pace*: at the same speed.

l. 101. *Balme*. Cf. 'Elegy on Mrs. Bulstrode', l. 10, and note (p. 183).

   The later Physitians say, that when our naturall inborn preservative is corrupted
or wasted, and must be restored by a like [balsam or balm] extracted from other
bodies; the chief care is that the Mummy have in it no excelling quality, but an
equally digested temper: And such is true vertue . . . we have Christianity, which is
the use and application of all vertue (*Letters*, pp. 97–9).

   Men like Harington (ll. 34–40), by their example, restore our virtue
'corrupted and wasted' by sin, and assuage the troubles to which fallen man
is prone.

ll. 105–10. A pair of compasses was a common Renaissance emblem; see note
to 'A Valediction: forbidding Mourning', ll. 25–36, in Gardner, *Elegies etc.*,
pp. 189–90. The closest analogue to Donne's use of the figure here is that
in Joseph Hall's *Epistles, The Second Volume* (1608), p. 176: 'Charity and Faith
make up one perfect pair of compasses, that can take the true latitude of a

Christian heart: Faith is the one foot, pitch't in the centre unmovable, whiles Charity walks about, in a perfect circle of beneficence; these two never did, never can go asunder' (F. P. Wilson, *Elizabethan and Jacobean*, 1945, pp. 30, 133). Jonson uses a similar image in the same year as Donne here (1614) in his Epistle (*Underwood*, xiv) to John Selden, ll. 31–3 (*Works*, viii. 159): 'And like a Compasse, keeping one foot still / Upon your Center, doe your Circle fill / Of generall knowledge.' See also J. Lederer, 'John Donne and the Emblematic Practice', *R.E.S.* xxii (1946), at p. 199.

l. 107. *still*: 'always', or 'at rest'.

l. 108. Cf. 'For they'are in Heaven on Earth, who Heavens workes do' (*The Second Anniversary*, l. 154).

l. 110. *man, the' abridgment*. Grierson quotes: 'the *Macrocosme*, and *Microcosme*, the Great and the Lesser world, man extended in the world, and the world contracted, and abridged into man' (*Sermons*, ix. 93).

ll. 111–30. 'The circles running parallel to the equator are all equally circular, but diminish in size as they approach the poles. But the circles which cut these at right angles, and along which we measure the distance of any spot from the equator, from the sun, are all of equal magnitude, passing round the earth through the poles, i.e. meridians are great circles, their planes passing through the centre of the earth.

'Harrington's life would have been a Great Circle had it completed its course, passing through the poles of youth and age. In that case we should have had from him lessons for every phase of life, medicines to cure every moral malady' (Grierson).

l. 112. *engrave*: mark out (by encircling), like the lines engraved on a map.

l. 114. *the' equinoctiall*: the earth's equator (*M. Blundevile his Exercises*, 1597, f. 143).

l. 121. *that*: the example of that happiness. 'The end of all consideration of all the actions of such leading and exemplar men . . . is assimilation too; That we may be like that man' (*Sermons*, vii. 280–1).

l. 124. *calentures*: fevers proper to the tropics, in which, through thirst, the delirious sufferer takes the sea for green fields and throws himself into it.

l. 126. *hydroptique*: abnormally thirsty (greedy). Cf. *The Second Anniversary*, l. 48, and note (p. 157).

l. 127. *scale*: measure; the standard provided by Harington's virtue.

l. 131. *Though as*. The syntax is loose: the main construction continues through 'If these' (l. 139) to 'So . . .' (l. 141).

small pocket-clocks. Donne bequeathed to his brother-in-law, Sir Thomas Grymes, 'that Strykinge clocke wch I ordinarilye weare' (Bald, p. 563). The compound 'pocket-clock' is not recorded in *O.E.D.*

l. 132. *mismotion and distemper*: irregular motion and maladjustment. 'Distemper' (*O.E.D.*, Sb¹. 4), a disorder of body or mind, carries on the analogy of the clock to a human body. This is the earliest example of 'mismotion' cited in *O.E.D.*

l. 133. *hand*. All the manuscripts (except *Lut*, *O'F*, *S 96*) have the singular; the plural in *1633* is a sophistication. Few clocks had both minute and second hands in the early seventeenth century; Grierson refers to illustrations in F. J. Britten, *Old Clocks and Watches and their Makers* (6th ed., 1932; e.g. pp. 148–9, 184–5), and quotes: 'he that makes a Clock, bestowes all that labour upon the severall wheeles, that thereby the Bell might give a sound, and that thereby the hand might give knowledge to others how the time passes' (*Sermons*, vi. 42).

   string: the cord or chain wound on the barrel of a watch (*O.E.D.* I. 9. a). 'In a Watch, the string moves nothing, but yet, it conserves the regularity of the motion of all' (*Sermons*, vii. 430).

l. 135. *flye*. In a non-striking clock or watch there is no fly (the winged portion of the striking apparatus which regulates the speed of the stroke).

l. 137. *rattle*: prattle.

l. 138. *idle*: foolish.

l. 139. *still*: continually (and so are 'overwound').

l. 140. *at every will*: i.e. by anybody and everybody who wants to tinker with the clock.

l. 146. *small clocks faults*. These were apparently plentiful in Donne's day. Sir Christopher Heydon says that 'common watches wherein the wheeles, teeth, axletrees, spring, &c. be not perfectly wrought, or not well set together, may breed errour, and drie weather or the spring new wound up, may cause the watch to goe faster' (*A Defence of Judiciall Astrologie*, 1605, pp. 143–4). Grosart cites a passage from Shakerley Marmion's *The Antiquary* (1641) about the time spent by gallants in checking watches: 'it helps much to discourse; for, while others confer notes together, we confer our watches, and spend good part of the day with talking of it' (I. i; *Dramatists of the Restoration*, ed. J. Maidment and W. H. Logan, vii, 1875, p. 204).

l. 150. *controule*: regulate.

l. 152. *such as*: such that.

l. 154. Grierson cites Webster, *The White Devil*, I. ii. 279–81 (*Works*, ed. F. L. Lucas, i. 120):

> The lives of Princes should like dyals move,
> Whose regular example is so strong,
> They make the times by them go right or wrong.

Like other images in the poem, this one is in the tradition of the emblem. J. Lederer, *R.E.S.* xxii (1946), quotes F. Picinelli's emblematic dictionary,

Mondo simbolico formato d'Imprese, 1669 (1st ed., 1653): 'l'horologio da sole . . . servirà per tipo d'huomo giusto, che non dal mondo, ma da Dio prende la direttione, e la luce.' Cf. Middleton, *Women Beware Women*, IV. i. 1–18 (*Works*, ed. A. H. Bullen, vi. 332–3).

l. 157. *not miracle, but Prodigie*: an abnormal and strange happening, but not a miraculous act of God; 'that is not a miracle which nature does' (*Sermons*, iii. 370).

l. 158. *where*: 'whereas'.

the ebbs, longer then flowings be. This is usually true of tidal estuaries. William Bourne, in a popular handbook, discusses the phenomenon, especially in the River Thames: the tide, 'when it is in, and hath taken his sway, then it cannot so soone reverse backe, untyll that the water is well descended or ebbed behynde it too the Seawardes, as it dooth manifestly appeare by experience' (*A Booke called the Treasure for Traveilers*, 1578, bk. 5, ch. 6).

l. 170. *Ants*. Donne reminds the citizens of London in his first Paul's Cross sermon that, on the death of Queen Elizabeth, 'every one of you in the City were running up and down like Ants with their eggs bigger then themselves, every man with his bags, to seek where to hide them safely' (*Sermons*, i. 217).

l. 172. A variation on the theme 'the good die young'. Cf. 'Elegy on Mrs. Bulstrode', l. 10.

ll. 174–5. Cf. 'this, where we are now, is the suburb of the great City, the porch of the triumphant Church, and the Grange, or Country house of the same Landlord, belonging to his heavenly Palace, in the heavenly Jerusalem' (*Sermons*, iii. 288).

l. 176. *utmost*: outermost.

ll. 177–246. The sustained imagery in this passage, developed from the familiar idea of the Christian life as a warfare (cf. 'Satire III', ll. 30 ff.; 'To Sir Henry Wotton', 'Here's no more newes', ll. 10–14), is based on the *ius triumphandi*, the law governing the award of a triumph, the greatest honour bestowed in ancient Rome upon a victorious general. St. Paul applies the term 'triumph' to Christ Himself ('having spoiled principalities and powers, he made a shew of them openly, triumphing over them in it'; Col. ii. 15), and hence to the victorious Christian ('Now thanks be unto God, which always causeth us to triumph in Christ'; 2 Cor. ii. 14; cf. *Sermons*, viii. 83). The idea is found occasionally in the Fathers (e.g. Lactantius; Migne, *P.L.* vii. 218–19), but Donne's treatment of it is his own. He applies the ancient rules to the soul of Lord Harington claiming entry as a triumphing general into 'Gods City, New Jerusalem' (l. 175). It is unlikely that he searched out these rules from the ancient sources, and indeed he had no need to do so, since several of the many Renaissance historians of ancient Rome assemble them more or less completely.

The most compendious accounts of triumphs I have found which include the conditions governing their award are in: G. B. Marliani, *Bartholomaei Marliani Patricii Mediolanensis Annales Consulum, Dictatorum, Censorumque ...*, with a section (pp. 115–36) called *Romanorum Virorum Triumphi cum commentario* (Rome, 1560); F. O. Panuvinio, *De Triumpho Commentarius* (Venice, 1571; also appended to his *De Ludis Circensibus*, Venice, 1600); Alexander ab Alexandro, *Genialium Dierum libri sex* (3rd ed., corrected, Paris, 1539; apparently the source of four later editions); and Flavio Biondo, *De Roma Triumphante* (originally *Triumphantis Romae libri*, 1472), which, after at least six editions and three Italian translations, appeared in *Blondi Flavii ... Historiarum ab Inclinatione Romanorum libri xxxi* (Basle, 1531; repr., 1559). Biondo includes all the details mentioned by Donne, except one (see note to ll. 230–5); the other three historians have one or two fewer of the relevant points. W. M. Lebans collects the ancient sources, *R.E.S.* xxiii (1972).

ll. 177–8. The fact that those seeking a triumph must not enter the City until the day appointed for the triumphal procession (if granted) is mentioned by almost all the Renaissance historians, e.g. by Panuvinio, f. 1ᵛ; cf. Livy, III. 63. 6, etc.

ll. 178–80, 229–30. The obvious reference is to the licence given to the soldiers of the triumphing general to indulge in scurrilous jests and songs at his expense; so, e.g., Biondo (1559), pp. 205, 216. Barnabé Brisson, in *De Formulis et Sollemnibus Populi Romani Verbis libri VIII* (2nd ed., Frankfurt, 1592), to which Donne refers in *Ignatius his Conclave* (Healy, p. 47) and *Essays in Divinity* (Simpson, p. 45), says (p. 352): 'Iocularia vero quaedam carmina & dicteria Milites in suos Imperatores triumphantes iacere solebant'; Brisson cites Dionysius of Halicarnassus (vii. 72. 11); Suetonius, *Julius* (xlix. 4); Pliny (*Hist. Nat.* xix. 41. 144); Livy, iv. 20. 2, v. 49. 7, xxxix. 7. 3 (cf. also vii. 38. 3); and Velleius Paterculus (*Hist. Rom.* II. lxvii. 4, where it is said that the triumpher endured 'execrationem civium'). Cf. also Martial, I. iv. 3–4, V. viii. 7–10. No Renaissance writer, so far as I know, mentions the perhaps relevant fact that 'Tribuni plebis antea solebant triumphum postulantibus adversari' (Livy, xxxviii. 47. 1).

ll. 183–4. Marliani (p. 117), Panuvinio (ff. 2ʳ, 3ᵛ), Alexander ab Alexandro (1539, f. 47ᵛ), and Biondo (pp. 203, 204) all make this point, which is based on Livy (xxviii. 38. 4, xxxi. 20. 4) and Suetonius (*Tiberius*, ix. 2). Biondo, quoting Livy, correctly defines magistracy: 'nulli licuit triumphare, qui nec dictator, nec consul, neque praetor res gessisset' (p. 203); Panuvinio (f. 1ᵛ) adds 'Imperator' to the list.

l. 185. *youthes foes.* Cf. l. 128, ll. 194–5.

l. 186. *that field*: high offices of State.

l. 190. *jealousies*: suspicions.

l. 191. *no title, to this triumph.* There were plenty of examples of a triumph's being granted in defiance of one or other of the usual conditions (as in the case of Pompey (ll. 233–5), a fact of which Donne makes complimentary use.

l. 199. *engines*: weapons, military contrivances (*O.E.D.*, sb. 5).

l. 200. *a divers Mine*. Each has a different way of undermining the virtue of the 'great'.

ll. 201–2. The four Renaissance historians are all aware of this condition on which triumphs were granted (and on which a triumphing general was 'admitted' to the City). The chief ancient source was Valerius Maximus, *Factorum Dictorumque Memorabilium*, II. viii. 7: 'quamvis quis praeclaras res maximeque utiles rei publicae civili bello gessisset . . . neque aut ovans aut curru triumphavit, quia . . . lugubres semper existimatae sunt victoriae utpote non externo, sed domestico partae cruore.' The most notorious breach of the rule was Julius Caesar's triumph after defeating the sons of Pompey; cf. *Julius Caesar*, I. i. 32–52, and Plutarch, *Caesar* lvi. 4.

ll. 203–6. Marliani (p. 117), Panuvinio (f. 3ᵛ), Alexander (f. 16ᵛ), and Biondo (p. 203) all state this condition, using the words of Valerius Maximus (II. viii. 4): 'ut pro aucto tantum imperio, non pro recuperatis quae populi Romani fuissent, triumphus decerneretur'. Cf. Livy, xxxvii. 60, xl. 38; and Ammianus Marcellinus, xvi. 10. 2.

l. 208. *those straits nature put thee in*: man's fallen state, corrupted by original sin (part of our human nature). Cf.:

in every man, there are two sides, two armies: the flesh fights against the Spirit. This is but a *Civill warre* [l. 201], nay it is but a *Rebellion* indeed [l. 222]; and yet it can never be absolutely quenched. So every Man is also a Souldier in that great and generall warre, betweene *Christ*, and *Beliall*, the Word of *God*, and the will of man. Every man is bound . . . to shut himselfe up against all overtures of peace, in such things, as are in their Nature irreconcileable, in differences where men differ from *God*. That warre *God* hath kindled, and that warre must bee maintained, and maintaind by his way (*Sermons*, iv. 194).

ll. 209–11. *deliver . . . intire*: based on the prayer of Oblation at Holy Communion (in the Book of Common Prayer since 1549): 'here we offer and present unto Thee, O Lord, ourselves, our souls and bodies, to be a reasonable, holy, and lively sacrifice unto Thee.'

l. 210. *vicariate*: responsibility as a deputy of God on earth, *O.E.D.*, sb. 1 (the earliest example quoted is from *Pseudo-Martyr*, p. 247).

l. 212. *takes endeavours*: accepts favourably our efforts to do so (*O.E.D.*, 'take', v. VI. 39).

ll. 217–18. Cf. l. 108, and note.

ll. 220–2. Marliani (p. 131), Alexander (ff. 16ᵛ, 150ʳ), and Biondo (p. 204) express this condition in Livy's phrasing: 'nisi perdomitam pacatamque provinciam tradidisset successori' (xxxix. 29. 5). Alexander also uses the phrase 'ut nihil inde rebellionis timere posset' (f. 16ʳ).

l. 226. *exemplar man*: one who sets us an example. Cf. l. 121, and note.

l. 228. *Tutelar Angels*: guardian angels; 'that Angel, which God hath given to protect thee' (*Sermons*, viii. 53). Cf. 'A Litany', l. 47: 'wee in Wardship to thine Angels be'; and Aquinas, *S.T.* Iᵃ pars, q. cxiii, art. 2.

l. 229. *this freedome*. Cf. ll. 178–80, and note.

ll. 230–5. I have not discovered any Renaissance or ancient source for this point about deference to the Senate's authority in connection with the *ius triumphandi*. It may be a reasonable deduction of Donne's own, in order to assert that God's proceedings with Harington must not be questioned (ll. 239–41). The lines are, however, quite specific and their tone is the same as that in which Donne refers to those rules concerning triumphs that can be documented; it is possible that he found authority for the statement in some systematic account of the law governing triumphs which I have not identified.

ll. 233–5. Pompey is appropriately selected as a notable example of the waiving of the ordinary rules for granting triumphs because, like Harington (who died aged twenty-one), he was youthful. He was awarded a triumph after victories in Sicily and Africa, though he was only twenty-four years old and not a magistrate. Biondo notes of him that he alone 'quod multi scripsere, eques Romanus, et priusque per aetatem consul fieri posset, bis triumphavit' (p. 204), citing Pliny, vii. 26 (96); cf. Livy, the Oxyrhyncus *Summaries*, lxxxix. Plutarch, *Pompey* xi–xiv, is the fullest ancient source; he says that Sulla at first opposed one request by Pompey for a triumph because he was not a magistrate and, as North's translation puts it, 'through his young yeares he was not yet a Senator' (cf. ll. 186–7).

l. 238. *abandon*: unlike 'tutelar angels', whose commission from God he shared (ll. 227–8).

ll. 240–1. *absolute Prerogative*: O.E.D., 'prerogative', I. a, unquestioned sovereign right. 'Prerogative is incomprehensible, and over-flowes and transcends all law' (*Biathanatos*, p. 48).

ll. 242–3. *natures lawes, which just impugners bee Of early triumphs*. The 'nature' of fallen man (cf. l. 208, and note) does not encourage us to believe that triumphs over sin will come early or easily; it is not 'natural' that a man who dies young should triumph, or deserve to do so, or be admired for doing so.

l. 244. *Lessen our losse, to magnifie thy gaine*. Donne refers to the mingled Consolation and Panegyric proper to Elegy (tempering Lament for the dead).

ll. 248–50. *testimonie of love . . . As Saxon wives*. In *Syntagma Iuris Universi* (Frankfurt, 1599, II. xiv. 17, p. 38) Petrus Gregorius Tholosanus says that 'alios [barbaros] vivas uxores cum cadaveribus maritorum in rogum iniicere solitos, ut Erulos'. He cites Procopius, *Hist. of the Wars*, VI. xiv, where, however, it is said of this Gothic tribe that 'when a man of the Eruli died, it was necessary for his wife, if she laid claim to virtue and wished to leave a fair name behind her, to die not long afterwards beside the tomb of her husband by hanging herself with a rope' (Loeb ed. iii. 405). Donne cites Tholosanus in *Biathanatos* (p. 54), but does not mention Saxon wives in his discussion of voluntary suicide. In the *Gallic Wars* (also cited in *Biathanatos*, loc. cit.) Caesar says that among the Gauls wives were immolated with their husbands, but only if the wife was suspected of having been involved in the husband's death (vi. 19). I have not found a printed source for Donne's attribution of the custom to the Saxons, or one connecting it with any other Germanic tribe; it may be that his memory was at fault.

Mr. W. M. Lebans, however (*R.E.S.* xxiii, 1970), notes the assertion by E. F. Henderson in *A Short History of Germany* (1902) that, on the evidence of ancient German graves, 'The fact that the wives and servants of great personages were immolated is proved beyond dispute'; and suggests that Donne might have heard of, or seen evidence of, the custom during his visits to Frankfurt and Heidelberg with Sir Robert Drury in 1612 (Bald, pp. 257–9).

l. 250. *French soldurii*. 'And we may well collect, that in *Caesars* time, in *France*, for one who dyed naturally, there dyed many by this devout violence. For hee says there were some, whom he calls *Devotos*, and *Clientes*, (the latter Lawes call them *Soldurios*) which . . . alwaies when the Lord dyed, celebrated his Funerall with their owne. And *Caesar* adds, that in the memorie of man, no one was found that ever refused it' (*Biathanatos*, p. 54). Donne refers in the margin to Caesar, *De Bell. Gall.* iii. [.22] and Tholosa. *Synt.* (see previous note), xiv. 10, n. 14. Caesar says that the forces of Crassus were attacked in Aquitaine by soldurii—men who took a vow to share all the fortunes, and the fate, of a chosen friend, and to kill themselves when he died. He mentions 'clientes' in relation to the Gauls, *De Bell. Gall.* vii. 40.

ll. 252–4. *great Alexanders great excesse*, etc. Plutarch tells that, as a sacrifice to his friend Hephaestion (who died of an ague at Ecbatana on Alexander's last Middle-Eastern expedition, 324 B.C.), Alexander the Great

unwisely tooke the chaunce of his death, and commaunded all the heares of his horse and mules to be presently shorn in token of mourning, and that al the battlements of the wals of cities should also be overthrown, and hong up pore Glaucus his Phisition upon a crosse. . . . In the end, to passe over his mourning and sorrow, he went unto the warres, as unto a hunting of men, and there subdued the people of the Cossaeians, whom he pluckt up by the rootes, and slue man, woman, and childe. And this was called the sacrifice of Hephaestions funeralls (*Life of Alexander*, *Lives*, tr. Thomas North, ed. W. E. Henley, 1895; iv. 380; cf. Aelian, *Var. Hist.* I. vii. 8).

ll. 253–4. Stones and other materials from conquered towns were taken to build a funeral pile and monument in honour of Hephaestion in Babylon.

l. 254. *became them best.* It was more fitting that they remained to protect the towns.

ll. 256–8. *interre my Muse . . . Behind hand . . . spoke her last.* The writing of this elegy had been delayed for some months by illness and misfortune (see Bald, pp. 276–80). In the meantime, Donne had written the verse letter 'To the Countess of Salisbury', dated August 1614, with some embarrassment (*Letters*, pp. 259–61). On 20 December 1614 he wrote to Sir Henry Goodyer announcing that he proposed to publish a volume of his poems, and asked his friend to send an 'old book' (presumably of copies of his poems); he wondered whether Goodyer had 'made use' of a verse letter to the Countess of Huntingdon: 'for I desire very very much, that something should bear her name in the book, and I would be just to my written words to my L. *Harrington*, to write nothing after that' (*Letters*, pp. 197–8). Donne's later poems were all on religious subjects: three Holy Sonnets, the three Hymns, the lines 'To Mr. Tilman', 'On the Translation of the Psalms', 'The Lamentations of Jeremy', a Latin epigram on the canonization of St. Ignatius, and the line of Latin verse placed under the portrait of Donne in *Deaths Duell* (1632); and the poem next following here.

An Hymne to the Saints, and to Marquesse Hamylton (p. 74)

MSS.: Group II (*A 18, TCC, TCD*); Group III (*Lut, O'F*).
Miscellanies: *Ash, Grey*; Brit. Lib. MS. *Add. 30982*; P.R.O., S.P. *9/51/17*; Bodleian MS. *Rawl. Poet. 26*; Univ. of Aberdeen Library, MS. *29*.

The poem is not in Group I; in *TCD* it is added in a different hand, and *N* (which does not contain it) was apparently copied before the poem was written into *TCD*. The copy in the Public Record Office is damaged; it appears among the state papers of Sir Joseph Williamson as part of a miscellany of poems on loose sheets, including 'Love's Usury'. William Drummond gave a copy, now lost, to the University of Edinburgh (see *Auctorium Bibliothecae Edinburgenae, sive Catalogus Librorum quos Gulielmus Drummondus ab Horthenden D.D.Q. Anno 1627*, Edin., 1627). Most of the miscellanies omit the phrase 'An Hymn to the Saints' from the title, but all associate the poem with the death of Hamilton.

My text differs from that in *1633* (and Grierson) only in l. 23. I have followed Grierson in altering the punctuation of *1633* at the ends of ll. 8 and 30 since, as he says, 'Four sustained periods compose the elegy' (ll. 1–8, 9–18, 19–30, 31–42).

A prose letter to Sir Robert Ker, or Carr (created Earl of Ancrum in 1633), accompanies the poem in *1633* and Groups II and III, and in P.R.O., S.P. *9/51/17*; in the last-named MS., in *TCD* (headed 'The Letter that was sent with these verses') and in *1633* the letter follows the poem. It occurs in

Bodleian Lib. MS. *Rawl. Poet. 116* without the poem, headed 'A friend of Dr
Dun desird him to make a paper of verses on the death of the marquese
Hambleton wch he did and wth it wrote thus. S^r / I presume', etc. As in
Group II, the letter is not addressed 'To Sir Robert Carr' in *1633*, and the
text in the edition is rather poor. Like Grierson, I emend fairly freely, with
support from the MSS.; my text is the same as his, except for 'subject', the
reading of all the MSS.:

To Sir Robert Carr.

Sir,
I presume you rather try what you can doe in me, then what I can doe in verse; you
know my uttermost when it was best, and even then I did best when I had least truth
for my subject. In this present case there is so much truth as it defeats all Poetry.
Call therefore this paper by what name you will, and, if it bee not worthy of him,
nor of you, nor of mee, smother it, and be that the sacrifice. If you had commanded
mee to have waited on his body to Scotland and preached there, I would have em-
braced the obligation with more alacrity; But, I thanke you that you would command
me that which I was loath to doe, for, even that hath given a tincture of merit to the
obedience of
Your poore friend and servant in Christ Jesus
J. D.

Donne, who had been Dean of St. Paul's for nearly three years, was clearly
reluctant to write a poem that would be likely to circulate in MS. That his
fears were justified is shown by John Chamberlain's remark about the elegy,
in a letter (23 April 1625) to Sir Dudley Carleton accompanying a copy of
the verses: 'though they be reasonable wittie and well don yet I could wish
a man of his yeares and place to geve over versifieng' (*Letters*, ed. N. E. Mc-
Clure, ii. 613). It says much for Donne's sense of the obligations of friendship
that he complied with the wish of his old patron and friend, who was
obviously anxious that his distinguished fellow Scot should be appropriately
honoured. Even so, Donne called the poem a 'Hymn', and in *1633* it appeared
among the Divine Poems. He could perhaps take some satisfaction in the
fitness of the Marquess, in character and reputation, to be celebrated in
verse by a famous divine.

James Hamilton was born in 1589 (*D.N.B.*), and succeeded his father as
second Marquess on 12 April 1604, and his uncle as Duke of Châtelherault
and Earl of Arran in March 1609. He entered the service of King James in
Scotland, came with him to England, and was spoken of as a possible husband
for Princess Elizabeth. He became a favourite courtier, prominent in court
affairs and on royal progresses. In 1619 he was created Earl of Cambridge in
the English peerage, and became a Gentleman of the Bed-Chamber in 1621.
He opposed the French War policy of Buckingham, and, when he died of a
fever on 2 March 1625, it was rumoured, unjustly, that Buckingham had
poisoned him. John Chamberlain voiced the general opinion of Hamilton
when he wrote (27 August 1617): 'I have not heard a man generally better
spoken of then that marques, even by all the English insomuch that he is
every way held the gallantest gentleman of both the nations' (*Letters*, ii. 98).

l. 1. *you*: the Saints.

l. 2. *Fill any former ranke*: take a place among the established orders of the angelic hierarchy and replace one of the angels who fell.

l. 4. *and* order *more*: an additional rank in the heavenly hierarchy (with a play on 'order'; cf. ll. 10 ff.). Cf. *The Second Anniversary*, ll. 357–8.

ll. 6–7. *if every severall Angell bee A* kind *alone.* Aquinas argues that each angel is of a single species ('impossibile sit esse duos angelos unius speciei'), *S.T.* Iª pars, q. l, art. 4. The angels took higher or lower rank on other principles (cf. Aquinas, *S.T.* Iª pars, q. cviii, arts. 3, 4).

l. 9. *accesse*: arrival in heaven.

l. 10. *our* orders: earthly hierarchies.

l. 14. Hamilton was made Lord Steward of the Household on 28 February 1624, and a Knight of the Garter on 15 April 1623.

l. 15. *Councell*. Hamilton was a member of the Privy Council.

l. 16. *Story*: history.

l. 18. *Gangreend*. The Group II MSS. suggest that this form of the word stood in the printer's copy. In the *Devotions* (Sparrow, p. 69), however, the spelling is 'gangred'.

Orders: especially orders of nobility, since Hamilton was duke, marquess, earl, and knight.

ll. 18–21. The Grolier editors say that the imagery in these lines was suggested by the symptoms of Hamilton's last illness that gave rise to the belief that he had been poisoned, quoting Arthur Wilson, *The History of Great Britain* (1653): 'the *Symptoms* being very *presumptuous*, his head and body swelling to an excessive greatness; the hair of his Head, Eye-brows, and Beard, came off being touched, and brought the *Skin* with them' (p. 285).

ll. 23–4. After the dissolution of the English monasteries by Henry VIII (1535–40) they soon fell into ruins. Cf. 'Satire II', l. 60: 'when winds in our ruin'd Abbeyes rore'.

ll. 25–30. Aquinas rejects the idea of 'certain Platonists' that 'the intellectual soul has an incorruptible body naturally united to it, from which it is never separated, and by means of which it is united to the corruptible body of man' (*S.T.* Iª pars, q. lxxvi, art. 7). Donne seems to be using, however, an idea like that which Aquinas denies, perhaps also recalling Aquinas's statement of the Platonic notion that all material things are presided over by immaterial Forms or 'ideas' (*S.T.* Iª pars, q. cx, art. 1). Hamilton's body, before its dissolution in the grave, sent its Form to represent it in the spiritual world (thus anticipating its resurrection at the Last Day and its reunion with the soul); his soul lives on earth in his reputation for Christian virtue.

l. 31. *first* Innocents: the Holy Innocents, slain by Herod (Matt. ii. 16), who were ranked in Heaven as martyrs for Christ's sake. They had not been old enough to sin wilfully.

l. 32. *Pœnitents*: *O.E.D.*, 'penitent', B. 2, 'in the early church, a member of one of four ranks into which those guilty of any of the mortal sins were divided'; and more generally (B. 1), a sinner repentant (and therefore in heaven).

l. 40. *thither*: to heaven (with Hamilton).

l. 42. *a* David . . . *a* Magdalen: sinners who achieved holiness by penitence. David, for example, used his authority to take Bathsheba for himself and have her husband killed (2 Sam. xi), but later repented. Mary Magdalen, 'a sinner', washed Christ's feet with her tears and was 'saved' by her faith (Luke vii. 37–50). Mrs. Simpson noted the parallel in a Whitsun sermon, which she dates to the same year as that of Hamilton's death (1625):

> But this, and all other reproofes, that arise in the godly, . . . have this comfort in them, that these faults that I indure in others, God hath either pardoned in me, or kept from me: and that though this world be wicked, yet when I shall come to the next world, I shall finde *Noah*, that had been drunk; . . . And *Mary Magdalen* that had been, I know not what sinner; and *David* that had been all; I leave none so ill in this world, but I may carry one that was, or finde some that had been as ill as they, in heaven; and that blood of Christ Jesus, which hath brought them thither, is offered to them that are here, who may be successors in their repentance, as they are in their sins (*Sermons*, vi. 22, 327–8).

EPITAPHS AND INSCRIPTIONS

In the transcriptions I have silently expanded most of the abbreviations. Any other variations are recorded below.

Epitaph for Elizabeth Drury (p. 76)

This epitaph survives on the south wall of the chancel in the parish church at Hawstead, Suffolk, on the monument of Elizabeth Drury (a photograph of which is reproduced in Bald, *Donne and the Drurys*, f.p. 69). The epitaph, and that immediately following on Sir Robert Drury, were first printed in Sir John Cullum's *History and Antiquities of Hawsted*, 1784, pp. 53–6 (included in John Nichols's *Bibliotheca Topographica Britannica*, v, 1790, and reprinted separately in 1813, when the epitaphs appear on pp. 52–5). An article in *The Suffolk Garland* (Ipswich, 1818, pp. 272–7) draws heavily on Cullum's account of the monuments and inscriptions, and includes a transcript of the epitaph on Elizabeth Drury (p. 274), followed by Donne's 'Funeral Elegy' upon her. The effigy that forms the main part of Elizabeth Drury's monument is clearly based on a portrait of her reproduced by Cullum (1784, f.p. 146), inscribed with ll. 244–6 of *The Second Anniversary*; by Gosse, i, f.p. 272; and by Bald, *Donne and the Drurys*, f.p. 68. Cullum notes two traditions concerning Elizabeth Drury, that she was destined to be the bride of Prince Henry, and that she died from the effects of a box on the ear (pp. 145–6): but rightly doubts both.

Of the epitaphs on Elizabeth and her father Cullum remarks that they 'are, I apprehend, from the pen of Dr. Donne'—an opinion repeated by S. Tymms in *Proc. of the Suffolk Inst. of Archaeology*, ii (1854), 7. Donne's 'connection with the family', says Cullum, 'makes the supposition probable; and the singularity of the expression "Anno sui Jesu", in both of these, and in his own [epitaph] written by himself, seems to confirm it' (p. 56). In a full study of the two Drury epitaphs ('Two Epitaphs by John Donne', *T.L.S.*, 26 March 1949, p. 208), Mr. John Sparrow points to other evidence of Donne's authorship: the antitheses, such as 'sine remis, sine remoris' in l. 18 of the epitaph on Elizabeth; the conceits, such as 'angelos aemulata etc.' (ll. 8–9); the unusual 'secessit' (l. 26), which occurs also in the epitaph on Ann Donne; and the phrasing in l. 18 of the epitaph on Sir Robert and in ll. 10–11 of the epitaph on Ann. He adds that the expression mentioned by Cullum is not known in other epitaphs of the period. The two Drury epitaphs were clearly composed by the same person. As Mr. Sparrow suggests, this rules out the only other likely author, Joseph Hall. Hall had left the living of Hawstead in 1608 and, although he remained on good enough terms with his former patrons, the Drurys, to supply introductory verses to Donne's *Anniversaries* (see above pp. xxx–xxxi), there is nothing to suggest that he was closely in touch with them as late as 1615, when Sir Robert died. Donne, however, was involved in the family's affairs until at least 1617 (Bald, pp. 310–11). His authorship of the two epitaphs may, I think, be taken as established.

In this and the following epitaph I have preserved the punctuation as the stone-mason left it (with one exception in the epitaph on Sir Robert Drury), on the assumption that he would not have inscribed punctuation marks upon marble unless his 'copy' required it. In this epitaph he made one error, carving 'extreuendo' for 'extruendo' in l. 23.

I offer the following translation:

Thou knowest not, wayfarer, whither thou goest. Thou hast come to the Cadiz of all men, even to thine own. Thou liest here thyself, if thou art virtuous; for indeed here lies Virtue herself, Elizabeth,—in that, as in beauty and innocence she had eagerly vied with the angels, she strove besides to excel them, nay even in this, that she lived sexlessly and wished on that account to restore to God an undefiled body, unimpaired as it was fashioned (an Eden without the serpent), not so much allured by the splendours of that palace that she was banished from her true self, nor so much made a cloister for herself that she denied herself to company, nor for all her endowments of body or fortune less endowed in intellect, nor for all her skill in tongues the less able to hold her peace; neither weary of, nor pursuing, life or death she followed God her guide without straining oars or hindering delays, and reached this haven after almost 15 years—by erecting this monument to whom

Robert Drury, Knight, and Anne his wife, stripped of their only daughter and thus of the very name of parents, vainly palliate their most grievous bereavement with the presence of some small fragment of their daughter (alas, utterly lost); she withdrew from the world in the tenth month of her fifteenth year, and in that of her Saviour 1610.

l. 2. *Gades*: Cadiz, as bourne or goal (the ultimate West).

l. 6. *cui*. I take this word as being governed by 'extruendo', l. 23.

l. 9. *sine sexu*. She could excel the angels because she voluntarily abandoned what the Angels, being sexless, could not enjoy.

l. 13. *aulae*: presumably 'the soul's palace', the body. She did not allow her bodily perfections to distract her from attending to her soul's welfare.

l. 20. *post XV fere annos*. Elizabeth Drury was baptized on 8 February 1596 (Redgrave Parish Register), and was buried on 17 December 1610 (Hawstead Parish Register).

l. 21. Robert Drury was knighted in 1591, and married Anne Bacon in 1592.

l. 22. The Drurys' elder daughter, Dorothy, had died in 1597, aged four years (Bald, p. 238).

l. 27. Elizabeth had died in London some days before her burial in Hawstead Church; she would, however, have completed ten months of her fifteenth year. See Bald, *Donne and the Drurys*, p. 68.

Epitaph for Sir Robert Drury (p. 77)

This epitaph is inscribed on the monument, on the north side of the chancel of Hawstead church, executed in 1617/18 by Nicholas Stone at Lady Drury's expense and in fulfilment of a clause in her husband's will (Bald, *Donne and the Drurys*, p. 145) to commemorate Sir William Drury and his son (Donne's patron), Sir Robert. See the commentary on the preceding epitaph.

In ll. 5–6 I read 'domi, . . . Rhotomagensi)' for the mason's 'domi) . . . Rhotomagensi,'. I suggest as a translation:

Anne, the wife of Robert Drury—than whom scarcely any other of his rank sprang from more noble forefathers; distinguished with the honour of knighthood in the year 1591 (and that not at home, but at the siege of Rouen) when he had neither come to man's estate nor left off the mourning garments for his father's death; whom military expeditions, travels abroad, and posts at Court had sufficiently trained (as envy itself, by which he was often touched but never broken, bears witness) whether for commanding troops, conducting embassies, or handling civil affairs; at last in his fortieth year, and in the year of his Saviour 1615, having given his soul to God with utmost and Christian constancy, having disbursed a goodly portion of his wealth to the poor five years before the fever by which he was carried off (and that for eternity)—made it her task in this spot to return to the earth (its rightful condition) the body, once the temple of the Holy Ghost, which must be restored to the soul as its rightful home.

[She was] neither barren nor yet a mother, having been bereaved of her daughters

Dorothy and Elizabeth; a descendant of the illustrious family of Bacon, to which lineage God gave this unparalleled honour, that father and son should discharge the same office, and that the most eminent, Nicholas the father that of Keeper of the Seal, Francis the son that of Chancellor as well; so, having faithfully discharged her duty to him who faithfully discharged his, she leaves this space on the stone tablet, to be filled in with those things which should be said of her (as God wills, and as they will) by those who come after.

ll. 3–5. Sir William Drury was killed in a duel with a fellow officer in 1590, when his son Robert was nearly fifteen. Robert Drury was knighted in the field by the Earl of Essex in September 1591 at the siege of Rouen, where English forces were supporting Henri IV (Bald, p. 237).

ll. 7–8. Sir Robert took part in military expeditions against Cadiz (1596), at Ostend (1596–7), in Ireland (1599) and in the Low Countries (1600). His foreign travels included a tour of Italy (1602–3) and a journey to Spain with the embassy of 1605, as well as the extensive tour in Europe (1611–12) on which Donne accompanied him (Bald, pp. 237 ff.).

l. 9. Sir Robert's posts at Court were far fewer and less important than he desired. He became a Gentleman of the Chamber soon after the accession of James I in 1605, and was a member of the King's first two Parliaments, 1605, 1611 (Bald, p. 238).

l. 15. Sir Robert died late in May 1615, and was buried in Hawstead church on 1 June (Parish Register).

ll. 17–18. The reference is to the establishment of a charitable foundation by Sir Robert in March 1610/11 to erect almshouses, and otherwise to provide, for six poor women from the villages on the Drury estates (Bald, *Donne and the Drurys*, p. 142).

ll. 23–4. The gap between these lines was left for the date of Lady Drury's death (5 June 1624). Though she was buried in the chancel of Hawstead church, the inscription was never completed (Bald, *Donne and the Drurys*, p. 156).

ll. 29–31. Lady Drury was the granddaughter of Sir Nicholas Bacon (1509–79), Lord Keeper of the Great Seal, and the daughter of Sir Nicholas his son (d. 1624), premier baronet, Sir Robert Drury's guardian. The younger Sir Nicholas was half-brother to Francis Bacon, who became Lord Keeper in March 1617 and Lord Chancellor on 7 January 1617/18 (*D.N.B.*).

Epitaph for Ann Donne (p. 78)

The text is from a surviving copy in Donne's handwriting among the Loseley manuscripts (MS. *L. b. 541*) in the Folger Shakespeare Library; it was presumably sent to Loseley for the approval of the More family. Other MS. copies are to be found: in the British Library, *Lansdowne MS. 984*, ff.

156-7 (included, with the epitaph which he composed for his own monument, in some brief 'Memoirs' of Donne), *Lansdowne MS. 878*, and in *Harleian MS. 3910*; and in *Lut* and *O'F* (both lacking l. 8) with the added note: 'In the Chancell of St. Clement Danes church without Temple Barr: Made by J. D. himselfe who was afterwardes notwithstanding [i.e. presumably, ll. 14-16] buryed in pawles whereof hee dyed Deane A.D. 1631.' (*O'F* also notes that the epitaph is 'Not Printed'.) The epitaph was first printed in *The Remaines* added to John Stow's *The Survey of London* (1633), p. 889b, introduced thus: 'A faire Monument in the Chancell [of St. Clement Danes] on the North side, at the upper end, with this Inscription'; see also Gosse, ii. 94, Grierson, ii. 235. The monument, which disappeared when St. Clement Danes was rebuilt, was made in 1617 by Nicholas Stone, who called it 'a letell tombe in a wall', for which he was paid '15 peces' (Bald, pp. 325-6). I translate:

John Donne, D.D., formerly (most sadly that can be said) her dear husband, to his dear Ann—daughter of George More, sister of Robert More, grand-daughter of William More, great-grand-daughter of Christopher More, Knights of Loseley; a lady most rare, most beloved; a wife most dear, most pure; a mother most dutiful, most tender; who, having completed 15 years of wedded life, seven days after bearing the twelfth of her children (of whom seven are living) was seized by a dire fever (at which he himself, speechless when confronted with the sorrow, commanded this stone tablet to speak)—commits her dust to be united with dust in a new marriage (may God bless it) in this place. She withdrew from the world in the 33rd year of her age and in the year of her Saviour 1617, on the 15th of August.

ll. 1-5. Ann More, Donne's wife, was the daughter of Sir George More (1553-1632) of Loseley Park, near Guildford, Surrey. His son Sir Robert (1581-1626) was the only one of Ann's brothers to survive to marry and have children. Ann's grandfather was Sir William More (1520-1600), son of Sir Christopher, the purchaser of Loseley Park, who died in 1549 (see A. J. Kempe's Introduction to *The Loseley Manuscripts*, 1835).

l. 9. According to his own statement (Gosse, i. 101), Donne's clandestine marriage to Ann took place 'about three weeks before Christmas', 1601. Ann died on 15 August 1617 (ll. 21-2), the marriage having therefore lasted for fifteen full years.

l. 10. Ann gave birth to her twelfth (stillborn) child on 10 August 1617; she and the child were buried in the same grave in St. Clement Danes on 16 August (Bald, pp. 324-5). The seven surviving children were Constance, John, George, Lucy, Bridget, Margaret, and Elizabeth.

ll. 12-13. Cf. 'Epitaph on Himself', l. 8: 'When we are speechlesse grown, to make stones speak'.

l. 18. Donne was made an honorary Doctor of Divinity by the University of Cambridge, as were Drs. Younge, Cheke, and Derham, by royal mandate in March 1615. The recently discovered entry of the degrees in the University's Grace Book E is reproduced in the catalogue of *An Exhibition to Celebrate the*

Work and Reputation of John Donne 1572–1631 (Cambridge University Library, 1972). See Bald, pp. 306–9.

Inscription in a Bible presented to Lincoln's Inn (p. 79)

The text is taken from the fly-leaf (vol. i) of the six-volume Latin Bible, with the *Glossa Ordinaria* and the Postills of Nicholas de Lyra (printed at Douai in 1617), which Donne presented to Lincoln's Inn and which is still preserved in the Library of the Inn; see Gosse, ii. 114, *Sermons*, ii. 3, and Bald, pp. 382–3. I translate:

That these six volumes of the entire Scriptures should be placed in the Library of Lincoln's Inn, London—most renowned in the City, in the whole World, a Society of those professing the Civil Law—is the wish (nay rather, the request) of John Donne, D.D., chaplain to the most serene and most generous King James; who, sent here in early youth to master the Laws, turning aside to other things—equally to other studies, to employments and travels, in the midst of which he notwithstanding never neglected the study of Theology—after many years impelled by the Holy Ghost and at the urging of the King being brought into Holy Orders, having fulfilled his duty of preaching often and earnestly in this place for five years, having set with his own hand the first stones of the new Chapel and well-nigh prepared the last, was bidden to transfer to the Deanship of the Cathedral Church of St. Paul, London, by the King (whom may God bless), in the 50th year of his age, and in the year of his Saviour 1621.

ll. 6–9. See note to l. 18 of the preceding Epitaph. Donne frequently and gratefully mentions the fact of his being persuaded to take Orders by James I; cf. Bald, pp. 300, 393 n., and *Sermons*, vii. 72.

l. 11. Donne entered Lincoln's Inn, after a year at Thavies Inn, as a law student on 6 May 1592 (Bald, pp. 54–5). He is not mentioned as a student of the Inn in the surviving records after the end of 1594, and he did not formally qualify as a barrister.

l. 13. On Donne's early studies of divinity see Walton, *Lives*, pp. 25–6, and Bald, pp. 67–9.

l. 15. Donne was ordained deacon and priest by Bishop John King on 23 January 1615 (Bald, p. 302).

ll. 16–19. Donne was chosen Reader (i.e. preacher and spiritual director) at Lincoln's Inn on 24 October 1616. The post required the preaching of about fifty sermons a year, but only twenty-one of Donne's sermons certainly preached at the Inn have survived (Bald, pp. 318–22). In 1617 the building of a new Chapel was actively undertaken by the Benchers, and Inigo Jones was commissioned to design the building (which still stands). In (? May) 1618 Donne preached a sermon at the Inn 'preparing them to build their Chappell' (*Sermons*, ii, no. 10). He was installed as Dean of St. Paul's on 22 November 1621, almost exactly five years (l. 17) after his appointment as Reader at the

Inn, though there is no mention of his resignation, or of his gift of the Bible, in the Inn records until 11 February 1622. The Chapel was consecrated on Ascension Day (22 May), 1623, when Donne, who preached the sermon (*Encaenia* . . . , *Sermons*, iv, no. 15), spoke of being 'a poore assistant in laying the first stone' (cf. l. 18; and see *Sermons*, ii. 1–8); he went on to say that he was 'a poore assistant again in this laying of this first formall Stone, the Word and Sacrament' (*Sermons*, iv. 371).

ll. 21–2. The King, as temporal head of the English Church, signed the orders for the election of Deans and Bishops. For James I's part in ecclesiastical appointments, and especially in Donne's, see Bald, pp. 374–80.

l. 23. The register of the parish in which Donne was born, St. Nicholas Olave, London, is not extant; the surviving evidence enables us to place the date of his birth between 24 January and 19 June 1572 (Bald, p. 35).

Inscription in the 'Album Amicorum' of Michael Corvinus (p. 80)

The text is taken from a leaf of Corvinus's autograph album in the library of Sir Geoffrey Keynes; it is reproduced in facsimile in Sir Geoffrey's *Bibliotheca Bibliographici* (1964) at p. 191. Corvinus's album was broken up and dispersed in 1952 by Winifred Myers; another leaf owned by Sir Geoffrey contains autographs by another John Donne (possibly the person of that name elected Junior Dean of Sion College in 1633; but not the poet's son) and by a continental pastor whose name is not apparent.

The identity of Michael Corvinus is not certainly known. He was possibly the 'Michael Corvinus Ungarus' of Krems, who matriculated at Wittemberg in November 1619, and was entered M.Phil. on 9 April 1622. One Heinrich Grimm composed a congratulatory song, the words of which were written by 'Josephus Guilhelmus Onoldinus Francus', Corvinus's friend; the words were printed on a single sheet at Wittemberg by Johann Gormann. (A copy of the four-page leaflet is preserved in the Hertzog August Library at Wolfenbüttel.) The title-page reads, in part: *Melos Gratulatorium . . . quod Honoribus novis Praestantissimi et doctissimi Viri-Juvenis Dn. Michaelis Corvini Cremnicensis Ungari, Philosophiae Candidati . . . ad V Idus Aprilis, Anno 1622, In incluta Witte[m]berg, Academia Summus in Philosophia gradus conferretur Honoris et amoris ergo congratulabundus admodulabatur Henricus Grimmius.* It seems possible that Corvinus, already a Protestant or converted to Protestantism at Wittemberg, found it impossible to return to Krems during the Thirty Years War, and travelled westwards, meeting notable Protestants. Donne's inscription suggests that Corvinus is a man no longer welcome among his own people, and expresses the wish that wherever he goes and in the church of Christ to which all Christians belong (*apud omnes*) he will be accepted into Christian communion, as Donne had welcomed him both in the Cathedral (as a communicant) and in his own house. I translate:

'He came unto his own, and his own received him not'. John i. 11

for what is spoken of Christ may be said of each and every Christian 'for all things are yours'. 1 Cor. iii. 22.

May God, most good, most great, grant that that most distinguished and most learned Hungarian, Michael Corvinus, may meet among all men with this Communion of Saints which is offered and pledged to him in St. Paul's and in his own house by John Donne, Dean thereof. September 27 1623.

ll. 2–3. For the importance of this idea in Donne's poetry, see General Introduction, pp. xviii–xix.

l. 4. The context is: 'Therefore let no man glory in men: for all things are yours; Whether Paul, or Apollos, or Cephas, or the world, or life, or death, or things present, or things to come; all are yours; And ye are Christ's; and Christ is God's' (1 Cor. iii. 21–3).

Epitaph for Himself (p. 80)

The text is from the inscription in St. Paul's Cathedral. There is almost no punctuation, and the mason made no attempt at an intelligent distribution of the words (breaking 'moni/tu', 'Iac/obi' and 'amplex/us' at the ends of lines); the text is entirely in capitals. I have tried to adjust such details to contemporary, and where possible to Donne's, practice. The inscription was first printed in *The Remaines* included with (and following) John Stow's *The Survey of London* (1633), p. 776b, where it is introduced by words which are still true: 'In the South side of the Quire of Saint *Pauls* Church stands a white Marble Statue on an Vrne, with this Inscription over it'; Stow omits l. 8. In *LXXX Sermons* (1640) the epitaph occupies a whole page (C1ᵛ) between Walton's *Life of Donne* and the 'Table' of sermons and texts; it was absorbed into the *Life* from the 2nd ed., 1658 (pp. 113–14), introduced by an account of the drawing of Donne in his winding-sheet in the days before his death: which drawing, Walton says, 'was then given to his dearest friend and executor Dr [Henry] King, who caused him to be thus carved in one entire piece of white Marble, as it now stands in the Cathedrall Church of S. *Pauls*; and by Dr. *Donn*'s own appointment these words were to be affixed to it as his Epitaph'. Whatever reservations one might have about Walton's account of Donne's last days, there is no reason to doubt that, apart from the actual date of his death, the epitaph is of Donne's authorship. It is inscribed on an entablature over the niche in which Nicholas Stone's effigy of the poet stands, and is itself surmounted by a coat of arms in which that of Donne impales that of the Cathedral. See Gosse, ii. 280–2; Grierson, ii. 248–9; Bald, pp. 533–5; and Sir Geoffrey Keynes's very full account in the Postscript to his edition of *Deaths Duell* (D. R. Godine, Boston, 1973), pp. 40–4.

Gosse (ii. 282) prints the following translation by Archdeacon Francis Wrangham (1769–1843):

John Donne, Doctor of Divinity, after various studies, pursued by him from his earliest years with assiduity and not without success, entered into Holy Orders, under the influence and impulse of the Divine Spirit and by the advice and exhortation of King James, in the year of his Saviour 1614, and of his own age 42. Having been invested with the Deanery of this Church, November 27, 1621, he was stripped of it by Death on the last day of March 1631: and here, though set in dust, he beholdeth Him Whose name is the Rising.

l. 2. Cf. the 'Epitaph for Ann Donne', l. 18 and note.

l. 7. Cf. the 'Inscription in a Bible presented to Lincoln's Inn', ll. 6–9 and note.

l. 9. *1614*: that is 1614/15; cf. the 'Inscription in a Bible . . .', l. 15 and note, and on Donne's age, ibid., l. 23 and note.

l. 12. *27⁰ Novemb.* This date is either an error in the copy of the epitaph which Donne's executors gave to Nicholas Stone and his assistants, or a misreading by the mason of the true date. This is clearly given in the notary's certificate, in Donne's Register as Dean, as 22 November (Bald, p. 381).

l. 16. *cujus Nomen est Oriens.* Cf. 'regem, orientem, justum' (Jer. xxiii. 5); 'Haec ait Dominus exercituum, dicens: ECCE VIR ORIENS NOMEN EIUS; et subter eum orietur, et aedificabit templum Domino' (Zech. vi. 12 *V*). The first text is taken as referring to Christ by St. Hilary, *Tract. super Psalmos*, Migne, *P.L.* ix. 728; the second by St. Gregory the Great, *Moralia*, xx. xxii, Migne, *P.L.* lxxvi. 167. Donne so applies the second text: 'The name of Christ is *Oriens*, *The East*; . . . still thy Prospect is the East, still thy Climate is heaven, still they Haven is Jerusalem; for, in our lowest dejection of all, even in the dust of the grave, we are so composed, so layed down, as that we look to the East' (*Sermons*, vi. 59). Similarly, in a letter to Sir Robert Ker, Donne refers to 'Oriens' as one of Christ's names (*Tobie Mathew Collection*, p. 305). Walton records that as the charcoal drawing of Donne in his winding-sheet was being made, Donne purposely turned his face 'toward the East, from whence he expected the second coming of his and our Saviour Jesus' (*Lives*, p. 78); the symbolism is, however, more closely connected with the root meaning of 'oriens' ('rising') and with the resurrection of the Christian in and through Christ. Hence the meeting of West and East as in 'flatt Maps', of death and resurrection, in the 'Hymn to God, my God, in my Sickness', ll. 13–15, and in the sermon and the letter to Ker referred to above; see the note on the lines in the 'Hymn' in Gardner, *Divine Poems*, p. 108.

ELEGIES UPON THE AUTHOR

The printer of *1633*, in an address 'to the Understanders' prefixed to the
poems, remarked that 'whereas it hath pleased some, who had studied and
did admire, him to offer to the memory of the Author, not long after his
decease, I have thought I should do you service in presenting them unto you
now . . . as an attestation for their sakes that knew not so much before, to let
them see how much honour was attributed to this worthy man, by those that
are capable to give it.' Of the twelve elegies in *1633*, two (those by Henry
King and Edward Hyde) had already appeared unsigned in *Deaths Duell*
(*1632*), pp. 45–7, after Donne's sermon. In *1635* the elegy by Thomas Browne
was dropped and replaced by the Latin verses of Daniel Darnelly; elegies by
Sidney Godolphin and John Chudleigh were added after Walton's verses;
and these fourteen elegies were reprinted in all the early editions after *1635*.

To the Memorie of my Ever Desired Friend Dr Donne (p. 81)

This elegy, by Henry King, was first printed (as 'An Elegie, on Dr. Donne,
Deane of Pauls'), with the sermon referred to in ll. 29–34, in *Deaths Duell*.
It appeared in *1633* and subsequent editions of Donne's *Poems*; in *Poems,
Elegies, Paradoxes, and Sonnets*, 1657, published anonymously, but entered in
the Stationers' Register as by King (reissued 1664; and in 1700 as *Ben John-
son's Poems* . . .); in Walton's *Life of Donne*, 1658, and in his collected *Lives*,
1670, 1675. For the MS. versions, see *The Poems of Henry King*, ed. Margaret
Crum (Oxford, 1965). The text here printed differs only in a few minor
details of spelling and punctuation from Miss Crum's; variants in the text
in *Deaths Duell* may be consulted in her edition.

Henry King (1592–1669), eldest son of John King, Bishop of London (who
ordained Donne), was educated at Westminster School and at Oxford. He
became Archdeacon of Colchester (1617), Canon of Christ Church (1624),
Dean of Rochester (1639), and Bishop of Chichester (1641). For a full account
of his career, see Miss Crum's Introduction, pp. 1–27. Like Donne, King was
a royal chaplain (by 1625) and a prebendary of St. Paul's (from 1616). The
two men were closely associated while Donne was Dean of the Cathedral;
King was an executor of Donne's will (cf. ll. 52–3), and assisted in the publica-
tion of *Deaths Duell*, the picture of Donne in his shroud (an engraving of which
was prefixed to this volume) having been 'given to his dearest friend and
Executor, Doctor *Henry King*' (Walton, *Lives*, p. 78; cf. Bald, pp. 391–2,
523–33).

ll. 22–9. Cf. Jonson's 'To the Memory of . . . Mr William Shakespeare' (1623),
ll. 7–12, 71. (Jonson's poem seems also, variously, to lie behind Valentine's
elegy, ll. 46–8, 51–2, and that by R. B., ll. 56–8.)

l. 34. Part of the full title of *Deaths Duell* reads: 'Being his last Sermon, and called by his Majesties houshold THE DOCTORS OWNE FUNERALL SERMON'; similarly Walton, *Lives*, p. 75.

ll. 44–5. Cf. Carew's elegy, ll. 28–9.

ll. 53–5. Cf. Donne's verse letter 'To Mr. T. W.' (Milgate, *Satires etc.*, p 60):

> For, but thy selfe, no subject can be found
> Worthy thy quill, nor any quill resound
> Thy worth but thine: how good it were to see
> A Poëm in thy praise, and writ by thee.

To the deceased Author . . . (p. 82)

These tasteless lines were not reprinted in *1635* or in later seventeenth-century editions of the *Poems*. The suggestion by Gosse, without supporting evidence (in his *Browne*, English Men of Letters Series, 1878), that the author was the famous physician of Norwich, is highly improbable, though Grierson accepted it (ii. 255). From 1631 until early in 1634 Sir Thomas Browne was a medical student at Montpellier, Padua, and Leyden. A much more plausible suggestion (Keynes, p. 196) is that the lines were written by Revd. Thomas Browne (1604–73), who was at Christ Church as an undergraduate from 1621, graduated M.A. in 1627, B.D. in 1637, and D.D. in 1643; he was appointed rector of St. Mary Aldermary, London (1638), Canon of Windsor (1639), rector of Oddington (1640), and was chaplain to the King at Oxford during the Civil War. Browne served in exile as chaplain to Mary, princess of Orange, and was restored to his appointments in 1660 (J. Foster, *Alumni Oxonienses*, I. i. 197). In 1637 he became domestic chaplain to Archbishop Laud, in which capacity he signed the *imprimatur* of Donne's *LXXX Sermons* (1640).

ll. 7–8. Donne himself feared that this might be true. 'For, as it is probably conceived, and agreeably to Gods Justice, that they that write wanton books, or make wanton pictures, have additions of torment, as often as other men are corrupted with their books, or their pictures' (*Sermons*, x. 190–1). Walton says that Donne, 'in his penitential years, viewing some of those pieces that had been loosely (God knows too loosely) scattered in his youth, . . . wish't they had been abortive, or so short liv'd that his own eyes had witnessed their funerals' (*Lives*, p. 61); and Ben Jonson told Drummond in 1619 that Donne, 'now since he was made Doctor repenteth highlie and seeketh to destroy all his poems' (*Works*, i. 136). It is probably, among other sins, the writing of wanton verses to which Donne refers in 'A Hymn to God the Father', ll. 7–8: 'Wilt thou forgive that sinne by which I wonne / Others to sinne? and, made my sinne their doore?'

On the death of Dr Donne (p. 83)

This poem appeared first (as 'an Epitaph on Dr. Donne') in *Deaths Duell*, 1632. The text given there varies somewhat from that in *1633*, and Hyde may have supplied an altered copy for the later volume; the main variants are noted in the apparatus.

Grierson (ii. 255) records the suggestion by C. E. Norton that these lines were written by Edward Hide (as he usually spells his name), son of Sir Lawrence Hyde of Salisbury. Born in 1607, Hide was educated at Westminster School and at Trinity College, Cambridge (M.A. 1633; B.D. 1640); he graduated D.D. from Oxford in 1643; in the same year he became rector of Brightwell, Berks., but was ejected two years later and spent the rest of his life in retirement, mostly in Oxford; he died in August 1659, at Salisbury (*D.N.B.*; Venn and Venn, *Alumni Cantabrigienses*, I. ii. 44). A more convincing case can, however, be made that the elegy was written by Hide's kinsman, Edward Hyde (1609–74), who became first Earl of Clarendon (for his career, see *D.N.B.*). The Revd. Giles Oldisworth (1619–78), annotating his copy of *1639* (now in the library of Sir Geoffrey Keynes), identified the author of this elegy as Sir Edward Hyde Kt. (J. Sampson, 'A Contemporary Light upon John Donne', *Essays and Studies by Members of the English Association*, vii, 1921), that is, the future Earl; Anthony Wood makes the same identification (*Athenae Oxonienses*, ed. Bliss, ii. 502). Sir Geoffrey Keynes also possesses a volume of MS. poems by Donne and Strode (*EH*) on the fly-leaves of which, at each end, are four signatures, partial or complete, of 'Edward Hyde'; a comparison of these with early signatures of Clarendon has convinced Sir Geoffrey that Clarendon was the owner of the MS. On the fly-leaf at the beginning the words 'On the death' are written twice, 'on the' again, and the word 'may' twice, near the word 'mame'; and these possibly have reference to the title of the elegy and to the awkwardness in sound of 'may aime' in l. 15 (see G. Keynes, 'A Footnote to Donne', *The Book Collector*, xxii, 1973, where the signatures are reproduced between pp. 166–7). At the time of Donne's death and the publication of *Deaths Duell* and of *1633*, after attending Westminster School and graduating from Oxford (1626), Clarendon was studying at the Middle Temple. He had written some verses prefixed to Davenant's tragedy *Albovine* (1629), was the associate of wits and scholars, and claimed friendship with Ben Jonson. As Grierson notes (ii. 255), Thomas Carew, Sir Lucius Cary, and Sidney Godolphin, whose elegies are also printed here, were among Clarendon's most intimate friends in the early 1630s.

ll. 3–4. Cf. King's elegy, ll. 53–5, and note.

ll. 5–8. Cf. Carew's elegy, ll. 9–10.

On Doctor Donne (p. 84)

This poem, first printed in 1633, was reprinted without variation in *Certain Elegant Poems, written by Dr. Corbet, Bishop of Norwich* (1647), edited by John Donne, the son of the poet; it is there entitled 'An Epitaph on Doctor Donne, Deane of Pauls'. It was included in *Recreation for Ingenious Head-peeces* (1654) as Epitaph no. 177; and in Walton's *Life of Donne* (1658) as 'An Epitaph written by Dr. *Corbet*, Bishop of Oxford, on his friend Dr. *Donne*', and also in the collected *Lives*, 1670, 1675. The poem is frequently included in MS. collections and miscellanies.

The career of Richard Corbett (1582–1635) is given in full in the edition of his *Poems* by J. A. W. Bennett and H. R. Trevor-Roper (Oxford, 1955), pp. xi–xli. He was acquainted with Ben Jonson and with many other poets and wits of the time; but there is no evidence, apart from Walton's statement, that he was a 'friend' of Donne. Corbett's appointment as Dean of Christ Church (1620) and Donne's as Dean of St. Paul's (1621) led John Chamberlain to record the remark 'that yf Ben Johnson might be made deane of Westminster, that place, Paules, and Christchurche shold be furnished with three very pleasant poeticall deanes' (*Letters of John Chamberlain*, ed. N. E. McClure, Philadelphia, 1939, ii. 407–8). Like Donne and Jonson, Corbett contributed verses to *The Odcombian Banquet* and *Coryats Crudities* in 1611. He became Bishop of Oxford in 1628; his elegy on Donne must have been written soon after the poet's death, since the title in 1633 implies that it was composed before Corbett's translation to the see of Norwich in April 1632. The text here printed is virtually the same as that in the edition of Bennett and Trevor-Roper.

On Donne's legal knowledge (ll. 7–8), see Bald, especially pp. 414 ff.

An Elegie upon the Incomparable Dr Donne (p. 84)

Henry Valentine matriculated from Christ's College, Cambridge, in December 1616, and graduated B.A. (1621) and M.A. (1624); he was incorporated at Oxford (1628) and took his D.D. there in 1636. Meanwhile he was made rector of Deptford, Kent, on 8 December 1630; and there he was buried on 18 January 1643. See Venn and Venn, *Alumni Cantabrigienses*, I. iv. 293. Among Valentine's publications were *Foure Sea-Sermons* (1635) preached at Deptford, and *Private Devotions* (1651).

l. 14. Cf. Carew's elegy, ll. 68–9.

l. 16. *Trump.* Cf. *Sermons*, ii. 166–70; for example: 'God shall send his people preachers furnished with all these abilities, to be *Tubae*, Trumpets to awaken them' (p. 167).

ll. 19–20. Probably suggested by Donne's 'An Hymn to the Saints, and to Marquess Hamilton', ll. 14–16. Donne became a royal chaplain in 1615, Dean of St. Paul's in 1621, and D.D. of the University of Cambridge in 1615.

ll. 21–2. Cf. Walton: 'beside an unnumbred number of others, many persons of Nobility, and of eminency for Learning, who did love and honour him in his life, did shew it at his death, by a voluntary and sad attendance of his body to the grave, where nothing was so remarkable as a publick sorrow' (*Lives*, p. 82).

ll. 25–8. Though the subject is commonplace enough, Valentine might be recalling Donne's last sermon, *Deaths Duell*, where much is said of 'the *death of corruption*, and *putrefaction*, and *vermiculation* . . .'; '*Christ is risen* without seeing corruption. Now this which is so singularly peculiar to him . . ., at his *second coming*, his coming to *Judgement*, shall extend to all that are then alive, their *flesh* shall not *see corruption*', etc. (*Sermons*, x. 235–6, 238).

ll. 37–8. Cf. Corbett's elegy, ll. 9–11.

ll. 38–40. For the image, cf. 'To the Countess of Bedford' ('Honour is so sublime . . .'), ll. 46–8: in circles, 'the peecelesse centers flow, / And are in all the lines which all wayes goe'.

ll. 46–8, 51–2. Cf. King's elegy, ll. 22–9 and note.

An Elegie upon Dr Donne (p. 86)

Walton revised his elegy from time to time. In its final form (*Lives*, pp. 87–9) it is dated 7 April 1631; it contains four lines added to the end in *1635* and retained in later editions of the *Poems* and of Walton's *Life of Donne*:

> Which, as a Free-will offering, I here give
> *Fame* and the *World*: and, parting with it, grieve,
> I want abilities, fit to set forth,
> A *Monument*, as matchless as his worth;

a new version of ll. 1–8 was supplied in the revised *Life* in 1658, and was retained in later editions:

> Our *Donne* is dead! and, we may sighing say,
> We had that man where Language chose to stay
> And shew her utmost power. I wou'd not praise
> That, and his great Wit, which in our vain days
> Make others proud; but, as these serv'd to unlock
> That Cabinet his mind, where such a stock
> Of knowledge was repos'd, that I lament
> Our just and general cause of discontent;

and the poem was varied throughout in wording and punctuation.

Walton also supplied lines engraved beneath the portrait of Donne reproduced in editions of the *Poems* 1635–54 (and in Gardner, *Elegies etc.*, f.p. 1; Bald, f.p. 54; etc.):

> This was for youth, Strength, Mirth, and wit that Time
> Most count their golden Age; but t'was not thine.
> Thine was thy later yeares, so much refind
> From youths Drosse, Mirth, & wit; as thy pure mind
> Thought (like the Angels) nothing but the Praise
> Of thy Creator, in those last, best Dayes.
>   Witnes this Booke, (thy Embleme) which begins
> With Love; but endes, with Sighes, & Teares for sin*n*s.

Izaak Walton (1593–1683), Donne's first biographer, was a parishioner of St. Dunstan's-in-the-West when, or soon after, Donne became vicar in 1624, though his personal acquaintance with the poet dates from a year or two later (see Bald, pp. 489, 503, 525). His admiration for Donne was, however, deep and lasting.

ll. 25–6. Walton was at pains, in his *Life* of Donne, in the lines just quoted above, and in this elegy, to make the composition of Donne's secular poetry an activity of his youth and early manhood. He speaks of 'those pieces which were facetiously Composed and carelesly scattered (most of them being written before the twentieth year of his age)', of which Donne in later life wished that they had been 'abortive' or 'short liv'd', whereas his love of 'heavenly Poetry' was 'in his declining age . . . witnessed . . . by many Divine Sonnets and other high, holy, and harmonious Composures' (*Lives*, p. 61). These two lines were revised to read: 'Did his Youth scatter Poetry, wherein / Lay Loves Philosophy . . .?'.

ll. 27, 35, 40. The *Satires* date probably from 1593–8; *La Corona* was probably written in 1607, 'A Litany' in 1608.

ll. 45–6. Cf. Valentine's elegy, ll. 37–8, and Corbett's, ll. 7–11.

ll. 47–8. There is no evidence that Donne visited the Holy Land, and indeed Walton elsewhere states that Donne intended to go there, but got no further than Italy (*Lives*, p. 26); 'went to see' apparently means 'set off with the purpose of seeing'.

ll. 64–6. Cf. *The Second Anniversary*, ll. 467–70.

l. 70. *seventy*. In 1631, when the elegy was apparently composed, Walton was thirty-eight years old, and comfortably far from the 'threescore years and ten' of Ps. xc. 10.

ll. 80–1. Cf. King's elegy, ll. 53–5, and note (p. 221).

An Elegie upon the Death of the Deane of Pauls . . . (p. 88)

This elegy, first printed in *1633* (as in later seventeenth-century editions of the *Poems*), appeared in *Poems. By Thomas Carew Esquire, One of the Gentlemen of the Privie-Chamber, and Sewer in Ordinary to His Majesty* (1640). Carew was born in 1594 or 1595, and was buried 23 March 1640; for what is known of his career, see the edition of his *Poems* by Rhodes Dunlap (Oxford, 1949), pp. xiii–xliv.

The text of the elegy published in 1640 is in many respects inferior to that in *1633* (see Dunlap's apparatus to the poem, pp. 71–4), and, accepting Grierson's suggestion that 'the poem was printed in 1640 from an early, unrevised version' (ii. 257), Dunlap takes *1633* as his copy-text; the text here printed is identical with his.

Carew's poem must have been written very soon after Donne's death, for, as Dunlap points out (p. 250), Aurelian Townshend writes (in a poem addressed to Carew on the death of Gustavus Adolphus in 1632) of Carew's

> Ambrosian teares,
> Which as they fell like manna on the Herse
> Of devine *Donne* (ll. 14–16; Dunlap, p. 207).

Similarly, Lord Herbert of Cherbury, in his 'Elegy for Doctor *Dunn*' (*Poems*, ed. G. C. Moore Smith, Oxford, 1923, p. 58), says:

> It rests that I should to the world declare
> Thy praises, *DUNN*, whom I so lov'd alive,
> That with my witty *Carew* I should strive
> To celebrate thee dead . . . (ll. 48–51).

The poem was apparently well enough known to influence, generally, several of the elegists in *1633*, for instance, Valentine and Sir Lucius Cary.

l. 4. *dowe-bak't*: cf. Donne, 'A Letter to the Lady Carey, and Mrs. Essex Rich', l. 20: 'In dow bak'd men'.

ll. 25–8. For the metaphor, cf. 'To Mr. Rowland Woodward' (Milgate, *Satires etc.*, p. 69), ll. 3–6:

> So'affects my muse now, a chast fallownesse;
>
> Since shee to few, yet to too many'hath showne
> How love-song weeds, and Satyrique thornes are growne
> Where seeds of better Arts, were early sown.

ll. 59–60. Carew paid a similar tribute to Donne in his poem 'In answer of an Elegiacall Letter upon the death of the King of Sweden from Aurelian Townsend' (the poem by Townshend referred to above), ll. 11–14:

> *Virgil*, nor *Lucan*, no, nor *Tasso* more
> Then both, not *Donne*, worth all that went before,
> With the united labour of their wit
> Could a just Poem to this subject fit.

An Elegie on Dr Donne (p. 91)

Sir Lucius Cary (1610?–43) succeeded in 1633 as 2nd Viscount Falkland; for his career, see K. B. Murdock: *The Sun at Noon* (New York, 1939). He had been educated at Trinity College, Dublin; 'His first years of reason were spent in poetry and polite learning, into the first of which he made divers plausible sallies, which caused him therefore to be admired by the poets of those times, particularly, first by Ben. Jonson, who hath an epigram upon him in his *Underwood* . . . , 2. by Edw. Waller of Beaconsfield, who highly extolls his worth and admirable parts; and, 3. By Sir John Suckling, who afterwards brought him into his poem, called, *The Session of Poets*, thus,

> He was of late so gone with divinity,
> That he had almost forgot his poetry,
> Though to say the truth (and Apollo did know it)
> He might have been both his priest and his poet.

(Anthony Wood, *Athenae Oxonienses*, ed. Bliss, ii. 566–7.) Falkland was, indeed, one of Jonson's most devoted 'sons' and wrote three verse tributes to his 'father'. Jonson's tribute to Cary (*Underwood*, lxx), mentioned by Wood, is the ode 'To the Immortall Memorie, and Friendship of that Noble Paire, Sir Lucius Cary, and Sir H. Morison'. Cary mentions Donne in 'An Elegy on Sir Henry Morison' (K. B. Murdock, *Harvard St. and Notes in Philol. and Lit.*, xx, 1938, p. 38) and refers to 'Satire II' and *Pseudo-Martyr* in his *Discourse of Infallibility*, 1651 (Keynes, p. 291). His elegy on Donne obviously takes its rise from that by Carew immediately preceding.

l. 9. *Gods Conduit-pipe*: cf. 'Satire I', l. 5, 'Gods conduits, grave Divines'.

l. 10. *Embassador*: cf. 'To Mr. Tilman after he had taken orders', ll. 37–8: 'What function is so noble, as to bee / Embassadour to God and destinie?'

l. 13. *Johnson*. Though Jonson wrote two poems addressed to Donne and one 'To Lucy, Countesse of Bedford, with M. Donnes Satyres' (*Epigrams*, xxiii, xciv, xcvi; also prefixed to the poems in *1635*), he did not write an elegy on Donne; nor did Archbishop Laud (l. 17) preach Donne's funeral sermon. Falkland is suggesting these as events which ought to have happened.

l. 28. *our soule is all in every part*: an idea of which Donne made use in 'The Progress of the Soul', ll. 334–5, and in the verse letter 'To the Lady Carey and Mrs. Essex Rich', l. 36.

On Dr Donnes Death (p. 93)

Jasper Mayne (1604–72) matriculated from Christ Church, Oxford, in 1624, and graduated M.A. (1631), B.D. (1642), and D.D. (1646). He became vicar of Cassington (1639) and of Pyrton, Oxon. (1649), but was deprived of his preferments by Parliament. At the Restoration he became, and till his death remained, Archdeacon of Chichester. See Foster, *Alumni Oxonienses*. Mayne was the author of sermons, of two plays (*The City Match*, 1639, published 1648; *The Amorous War*, 1658) and of a quantity of indifferent verse, including complimentary poems on Jonson and Cartwright. He was the translator, and probably the composer (Chambers, ii. 309–10), of Latin epigrams published in 1652 by the younger John Donne with his father's *Paradoxes, Problems, Essayes, Characters* . . . (Keynes, pp. 94–5).

l. 2. Cf. King's elegy, ll. 53–4.

l. 4. *Anniverse*: the *Anniversaries*.

ll. 13–18. For similar sentiments, cf. King's elegy, ll. 4, 9–17, 47–50; Hyde's, ll. 3–10; and Carew's, ll. 9–10.

Upon Mr J. Donne, and his Poems (p. 95)

Arthur Wilson (1595–1652), historian and dramatist, spent much of his life in the service (1614–31) of Robert Devereux, 3rd Earl of Essex, and (from 1633 until his death) in that of Robert Rich, 2nd Earl of Warwick (a friend of Donne, for whose sisters Donne wrote the verse letter 'To the Lady Carey and Mrs. Essex Rich'). In the interval, 1631–3, Wilson was studying at Trinity College, Oxford. His most important work was *The History of Great Britain* (1653), but he also wrote three plays (*The Inconstant Lady*, *The Corporal*—not extant—and *The Swisser*) and some lines prefixed to Benlowes's *Theophila*. For his biography, see *D.N.B.*; Wood's *Athenae Oxonienses*, ed. Bliss, iii. 318–23; and A. Feuillerat's introduction to his edition of *The Swisser* (Paris, 1904).

ll. 8–9. Probably a faulty reminiscence of Donne's 'Elegy on the Lady Markham', ll. 21–2: 'As men of China,'after an ages stay, / Do take up Porcelane, where they buried Clay'.

ll. 17 ff. The 'objects' which Wilson assembles, with a fine disregard for context, are nearly all mentioned in the poems published as Donne's in *1633*; but not speaking cherries, or roses amidst snow.

ll. 33–6. The alchemical belief that minerals strive, under the influence of the sun's rays, to become gold is used by Donne in 'Resurrection, imperfect', ll. 9–16, 'Epitaph on Himself', ll. 11–14, in the Eclogue prefixed to the Somerset 'Epithalamion', ll. 61–4, and in 'Elegy on the Lady Markham', ll. 23–8 (on which see note, p. 179).

l. 40. Cf. *The First Anniversary*, ll. 278–9.

In Memory of Doctor Donne (p. 97)

The author of this elegy is identified by Giles Oldisworth in his copy of *1639* as Richard Busby (J. Sampson, 'A Contemporary Light on John Donne', *Essays and Studies*, vii, 1921). Busby (1606–95) was a contemporary of Donne's eldest son John, and probably of his second son George, at Westminster school, and, like the younger John Donne, Busby was a King's scholar. (Among Donne's elegists, Henry King, Richard Corbett, Jasper Mayne, and Clarendon had also been educated at the school.) Entering Christ Church, Oxford, in 1626, Busby graduated M.A. in 1631, and was for a time a tutor at his College. In 1639 he became rector and prebend of Cudworth, Somerset. Meantime he was appointed headmaster of Westminster school in 1638 (confirmed 1640). He was ejected from his posts by Parliament, but at the Restoration became a D.D., canon of Westminster and residentiary and treasurer of Wells. Busby is not otherwise known as a versifier, his publications being mostly pedagogical editions of the ancient classics. See *D.N.B.*

ll. 16–17. Cf. Carew's elegy, ll. 75–7, and Valentine's, l. 5.

ll. 21–4. Cf. Valentine's elegy, ll. 37–8; Corbett's, ll. 9–11; and Walton's, ll. 43–8.

l. 61. *late.* Donne was forty-three years old when he was ordained.

ll. 70–2. Henry Wriothesley, 3rd Earl of Southampton, died in 1624; the only other evidence of his friendship with Donne is that the poet lent the Earl a copy of one of his sermons (*Letters*, p. 200); and Southampton's arms (with those of the Earls of Pembroke, Bridgewater, and Carlisle) are included in a stained-glass window in the Chapel of Lincoln's Inn, part of which was a gift of Donne (Bald, p. 385). James Hamilton, Marquess of Hamilton and Earl of Arran, was the subject of Donne's 'Hymn', 1625 (see the commentary on the poem, pp. 208—11 above). William Herbert, 3rd Earl of Pembroke, had died in 1630; for his relations with Donne, see Bald, pp. 351, 385. Richard Sackville, 3rd Earl of Dorset, appointed Donne as vicar of St. Dunstan's on 18 March 1624, but died ten days later; Edward Sackville, the 4th Earl (d. 1652), then became Donne's patron (see Bald, pp. 295, 318, 324, 455). To Elizabeth Stanley, wife of the 5th Earl of Huntingdon, Donne addressed two verse letters; she died in 1633. Lucy Harington, Countess of Bedford, was Donne's patroness and friend from about 1607; she died in 1627.

ll. 81–2. Cf. Hyde's elegy, ll. 9–11.

Epitaph upon Dr Donne (p. 100)

Endymion Porter (1587–1649) was brought up in Spain, and entered the service of Edward Villiers, and then of his brother George, Duke of

Buckingham. He became Groom of the bedchamber to Charles I. From 1622 his knowledge of Spanish led to his being chosen to accompany important diplomatic missions to the Continent. For his career, see G. Huxley, *Endymion Porter: the Life of a Courtier* (London, 1959). He is chiefly remembered as a 'great patron of all ingenious men, especially of poets' (Wood, *Athenae Oxonienses*, ed. Bliss, iii. 2), and evoked tributes from Herrick, Dekker, Randolph, and others. He himself wrote verses, for example the lines prefixed to Davenant's 'Madagascar'. There is no evidence, however, that he was personally acquainted with Donne.

In Obitum Venerabilis Viri Iohannis Donne (p. 101)

Daniel Darnelly (1604–59) was born in London, and matriculated from New College, Oxford, in November 1623; he graduated B.A. in 1627 and M.A. in 1630 (incorporated at Cambridge, 1634). He became rector of Curry Mallet, Somerset, in 1632, and of Walden St. Paul, Herts., in 1634. He was rector of Teversham, Cambridgeshire, from 1635 until 1646, when the living was sequestered (Foster, *Alumni Oxonienses*). The title suggests that Darnelly wrote his elegy in response to a request, but it is not known on whose part.

Elegie on D.D. (p. 104)

The poems and translations of Sidney Godolphin (1610–43) were not collected until G. E. B. Saintsbury included them (with the exception of this one, and of a verse tribute to Jonson in Herford and Simpson's *Jonson*, xi. 450) in *Minor Poets of the Caroline Period*, ii (1906), 227–61. Godolphin studied at Exeter College, Oxford, from June 1624 until 1627; according to Wood (*Athenae Oxonienses*, ed. Bliss, ii. 44–7) he entered one of the Inns of Court. After travel abroad, Godolphin was a member of Parliament in 1628–9 and in the Short and Long Parliaments (1640). He raised a Cornish troop and fought as a Colonel on the King's side in the Civil War, until he was killed in a skirmish at Chagford, Devon (*D.N.B.*). He was intimate with Clarendon and Falkland, and appears in Suckling's 'A Sessions of the Poets', but no evidence survives that he was acquainted with Donne.

On Dr John Donne . . . (p. 105)

The author of this elegy was probably the John Chudleigh who in *TCD* (2) is credited with the authorship of Donne's 'A Fever' and two other poems, and in British Library *Add. MS. 33998*, fo. 62ᵛ, with the authorship of another. He may be identified with some probability as John, the son of George

Chudley of Asheriston, or Ashton, Devon, who was born in 1606, matricu-
lated from Wadham College, Oxford, in 1621 and graduated B.A. in 1624,
and M.A. in 1626 (incorporated at Cambridge, 1629). He was a member of
Parliament in 1626, and in 1627–8; but died before 10 May 1634 (Foster,
Alumni Oxonienses). If he was the author of this elegy, which first appeared in
1635, he must have written it at least a year before, and possibly without
thought of, its publication.

Verbal Alterations in the *Epithalamions* and *Epicedes* in the edition of 1635

THE edition of Donne's poems issued in 1635 has a text which often differs from that in *1633* in the poems which they have in common. It has been shown by Helen Gardner (*Divine Poems*, pp. lxxxix–xc) that the printer's copy in *1635* was, for these poems (except for the *Anniversaries*[1]), a conflation of *1633* and *O'F*, and that *O'F* itself had previously had some of its Group III readings changed to those in *1633*. The resulting text in *1635* is thus a rather haphazard mixture of Group I readings, or elsewhere of Group II readings, with readings from Group III. Apart from its punctuation, therefore, *1635* has little importance for the modern editor. It was, however, the basis of all later editions of the poems until the Grolier editors and Grierson returned to *1633*; and its readings are of some interest to students of the poet.

This list continues those in Gardner, *Divine Poems*, Appendix B, in *Elegies etc.*, Appendix A, and in Milgate, *Satires etc.*, Appendix A, and will both illustrate the explanation of the text of *1635* given above and show the consistency with which the editor of *1635* did his work. It will be seen that, apart from misprints, errors, and obvious corrections, all but two of these readings are in *O'F*; most are Group III readings, but some are found only in *Lut* and *O'F*.[2]

EPITHALAMIONS

1633	1635	MSS. agreeing with 1635

'Epithalamion made at Lincolnes Inne'

1633	1635	MSS. agreeing with 1635
26 these	those	TCC, TCD, Dob, Lut, O'F, S 96, B
59 come	runne	W, Dob, Lut, O'F, S 96, O 2, P, B, A 34
worlds	heavens	Lut, O'F
60 *but*	*put*	All MSS.
95 maime	name	Σ—W (O'F corr. to 'maime')

---

[1] The few variations in *1635* from the text of the *Anniversaries* in *1633* are due to printer's errors and misreadings of *1633*.

[2] I list the MSS. alphabetically in their groups, omitting *SP*, *A 18*, *N*, and *D 17* since they are direct copies of *D*, *TCC*, *TCD*, and *ℐC*, and ignoring *O 1* and most of the miscellanies as valueless. The sign 'Σ—' means 'all MSS. containing the poem, except . . .'.

1633	1635	MSS. agreeing with 1635

'An Epithalamion, Or Mariage Song . . .'

Title married	mared	—
21 foules	fowle	—
60 store	starres	O'F (*corr. from* 'stores'), Hd
67 too late	late	Σ—Group I, S 96, JC
94 acquittance	acquittances	TCD, Dob, Lut, O'F, O2, P, JC, Hd

'Epithalamion at the Marriage of the Earl of Somerset'

Heading		
absence thence	Actions there	H 49, TCC, TCD, Dob, Lut, O'F, B, Hd
5 small	smaller	—
12 Have	Having	—
34 places	plotts	Σ—C 57, Lec
54 one	owne	Σ—D, H 49, O'F corr.
55 I am not	And am I	Lut, O'F
72 abroad	aboad	—
108 by	from	—
145 Are	Wert	Lut, O'F

EPICEDES

'Elegie on the Lady Marckham'

12 *Noe*	No	Dob, Lut, O'F, Hd

1633 alone omits ll. 44–5

48 sometimes	sometime	S 96
58 woman	women	Σ—Cy

'Elegie on Mʳⁱˢ Boulstred'

6 dishes	dish'd	L 74, TCC, TCD, Lut, O'F, S 96
15 by	the	—
27 life	lives	Dob ('lifes'), Lut, O'F, S 96 ('lifes'), Cy, O 2, P, HN ('lifes'), B, S
34 to	for	Lut, O'F, A 25
41 King	Kings	Dob
74 but	though	Σ—Group I, H 40, DC (Cy, 'and'; B, 'yet')

'Elegie upon the Death of Mistress Boulstred'

2 sorrow	sorrowes	Lut, O'F, S 96, S
21 to	for	All MSS.
26 for in her	in her we	Lut, O'F
28 They . . . that	That . . . who	Lut, O'F, B, ('That . . . that', S 96, O 2, P, S)
34 The	That	Lut, O'F, S 96, B, S
53 body	bodie's	Lut, O'F, S 96, Cy, S ('Body'is', B; 'body is', O 2, P)
57 woes	wooes	All MSS.
62 waste	breake	Lut, O'F, S 96, B, S, HK 1

'Elegy on Prince Henry'

34 through	to	Lut, O'F
42 did	should	Lut, O'F

1633	*1635*	*MSS.* agreeing with *1635*

'Obsequies to the Lord Harrington'

7 mans	mens	Σ—Group I
39 living	beeing	Σ—Group I, *TCD*
53 feeds	feed	Σ—*C 57*, *Lec*
63 would	should	*Lut, O'F*
69 to have	to'have had	*Lut, O'F, B*
130 tell	sett	*Dob, Lut, O'F, S 96, B*
135 *flye*	*flee*	—
161 was	were	Σ—*C 57*, *Lec, A 25*
165 grow	am	Σ—Group I, *DC*
192 usurp'st	usurpe	*Lut, O'F, JC, A 25*
193 That	Then	Σ—*C 57*, *Lec*
257 Who	Which	*Lut, O'F*

'An Hymne to the Saints . . .'

1, 3 Whither	Whether	All *MSS.*
12 are	is	*Lut, O'F*
18 Gangred	Gangreend	All *MSS.*
23 one	an	All *MSS.*
25 this	his	*Lut, O'F*

The Elegy 'Death be not Proud'

THE extravagance of language in which, in the 'Elegy on Mrs. Bulstrode' ('Death I recant'), the powers of death are described seems to have called forth a reply, possibly from the Countess of Bedford herself. A poem beginning 'Death be not proud' was first printed in *1635* as 'Elegie on Mistris Boulstred'. In *RP 31* it is called 'Elegie on the Lady Marckham. By L: C: of B:' (presumably Lucy, Countess of Bedford); in *H 40* it is said to be 'by C: L: of B.'. In *B* it follows the 'Elegy upon the Death of Mistress Bulstrode' ('Language thou art too narrow'), and is attributed to 'F. B' (? Francis Beaumont). In *Cy*, *Lut*, *O 2*, *P*, however, the poem appears as a continuation of 'Death I recant' (in *O'F* it follows immediately upon the latter poem with a separate title, 'Elegie'), and is followed by the 'Elegy on the Lady Markham'. Grierson is clearly right (ii. cxliv) in regarding 'Death be not proud' as a separate poem; there is no preparation at the end of 'Death I recant' for a change of direction, nor is there anything to suggest that Donne's elegy does not properly end at line 74. Indeed, 'Death be not proud' is fairly clearly an answer to Donne's poem. It is even more clearly not by Donne, being, as Grierson says, 'slighter in texture, vaguer in thought, in feeling more sentimental and pious, than Donne's own *Epicedes*. Whoever wrote it had a warmer feeling for Mris. Boulstred than underlies Donne's frigid hyperboles.' Though no manuscript explicitly ascribes it to Donne, it is easy to see how a reply to 'Death I recant' could have become attached to Donne's verses if the two poems were copied together from the Countess's papers, or from his own, and how 'Death be not proud' could have been included as his in *1635*.

We know that the Countess did write verses (though none certainly from her pen have survived) and that Donne had seen some of them. In a letter to her, dating probably from 1609, Donne writes: 'I have yet adventured so near as to make a petition for verse, it is for those your Ladiship did me the honour to see in *Twicknam* garden, except you repent your making. . . . They must needs be an excellent exercise of your wit, which speake well of so ill'

(*Letters*, p. 67). These verses could not have been connected with Miss Bulstrode's death; but it is possible, as Bald suggests (p. 179), that 'Death be not proud' is referred to in a letter of Donne to Sir Henry Goodyer, dated 14 August (almost certainly 1609, and therefore ten days after Miss Bulstrode died): 'instead of a Letter to you, I send you one to another, to the best Lady, who did me the honour to acknowledge the receit of one of mine, by one of hers' (*Letters*, p. 117). Donne's letter to the Countess may have enclosed 'Death I recant' and hers to him may have accompanied 'Death be not proud'. The somewhat Calvinistic tone of the latter poem would accord with what we know of the Countess's religious bent, especially as it was later shown in her association with Dr. John Burgess (see P. Thomson, 'John Donne and the Countess of Bedford', *M.L.R.* xliv, 1949). It would have been a nice touch that (as Helen Gardner suggests, *Divine Poems*, pp. xlvii–xlviii) she should begin an answer to Donne's elegy with the opening words of one of his Holy Sonnets, which she would have had the opportunity of reading, and in which he treated the subject of death in a manner both more confident and more obviously orthodox in its Christian feeling. Grierson's suggestion that the Countess wrote the following lines is therefore quite plausible.

I print the verses from *1635*, the chief variations from which (well supported in the manuscripts) are noted beneath the poem.

> Death be not proud, thy hand gave not this blow,
> Sinne was her captive, whence thy power doth flow;
> The executioner of wrath thou art,
> But to destroy the just is not thy part.
> Thy comming, terrour, anguish, griefe denounce;   5
> Her happy state, courage, ease, joy pronounce.
> From out the Christall palace of her breast,
> The clearer soule was call'd to endlesse rest,
> (Not by the thundering voyce, wherewith God threats,
> But, as with crowned Saints in heaven he treats,)   10
> And, waited on by Angels, home was brought,
> To joy that it through many dangers sought;
> The key of mercy gently did unlocke
> The doores 'twixt heaven and it, when life did knock.
>   Nor boast, the fairest frame was made thy prey,   15
> Because to mortall eyes it did decay;

5–6 denounce . . . pronounce] denounces . . . pronounces *1635*

A better witnesse than thou art, assures,
That though dissolv'd, it yet a space endures;
No dramme thereof shall want or losse sustaine,
When her best soule inhabits it again.   20
Goe then to people curst before they were,
Their spoyles in Triumph of thy conquest weare.
Glory not thou thy selfe in these hot teares
Which our face, not for hers, but our harme weares,
The mourning livery given by Grace, not thee,   25
Which wils our soules in these streams washt should be,
And on our hearts, her memories best tombe,
In this her Epitaph doth write thy doome.
Blinde were those eyes, saw not how bright did shine
Through fleshes misty vaile the beames divine.   30
Deafe were the eares, not charm'd with that sweet sound
Which did i'th spirit-instructed voice abound.
Of flint the conscience, did not yeeld and melt,
At what in her last Act it saw, heard, felt.
    Weep not, nor grudge then, to have lost her sight,   35
Taught thus, our after stay's but a short night:
But by all soules not by corruption choaked
Let in high rais'd notes that power be invoked.
Calme the rough seas, by which she sayles to rest,
From sorrowes here, to a kingdome ever blest;   40
And teach this hymne of her with joy, and sing,
    The grave no conquest gets, Death hath no sting.

22 spoyles ... of ... weare] soules ... to ... beare *1635*   24 hers] her *1635*
30 the] those *1635*   32 spirit-instructed] spirits instructed *1635*   34 saw,
heard, felt] saw and felt *1635*

Whether the Countess of Bedford replied to, and indeed reproved,
Donne in this poem, or had shown other signs of dissatisfaction with
'Death I recant', we do not certainly know. Even without her
prompting, however, the poet who had not long before written
most of the Holy Sonnets could hardly have remained satisfied with
the tone of his first attempt at commemorating Miss Bulstrode.
Donne probably felt that even by recasting 'Death I recant' it was
not possible to re-handle the theme of Miss Bulstrode's youth
and premature death (and it may not be ungallant to suggest that
insistence on her 'youth' at the age of thirty might not have seemed
to him worth a second try). In 'Language thou art too narrow' he
takes quite another direction.

INDEX OF FIRST LINES

(*Poems not by Donne are marked* ★)